The Effects of Agency Problems on the Financial Behavior, Performance, and Efficiency of German Industrial Stock Corporations

European University Studies
Europäische Hochschulschriften
Publications Universitaires Européennes

Series V
Economics and Management

Reihe V Série V
Volks- und Betriebswirtschaft
Sciences économiques, gestion d'entreprise

Vol./Bd. 2424

PETER LANG
Frankfurt am Main · Berlin · Bern · New York · Paris · Wien

J. Benedict Wolf

The Effects of Agency Problems on the Financial Behavior, Performance, and Efficiency of German Industrial Stock Corporations

PETER LANG
Europäischer Verlag der Wissenschaften

Die Deutsche Bibliothek - CIP-Einheitsaufnahme

Wolf, J. Benedict:

The effects of agency problems on the financial behavior, performance, and efficiency of German industrial stock corporations / J. Benedict Wolf. - Frankfurt am Main ; Berlin ; Bern ; New York ; Paris ; Wien : Lang, 1999
(European university studies : Series 5, Economics and Management ; Vol. 2424)
Zugl.: Augsburg, Univ., Diss., 1998
ISBN 3-631-34574-7

D 384
ISSN 0531-7339
ISBN 3-631-34574-7
US-ISBN 0-8204-3241-5

Author's note

The following thesis was accepted as my dissertation in July 1998 by the Faculty for Economics and Sociology of the University of Augsburg. I would like to thank my mentor and academic teacher Prof. Dr. Manfred Steiner for supervising my thesis. I am very grateful to him for leaving me the liberty to realize my concept of analysis and always being available for fruitful discussions.

I would like to thank Prof. Dr. Louis Perridon for co-mentoring of the thesis and for his collaboration in all problems in connection with the coordination of the European Union's Socrates program at the faculty. I am also grateful to Prof. Dr. Günter Bamberg for chairing the examination committee and for giving me many helpful comments.

My colleagues at the Department of Finance and Banking were most helpful to me, both through their support and their friendship. They made my time enjoyable, despite all the work writing a dissertation involves. I would especially like to thank Dr. Hermann-Josef Tebroke and Sebastian Schneider for their support and involvement, as well as Dr. Martin Wallmeier and Thomas Dittmar for their assistance in theoretical and empirical questions.

Finally, I would like to thank my parents for their love and support over all these years, and my dear wife Ursula for her TLC. I dedicate this book to them.

Augsburg, December 1998 J. Benedict Wolf

Contents

Figures

Tables

Abbreviations

3SLS	three-stage least squares regression
adj.	adjusted
AG	Aktiengesellschaft
AktG	Aktiengesetz
ANOVA	analysis of variance
APT	arbitrage pricing theory
arg	is an argument of
AUS	Australia
BörsG	Börsengesetz
CAPM	capital asset pricing model
CEO	chief executive officer
cf.	see
classifica(t).	classifications
COLS	corrected ordinary least squares regression
c. p.	ceteris paribus
CPA	certified public accounting
DEA	data envelopment analysis
diff	difference
DM	Deutsche Mark
DVFA	Deutsche Vereinigung für Finanzanalysen und Anlagenberatung
ed., eds.	editor(s)
e. g.	for example
F	France
f., ff.	following page(s)
G	Germany
GB	Great Britain
GLS	generalized least squares regression
GmbH	Gesellschaft mit beschränkter Haftung
i. e.	that is

Inc.	incorporated
km	kilometers
KonTraG	Gesetz zur Kontrolle und Transparenz im Unternehmensbereich
KWG	Kreditwesengesetz
LEN	Linear production function, Exponential utility function, Normally distributed state variable
LISREL	linear structural relationships
max, maxim.	maximum
min, minim.	minimum
ML	maximum likelihood
N/A	not applicable; non available
NLS	non-linear least squares regression
no.	number
NPV	net present value
OLS	ordinary least squares regression
p., pp.	page(s)
q. e. d.	quod erat demonstrandum
R&D	research and development
ROC	return on capital
ROE	return on equity
ROI	return on investment
sig	significance
SG	Schmalenbach-Gesellschaft
std. dev.	standard deviation
SURE	seemingly unrelated regression
TM	trademark
US, USA	United States of America
Vol.	volume
vs.	versus
WACM	weak axiom of cost minimization

Symbols[1,2]

!	faculty (after a number)
'	first derivative
"	second derivative
$\bar{}$	mean
^	estimate
*	optimal
#	number
∇_f	vector of first partial derivatives of f
$\in$	belongs to
§	paragraph (section)
&	and
a	work effort future value of investments
agency1...agency7	agency conglomerate variable (seven in all)
α	proportion homogeneity factor
B	vector of parameters
b	present value of investment
β_i	coefficient of i
C	costs
$C(\cdot)$	cost function
c	constant
D	value of debt
d	derivative dividend
d_l	long-term debt
d_s	short-term debt

---

1 Vectors are written in bold type.

2 Letter symbols are written in italics in the text where necessary to to distinguish them from normal letters.

Δ	difference
δ	partial derivative
δ_i	coefficient of i
E	value of equity
$E(\cdot)$	mean
e	equity
ε	error term
η	placeholder for term
$\eta_{i,j}$	price elasticity for inputs i and j
eval	eigenvalue
evec	eigenvector
F	value of perquisite consumption
$f(\cdot)$	function
fa	fixed assets
fcf	free cash flow
$\Phi(\cdot)$	cumulative normal density function
$\phi(\cdot)$	normal density function
g	growth
γ_i	coefficient of i
H	Hessian matrix
I	investment
i	interest rate index: company or case
L	outcome of a lottery liquidity leverage modified likelihood ratio
$L(\cdot)$	Lagrange function
λ	$\frac{\sigma_u}{\sigma_v}$ $\frac{U_p}{V_s}$ input multiplier

λ_i	Lagrange multiplier
ln	natural logarithm
LR	likelihood ratio
M	market index return number of cases
m	index of M
μ	mean
N	number of cases
n	number index of N
n_i	number of cases in sample i
P	payment obligation retirement price of debt
p	price profit probability
q	Tobin's q; ratio of market value to book value of assets discount factor
$\mathbf{q}_i$	quality vector of outputs for i
R^2	measure of linear determination
r	return
r_F	risk-free interest rate
Σ	sum
s	estimated standard deviation state staff expenditures
$s(\cdot)$	salary function
σ, σ_i	standard deviation (of i)
σ^2	variance
σ_{iM}	covariance between i and M
T	number of periods
t	index for period student-distributed test variable
Θ	set of possible future states

θ	future state
θ_t	coefficient of t
U	utility isoquant
$U(\cdot)$	utility function utility function of ownership
u	inefficiency
V	value of firm value of growth possibilities
$V(\cdot)$	utility function of management input requirement set
v	real error
$VI(\cdot)$	inner input requirement set
$VO(\cdot)$	outer input requirement set
w	input price
X	input factor set
x	independent variable, input factor
xineff	measure of x-inefficiency
Y	output factor set
y	dependent variable, output factor
z	normally distributed test variable
ζ_i	coefficient of i

1 Introduction

The late 1990s in Germany are marked by an increase of small investor activity in the capital markets. Investment funds provide easy access to the stock markets for low-budget investors who neither have the time nor inclination to daily follow stock market developments.[1] The partial privatization of the Deutsche Telekom AG in 1997 brought stock investments to the attention of the German public. With an ever larger volume of capital surging into the markets from all over the world,[2] causing stock indexes to reach unprecedented levels, investors are becoming increasingly sensitive to the management of their money. These developments have created a renewed demand for shareholder value-increasing management,[3] and an interest in the control over and verification of the management's activities.

Not long before, the rising popularity of neoinstitutionalistic economic and financial theories for the first time challenged the heretofore prevailing neoclassical view of markets and institutions. In an effort to explain the existence of institutions and instruments that the neoclassical theory could only describe, researchers abandoned the perfect market conditions of neoclassicism and studied the effects that more realistic assumptions would have on the models of economic actions. In particular, it was hoped that theoretical explanations could be found for the existence of institutions in reality, giving rise to the so-called neoinstitutionalistic theories, the transaction cost theory,[4] the property rights theory,[5] and the agency theory.[6]

---

1 Cf. BVI (1994).

2 Cf. Horn (1994).

3 Cf. Bühner (1996).

4 Cf. Williamson (1974; 1985).

5 Cf. Alchian/Demsetz (1973).

One of the most promising and fruitful directions taken in neoinstitutionalism is the result of the introduction of an imperfect information level for some of the parties in transactions. This asymmetric information distribution, coupled with an adherence to rational, utility-maximizing behavior, is well suited to describe the relationship between investors in a stock corporation and the non-ownership management. In this principal-agent relationship, the owner-principals charge the agent-management with the management of their firm, but cannot costlessly observe the management's activities. The by assumption rational management can be expected to try to exploit this information gap to increase its utility over and above that utility it can achieve by following the ownership's best interests. Unless there are monitoring and control mechanisms in place, or incentives have been included in the work contract that align the management's interests with the ownership's, measurable differences in the operational characteristics of stock corporations should be detectable by an outside analyst.[7]

Of the myriad company activities and results that can be used to measure agency problem-related differences, three categories are chosen here for closer analysis. These are the financial behavior (in Chapter 3), which studies the different preferences of the agency groups regarding the choice of financial instruments, the performance (Chapter 4), and the x-efficiency, or management-related efficiency (Chapter 5). The study of these areas will hopefully provide valuable insights for both researchers and investors concerned with this most current field of corporate finance.

The main body of the thesis is divided into four big chapters. The first of these, **Chapter 2**, contains an overview over the neoinstitutionalistic theories: transac-

---

6 Cf. Jensen/Meckling (1976). Berle/Means (1932) discuss managerial ideas without actually coining the principal-agent terminology; also see Coase (1937). Smith (1986, reprint of the original from 1776), is usually quoted as the earliest and seminal study in recent times concerning agency problems.

7 Cf. Jensen/Meckling (1976).

tion cost theory, property rights theory, agency theory, and include a separate discussion of the asymmetric information condition.[8] The theoretical analysis of agency problems, agency costs and the ability to identify agency problems is given a detailed treatment. The management is seen as the agent in this context, while the owners and the debtors constitute separate principal groups. It is possible for each group to exert control over the companies' dealings, where managerial control and ownership control are considered to exclude each other, as do manager control and creditor control. By nature of the control types, owner control and creditor control are not seen as mutually exclusive. Mechanisms to reduce agency problems from the theoretical point of view are then presented and evaluated.

The joint nature of the following empirical hypotheses is discussed, insofar as the suitability of the agency variables chosen to identify or quantify agency problems is assumed as given, whereas the hypotheses concerning the financial behavior, performance, and efficiency of the companies are submitted to statistical tests.

In addition, the data sample used in the subsequent analyses, which covers 237 German stock corporations in the seven years from 1986 to 1992, is presented to the reader, and the theoretical considerations concerning influences on agency problems, both in creating and reducing them, are applied to the data. This results in the choice of agency variables for the following research which are first presented and then further aggregated using various methods, one of them genetic algorithms.

The first main chapter ends with a description of the statistical methods germane to all following chapters, i. e., t-tests for differences in group means and logistic

---

8 Cf. Milgrom/Roberts (1992).

regressions. Additional, chapter-specific methods are discussed in the relevant chapter.

The second main chapter, **Chapter 3**, is the first of the chapters containing empirical research, and begins with a theoretical analysis of the financial behavior of stock corporations with and without agency problems. The analysis does not go so far as to postulate the existence of an optimal leverage ratio, but ranks financial instruments by order of preference and sees financial decisions as the choice of that instrument that is the most preferred among those available. This entails the analysis of the effects of financial decisions on the wealth positions of principals and agents, for which some thoughts are borrowed from the option pricing theory. The financial decision-making process described in the managerial theory of finance[9] follows the categorization of internal vs. external financing and equity vs. debt financing.

The theoretical analysis results in the ranking of four financial instruments by preference, which are the internal finance by free cash flows (i. e., cash flows remaining after the normal investment program is accounted for), external equity, and external short- and long-term debt. The rankings differ for the three agency control groups: managers, owners and creditors, giving differences in volume for companies controlled by the various groups.

The financial behavior is analyzed for the full sample and then again separately for five of the most populous industrial sectors in the dataset. These are the chemicals, machinery, electronics, food & beverages, and utilities industries. The sectoral analysis allows for additional, sector-specific hypotheses to be tested, too.

In the second empirical chapter, **Chapter 4**, the performance of the firms is addressed. The performance is understood here as an aggregated measure, based

---

9 Cf. Griner/Gordon (1995); Myers/Majluf (1984).

on either accounting values or market prices. The managerial performance hypothesis and other agency-related considerations that are presented in the theoretical section of the chapter assume uncontrolled managers to lead their companies to lower performance levels than principal-controlled companies.[10]

Four performance measures that cover the range of options for such measures are chosen for the empirical research: the returns on equity and capital, the Sharpe ratio and Tobin's q. As for the previous chapter on financial behavior, the full sample as well as sectoral subsamples are submitted to the hypothesis tests. Sector hypotheses are evaluated in this chapter, too. In addition, a time-related hypothesis is constructed and tested using cross-sectional yearly data.

The third and final empirical **Chapter 5** concerns itself with the efficiency of the stock corporations from an agency viewpoint. Therefore the x-efficiency, which is the efficiency that is due to managerial effectivity, is the object of this research chapter. The efficiency is understood as a disaggregate measure of the situation of a firm, which contrasts with the aggregated view of the firms' performance in chapter 4. The cost efficiency is used here to capture the x-efficiency. It is estimated directly from the costs of the firm.[11]

The estimation process involves the theoretical description and construction of a production function for the firms, and the derivation of a dual cost function from this production function. The estimation of the stochastic frontier cost function with an efficiency error term component that follows a one-sided distribution requires more elaborate maximum likelihood estimation techniques. These are described at the beginning of the empirical section of the chapter.[12]

---

10 Cf. Marris (1968).

11 Cf. Farrell (1957).

12 Cf. Greene (1993).

Just as for the performance chapter, cross-sectional estimations that allow for developments over time are used to test for time-related hypotheses, but also the standard hypotheses are tested here. The full sample and sectoral sample tests, which call for slight variations in the estimation functions, follow in the accustomed manner.

A thorough summary of the results is followed by an appendix in which many of the tables were placed. This should make the body of the thesis more readable while not compromising the openness of the research.

2 The Agency Theory and its Empirical Implementation

2.1 Overview over the Neoinstitutionalistic Theories

The neoclassic financial theory is based on the assumption of perfect markets, which are defined as having the following characteristics:[1]

- full information for all parties,
- instantaneous transmission of information,
- no transaction costs,
- no taxes,
- rational investors,[2] and
- homogeneous expectations.

Under exclusion of marring factors such as taxes and transaction costs[3], financial actions and relations can be studied in a clean form, more clearly than they are observable in reality. This makes the neoclassical theory of finance a very valuable tool in education and as a foundation for further deliberations. However, the rigidity and unrealistic nature of the assumptions not only lead to the inability to empirically test propositions derived from them, but also prohibit the explanation of financial institutions such as banks, insurance companies, rating agencies,[4] and financial laws.[5] Institutions can generally be defined as a system of norms constructed for a certain purpose and they include the instruments that are necessary to sustain the system and enable the achievement of the goals for which the institution was created.[6] From the neoclassical point of view, markets should be able to fulfill the functions of existing institutions, such as the dissemination of the information a rating agency processes. The existence of financial instruments are also inexplicable, if they can be synthesized from simple ones.[7] Many instruments and institutions therefore can only be described, but not explained, in the neoclassical theory of finance.

---

1 Cf. Oberender (1987), p. 1240.

2 Williamson (1985) speaks of three types of rationality, the strong rationality in neoclassicism, bounded rationality which denotes utility maximization under imperfect information, and organic rationality.

3 See below 2.1.1.

4 Cf. Steiner/Heinke (1996).

5 Cf. Schmidt (1988); Hax/Hartmann-Wendels/von Hinten (1988).

6 Cf. Richter (1990), p. 572.

7 Cf. Schmidt (1981), p. 136.

The neoinstitutionalistic theory tries to address these open questions. In doing so, it must forego the assumption of perfect markets and allow for imperfections. These imperfections ultimately explain the existence of the observable financial institutions and instruments.

Figure 2-1 shows a systemization of the neoinstitutionalistic theories.[8] All theories are based on the relations between different parties, their explanation and their optimal design. The first distinction that can be made is between incentive-based and transaction cost-based theories. The names of these branches give the decisive factor in each theory that is used to explain the object of the analysis. The incentive-based theories are further subdivided into the property rights theory, and the agency theory, whose financial and organizational branches are used to supply the theory used in this study. Several studies are also based on the sole assumption of asymmetric information,[9] although this condition is very common and also used in addition to others in other branches, such as the transaction cost theory branch.

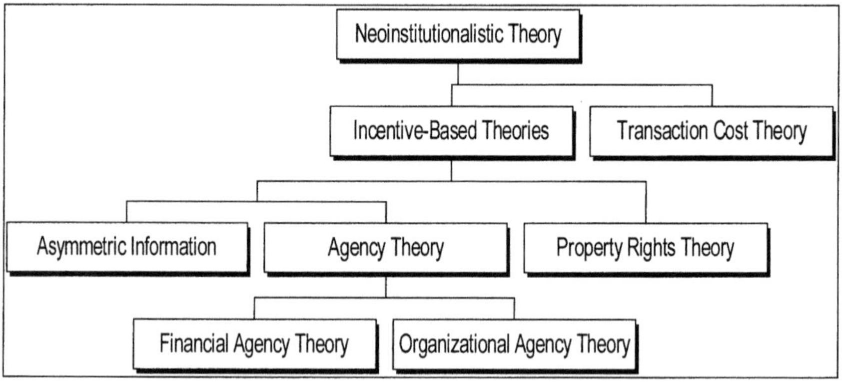

Figure 2-1: Systemization of the neoinstitutionalistic theories[10]

8 Also see Schmidt/Terberger (1996), pp. 392 ff.

9 Asymmetric information in this context is defined as a situation in which one or more parties have more information than others, and the others know about this advantage. Cf. Schmidt/Terberger (1996), p. 387.

10 Cf. Williamson (1985), pp. 23 ff.

2.1.1 Transaction Cost Theory

The transaction cost theory[11] obviously rejects the assumption of non-existing transaction costs of the perfect markets and studies the effect of this imperfection on economic relations. The theory does not require an asymmetric information distribution.[12] It posits that transactions occur there where they are most efficient, i. e., where the transaction costs are minimized.[13] This can be on the market or inside a company.

Transaction costs can be divided into

- costs of coordination and
- costs of motivation.[14]

Coordination is necessary for the involved parties to agree on a transaction, and can include costs of gathering information (search costs), but also communication costs, and location costs such as rent when it is necessary to get the partners together. Opportunity costs in the sense of lost utility due to imperfect matches and deals are also counted toward transaction costs of coordination.

Motivational costs are due to information asymmetries, where one party is not sufficiently motivated to enter a deal because of an inability to oversee the situation. A very popular example is the used car market.[15] Unsure about the quality of the cars, buyers assume a car is of average quality and are only willing to pay the price for an average quality car. This forces the sellers of above average quality cars out of the market. Motivational costs occur before a transaction is sealed and are also called costs of hidden information.[16]

Imperfect commitment is another motivational problem, which occurs after a transaction is agreed upon. It causes costs of hidden action. If one contract partner is unable to observe the other partner's activities, or accurately attribute the results of the actions to the partner's efforts or outside circumstances, this opens up a moral hazard for the unmonitored partner to exploit his advantage to the detriment of the other. This post-contractual situation is in the center of this study, as the management of the stock corporations to be analyzed have for the most part already been hired at terms that have been agreed upon, and the ques-

---

11 Described by Coase (1937).

12 Cf. Schmidt/Terberger (1996), p. 389.

13 Cf. Theuvsen (1997) on internal transaction costs of companies.

14 Cf. Milgrom/Roberts (1992), pp. 29 f. Picot (1982) speaks of costs of negotiation, costs of control, and costs of adaptation.

15 Cf. Akerlof (1970).

16 Cf. Arrow (1985, 1986).

tion concentrates on how to keep the management in line without tampering with contract possibilities.

Transactions themselves have several dimensions, all of which can affect the cost levels and therefore play a role in the transaction cost theory. These are the[17]

- specificity of the underlying of a transaction,
- uncertainty or complexity of a transaction and its control,
- frequency of the transaction, and
- degree of connection of one transaction to other transactions.

Specific assets are those that cannot be transferred to another company or even used in another function without incurring a major reduction in value. Constructing a custom-built machine is more specific than producing assembly-line gadgets, making the contract partners more sensitive to the well-being of the respective partner. The higher the specificity of a transaction is, the more it makes sense to incorporate the transaction into a firm (buy up the contractor), and not carry it out via markets. A firm is understood in this case as a nexus of contracts.[18] Moving the circumstances of the contract making from the market to the company provides a different set of control and enforcement options that reduces the risk of the seller of being saddled with the loss of the specific value of the asset due to contractual loopholes. Motivational and coordination costs are both affected by these decisions.

Related issues are the complexity and uncertainty of a transaction. The complexity will cause high costs of coordination. An example for an uncertain transaction is a purchase of a resource for which the exact volume of the resource required might be unclear until shortly before its delivery is due. High levels for either factor, complexity and uncertainty, speak for the transferal of the transaction in question away from the market to the inside of a company.

Setting specificity and complexity aside, even fairly basic transactions can more reasonably be incorporated into a firm under certain circumstances. If a transaction frequently reoccurs, but for each occurrence still produces transaction costs on the market, it might be cheaper to transfer this transaction to the company. If the transaction is linked to other transactions, especially those including different parties from those involved in the original transaction, coordination costs can increase dramatically if multiple negotiations must be conducted via the market.

---

17 Cf. Milgrom/Roberts (1992), p. 30.

18 Cf. Jensen (1983); Pfaffmann (1996).

All of the factors presented can affect transaction costs.[19] The main principle that emerged here is that high transaction costs for carrying out a transaction on the market provide a reason to transfer the transaction into the company. The Coase theorem describes this conclusion:[20]

> If parties are bargaining to an efficient agreement and their preferences have no wealth effects, then their bargaining power or assets owned at the beginning of the negotiations will not affect the outcome. Efficiency alone governs the choice, while the other factors only affect decisions about the sharing of the costs and benefits.

The transaction cost theory ultimately leads into a theory of vertical integration of firms.[21]

2.1.2 Property Rights Approach

In the Coase theorem above, the efficient solution described is only achieved if the rights to the assets mentioned are clearly defined. These rights comprise the rights of ownership, disposition and barter.[22] If they are not secure, this can affect the solution found and divert it away from the efficient solution. The branch of theory treating this variant of the problem is called the property rights theory.[23,24]

The property rights theory belongs to the incentive-based approaches of the neoinstitutionalistic theory because it addresses the effects unclear or unassigned property rights have on the incentives of the involved parties.[25] It assumes individual utility maximization, the existence of property rights, transaction costs, and external effects.[26] The transaction costs arise due to the formulation, allocation, transferal, and assertion of the property rights. The higher the transaction costs are, the less likely it is that the property rights will be exercised.[27] The

---

19 An application of this theory to financial transactions can be found in Münchow (1995), pp. 68 ff.

20 Cf. Coase (1937); Coase (1960).

21 Cf. Oberender (1994).

22 Cf. Fischer (1994); Schenk (1984).

23 Cf. Coase (1960); Alchian, (1965); Demsetz (1967); Alchian/Demsetz (1973). Gäfgen (1984) prefers to call it property rights analysis.

24 Financial applications of the property rights theory are discussed in Schmidt (1988).

25 Cf. Kaulmann (1987); Buhbe (1980).

26 Cf. Gäfgen (1984).

27 Cf. Schüller (1983).

non-allocation of the effects of certain assets to the owner of the asset or another party causes external effects. These are the positive or negative results of actions for which nobody can be held responsible. Both high transaction costs and high external effects are signs that a situation can be improved.[28]

Another problem that arises due to an inadequate property rights distribution is the free rider problem or public good problem. If the right of use of an asset is not allocated, or the enforcement of the existing property rights is not possible, other parties can use the asset without having to pay for the use.[29] Here, the property rights theory discusses who is best assigned the rights in order to make them enforceable. Innovation and the taking of risk are both discouraged on markets where the property rights are not clearly allocated or enforceable. This is basically a form of the free rider problem, where imitators for example can profit from an innovative firm without themselves incurring the risk of the innovation.[30]

2.1.3 Asymmetric Information

Studies uniquely rejecting the assumption of perfect information for all parties as stated for perfect markets constitute another of the incentive-based branches.[31] There are many studies, especially in finance, that take this approach. Here, the lack of information is assumed to be on the side of owners who are not at the same time managers of a firm. The information asymmetry between the well-informed management and the ill-informed owners can produce several types of behavior. Assuming that the management is acting in the owners' interests,[32] managers of successful companies can try to reduce the information asymmetry by producing costly signals their less successful competitors cannot afford to copy. An example is a dividend raise.[33] This informs the management that their company is well off. The signaling theory, which is the

---

28 Cf. Picot (1991), pp. 145 f.

29 Cf. Milgrom/Roberts (1992), pp. 294 f.

30 An overview over empirical research in this area is given by de Alessi (1980).

31 Cf. Ross (1977); Ross (1978).

32 Strictly speaking, this assumption might be said to contradict the assumption of rational participants in the perfect market theory. As long as there are no mechanisms in place to align a manager's interests with the investors', they will only by coincidence have the same utility function. The management therefore will under normal circumstances not be maximizing its own utility by maximizing the owners'.

33 Cf. Denis/Denis/Sarin (1994); Milde (1990).

analysis of such signaling instruments, constitutes one branch of the studies based on asymmetric information.[34]

Another branch more specifically addresses the financial behavior of the management of such firms and studies the signals finance decisions, in connection with investment decisions[35] or unusual actions such as stock repurchases,[36] can send to the investors. This so-called pecking order theory[37] is described in more detail in chapter 3.2.

Apart from signaling, the studies in the field of asymmetric information discuss other possibilities of reducing the information asymmetry. Whereas signaling is an option also suited to reduce hidden action problems and therefore belongs to the situation after the contract is sealed, the self selection and screening solution alternatives belong to the pre-contractual hidden information problem.

Self selection means that the less-informed party confronts the one with hidden information with the choice between several options, which respectively are suited to different quality levels of the party with the hidden information. The choice of alternative will reveal to the less-informed side what quality level the other side possesses.[38] An example can be found in the health insurance industry. Some people are prone to sickness, others not, but the insurance firm does not know this in advance. By offering the choice between low payments but incomplete coverage of treatment and high payments but complete treatment compensation, the hidden information can be uncovered. High health-risk people will choose the full coverage, low risk people the low rates.

Screening simply stands for the elicitation of the help of third parties to acquire more knowledge on the situation at hand where an informational asymmetry prevails. The third party can for example be an auditing or CPA firm. Screening can also refer to the uninformed party's own efforts to reduce the information gap.[39]

---

34 Cf. Ross (1978).

35 Cf. Moses (1991); Noe (1988); John (1987).

36 Cf. Vermaelen (1981); Constantinides/Grundy (1989).

37 Cf. Myers/Majluf (1984).

38 Cf. Perridon/Steiner (1997), p. 522.

39 For a slightly differing description of the signaling, self-selection, and screening concepts, cf. Milgrom/Roberts (1992), pp. 154 ff.

2.2 Agency Theory

2.2.1 Typology of the Agency Theory

The agency theory is marked as a parallel branch of the asymmetric information studies in Figure 2-1, as it can be defined as a theory based on the asymmetric information assumption and in addition the assumption of rational managers maximizing their own utility.[40] The definition of a principal-agent relationship is a relationship in which the principal instructs the agent to conduct affairs of the principal, under delegation of some decision-making authority.[41] In this study, the principal is often the less well informed owners of the firm, or also the creditor; the management has the role of the agent. The terminology led to the name of principal-agent theory or simply agency theory for this neoinstitutionalistic theory.[42]

2.2.1.1 Owner-Manager Conflicts

In the owner-management principal-agent relation, and given the utility-maximizing behavior of the management, the decisions the management makes will not necessarily be in the best interests of the owners of a firm. This is the case if it is difficult or expensive for the owners to verify the agent's actions, or if no measures have been taken to realign the management's and the ownership's interests. This causes an agency problem. Managers who are hired to run a company will quite naturally have an information advantage over the non-managing owners.[43] Another type of agency problem occurs if the principal and agent have different propensities for risk, and must share the risk of an investment or of the firm.[44]

While managerial decisions are made in all areas of a company's activities, and all can be influenced by agency considerations, those affecting the financial area produce effects that are most accessible to outside empirical analysis. The study

---

40 Called opportunistic behavior. Cf. Williamson (1985).

41 Cf. Pratt/Zeckhauser (1985).

42 Jensen/Smith (1985) suggest using the term principal-agent theory for the mathematical branch and (positive) agency theory for the empirical branch of this neoinstitutionalistic theory (detailed below). Under this distinction, the following study belongs to the agency theory. See, though, 2.2.2.3, which pertains to the principal-agent-theory.

43 Cf. Schmidt/Terberger (1996), p. 435.

44 Cf. Eisenhardt (1988).

of these activities is classified as the financial branch of the agency theory.[45] Another take on the agency problem is organizational, where the effect of organizational structures on the magnitude of agency problems is analyzed. This view especially allows normative recommendations to be made concerning the optimal organizational structures in a firm in view of agency conflicts. In this study, both elements will be addressed.

Both the financial and the organizational branches of the agency theory produce mathematical and empirical studies.[46] The mathematical principal-agent studies are able to make precise assumptions regarding the utility and risk functions of the principals and agents.[47] Based on these assumptions they can come up with detailed recommendations on what arrangements are optimally suited to which principal-agent constellation. In this sense, the mathematical studies are often normative in nature. On the downside, their inclusion of utility functions makes these models useless for empirical testing, and thus non-falsifiable, apart from errors in the mathematical calculations.[48] This study on the other hand is intended to be empirical in nature and test a number of agency hypotheses for the German capital market. The importance and role of the utility in the agency theory will be addressed (see 2.2.2.3), but it cannot play the central part in the formulation of hypotheses. The hypotheses must be based on less precisely defined relationships that are generally accepted as applying to the party being analyzed. This means for example that managers will be assumed to be risk averse, without specifying their actual utility functions. The empirical research can of course also depart from purely positive analyses toward normative recommendations, which have the added advantage of being founded on the analysis of actual practices that were observed and measured in reality.

2.2.1.2 Creditor-Owner and Other Agency Conflicts

Apart from the owner-manager relationship, there are also other principal-agent relationships in a firm.[49] The next most important one from the point of view of this study is that between the creditors as the second major class of financier and

45 The pecking order theory parallels this branch of the agency theory. Cf. Griner/Gordon (1995).

46 Cf. Jensen (1983); Wenger/Terberger (1988); Elschen (1991).

47 For an example, see Kürsten (1993).

48 According to the theory of science called critical rationalism, an important characteristic of the quality of every theory is its empirical content. That means that a theory must be formulated in a fashion that allows its empirical falsification. The verification of a hypothesis is not possible; it can only not be rejected. Cf. Popper (1966).

49 Cf. Hackett (1985).

the owners. In this type of study, the management is usually assumed to have the same interests as the ownership, otherwise the analysis would become too complicated. In this case, the creditors are the principals, and the owners (with the managers) the agents.[50] The interests of owners and creditors can collide in four areas:[51]

- Dividends: A dividend hike will be good news to shareholders, but leads to the payout of assets that alternatively could be used to ensure the repayment of the debt to the owners.[52]
- Claim dilution: Procuring new debt (bonds) at higher priority or seniority than the existing debt will lead to the devaluation of the old debt, if the possibility of further issues was not included in the price of the old debt.
- Asset substitution: Investing in risky investments increases the payout to shareholders,[53] and also increases the default risk borne by the creditors (cf. chapter 3.2).[54]
- Underinvestment: Low positive NPV investments, whose profits must be used for amortization purposes will be foregone since they do not benefit the owners (cf. chapter 4.1.2).[55]

Nevertheless, both owners and creditors will be interested in curbing the management's perk consumption and shirking. Also, if the management is uncontrolled by the ownership, the actions listed above will not necessarily occur, as the management will not be maximizing the owners' utility. Therefore, the ownership-creditor conflict can be smaller than the degree of ownership-creditor agreement on corporate policy.[56]

Other principal-agent relationships that will not be analyzed more closely in this study are between other stakeholders and the management or management/ownership of a firm (cf. Figure 2-2).[57] There can also be conflicts inside of

---

50 Cf. Hax/Hartmann-Wendels/von Hinten (1988), p. 708.

51 Cf. Smith/Warner (1979).

52 Cf. Kalay (1982).

53 Cf. Mülbert (1997), pp. 16 ff.

54 One can question if managers really are willing to let their company default. In the new German insolvency proceedings code, effective in 1999, incumbent managers must as a rule relinquish control of the firm. Cf. Drukarczyk/Schmidt (1997). Cf. Steiner (1994) for financial strategies in crises.

55 Cf. Myers (1977).

56 Cf. Parrino/Weisbach (1997), who only find small effects of owner-creditor conflicts.

57 Cf. Hill/Jones (1992); Cornell/Shapiro (1987).

the ownership or creditor groups, especially among current and new owners or creditors. An important stakeholder, also from an ethical point of view, are the workers in a company.[58] The market partners of a firm in both the sales as well as the resource markets constitute further stakeholder groups, i. e., both customers and suppliers can be seen as principals or agents.[59]

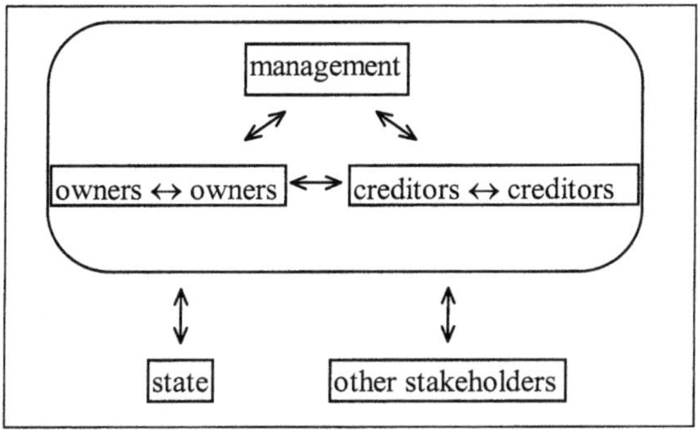

Figure 2-2: Financial principal-agent relationships in a company[60]

2.2.2 Agency Problems and Agency Costs

2.2.2.1 The Concept of Agency Costs

Berle and Means are credited with having drawn attention to the effect of ownership control on firm performance in this century.[61] In their seminal article, Jensen/Meckling (1976) link capital structure to agency costs and thus performance and revived the interest in the ownership/performance question. They start their analysis by taking a company owned to 100 % by the manager (e. g., a family firm) and study the behavior of the manager as he slowly sells shares of his firm and continues to maximize his utility. He not only derives utility from the profit of the firm, but also from the consumption of non-pecuniary perquisites which reduces the profits and value of the firm.

---

58 Cf. Valentiner-Branth/Weiler (1991); Hax (1981).

59 Cf. Titman (1984).

60 Cf. Noth (1996), p. 129.

61 Cf. Berle/Means (1932). For Germany, see Rathenau (1916).

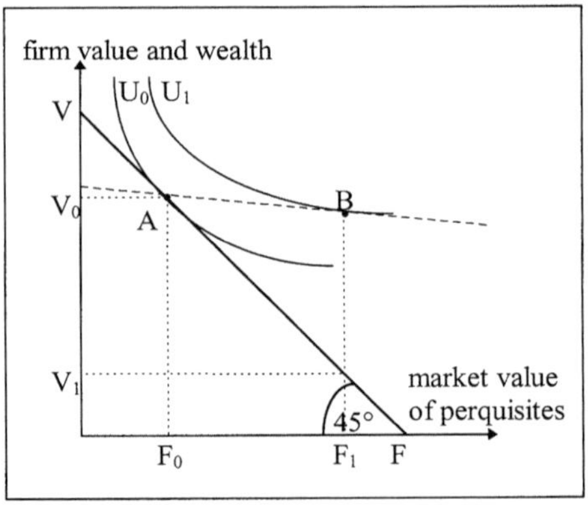

Figure 2-3: Development of the firm value by degree of managerial ownership[62]

Figure 2-3 shows the relationship between the firm value and the level of perquisites a manager enjoys. Even when the manager is the full owner of a firm, his utility function for which two indifference curves U_0 and U_1 are drawn will make him decide to enjoy some perks in order to maximize his utility. The level of perquisites F_0 he will choose is defined at the point A where the trade-off line VF between firm value and perks is a tangent to one of his utility indifference curves, here U_0. The consumption reduces the firm value dollar for dollar from its maximum possible value of V to V_0, which is the price an outside investor would pay for the company.

If the manager were to sell a portion α of the company ($0 < \alpha < 1$), increasing consumption by one dollar would not cost him one dollar in firm value, but only $(1 - \alpha)$ times one dollar. The remaining α times one dollar loss would be borne by the outside investor. This is an incentive for the manager to increase his consumption. In Figure 2-3, this is marked by the new trade-off line between firm value and perquisite consumption for the manager going through A and B. Its slope is $-\alpha$, showing that the manager's wealth invested in the firm only declines by α for every unit of additional consumption. Again assuming utility-maximizing behavior, the manager will increase consumption to the point where this new trade-off line is a tangent to an indifference curve. This is at point B in Figure 2-3, where the manager reaches a new utility level U_1 by consuming F_1, because the outside investor is bearing some of the costs his increased consumption is producing. The firm value for outsiders, however, drops from V_0 to V_1. This drop in firm value constitutes agency costs (see 2.2.2.2.3).

62 Cf. Jensen/Meckling (1976), p. 316.

2.2.2.2 The Categorization of Agency Costs by Jensen/Meckling

2.2.2.2.1 Monitoring Costs

To reduce agency costs, the outside ownership can decide to take measures suitable to monitor and control the management and enforce their interests. These so-called monitoring costs can consist of the retrieval of additional information on the company's prospects and information requirements for shareholders' meetings.[63] The control can also consist of simple restrictions on certain activities, such as limiting the amount of profits that may be retained. Such actions can cause follow-up opportunity costs if the optimal action for the company is unknowingly excluded from the manager's choices. Since the measures usually produce costs, it is not possible for outside owners to achieve perfect monitoring short of simply taking over the management positions. A balance must be found where the additional marginal cost of an extra unit of monitoring exactly offsets the marginal savings due to reduced agency costs (see Figure 2-4). This assumes that for the first units of monitoring, monitoring costs reduce agency costs by more than the cost of monitoring, and that the relationship is reversed as monitoring increases, as is visible by the rising marginal costs of monitoring. As a result of such reasoning, the agency theory is a theory of the second best, where the costless optimum is not the target, but the minimization of costs is.[64]

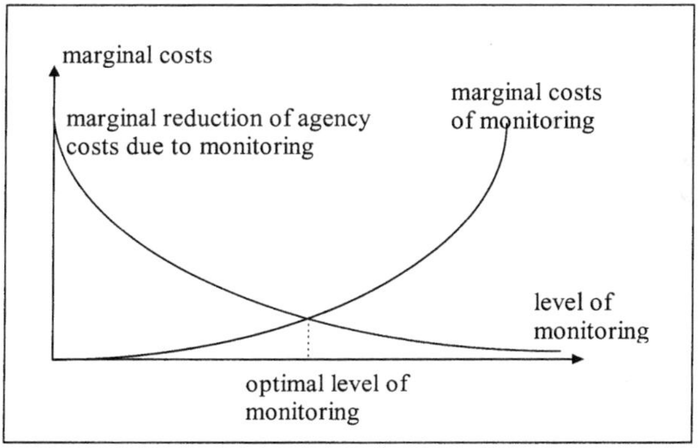

Figure 2-4: Graphical representation of the optimal level of monitoring

---

[63] Jensen/Meckling also count such things as compensation policies and budget restrictions to monitoring. Cf. Jensen/Meckling (1976), p. 308, footnote 9.

[64] Cf. Schmidt/Terberger (1996), pp. 400 ff. See Lipsey/Lancaster (1956) on the theory of second best.

2.2.2.2.2 Bonding Costs

The second category of agency costs described by Jensen/Meckling (1976) are bonding costs, which are incurred by the agent (manager), and consist of the costs the manager bears in order to demonstrate to the principals his intention of maximizing their utility and not his. Such measures could be voluntary contractual self-restrictions. But bonding costs can also consist of costs the agent causes to the firm and the owners, not to himself. An example for this can be found in the signaling theory that assumes asymmetric informational distribution between owners and managers of a firm, but not a divergence of interests between the two parties.[65] In order to reduce the information gap of the less well informed owners concerning the future prospects of the firm, a dividend raise can signal to the owners that the management is confident of being able to finance the dividend raise now and in the future, i. e., the prospects of the firm are good and will remain so in the future. Such a signal must be costly in order to deter companies that are not as well off from copying the signal and rendering its informational value nil.[66]

Incentive pay can be seen as another form of bonding a manager's interests to those of the ownership (see 2.2.3.2). Yet performance-dependent payment contracts will produce costs through the extra effort needed to construct a workable contract acceptable to both parties. Also, incentive pay can produce a loss of utility on the part of the manager whenever he feels that the payment does not compensate the extra effort.[67]

2.2.2.2.3 Residual Loss

The cost factor of residual loss[68] was already partially described above in 2.2.2.2, as the drop in firm value incurred when the management increases its consumption of perquisites in order to maximize its own utility after having sold a proportion α of the firm. In Figure 2-3, the residual loss due to perquisite consumption is depicted as the drop in firm value from V_0 to V_1.

The description that evolved around Figure 2-3 shows that non-managerial ownership of a company will produce increased costs, in the form of perquisite consumption, that reduce the firm value. In addition, shirking becomes a problem in

---

65 For more on signaling cf. Padberg (1995), pp. 119 ff.

66 Cf. Hartmann-Wendels (1986).

67 Studies of the relationship of incentive pay to performance are e. g. Riahi-Belkaoui (1992), Murphy (1985), Coughlan/Schmidt (1985).

68 Cf. Jensen/Meckling (1976), p. 308.

companies not managed by the ownership, as managers optimize their utility in a tradeoff between working and leisure. The resulting decrease in value is also called residual loss. Residual loss consists of other elements, too. Not only can it be expected that a manager will increase his consumption, but he may also, in maximizing his utility, make managerial decisions that are not in the best interests of the ownership of the firm, the principals. This, too, can be measurable in a loss of firm value.

Credit-sided agency problems can lead to residual loss if the optimal investment policy is not achieved (cf. 2.2.1.2). It can also lead to the phenomenon known as credit rationing.[69] This occurs as the result of the moral hazard creditors are confronted with. If they cannot be sure managers will implement the promised level of risk in their investment policy, the creditors might raise the interest rates demanded to account for this uncertainty. This can lead to the adverse selection effect as good debtors leave the too expensive credit market.[70]

Finally, the term residual loss also applies to the costs required to optimize the risk allocation among bearers with different risk propensities (owners, managers, creditors).[71] A suboptimal investment policy due to a faulty allocation of funds will reduce the company's profits and create additional residual loss.

2.2.2.3 Risk Allocation and Utility Maximization as Agency Problems under Asymmetric Information

2.2.2.3.1 Risk Allocation

When considering alternate investments i, a simple decision rule is to choose the one for which the highest weighted average return r_i is expected. Possible returns r_θ are estimated for Θ different possible future states, and for each state θ, its probability of occurring p_θ must also be judged. The probability of the state's occurring is used to weight the returns, see Equation (2-1).[72,73]

$$r_i = \sum_{\theta} p_{i,\theta} \cdot r_{i,\theta} \tag{2-1}$$

---

[69] Cf. Terberger (1987).

[70] Cf. Neuberger (1989), pp. 132 ff; Stiglitz/Weiss (1981).

[71] Cf. Kürsten (1993), pp. 179 f. Also see 2.2.2.3.

[72] Cf. Myerson (1991), p. 12.

[73] This criterion is also called the Bayes criterion and provides a simple and intuitive method for comparing investments.

In modern financing theory, it is recognized that high returns alone do not give full information on the performance of a firm. High returns are often achieved at the price of high risk incurred, and comparing return values with each other without allowing for different risk of the projects is only possible with risk-neutral investors. Otherwise, it is necessary to norm the return values by the units of risk each return value entails. The variance or standard deviation of the possible returns of an investment is the most commonly used measure for risk.[74]

For a manager, the risk of the investments he is willing to sustain is curbed by two factors. One is the lack of diversification of his own investments, given that his so-called human capital is bound in the firm he works for. This situation is exacerbated if part of his knowledge is specific, meaning that it cannot be used in another company or context, which reduces the outside value of that knowledge. For this reason, managers will be concerned with the total risk of a firm, not only its non-diversifiable portion.[75] The other factor that increases the risk aversion of a manager is the proportion of his salary that is not fixed, but paid out as shares in or options on the firm (cf. 2.2.3.2). While risky and highly profitable investments could sharply increase the value of these shares or derivatives, an even greater portion of the manager's capital is thus tied to the company. Failures will hit him even harder this way.

There are different positions on the level of risk desired by the ownership of a company. On the one hand, most people are risk averse, meaning that they are only willing to assume more risk if they are compensated for this. Risk-neutral people do not require an increased compensation for them to assume more risk, and risk-loving people will even be content with a reduction in compensation.[76] Figure 2-5 shows a possible utility function of a risk averse person. If a person is offered the choice between two equally probable risky profits p_1 and p_2, or alternatively one sure profit $0.5 \cdot (p_1 + p_2)$, he will prefer the latter. His utility function is concave.

74 Cf. Milgrom/Roberts (1992), p. 209.

75 Cf. Reagan/Stulz (1983).

76 Also see e. g. Blohm/Lüder (1995). One can also define risk aversion as requiring an over proportional compensation for assuming more risk, and risk propensity as being content with a subproportional increase in compensation, but an increase nonetheless.

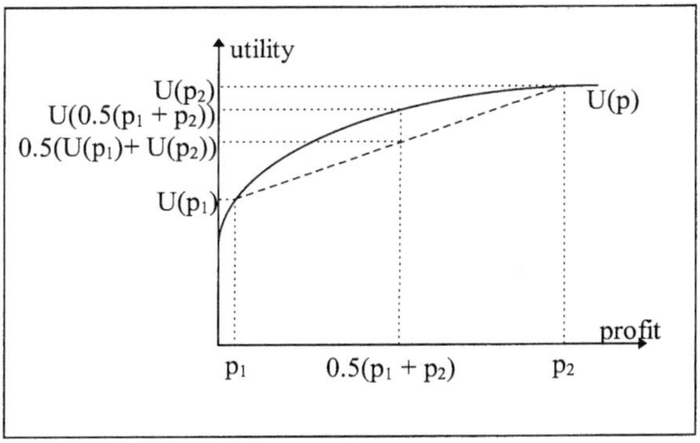

Figure 2-5: Exemplary sketch of the utility function of a risk averse person[77]

On the other hand, in the case of a stock corporation the owners often have a much smaller proportion of their wealth invested in the company, in particular none of their human capital. They also only have limited liability in the case of default, reducing their stakes in the company. In addition, they can profit from diversification, which means that by investing in many different companies, the firm-specific risks each company entails are reduced by those risks of the other companies invested in that have a non-perfect correlation to each other. This can lead to a greater risk propensity than the management may have, as the owners participate fully in the company's success and in a corporation only risk limited liability in failure.[78]

Owners might have another interest in increasing the risk of their investments if the companies they participate in are not wholly financed by equity. Then their stake in the company can be interpreted as a call option on the whole firm (see below chapter 3.2.4).[79] If a company's returns are high and exceed the amortization of the debt, owners can repay the debt and keep all remaining proceeds. If the company fails, owners only lose their shares through their limited liability. Call options increase in value if the standard deviation of the underlying increases, as the expected profits of new possible states increase, while the loss in the case of failure is fixed.[80] It is assumed here that owners are less risk-averse than managers, but remain risk-averse or are risk neutral.[81]

---

77 Cf. Perridon/Steiner (1997), p. 114.

78 An empirical application of the risk aversion measure can be found in Campbell (1996).

79 Cf. Merton (1974).

80 Cf. Galai/Masulis (1976).

81 Cf. Shavell (1979), p. 66.

If the risk propensities of owners and managers diverge, agency problems can arise through the problem of distributing the risk of investments to those who are most capable of bearing that risk. This means that binding a too large portion of a manager's salary to the company's profit via incentive pay can collide with his risk aversion and be a suboptimal solution.[82] Thus, a conflict arises between the optimal (efficient) risk allocation and the optimal incentive negotiation.[83] Rising managerial ownership can initially be beneficial to performance and shareholder value, but then decrease it again as the manager becomes more and more risk averse in order to secure his rising nondiversifiable capital stock invested in the firm.[84]

2.2.2.3.2 Utility Maximization

Before the manager enters a contract with the owners, the contract specifications must be agreed upon and should allocate risk optimally. A simple set of axioms for a utility function is supplied by:[85]

1. There is a complete, reflexive and transitive order of preferences for a set of possible outcomes to an investment.[86]
2. The preference order for the outcomes L_i is continuous: if $L_1 > L_2 > L_3$, there is an α, $0 < \alpha < 1$, such that $L_2 = (L_1, \alpha, L_3)$.[87]
3. The preference order is independent from irrelevant alternatives: if $L_1 > L_2$, and $0 < \alpha < 1$, then $L' = \alpha L_1 + (1-\alpha)L_3 > \alpha L_2 + (1-\alpha)L_3$ for any given L_3.

The ownership will award a compensation to the management and in return demand a level of work input from the management that maximizes the ownership's utility function. The owners' utility is a function of the profits achieved, minus the profit-dependent salary of the management. The profits in turn rise with the work level of the management, so the ownership will demand a maximum work effort.[88]

---

82 Cf. Bühner (1989).

83 Cf. Neus (1989); Milgrom/Roberts (1992), p. 208.

84 Cf. Morck/Shleifer/Vishny (1988); Chen/Hexter/Hu (1993); Rosen (1990). This nonlinearity could explain the nonsignificant result of a linear test of differences in risk between owner and manager-controlled firms for Germany in Thonet/Poensgen (1979).

85 Cf. von Neumann/Morgenstern (1947). These are the von Neumann/Morgernstern axioms, sometimes called the Bernoulli Principle.

86 The outcomes are generally called lotteries.

87 In contrast to Figure 2-5.

88 Cf. Blickle-Liebersbach (1990).

The management's choice of work level on the other hand will be governed by the compensation it receives, which increases with the effort a manager puts into his work. However, a rising work effort decreases the management's utility, causing its maximum utility to lie at a lower work effort than the effort needed for the maximum utility of the ownership.

Due to the problems in making the management into owners in order to equalize the risk propensities of owners and managers as mentioned above in 2.2.2.3.1, the different choices of work effort will prevail in an asymmetric setting with hidden information.[89] The optimal effort depends on the risk of the investment, by way of the risk aversion measures. The lower the manager's risk aversion, the higher his effort will be (and also the proportion of his profit-linked salary).[90] Overall, though, the management will not work as hard as the ownership would like them to. Therefore, agency costs will arise that in the Jensen/Meckling (1976) context could be termed as residual loss.

2.2.2.4 The Measurability of Agency Costs

For the purposes of this study, it is not only necessary to categorize the agency costs, but also to empirically measure them, especially in view of the performance and efficiency analyses. This calls for a subsequent appraisal of the practicability of determining the different cost categories.

Monitoring activities in the form of information retrieval and expense of time can be expressed and measured in monetary values, e. g., the cost of shareholders' meetings, and the cost in man-hours necessary to supply outside owners with information on the firm's investment possibilities. The implementation of restrictions on actions or policies is slightly more difficult to evaluate in objective terms. However, even the quantifiable portions of this cost category are hardly observable by an outside analyst. The ownership or other monitoring instance itself would have to be interviewed by the analyst for this. Therefore, the concrete concept of monitoring costs is rather difficult to numerically evaluate by an outsider.

Bonding costs in the form of signals sent via capital issues or dividend hikes produce costs that can directly be identified, such as printing costs to inform investors of the issue or bank fees for the placement. Contractual restrictions on behavior and activities of the management cost time and money to negotiate; however, the effects of the restrictions are more elusive. The loss in utility of the management is difficult to quantify, as is typical for all utility, but it can also be

---

89 Cf. Arrow (1986).

90 Cf. Blickle-Liebersbach (1990).

argued that from the point of view of the principals of a company, this loss is not relevant.

The residual loss is the category of agency costs that is seemingly most difficult to measure. They are defined as the drop in value from the ideal value of the firm. This ideal value is of course not known in the real world, only the actual firm value.[91] Alternate situations cannot be played through with single parameters changed and all else equal. The residual loss however can be determined to a degree by replacing the ideal firm value with the average firm value of similar companies without agency problems. Given a sufficiently large sample, the reduced value of the company with agency problems can be interpreted as residual loss, where the difference can of course also include unspecified monitoring and bonding costs. This practice will be applied in the following empirical sections. It will be both used in connection with performance and efficiency measures which are directly affected by agency costs, as well as a general procedure in determining differences in the financial behavior of the firms. The loss in utility of the management or ownership due to suboptimal risk allocation is not necessarily expressable in monetary terms, and therefore remains unobservable. This shows that agency cost can at the same time be observable, but not immediately and by consequence avoidable.[92]

2.2.3 Mechanisms to Reduce Agency Problems

Aside from identifying and (indirectly) measuring the level of agency problems and the associated agency costs, the agency theory in both its positive and normative forms also concerns itself with the description and evaluation of mechanisms that are suitable for reducing the level of agency problems and costs in a firm.[93]

The mechanisms discussed in this context are subdivided into control and incentive mechanisms. The control mechanisms fall into two groups, the first being the internal control mechanisms, which originate inside of a company. The second type of control mechanism is external, if it originates from outside the company and functions independently from the company's influence. Each category will be presented below, followed by a discussion of which mechanisms will be captured in what way in this study.

---

91 And even that only in the case of publically traded stock corporations.

92 Cf. Schneider (1987).

93 An interesting study for the current situation in Germany after the publication of the law concerning control and transparency in companies (Gesetz zur Kontrolle und Transparenz im Unternehmensbereich, KonTraG) in March 1998 is in Förschle/Glaum/Mandler (1998).

2.2.3.1 Monitoring and Control Mechanisms

The control mechanisms to reduce agency problems belong to those that produce monitoring costs in the sense of 2.2.2.2 above. This means that the principals, who for the purposes of this study are exclusively understood to be the ownership and the creditors of a firm, can choose methods within their means to gather information on the activities of the management. The monitoring activity therefore directly reduces the information asymmetry. If the information gathering process were not costly, the principals could completely reduce the information asymmetry to zero and would create a situation very similar to the original manager-owned firm used as the outset of Figure 2-3.

The monitoring actions taken do not fundamentally affect the utility function of the management. Instead, they limit the range of actions open to the management, within which he will still try to maximize his utility.

2.2.3.1.1 Internal Control Measures

As said above, principals can be divided into owners and creditors, who have different monitoring possibilities at their disposal. The owners will be treated first in this section. Insofar as the owners use their rights or power to demand insights into the options and information of the management, they can be considered to be exercising direct and internal control measures. The same owners, by selling their shares and causing the stock prices to decline, are triggering indirect external control measures as discussed below in 2.2.3.1.1.4.

2.2.3.1.1.1 Shareholder Voting and Block Ownership

The ownership of a corporation on stocks in Germany have several institutional possibilities of internally gaining insight into the corporate workings and reducing the information asymmetries. Every year, the company must hold a Hauptversammlung, a general meeting of the stockholders.[94] At this meeting, the management must detail the position of the company and describe its plans, and subject them to the approval of the shareholders.[95] It is possible for different types of stock to have different voting rights;[96] in Germany, common stocks have one vote and preferred stocks (Vorzugsaktien) are usually without vote.[97]

---

94 §§ 118-137 AktG.

95 § 120 AktG.

96 Cf. Partch (1987).

97 Preferred stock are described in §§ 139-141 AktG. Cf. Doerks (1992) for an analysis between pricing differences between common and preferred shares in Germany.

The self-organizational capabilities of the principals are an important factor for their monitoring potential, especially in view of proposing and passing resolutions in the Hauptversammlung. The nature of the shareholder gives a first insight into this characteristic. Table 2-1 shows the comparative distribution of share ownership in Germany and the US, by ownership category. The financial sector in the US holds a larger portion of shares than the German financial sector. This is especially due to the pension funds, which replace the pension liability accruals (Pensionsrückstellungen) in German companies. Banks in the US are unimportant as shareholders. It is especially interesting from the point of view of external monitoring that German private households are much less involved in stock ownership than US private households. All other categories listed usually have the capability of organizing the monitoring of the management. This means that from the point of view of the nature of the shareholders, the monitoring situation is more of a problem in the US[98] than in Germany.

owner category	Germany	US
non-financial sector	61.0	51.4
government households	4.3	0.0
private households	14.6	36.4
companies	42.1	15.0
financial sector	30.3	44.5
banks	10.3	0.2
insurance and pension funds	12.4	31.3
other financial institutes	7.6	13.0

Table 2-1: Distribution of share ownership in the US and Germany, in percent by owner category[99]

Block ownership is another major factor in determining the monitoring clout of the owners. Only block owners will generally be invested in a firm to such a degree that the costs of monitoring will be outweighed by the expected savings in agency costs of that same owner. For other owners with smaller stakes in a firm, the calculation might not turn out in favor of monitoring. For these small owners, the existence of a block owner offers the possibility of being a so-called free rider, who benefits from the monitoring efforts of the block owner, without being able to be forced to participate in the monitoring expenses incurred. Block ownership also confers legal possibilities to control the management that a small

98 Cf. Strickland/Wiles/Zenner (1996).

99 Cf. Deutsche Bundesbank (1997).

owner does not have. For example, a 5 % ownership is necessary to be able to call in general assemblies.[100] Further rights are conferred for 10 % of the stock ownership,[101] and the simple majority (50 %),[102] and the three-quarter majority.[103] The opposing 25 % of shares for decisions requiring a three-quarter majority is important as it can block such decisions (Sperrminorität).[104] There has been some criticism about the extent of manager control in the absence of blockholders, but that view has not been echoed in other research.[105]

2.2.3.1.1.2 The Supervisory Board

In stock corporations, there is a supervisory board[106] charged with the supervision of the management.[107] The members of the board represent the shareholders of the firm. Major shareholders will usually have a seat on the supervisory board.[108] As the board can also vote on calling a general assembly, shareholders with a supervisory board seat but less than 5 % of the shares also have a possibility of calling in an assembly, subject to the approval of the simple majority of the board members.[109] The employees of the stock corporation also have a representative in the supervisory board of the firm.[110] This ensures the participation of a major stakeholder of the firm in corporate activities.[111]

Looking at the legal concept, it appears that the supervisory board should be an ideal institution to monitor the management of a stock corporation. However, the supervisory board usually is not an ex-ante controller of the management's ac-

---

100 § 122 AktG.

101 §§ 137-138; 142 AktG.

102 §§ 121; 133; 147 AktG.

103 §§ 141; 182; 193; 202; 222; 319; 340c; 362 AktG.

104 Cf. Iber (1987); for an example see Volmer/Lorch (1991). With an average participation of 75 % at shareholder meetings, this means that on average less than 18 % block ownership constitutes a blocking stake. Cf. Böhm (1992).

105 Cf. Pitelis/Sudgen (1986); Stiglitz (1985).

106 Cf. §§ 96-116 AktG.

107 § 111 I, II AktG.

108 Cf. Steinbeck (1992).

109 § 111 III AktG.

110 § 96 AktG.

111 Cf. Steinmann/Gerum (1980).

tivities, but only exercises its monitoring function after a crisis has erupted.[112] Also, cross-interests of board members can severely influence the interests of the board members.[113] If two companies are interlinked through stock ownership in each other, and respectively have one of their own people on the other company's board, all to critical control might not be exercised by either company in the interest of not provoking a similar monitoring effort in one's own company.[114] Table 2-1 shows that 42 % of the shares in Germany are held by other companies, creating numerous occasions for the interlinking of firms and making interlinking a major concern for this country.

2.2.3.1.1.3 Internal Monitoring and Control by Non-Bank Creditors

Control over the management can also be exercised from the creditor side of the capital suppliers of a firm. While the creditors typically will demand a lower return on their capital than the shareholders, because they only bear a lesser risk than these do, they still have a vested interest in the well-being of the firm they have given credit to. In particular, a default of the company would hit the creditors very hard.

Therefore, creditors will be interested in the health of a firm they are giving credit to. Unlike for the ownership of a firm, it is not said that the creditors possess the wherewithal to actually implement this control. This can be especially true for state-owned companies.[115] Creditors do not have the same legal possibilities as owners to gain insight into the corporate workings and thus reduce information asymmetries. Banks as an important source of credit for companies are treated below in 2.2.3.1.3.1. Other creditors include bondholders, the suppliers of a firm with accounts payable, in the case of tax payments due the government and in view of pension accruals the employees of the firm. The holders of bonds do not have special rights to company information, meaning that they are not effective internal controllers. The market valuation of the bonds however is an issue that will be addressed in the following section.

Not all creditors are equally concerned with controlling the management. The time frame under which this capital is given is also of importance. Creditors giving money for a longer period of time will demand more information on the status of a company during the capital issuance procedure than short-term lend-

---

112 Ex-ante involvement is required by §§ 59; 204 AktG, also see § 111 AktG. Major ex-post investigations are very rare. Cf. Vogel (1980).

113 Cf. Lin (1996); Kallfass (1992); Jehle (1982).

114 Cf. Leimkühler (1996).

115 Cf. Bertero/Rondi (1997).

ers. On the other hand, short-term lenders receive the chance to demand such information much more often, assuming short-term debt is revolved in some way. Short-term creditors can "vote with their feet" by refusing to revolve debt or only do so at higher interest rates. Still, long-term creditors will usually have the greater interest in the debtor company's dealings.

The interests of the creditor are also a relevant factor. Suppliers for which accounts receivable are created will often not want to get involved in monitoring the management of their client firm. Pension accruals, the German counterpart to pension funds, are entered in the companies' own books, creating a position that constitutes debt to the employees. This voluminous debt position hardly conveys controlling power to the employees of the firm, but creates financial maneuvering space for managers.

The creditor status of the government normally carries no weight from a monitoring point of view, as all companies are equally tax debtors to the state and the government is not disposed to make use of its creditor status and control every company. Major lapses in tax morale will lead to legal repercussions, though.

Apart from the representative in the supervisory board, the employees of a firm have another monitoring possibility. They are, through the pension accruals the company makes, creditors of the firm. But the supervisory board member already has sufficient influence in representing the employees' interests, so that there is no reason to link the level of monitoring by the employees to the weight of the pension accruals.

Finally, creditors from accounts payable are not in that position for control reasons, as it is normal practice to run up short-term (< 3 months) payables. These creditors will not become active if the debt is regularly paid on time, and in the case of problems they have little other claim than to their outstanding debt, meaning that their rights to internal monitoring and information gathering are non-existent.

As far as passive control is concerned, debt also has another regulatory effect, which pertains to all types of external debt, but works internally. The importance of debt as an internal control mechanism lies in the fact that higher debt levels leads to higher obligations of debt servicing (interest and amortization), meaning that the cash outflows of the company are raised.[116] The increased outflows in turn reduce the discretionary possibilities of a manager, who must always choose his actions under the condition that he is able to service the debt at all times.[117]

---

[116] This can affect investment policies. Cf. Forsyth (1996).

[117] Cf. Jensen/Meckling (1976), Crutchley/Hansen (1989).

2.2.3.1.1.4 Bottom-Up Monitoring

The final method of internal monitoring to be mentioned is the bottom-up monitoring.[118] This form of monitoring refers to the in-company competition between the managers of various levels in the company hierarchy. Management decisions that stray too far from the company value-maximizing path will be uncovered by other managers intent on bettering their own position. This internal method contrasts with the external market for manager control described below in 2.2.3.1.2.3. The effectiveness[119] and ethicality of this method of control remains open to discussion.

Therefore, internal monitoring in stock corporations is mainly to be expected in companies with block owners who have representatives in the supervisory board and starting at ownership levels greater than 5 % of the shares have further legal possibilities for monitoring their firm. The small amount of private stock ownership in Germany speaks for effective monitoring. But the efficacy of monitoring is reduced by the large amount of interlinking ownership between companies. Non-bank creditors have little monitoring interest or possibilities in a firm.

2.2.3.1.2 Markets as External Control Mechanisms

While internal monitoring is only possible for important owners or creditors, stock corporations provide some possibilities for indirect or external control. Market mechanisms act as the information bourse in this case. As for the internal control mechanisms, the external control mainly works via the reduction of information asymmetries. In a functioning market, the important information is condensed into one number, the price. How much information actually is incorporated is the subject of market efficiency studies.[120] They distinguish three levels of market efficiency:[121]

1. Weak market efficiency, where all past information contained in earlier prices is contained in the current price. That implies that technical analysis is unnecessary.
2. Semi-strong market efficiency, where all public information on a company is evaluated in the firm's share price. That would make fundamental analysis superfluous.

---

118 Cf. Jensen/Smith (1985), p. 102.

119 Cf. Hackett (1985).

120 Cf. Strong/Walker (1987), pp. 126 ff.

121 Cf. Fama (1970), and the more differentiated version in Fama (1991).

3. Strong market efficiency, where all information is incorporated in the share price. That would mean that insiders cannot exploit their position, as insider information does not exist for substantial periods.

2.2.3.1.2.1 The Market for Corporate Control

For stock corporations, the quotation of their shares on the market provides a quick and convenient insight into the company's overall standing, all condensed into the one share price. The German stock market structure is comprised of four market segments,[122] the official continuous trade market, the official daily trade market with prices fixed at one time per day for odd lots and infrequently traded securities, the regulated and the unregulated free trade (including telephone trading). The inclusion in the segments can entail additional information obligations to the public.

The admission criteria to the official continuous trade market are listed in §§ 36-44d BörsG together with the stock market admission guide; the most important requirements are a minimal combined value of DM 2.5 million of the shares to be issued, a public spread of at least 25 %, a comprehensive issue prospectus and at least one interim report per year. The regulated free trade is meant for those corporations who cannot or will not fulfill these requirements. There are no admission criteria for stock corporations wishing their shares to be traded the unregulated market.

In addition, the frequency of trading diminishes from one market segment to the next. Buying and selling orders might not coincide, or one trading side can lack completely for small shares. In a free market with full informational efficiency, the price of a share is the only information needed by investors to base their trading decisions on, as the price reflects all relevant information the investor might need. Prices of share that are infrequently traded are estimated, often at preday levels, where necessary. That means that the information incorporated in the price is old, possibly outdated, and subject to the subjective feeling of the trader who is estimating the price without input from prospective buyers or sellers.[123] Foreign institutional investors such as investment funds who play a major role in German stock trading usually confine their activities to the official continuous trading segment. While instances of infrequent trading are already visible for shares in the official continuous market, they are quite common in the other segments. The informational asymmetry remains very high there, despite the open market trading. This means that larger companies, traded in the official

122 The so-called "new market" for innovative firms introduced in 1997 is not relevant for the time period studied here.

123 Cf. Beiker (1993).

continuous market, will generally suffer less from information asymmetries due to pricing efficiency and scrutiny by market participants than smaller companies.

Discontentment with a company's standing or outlook can lead to a decline in a stock's quotes. Continued poor stock performance in itself acts as an alarm for the major blockholders and supervisory board that the management is having problems. This will lead to increased internal monitoring activities by these parties.

Poor stock performance for which the management is responsible can lead to external monitoring activities by corporate raiders who specialize in identifying companies that are undervalued with regard to their assets.[124] Corporate raiders would buy up the undervalued company and either replace the management or sell the company in components for a greater sum than they had to pay to purchase the company.[125] The managers stand to lose their jobs in the process,[126] so they will strive to maintain a performance level high enough to deter raiders, besides considering other takeover defenses.[127]

There has been some criticism as to the effectivity and efficiency of this market for corporate control.[128] The first concern is the information efficiency itself. In Germany, the strong and sometimes the semi-strong market efficiency concepts are rejected.[129] Some studies even dispute the weak efficiency.[130] Criticism of the market for corporate control is also due to the costs and effort a takeover entails.[131] High debt ratios further increase the cost of a takeover.[132] In Germany, this has been especially thought to be true, as there is a very low record of

---

124 Cf. Fama/Jensen (1983).

125 Cf. Kessel (1995) for an agency-theoretical analysis of leveraged buyouts. Also see Jensen (1988); Brealey/Myers (1996), pp. 937 ff.

126 On the connection between management buyouts, where the managers buy their own company, and agency problems, see Schmid (1994); Berger (1993), pp. 101 ff. Thompson/Wright (1989) provide an extension of the Jensen/Meckling (1976) model to management buyouts.

127 Cf. Jarrell/Poulsen (1987).

128 Cf. Wenger (1994). Cf. Jensen/Ruback (1983) for an overview of the results from 13 US studies.

129 Cf. Lerbinger (1984). Schmidt/May (1993) and Sahling (1981) support the semi-strong efficiency, Hawawini (1984), Mühlbradt (1978), and Brandi (1977) reject it.

130 Cf. Schnittge (1989); Frantzmann (1987).

131 Cf. Fama (1980), Williamson (1969).

132 Cf. Stulz (1988); Israel (1991).

hostile takeovers for this country.[133] Crossholdings make it difficult for hostile investors to gain a stake in a company, but there does seem to be more interest in hostile takeovers in the German capital market than previously thought.[134]

Other arguments can be raised against the effectivity of takeovers.[135] Since only shareholders who do not sell their shares can participate in the creation of value subsequent to the takeover, the takeover bid can easily fail. The takeover will only succeed if the firm taking over pays too much for its target. In addition, managers in the target firm are in a position to take measures to deter potential hostile takeovers. These measures can reduce the agency problem, which would produce the desired result after all, but other measures are possible. These include acquisitions that will result in antitrust violations if the firm takes over the target, poison pills, or golden parachutes.[136]

2.2.3.1.2.2 The Bond Market

The bond market offers another possibility for outsiders to monitor a company's performance without the need for high information gathering costs. In Germany, the bond market is relatively unimportant, as only about 10 % of the companies' external debt is raised on the bond market.[137] Its efficiency has also been debated.[138] However, the information contained in the bond prices is basically already in the stock prices, if that market has reached a sufficient efficiency level. The only difference will be in the target audience for bond prices, which is creditors who expect fixed interest payments in advance but at lower rates than the residual returns demanded by investors.

Based on agency considerations, creditors differ from shareholders not only in the payment schedules they expect from the company, but they will also have different risk profiles. Given a positive risk-return relationship, the lower return demands of creditors will go hand in hand with a greater risk aversion. In chapter 3.2.3, I detail that shareholders in collusion with the management are able to extract the creditors' wealth by risky investment policies. The limited liability of

---

133 There were three hostile takeovers of non-financial corporations in Germany between 1945 and 1994. Cf. Franks/Mayer (1997). Hostile takeovers in Germany could be less frequent than in the US due to blockholding by banks, the issuance of preferred stock, and codetermination of labor.

134 Cf. Jenkinson/Ljungqvist (1997).

135 Cf. Stiglitz (1985).

136 The acquiring company guarantees the management of the acquired company a lucrative payoff.

137 Cf. Wiendieck (1992); Wiegers (1987).

138 Cf. Bester (1987a); Terberger (1987).

shareholders makes the default risk more important for creditors than for owners. That means that increasingly risky investment policies can positively affect stock quotes but negatively impact bond prices. Even the knowledge that the management and the ownership are colluding with each other can be a signal that creditors as the third party in the triangle relationship are set to be put at a disadvantage, sending bond prices downward.

2.2.3.1.2.3 The Market for Managers

Apart from the capital markets, there is another market that can exert external control over the management. Managers seeking a new position will find their chances of finding a satisfactory offer hurt if knowledge of poor performance records or even general behavior in opposition to the ownership's interests is available on the job market. Similar to the bottom-up control mentioned in 2.2.3.1.1.4, this will force the managers to pursue policies favorable to owners' preferences even if the ownership itself cannot immediately monitor the manager's activities.

This control mechanism will only work if the market for managers is efficient enough for past successes and especially failures of a manager to be known without the manager himself having to disclose that information. It does not seem, however, that this market is very transparent, so the effectiveness of this controlling mechanism should not be overrated.[139]

2.2.3.1.3 Banks as Controlling Instances in German Industrial Stock Companies

In Germany, banks have several possibilities for influencing a company's management, which has given rise to discussions on the possible excess of the power of banks in Germany.[140] These comprise the role of banks as creditors, but also as shareholders, which includes such follow-on powers such as the possibility of exercising proxy voting rights or having representatives on the supervisory boards.[141]

---

139 Cf. Harris/Raviv (1991); Wosnitza (1991), p. 36.

140 Cf. Förschle/Glaum/Mandler (1998); Wiendieck (1992); Wenger (1990).

141 Management control in German banks themselves is discussed in Köhne/Tebroke (1995). Also see Krahnen (1985).

2.2.3.1.3.1 Banks as Creditors

Bank credit plays an important role for corporate finance in Germany. The proportion of bank credit to the total liabilities of the firms analyzed here is over 21 %.[142] Banks are obliged by law to demand continuous insight into the annual reports of companies to which credits in excess of DM 100,000.-- are granted.[143,144] This major information-gathering prerogative loses some of its importance for the stock corporations analyzed here, as those listed in the official continuous trade are obliged to publish an annual report anyway.[145]

In Germany, the influence of banks as creditors is bolstered further by the house bank system.[146] This means that one bank plays a major role as the creditor of a firm, in return for extended insights into the company's financial standing. The bank can also share information with other prospective creditors.[147] That means that house banks will be able to greatly reduce the information asymmetry between the creditor (principal) and the manager (agent).[148] The role of the house bank has declined in recent years, though, as competition between banks is heating up and the banks find their own fates too closely linked to the well-being of the firm they are involved in as a house bank.[149] The house bank system makes it easier for companies to gain a reputation as a good debtor, and one who does not favor the ownership principals over the creditor principals.[150]

2.2.3.1.3.2 Banks as Shareholders

In Table 2-1 above, one can see that over 10 % of the shares of German companies are in the hands of banks.[151] For a universal bank, this can be the result of

---

142 The proportion of bank credit to total external debt is about 60 %.

143 For the time period before 1993. The limit has since been raised to currently DM 500,000.--.

144 § 18 KWG. Exceptions are permitted for collateralized loans, as well as a recent additonal permitted exception if the interest and amortization payments occur without problem.

145 § 44b BörsG. Cf. 2.3.2.2 below.

146 Cf. Neuberger (1994), pp. 167 ff.

147 Cf. Pagano/Jappelli (1993).

148 Cf. Münchow (1995), pp. 177 ff.

149 Cf. Fischer (1990).

150 Cf. Diamond (1989).

151 Cf. Münchow (1995), pp. 148 ff. for a more detailed analysis of bank ownership in nonbanks in Germany.

simple value-maximizing policy.[152] Bank ownership is sometimes interpreted as a bonding measure of the banks to more closely link the company to the bank.[153] § 12 KWG (Kreditwesengesetz) determines that a maximum of 15 % of the liable equity of a bank may be invested in a non bank participation, per company participated in. Over all non banks participated in, this figure may rise to a maximum of 60 % total participation. While 1990 about 25 % of the capital in Germany was held by banks,[154] i. e., enough to prevent unfriendly takeovers, this value shrank to 10.3 % in 1996.[155] A tendency toward shrinking bank participation in Germany is evident,[156] which can be traced back very far.[157]

Bank participation as a shareholder can very often lead to banks holding at least one seat on the supervisory board. In Germany in 1986, this is the case for over 80 % of non-bank corporations.[158] This confers an important role to banks in corporate control by owner-principals.

2.2.3.1.3.3 Proxy Voting and Conflicts in the Principal Roles of Banks

Banks have the possibility of expanding their influence even further than their own ownership due to the possibility of proxy voting (Depotstimmrecht) for small investors in the general assembly.[159] In actual practice, 95 % of small shareholders allow the banks free reign in how to exercise their proxy voting powers.[160] The banks do not have to report their proxy votes.[161]

It is not said that the banks always act in the interests of the small shareholders when exercising their proxy rights, so one must speak of a further principal-agent constellation in companies, that between banks and small shareholders. This relationship alone is worth detailed analyses.[162]

---

152 Cf. Mülbert (1997), pp. 22 ff.

153 Cf. Neuberger (1994), pp. 90 ff.

154 Cf. Steinmann/Gerum (1980).

155 Cf. Table 2-1 above.

156 Cf. Börner (1996), p. 57.

157 Cf. Bundesministerium der Finanzen (1974).

158 Cf. Böhm (1992), pp. 194 ff.

159 § 135 AktG.

160 Cf. Schrader (1991).

161 Cf. Becht/Boehmer (1997), pp. 26 f.

162 Cf. Neuberger (1994), pp. 172 ff.; Schmid (1996).

The fact that banks can be involved in one and the same firm both as owners and as creditors can lead to conflicting interests inside the bank.[163] The conflict is exacerbated if the bank is not only a large shareholder in its own right, but also the proxy representative of small investors. If it compromises its shareholder positions in favor of its creditor interests, the bank is deceiving the small investors it represents. This conflict can arise for example with regard to the riskiness of the investment policies pursued. There is a theory of credit rationing by banks with the purpose of risk avoidance.[164] Well diversified investors however will welcome risky investments, causing a dilemma for the owner-creditor bank.

Also, while the retention of profits can be a favored method of finance for all shareholders (cf. chapter 3.2.1), banks as creditors can have a special interest in retaining profits in order to secure their loans to the company. Other investors will demand a payout of funds that cannot be invested at the desired rate of return.[165] Finally, banks themselves can suffer from agency problems, and therefore pursue suboptimal policies themselves.[166]

2.2.3.2 Incentive and Bonding Mechanisms

Whereas the monitoring mechanisms discussed above are used to reduce the information asymmetry between the management and the principals (owners or creditors), the utility functions of the parties remain untouched. The management is simply not allowed to maximize its own utility, but must follow the directives of the principals. The preferences of principals and agents are only aligned in the sense that punishment up to the loss of the job is threatened in the case of non-obedience to the principals' wishes.

In the case of incentive-based mechanisms to reduce agency problems, the level of information asymmetry remains untouched, while the point of attack is the difference in the utility structure. Incentive methods try to find ways of aligning the principals' and agents utility functions and preference systems so that the management will act in the best interests of the principals, despite the fact that the information asymmetry remains, and the principals are subject to the hidden information problem. The management will just not desire to exploit this situation to the principals' detriment, because the management no longer stands to gain more from that behavior than from maximizing the principals' utility.

---

[163] Cf. Payne/Millar/Glezen (1994).

[164] Cf. Jaffee/Russell (1976); Mühlhaupt (1956).

[165] Cf. Münchow (1995), p. 226.

[166] Cf. Mülbert (1997), p. 12.

2.2.3.2.1.1 Compensation Agreements and Managerial Ownership

A common suggestion to align owners' and managers' interests and provide the right incentive for managers is to make managers participate in the success of the firm.[167] This can happen in two ways. First, the managers can receive a kind of incentive payment. This can be in the form of performance-linked bonuses that are only paid out if a certain performance is reached, or that grow together with the performance of the firm.[168] The performance can either refer to market or accounting-based performance measures.[169] These can be interpreted using the option price theory.[170] Another possibility is to make the managers co-owners of the firm by paying part of the salary in the form of stock options or shares.[171] The seminal article in recent years on this subject is from Morck/Shleifer/Vishny (1988). They test the influence of board ownership on Tobin's q[172] in a piecewise regression to simulate nonlinearities. Purely fixed salaries induce managers to invest more risk adversely, invest less and reduce debt, all in order to secure their financial claims. Increasing the performance-based portion of the compensation will lead the management to participate in high profits, inducing it to increase the riskiness of investments, the overall investment activity, and leverage in order to achieve those profits. A too high performance-based remuneration however will backfire, causing a manager to become extremely risk adverse, as not only his human capital, but also most of his financial capital is bound in the one company.[173] The causality of the link between performance and managerial ownership can be disputed, though; high performance levels can also be the cause, not the effect of managerial ownership.[174]

The risk optimization efforts of the management concerning investment policies, depending on the portion of performance-based compensation, can be posited to be U-shaped:

---

167 Cf. Böbel/Dirrheimer (1984).

168 See e. g. Rayton (1996); Baker/Jensen/Murphy (1988).

169 Cf. Smith/Watts (1982).

170 Cf. Grinblatt/Titman (1989).

171 Cf. Bernhardt/Witt (1997). Managerial ownership is also referred to as inside equity; cf. Servaes/Zenner (1994).

172 See chapter 4.3.1.4 for a definition of this performance measure.

173 Cf. Morck/Shleifer/Vishny (1988).

174 Cf. Loderer/Martin (1997); Kole (1993).

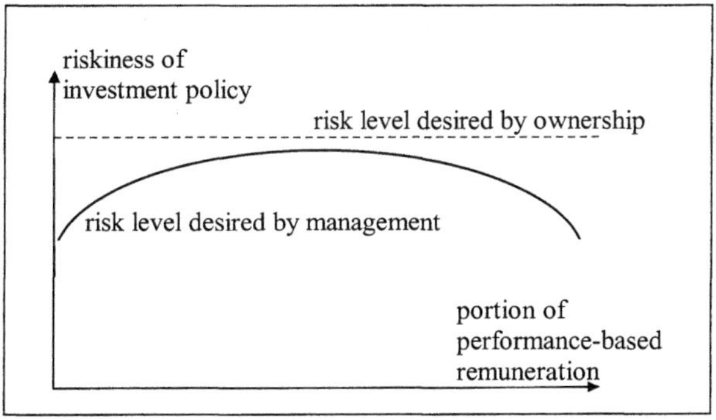

Figure 2-6: Riskiness of investment policy of the management depending on the portion of performance-based compensation

Such payment incentives are more effective with young managers, who stand to gain or lose more due to adjustments to future salaries than older managers close to retirement age.[175] The older managers' horizon with the firm is much shorter than that of investors, so payments beyond the managers' horizon will count much less for managers than for the investors.[176] Promotions, too, will be more effective with younger managers.[177] Executive compensation has been the subject of many studies in the US, where information on managers' pay is more accessible.[178]

2.2.3.2.1.2 Contractual Clauses in Debt Finance

A bonding measure to reduce agency problems can be found in contracting measures.[179] In these contracts, the agent agrees to certain restrictions to his actions, which give the principal the security that the principal's interests are not being ignored. In the creditor-owner conflict, the agency problem-reducing contract can have clauses providing seniority or collateral for the credit.[180] Contracting can be used very effectively as a self-selection mechanism. By offering the agent a low-interest debt with a high level of securities and a high-interest debt

---

175 Cf. Jensen/Smith (1985), p. 103.

176 Cf. Jensen/Meckling (1979).

177 Cf. Baker/Jensen/Murphy (1988).

178 Cf. e. g. Akhigbe/Madura (1996).

179 Cf. 2.2.3.2 for compensation agreements.

180 Cf. Pottschmidt (1995) for types of collateral.

with few securities, the good agents can be separated from the bad.[181] Collateral punishes the debtor in the case of default, making it an ideal tool to reduce the riskiness of the investment policies.[182] It also deters owners from driving the leverage up too high.[183] Guarantees by the mother concern are also a suitable contractual clause to reduce creditor-owner agency problems.[184] Finally, outright negative clauses in which the debtor agrees to refrain from certain investments or dividend policies constitute contractual clauses.[185]

2.2.3.2.1.3 Signaling as a Bonding Mechanism

It is possible for managers either through incentives or altruistic behavior to strive to act in the owners' best interests.[186] The only agency problem that exists is that the investors cannot be sure the management is not hiding information from them and acting in his own interests, even though he is not. In that case, the managers will be interested in reducing the level of information asymmetry between them and the investors, and thus will be likely to take bonding measures if possible.

A signal as a bonding instrument only conveys information about a firm when it cannot be copied by somebody else whose firm is not in the same situation.[187] One such occasion for bonding is when the future prospects of a firm are favorable, giving the management reason to believe that a higher level of dividend payouts is sustainable. An increase of the volume of the dividend payout (this can also be achieved by stock splits) is a possible signal to investors.[188] Such a dividend hike is costly, especially as subsequent reductions are harder to implement.[189] A one-time raise in dividends leads to a long-term raise in cash outflows. This signal cannot be copied by an ailing firm, because it cannot afford the expenses involved. This precludes any imitation of the signal by firms without favorable future prospects. Therefore the signal is believable and investors

181 Cf. Bester (1987b), Clemenz (1988).

182 Cf. Stulz/Johnson (1985).

183 Cf. Franke (1995).

184 Cf. Pottschmidt (1995).

185 Cf. Swoboda (1987).

186 In the latter case, the assumption of rational behavior is abandoned.

187 Cf. Ross (1978).

188 Cf. e.g. Amihud/Murgia (1997), Easterbrook (1984), Rozeff (1982).

189 For dividend reductions cf. Jensen/Johnson (1995). An analysis for the German capital market is provided by Gerke/Oerke/Sentner (1997).

can with some certainty assume that the company raising the dividends is doing well and expects to stay that way.

2.2.3.3 Comparative Summary of the German and US Systems of Corporate Governance

governance system	Germany	US
ownership	concentrated (family, corporate, bank)[190]	diffuse/non-corporate
supervisory board	codetermination	primarily outsiders
capital markets	relatively illiquid	very liquid
takeover/control market	minor role	major role
executive compensation	moderate/low influence	high influence
banking system	universal banking	fragmented

Table 2-2: Comparison of the effectivity of the main German and US governance systems[191]

Table 2-2 gives a final overview over the governance systems in the US and Germany, with a description or valuation of the effectivity of each system. The ownership levels in Germany are high, with families, other corporations or banks as principle block owners, which facilitates management control, although the cross-involvement of corporations reduces the effectiveness of the block ownership. The appointment of outsiders to the board of directors in the US encourages impartial control, but also allows for incompetent monitoring compared to Germany. The liquidity of the capital markets in the US greatly reduces information asymmetries on that market, giving the market for corporate control and takeovers an important role in the US. In Germany the relatively illiquid capital market forestalls any major role for corporate takeovers. This is also a negative consequence of the high block ownership levels in Germany. The executive compensation is also a less effective incentive measure in Germany, although this could be due in part to the lack of data on German managers' compensation plans. Finally, the universal banking system in Germany gives the German banks more possibilities to influence a company than the specialized

190 Also see Horn (1994).

191 Cf. Kaplan (1997).

bank system in the US.[192] The superiority of the universal bank system in providing corporate governance has been disputed however.[193] In this quick review, the US governance has the controlling edge over the German systems, except for lower ownership concentration and the banking system.

2.3 The Dataset

2.3.1 Raw Data

2.3.1.1 Databases

The data on the German stock corporations used in this analysis was drawn from the annual report and stock price databases of the Deutsche Finanzdatenbank.[194] In addition, employee numbers for the companies used in the efficiency analysis were drawn from the Finanz- und Börsendatenbank from Hoppenstedt GmbH.[195] The employee numbers are available from 1986 onwards, while the annual statements and stock quotes go until 1992. The seven year period from 1986 to 1992 covered by both datasets will effectively be studied in this analysis. In 1987 a new law for accounting procedures was implemented for the first time, so the accounting practices differ slightly for the 1986 data.[196]

Banks and insurance companies are excluded, because their annual reports are not comparable to those of industrial firms.[197] After outlier corrections due to faulty data this left 237 companies in the sample (see Table A-1 in the appendix). These are generally the larger companies of those traded at the Frankfurt stock exchange.[198] For the smaller companies, trading is so infrequent that the share quotes contain little information.[199] Stock corporations constitute only a

---

192 Also see Carney (1997).

193 Cf. Macey/Miller (1997).

194 Cf. Bühler/Göppl/Möller (1993).

195 Cf. Hoppenstedt (1996).

196 Cf. Stein (1994) for a discussion of the Bilanzrichtliniengesetz.

197 Cf. Hannan/Mavinga (1980) for a study of banks in the US.

198 At the end of 1990, 545 German stock corporations were traded at stock markets. Cf. Statistisches Bundesamt (1992).

199 In 1996, the 10 most heavily traded companies accounted for 63.4 % of total turnover at the Frankfurt Stock Exchange, the top 25 for 94.1 % of the turnover. Cf. Hansen (1997).

small portion of all corporations in Germany.[200] However, the largest corporations are all stock corporations (AGs), which are on average 120 times larger than GmbHs.[201]

For the determination of the levels of competitivity in the separate sectors, employee and sales numbers by sector were drawn from data published by the Statistisches Bundesamt.[202]

2.3.1.2 Return calculation

The share prices were adjusted for dividend changes and capital issues or changes in the face values of the shares according to a correction factor supplied by the Deutsche Finanzdatenbank. While the stock prices are available on a daily basis, the share prices were aggregated in order to obtain data with the same frequency as annual reports. Annual returns are calculated as the product of the 12 monthly logarithmed returns of the stocks in each year (geometric series). Higher frequency returns are not used, as many German stocks are infrequently traded, reducing the quality of the return data. If a share price was needed for the year, the end of year quotes were used. The monthly returns $r_{i,t}$ for a firm i in the month t were calculated using adjusted end of month quotes according to the following formula:

$$r_{i,t} = \ln\left(\frac{p_{i,t} + d_{i,t}}{p_{i,t-1}}\right) \tag{2-2}$$

where p is the share price and d a dividend payment, purchase rights issues or other occurrences of value pertaining to the shares.

2.3.1.3 Sector Classification

The companies were grouped into sectors according to their main field of activity, based on the classifications used by the Statistisches Bundesamt.[203] Table 2-3 shows the distribution of the companies in the dataset by sector and year. About 15 % of the data (about 225 companies) can be found in each year, except for 1992, where only 10 % of the data is located. The five most populated sec-

---

200 For example, on December 31, 1993, there were 543,444 GmbH registered in Germany. Statistisches Bundesamt (1995), p. 138.

201 Cf. Becht/Boehmer (1997), pp. 21 f.

202 Cf. Statistisches Bundesamt (1994).

203 The Saling Aktienführer classification was used where no clear decision could be made. Cf. Hoppenstedt GmbH (1986-1992).

tors that will be used in the sectoral analyses are shaded in the table.[204] These are the chemicals, machinery, electronics, food & beverages,[205] and utilities[206] sectors. For each of the three empirical analyses, after the additional removal of outliers according to the variables studied, the sample analyzed was accordingly reduced from the total shown here.

	1986	1987	1988	1989	1990	1991	1992	Total Cases
1. Chemicals	23	22	22	22	22	22	13	146
2. Plastics and Rubber	3	3	3	3	3	3	1	19
3. Mining and Ceramics	12	11	11	11	11	11	8	75
4. Metallurgy	11	11	11	11	11	11	7	73
5. Machinery	29	29	29	29	30	30	24	200
6. Automotive	6	6	6	6	6	6	3	39
7. Electronics and Precision Mechanics	15	16	16	16	16	15	11	105
8. Wood, Paper, Printing	6	4	4	4	4	4	2	28
9. Leather, Fabrics and Apparel	9	7	8	8	8	8	6	54
10.Food & Beverages*	29	28	28	29	25	25	13	177
11.Construction	7	7	7	7	7	7	6	48
12.Trade	6	6	6	6	6	6	4	40
13.Utilities	15	15	15	15	15	15	13	104
14.Holdings, Participation Acquisition,[207] Property Management	40	40	39	41	42	41	31	274
15.Others, including diversified companies	21	20	19	19	19	19	9	126
Total	232	225	224	227	225	223	151	1507
Total in %	15.4	14.9	14.9	15.1	14.9	14.8	10.0	100.0

* Excluding the tobacco industry.

Table 2-3: Number of companies in the sample, by sector and year[208]

[204] Holdings, although left in the full sample, were not studied separately, because the peculiarities of their annual statements.

[205] Excluding the tobacco industry. Many companies in the sector that are contained in the dataset are breweries.

[206] Water and energy.

[207] Cf. Horn (1994), pp. 93 ff.

2.3.2 Agency Indicator Variables for the Empirical Research

2.3.2.1 Classification of the Agency Indicator Variables

In order to determine which variables can be used to represent agency problems, it is important to first clarify that no proof can be given that the variables presented below are trustworthy indicators of agency problems in a company. Agency problems cannot be directly identified, only indirectly through variables that represent agency problem-causing circumstances or variables that represent effects of agency problems. In Figure 2-7 this is expressed by the two circles denoting the agency-related areas that are measurable. The agency problems themselves in the box remain immeasurable and thus removed from a researcher's reach.

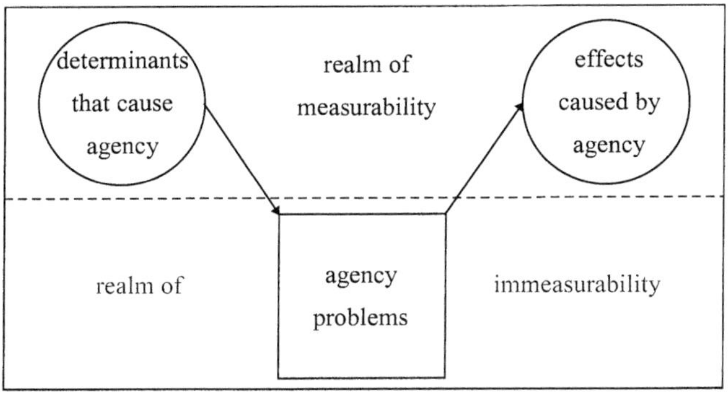

Figure 2-7: Causality and measurability of agency problems

The objective of this analysis is to test the validity of the right-hand side of Figure 2-7, to see if the effects of agency problems (the arrow leading away from the agency problem box) are significant. Such a significance can be ascertained by testing for correlations between the two elements on either side of the arrow, in this case, the agency problem box and the agency effects circle.

Unfortunately, the agency problem box belongs to the realm of immeasurability. That means that in order to test the effects of the agency problems for significance, it becomes necessary to include the left-hand side of Figure 2-7, the measurable agency problem-causing influences to the agency problems in the reasoning.

---

[208] Shaded sectors are used in the sectoral analysis.

The left-hand side however cannot be the object of this study. Including agency problem causing variables, or agency variables for short, can either be to validate the left-hand branch or the right hand one, but not both. Therefore, the decision has to be made which branch to study and the right one is chosen, like this was done in the other studies in the field. The agency problems themselves remain elusive and it can only be hoped that by "surrounding" the problems as shown here they can be credibly identified.

This is a problem with which all empirical agency studies have to contend, although not all studies directly address this problem. In all cases this inadequacy has to be accepted. The agency variables used by the authors of course are well founded in theoretical analyses.[209]

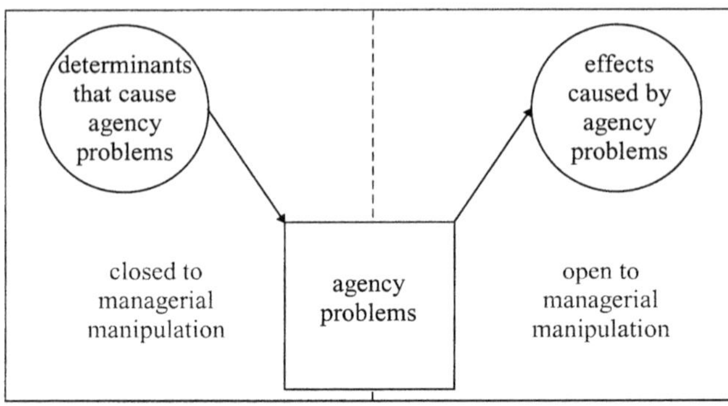

Figure 2-8: Susceptibility of the agency problem context to short-term managerial actions

The situation described means that the hypotheses concerning effects of agency problems to be tested, e. g., differences in the financing behavior of firms with and without agency problems, are always strictly to be understood as joint hypotheses. The second hypothesis is always the assumption that the indicators for causes of agency problems used are valid and reliable.

One central element to a credible choice of agency variables is to ensure that they in general stem from areas of the company that the management cannot affect in the short run, as shown in Figure 2-8.[210] If the variables chosen can easily

---

209 Typically block ownership. Cf. e. g. Schreyögg/Steinmann (1981); Steinmann/Schreyögg/Dütthorn (1983).

210 Again, an example is block ownership. Cho (1998) suggests, though, that block ownership is also an endogenous variable, affected by investment policies.

and quickly be manipulated at little or no cost, then it is evident that a manager wishing to conceal the existence of agency problems from the ownership will do what is possible to hide any obviously damaging evidence.[211]

In the case that a hypothesis must be rejected, this usually means that no differences between firms with and without agency problems can be identified with statistical significance. But the actual hypothesis from the two joint hypotheses that is rejected cannot be identified. Either there actually are no differences in the behavior between the two company groups, or worse, the agency variable used is inadequate.

In this study three partly related approaches are taken to minimize the problem potential just described. First, I try to include in the analysis all variables that capture a significant portion of agency problems. This also bears tribute to the many facets of agency problems. This variety means that some aspects of agency problems might bear on the hypothesis analyzed where others do not, giving mixed results for the hypothesis tests, depending on which agency variable is used. It is to be hoped, however, that the majority of the agency variables will produce the same result, thus adding additional weight to the truth of the implicit second of the joint hypotheses, namely that the agency variables used are adequate.

This first remedy entails the problem of providing five or six different takes for one hypothesis and possibly completely contradictory results. Therefore, in a second step conglomerate agency variables are developed that incorporate elements of all the agency variables. Thus, they provide a sort of weighted majority vote on the level of agency problems in a firm. The type of weighting to be used is discussed in more detail below. These variables will, by nature of their comprehensiveness and their relative clarity, be given preference to most of the single agency variables.

Finally, the breadth of the hypotheses which will be tested in this thesis can also help give credence to the choice of agency variables. If hypotheses from all the various fields should pan out and be confirmed, it can be taken as a justification of sorts for the hypothesis that the agency variables used do capture agency problems.

There are several aspects of agency problems which can be covered by the agency variables. First, recalling that agency problems are only possible under the prerequisite that there is a situation of informational asymmetry between the management and ownership, it makes sense to include variables that point to that informational asymmetry.

---

211 Cf. Coenenberg/Schmidt/Werhand (1983).

While such variables will be called agency variables here for purposes of simplicity, information asymmetry is not a sufficient condition for agency problems in a firm. Taken alone, it can be an indicator that while the management is trying to act in the best interests of the ownership, they are unable to communicate this to the distrustful owners. This situation gave rise to such theories as the pecking order hypothesis for corporate financing decisions.

In addition to these information asymmetry variables, there are other variables that reflect the amount of control the ownership of a firm has over the management. Lack of control possibilities is another prerequisite for agency problems. Also, it would be necessary to account for the other method of mitigating agency problems, which is the incentive solution. For this it would be necessary to have access to the contractual information in the top management's agreements which pertains to success-oriented payment schedules. Unfortunately, as mentioned before, this information is not available for the German capital market, so no such agency variables are proposed.

2.3.2.2 Information Asymmetry Variables

Because information asymmetry is at the base of agency problems, in the sense of being a necessary but not sufficient condition for such problems, variables representing this kind of asymmetry will be presented first.

The *market segment* with its specific information requirements the company is traded in indicates varying degrees of information asymmetry between owners and management. Assuming that managers exploit the leeway given to them by information asymmetries (which constitutes the sufficient criterion for agency problems to exist in a firm), companies in the free trade segment will have the largest agency problems, those in official trade the least. The market segment variable used in the empirical part of the study is designed as a dummy variable, reducing the four market segments to two categories. Companies traded in the official continuous market receive a market segment value of one, and all other firms are given a zero. Thus the higher value of the variable points to lesser agency problems. This choice of division follows the greatest gap in trading frequency between segments.

About 40 % of the firms in the sample are continuously traded, while about 30 % are in the official daily trade, and the remaining 30 % in the free trade segment. This distribution is fairly stable over the period observed. Therefore, no time effects should be expected for this agency variable in the analyses.

Another variable representing the degree of information asymmetry between management and ownership in a firm is the *dividend signal*.[212] This variable operates more as a short-term corrective to the long-term information level described by the market segment. In every year in which the dividend per share exceeds the previous year's dividend, the dividend signal dummy is set to one, otherwise it initially is set to zero.

This variable is problematic in that in return every company is regarded as having agency problems that did not raise the dividend per share in that year. Even agency problem-free companies will not increase the dividends every year. Using this variable alone should therefore produce poor results. As a solution to this, the signal is considered to count in the year in which dividends were raised and also in the following year. For the first year, 1986, dividend data from 1985 was processed, too.

To sum up, the market segment variable describes a general and constant level of informational asymmetry. The dividend signal, on the other hand, shows short-term changes in the asymmetry level that subside after some time, leaving the company at its original asymmetry level described by the market segment.

2.3.2.3 Ownership Control Variables

Block ownership is probably the most accepted and common of all agency variables used, and hence will be given more attention in the interpretation of the results in the empirical section of the thesis.[213] For organizational reasons, small investors will hardly be willing to monitor the management of a firm, as the expense either of organizing the investors or of implementing a monitoring plan of one's own is too high for each individual investor to bear, compared to the amount of funds he has invested in the company.

Thus, barring major crises, the management of a firm will only be controlled by the ownership if there is at least one block owner, for whom the expense of instituting and maintaining a monitoring instance is less than the gains he can expect from owning shares in an agency problem free company.

I assume such control to exist in a company if the block ownership of a company's outstanding shares is 25 % or more. These shares can be owned by one or more investors. Others already assume ownership control if the level of block ownership is 5 % or more of the firm's stock. It is not sure if a 5 % ownership

---

212 The signaling theory is described in Padberg (1995), pp. 119 ff.

213 Cf. e. g. Ware (1975), McEachern (1975), Kim/Sorensen (1986), Friend/Lang (1988), Morck/ Shleifer/Vishny (1988); for Germany Thonet (1977), Bühner (1984), Kaulmann (1987), Lipka (1995); Padberg (1995).

already constitutes a level for which the expense of monitoring the management is already worthwhile.[214] Due to the German web of companies and banks holding interest in each other, using the 5 %-rate would also make most companies studied here agency problem free, and block ownership would be a useless criterion.[215]

Despite the demands on minimum public spread (25 %) mentioned in 2.3.2.2, the two variables market segment and block ownership are not perfectly correlated. The requirement is applied to companies entering the continuous official trade segment, while the rates may change once accepted. In the study, I disregard that companies holding interest in each other might not actually exercise the degree of monitoring over each other that their levels of block ownership lead one to expect, due to collusion between the companies.[216]

2.3.2.4 Creditor Control Variables

The possibilities to control the management are initially linked to the amount of capital the company is receiving from the creditor. A high debt-equity ratio speaks for a higher level of creditor interest in the activities of a company's management. But the *leverage* value itself is not fully informative in and of itself.

The organizational level of the creditors is a key issue. Just as the benefits of control must outweigh the costs for owners to monitor their managers, monitoring must also be worthwhile for the creditors. Bank debt is a debt type with a highly organized backing, as banks' credit employees have the explicit task to monitor companies' activities, at least at the time of the credit negotiations.[217]

The only type of debt that is open to the control of market forces is industry bonds, which through sales price and rating changes convey to investors information on what the situation in a company is like. This can also, but will not exclusively, include information on the agency situation of the firm. Infrequent trading can be a problem for the informational level of industry bond prices.[218]

---

[214] Cf. Demsetz/Lehn (1985).

[215] Ownership structures in Germany are described in Iber (1985). From 1963-1983, the percentage of companies with a block owner rose from 55 % to 65 %. Still, ownership control is not considered adequate. Cf. Steinmann/Schreyögg/Dütthorn (1983), Jehle (1982).

[216] Simple analyses of the control situation in companies are given in Berle/Means (1932) and for Germany in Schreyögg/Steinmann (1981) and Steinmann/Schreyögg/Dütthorn (1983).

[217] Cf. Chirinko/Elston (1996).

[218] Cf. Heinke (1998).

German firms issue a lower percentage of their debt as bonds than their American counterparts do, making an agency variable uniquely based on this information too specialized. Therefore the two types of controlling debt, publicly issued bonds and bank debt, will be added together and the assumption will be made that from a certain *ratio of the monitored to the unmonitored debt* on, a company will be counted to the low agency problem category. There is no explicit theory or law governing the choice of this level, so I determine 10 % to be the boundary level for the ratio of monitored to unmonitored debt.

The leverage variable will be used in addition as a measure of creditor control. Preference will be given to the ratio of monitored to unmonitored debt, though, for the interpretation of creditor-related results, as the monitored debt ratio more cleanly represents creditor control. Where the variable monitored debt ratio describes the degree of control creditors exercise in the context of the debt a company has assumed, the leverage variable relates the debt to the equity and thus to the whole firm value. The leverage variable will be addressed again in the next point 2.3.2.5, since it can also be counted as an internal control variable in addition to its interpretation as an external control variable given in this section.

2.3.2.5 Internal Control Variables

Leverage as the ratio of debt to equity can be used as an internal control variable in the agency context, although it also represents the influence of creditors on a firm. I take an above average leverage as an indicator of lesser agency problems. The average leverage in this case is computed per year and there per sector, as different sectors support different debt-equity ratios.

The leverage variable is computed from elements also used in some of the financing variables that are studied in the test of the managerial financing hypothesis following in chapter 3. This could cause 'wrong' signs from the point of view of the managerial financing hypothesis described there. Hence, in that section of the thesis the leverage variable cannot be accorded the greatest significance of the agency variables.

The leverage variable includes only the interest-bearing components of the debt a company assumes, as only these can restrict the management as described. In particular, pension accruals are not used to compute leverage.

2.3.2.6 External Control Variables

The effectiveness of the internal control mechanisms has been disputed.[219] Therefore it is important to capture external mechanisms, too. The company *size*

---

[219] Cf. Jensen (1993) for the US.

as measured by total assets indicates which companies are more in the spotlight of public attention and thus have less agency problems. For lack of size classifiers founded in theory, I choose DM 100 million total assets as the boundary value to distinguish companies with greater agency problems from those with less problems. This round number should capture the psychological, not economical trigger that causes the public to decide when a company is large, i. e., important enough, to merit attention from the media or other external monitoring agents. The company size is also related to the market sector it is traded in (cf. chapter 2.2.3.1.2.1), giving an additional indication of the pricing efficiency that pertains to the shares.

On the other hand, it can be argued that a manager invests a great part of his human capital in a company. Bankruptcy would devaluate his company-specific know-how. For this reason the management will prefer to diversify their company as much as possible to minimize their human capital risks.[220] This can, but need not, lead to a larger size for management-controlled companies. There is also a psychological factor of managers equating size to power, and therefore striving to maximize firm size. This can be compounded if managerial performance is judged by such factors as sales growth. The empirical analysis must show which influence prevails.

The industrial *sector* a company is in can also be seen to be a pointer to agency problems, although of course this variable encompasses much more than just agency problem-related information. The capital and asset structure of a firm is partly determined by its field of production. The market conditions both on the demand and the supply side for a company's goods, from the point of view of the firms, are sector-specific, if one considers the sector to actually demarcate the relevant market of a firm.[221]

Through free competition, the supply side of the sales or products market can exert pressure on a company to produce more efficiently.[222] On the customer side of the sales market, monopsonistic customer structures can force a company to adapt to external wishes. On the supply side of the sales market, the company can face stiff competition from other companies. Both sides of the sales market act as external control instances that can reduce agency problems in a company.

Also, since the companies themselves are active in markets as customers, for example when purchasing raw and unfinished materials which the company

---

220 Cf. Wolf (1995a) and Wolf (1995b) for a description of diversification measures.

221 This is, of course, a very generalizing assumption that completely ignores geographical and other factors. Foreign competition for example is an important factor. On relevant markets see Meffert (1998).

222 Cf. Kovenock/Phillips (1995), p. 403.

processes, the companies can be controlled from two sides, depending on the specific circumstances of the sales and the supply markets.

Figure 2-9 shows the total number of companies with more than 20 employees[223] for five sectors that will be analyzed separately. These are the chemicals, machinery, electronics, food & beverages and utilities sectors. In addition, the figure shows the number of employees per sector, which gives an alternate first impression of the size of a sector. The chemicals and utilities firms are the least numerous in number and have the lowest employee figures.

The number of companies or employees per sector alone cannot be taken per se as an indicator of the competitive situation of a market, as a small number of companies might be extremely competitive on a small market which just supports just that number of competitors. One could also argue that companies under great competitive pressure will tend to hold less resources and thus employ fewer workers. The alternate view, equally valid, would be to state that only successful companies that stand firm in competition will be able to grow in size. So the numbers must be processed further to be interpreted for the purpose of estimating the level of competition.

Figure 2-10 shows again, for 1992, the number of employees per company in thousands, which is used as a measure of the company size.[224] This information is overlaid by the sales per employee. By putting the employee figure in the denominator, the company size is factored out of the sales number. Therefore this ratio can serve as an indicator for the degree of concentration on the sales market of the firms in the sector.[225] High sales per employee stand for low competitive pressure, allowing companies to secure larger portions of the total market for themselves and raise the concentration, taking into consideration the actual size of the company.[226]

While the chemicals companies and the utilities are in the same ballpark regarding the number of employees per firm, the chemicals firms have about 40 % lower sales per employee. This shows that the chemicals firms are in much more competitive markets than the utilities. With the highest sales per company for the sectors analyzed here, the firms in the utilities sector can be assumed to lack

---

223 This data is very highly correlated with the total number of companies, as determined in the 1987 total census (cf. Statistisches Bundesamt 1989). There is a difference between the two sets of data of about one magnitude.

224 Cf. Bleymüller/Gehlert/Küting (1987), p. 1071.

225 Cf. Bruckmann (1988) for more information on concentration ratios, which need more data than is available here.

226 See also Jeger (1994) on using employment figures to estimate market shares.

competitive pressure, and so they will be more susceptible to agency problems.[227]

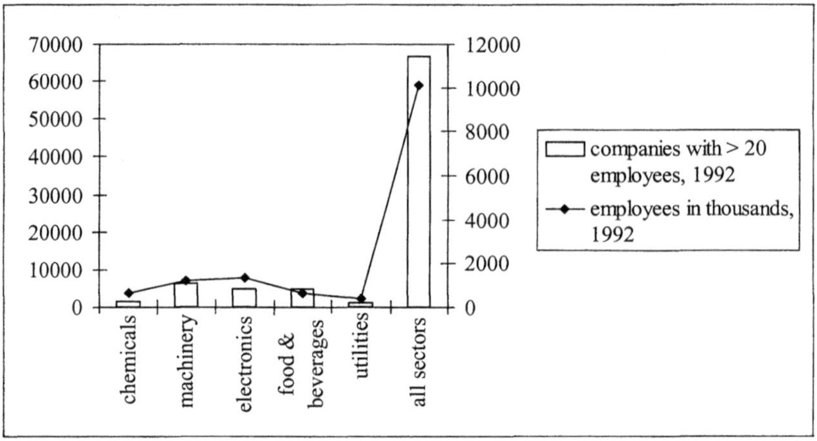

Figure 2-9: Company and employee numbers, 1992[228, 229]

The lowest sales per employee are achieved in the export dependent machinery industry, although these companies are not the smallest. Accordingly, the highest level of competition and thus the greatest level of external control can be expected for this sector. The electronics sector is the second most competitive, only slightly better or worse off than the machinery sector, depending on one's point of view. The food & beverages sector is the second least competitive. These small companies, mainly breweries, do not face nationwide competitive pressure to the same degree as most other sectors. That gives the following ranking of the sectors by assumed degree of competitivity on the sales market (Table 2-4). These ranks also identify the degree of agency problems assumed to affect the sectors: the machinery firms should have the least and the utilities the greatest.

---

[227] Foreign competition can play an important role, but that is not tracked here. It would affect the utilities sector less than the chemicals or machinery sectors, basically supporting the evaluations made with the national data.

[228] Left axis: number of companies, right axis: number of employees in thousands.

[229] Source: Statistisches Bundesamt (1994).

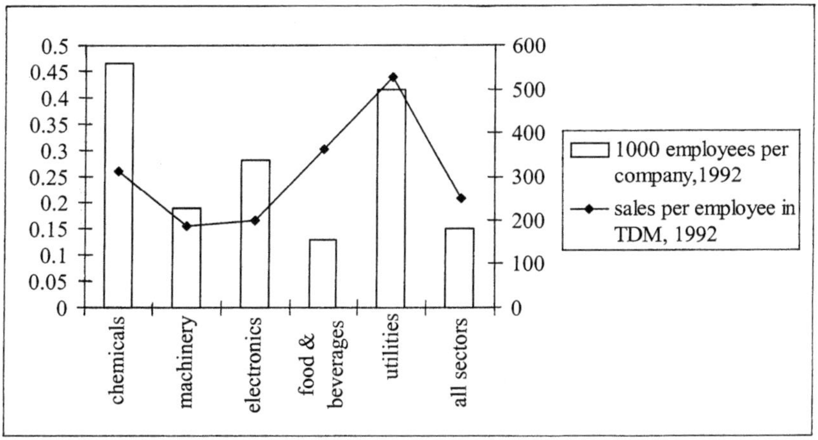

Figure 2-10: Descriptive statistics for the sectors studied, values for 1992[230,231]

sector	rank by competitivity in sales market
machinery	1
electronics	2
chemicals	3
food & beverages	4
utilities	5

Table 2-4: Ranking of the sectors by degree of competitiveness in the sales market[232]

To end this subsection, Table 2-5 shows the correlations of the agency measures except for the sector designation. A number of low correlations and negative signs shows that the variables do not copy each other, but complement each other by contributing different pieces to the big picture of agency problems in a firm. Especially the negative correlations show that while a company may be

230 With the left axis for the number of employees per firm in thousands and the right axis for the sales per employee in thousands of DM.

231 Source: Statistisches Bundesamt (1994).

232 Using 1992 data. 1 = most competitive, 5 = least competitive.

unmonitored from one point of view, another aspect that reduces agency problems might be strongly represented and in effect ensure lower agency problems.

	size	market segment	dividend signal	leverage	monitored debt ratio
block ownership	-.2598 ***	-.1987 ***	-.0037	.0161	-.1906 ***
size	1.000	.3826 ***	.0700 **	-.0492 *	-.1703 ***
market segment		1.000	.0731 **	-.1187 ***	-.0798 ***
dividend signal			1.000	.0131	-.0139
leverage				1.000	.1784 ***

N = 1119; *** = significant at 1 %-level (** = 5 %; * = 10 %)

Table 2-5: Correlations of the agency measures, 1986-1992[233]

This interpretation makes a full understanding of a company's agency situation only possible if all the variables are considered simultaneously. An attempt to do so is presented in the following section 2.3.2.7.

There are other influences that are relevant in the agency theory but could not be included here. In the first place this is the level of bank control. While the ratio of monitored to unmonitored debt is primarily determined by bank credit levels, bank control was seen to extend to block ownership, proxy voting and supervisory board seats, too (see 2.2.3.1.3). This much more varied picture with its many facets would make an analysis solely into bank influence worthwhile.

The degree of managerial ownership is another important element. It can be understood in two ways, both as the amount of shares a manager holds as a block owner in a company, as well as the proportion of remuneration the manager receives in the form of ownership participation. This can be a minute amount of the firm value, but still constitute a sizable portion of the management's pay. Such payment schedules can greatly affect the risk propensity of the management. The age of the management was also not available, but impacts the effectivity of incentive mechanisms via adjustments to future compensation.

The ratio of intangible to total assets could be another variable to include in future analyses. This ratio could represent another indicator of the degree of information asymmetry existing in a company. In most studies, the intangibles are more accurately expressed by the running expenses for R&D and for advertising. This indicates not so much any existing level of good will in a company, as intangible assets do, but the ongoing efforts to improve the company's future

233 Note that the market segment variable is only ordinally scaled.

prospects. Both expense variables, R&D and advertising, are not available for the bulk of German firms,[234] which leads to the exclusion of this effect in the study presented here.

2.3.2.7 Conglomerate Agency Variables

2.3.2.7.1 Aggregation of the Indicator Variables

In order to reduce the information overflow that may arise over the plethora of agency variables, and in an effort to combine the facets each agency variable introduces into the big picture of the agency situation in a firm, the agency variables are also incorporated into conglomerate agency variables.

Two kinds of aggregated agency variables are created. There are variables that capture the reduction in information asymmetry, variables describing the degree of ownership control, and a variable to ascertain if the creditors of the firm can effectively monitor it. It is generally accepted that the information asymmetry-reducing measures and the ownership control activities work in the same direction; after all, it is mainly the ownership which profits from the reduction of the information gap. Therefore these two groups of variables can easily be combined.

Creditors have been shown above to follow different agendas than the ownership of a firm. They desire to secure their interest payments, for which a certain level of effort is required from the management. Returns over and above those necessary to pay the interest and retire the debt are of lesser importance. This aligns the creditors' goal somewhat closer with the management's than to the ownership's, which reaps the benefits of high returns. Neither managers nor creditors are necessarily interested in maximum performance. Nevertheless, the creditors of a company will not tolerate inefficiencies that threaten to bankrupt a company if they remain unchecked over time. The management's desire to avoid work and increase consumption remains oppose both the owners' and the creditors' best interests.

Assuming that the interests of the owners and creditors are more similar than dissimilar, and that the results of creditors' (in Germany usually banks) monitoring of a firm also resemble the ownership-sided control more than they are different, it is possible to combine all three variable groups into one composite. If this is not the case, then the ratio of monitored to unmonitored debt must remain removed from the composite variable. Both approaches are followed here, the monitored debt ratio variable initially being included in the conglomerate vari-

---

234 Chemical and pharmaceutical firms often report R&D expenses.

ables (*agency1* through *agency4*) and excluded in the later variables (*agency5* through *agency7*).

Due to the double significance of the leverage variable, it is not excluded from the *agency5* through *agency7* variables. Its internal control effect is important enough to warrant its inclusion.

The agency variables exclude the sector dummies. It does not make sense to include, say, 10 % of the chemicals dummy in the conglomerate agency variable which is later used for the food & beverages and all the other sectors.

The agency variables are combined by taking them in form of a dummy variable, where the value of 0 signifies "has agency problems" and 1 stands for "does not have agency problems" according to that variable's information content. Alternatively, the values can also be understood to stand for greater or only lesser agency problems. They are then weighted by certain percentages and added together. The resulting value lies between zero and one and is then rounded to one of those values. The result is the conglomerate variable, which is dichotomous.

In aggregating the agency variables, two procedures are followed. First, the variables are combined equally weighted and rounded, with the exception of the block ownership variable, which was weighted more heavily due to its importance. The details for the two agency conglomerates, one with the monitored debt ratio and one without, are given below in Table 2-6.

	block ownership	market segment	size	leverage	dividend signal	monitored debt ratio
agency1	25 %	15 %	15 %	15 %	15 %	15 %
agency5	40 %	15 %	15 %	15 %	15 %	0 %

Table 2-6: Percentages of agency variables in conglomerate agency variables, using predetermined percentages

The second approach taken to determine the composition of the aggregate variables is to employ genetic algorithms, which are described below.

2.3.2.7.2 Genetic Algorithms

2.3.2.7.2.1 A Brief Description of Genetic Algorithms[235]

Genetic algorithms are a method of problem solving, that, as the name implies, try to optimize a problem set using a method observed in natural biological processes.[236] The processes simulated in most software packages[237] include crossbreeding and the evolutionary principle of survival of the fittest. Mutations, diversity[238] and extinctions can also be implemented to imitate all possibilities of evolution found in nature. The inclusion of unnatural processes such as inversion are also possible.

The selection process of a genetic algorithm is simulated by first formulating the problem set so that it can be expressed in chromosomal terms. This means that the variable parameters of the problem set are declared as chromosomes. The chromosomes are composed of genes, which the software user cannot directly address. The chromosomes combine to make up one individual. One individual thus stands for a set of variable values which are one possible solution to the problem at hand. The variables or chromosomes are modeled in a formula that is declared as the target equation. The target equation or fitness function specifies how the chromosomes of an individual are to be processed, with the goal of optimizing that equation.

The chromosomes are also used to describe restrictions, such as the bounds in which the sum of the chromosome values may lie. When a number of restrictions are necessary, the first generations created by the algorithm might not satisfy all restrictions.[239] I. e., if the sum of the chromosome values must be equal to one, the first generation's chromosomes can easily add up to be unequal to one.

The genetic algorithm when started initially randomly creates a pool of individuals,[240] or combinations of chromosomes. These first genes will only by the greatest chance fulfill the optimization requirement. Comparing the results each

---

235 More details can be found in Wittkemper (1993), pp. 66 ff.

236 The theory followed here is the evolutionary one as opposed to the creationist point of view.

237 The software used is GeneHunter™, release 1.0 from Ward Systems Group. Inc., 1995.

238 Diversity means population-wide slight mutations that do not preclude the familiar single-chromosome mutations. Ward Systems Group, Inc. (1995), p. 14.

239 Contrary to Ward Systems Group, Inc. (1995), p. 15.

240 Twelve chromosomes make up the first pool in Wittkemper (1993), p. 69. A pool size of fifty was used in this study.

individual produces using the fitness function allows the individuals to be ranked by goodness of fit. The poorest performing individuals are deleted from the pool in the so-called selection stage.

The selected or "surviving" individuals are then "mated" with each other, again following nature's example. GeneHunter uses the crossover technique, which mimics sexual breeding (see Figure 2-11).[241] This means that two individuals are split into two parts, say the top and the bottom chromosome sections, at a randomly determined place along their string of chromosomes. The position for the split is the same for the two individuals. The top section of chromosomes from the first individual is then mated to the bottom chromosomal section of the other individual and vice versa.[242] This is repeated for all individuals, creating a new pool of individuals. Exceptional (elite) individuals are not only mated, but also survive intact into the next generation.[243]

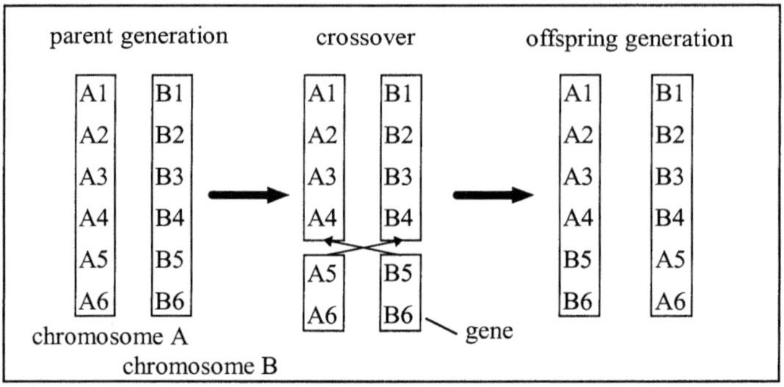

Figure 2-11: Crossover breeding

In addition to this crossbreeding technique, a small chance for mutations is allowed for. This means that the value (allele) of one or more genes in some of the offspring chromosomes can be changed randomly. Mutations often are unsuccessful, and lead to the elimination of that individual, but sometimes do improve the results. They can be seen as valves that introduce fresh genes into the optimization process and mathematically speaking can keep the genetic algorithm from converging on a local optimum obtainable by the initial chromosomes and their combinations.

241 Cf. Ward Systems Group, Inc. (1995), p. 13.

242 For more complex crossbreeding variants see Syswerda (1993).

243 Cf. Ward Systems Group, Inc. (1995), p. 14.

The population-wide form of mutation called diversity proceeds according to the same rules but mutates a whole population. The chances for diversification are intentionally kept very small. Extinction can be allowed to occur when new generations repeatedly do not improve over old ones. In this case, all but the elite individuals are deleted.[244]

Inversion as a process not found in nature means that the alleles (bit values) of the genes are inverted in the crossover process.[245]

The selection process is then applied to the new generation, followed by a new round of crossbreeding and possible mutations or diversification. The offspring generation again undergoes the selection process, and so it continues until the chosen cutoff criterion is reached. This can be after a specified amount of time, a specified number of generations have elapsed, or if the goodness of fit remains unchanged over a certain number of generations.

In continuous chromosomes, as are used here, the number of genes per chromosome determines the number of values the chromosome (variable) can assume inside its constraints. So the variable is not really continuous after all. An 8-bit chromosome for example only allows for 2^8 or 256 different values.

2.3.2.7.2.2 The Genetic Algorithm Design Used

For the purposes of this analysis, the goal is to find percentages with which the agency variables should enter a conglomerate agency problem indicator. That implies that the weights of the variables make up the chromosomes of the problem set. It also immediately becomes apparent that a restriction calling for the sum of these weights to equal one is necessary.

Some fitness function must be given, so the sum of the weighted absolute correlations of the agency dummies to the performance and finance variables studied was chosen as the target function to be optimized.[246] As the available GeneHunter release 1.0 only allows a single target equation to be optimized, it was necessary to combine the sums of the correlations to both the finance and performance variables and maximize their absolute values.

---

244 Cf. Ward Systems Group, Inc. (1995), p. 14. Extinction was not an option in the software implementation used.

245 Cf. Radcliffe (1993) for more operators.

246 Efficiency measures were excluded here.

A pool size of 50 was chosen, along with 16-bit chromosomes.[247] The mutation rate was set to 1 %. The percentage value of each variable in the conglomerate was obviously set to be greater than or equal to 0 % and less than or equal to 100 %. In addition, a restriction on the value of the block ownership was introduced in some cases, limiting it to at least 10 %, and the size and leverage variables were limited to a maximum of 60 %, as the algorithms tended to break out far past the values mentioned. Block ownership sometimes got reduced to 0 % while the other two variables in separate instances approached 90 %.

An additional restraint had to be added when it became apparent that the correlations could be maximized by choosing the variable weights in a way to maximize the number of agency conglomerate values of one. That means that if as many companies as possible were classified as not having agency problems, the correlations to financing behavior and performance were the highest. That made the restriction necessary that each group, that of agency problem companies and that of agency problem-free companies, had to represent at least one third of the sample.

2.3.2.7.2.3 Results of the Runs

The results of the runs for the conglomerates that include the ration of monitored to unmonitored debt are shown below. Three versions were chosen that produced sufficiently varied mixes to assure that the results would not automatically be identical. The lowest input proportion is for the dividend signal, which represents five percent of the *agency2* and *agency3* variables. Block ownership is the strongest variable in *agency2*, leverage in *agency3* and size in *agency4*.

	block ownership	market segment	size	leverage	dividend signal	monitored debt ratio
agency2	31.0 %	26.5 %	15.2 %	7.3 %	5.0 %	15.0 %
agency3	12.0 %	9.5 %	7.9 %	59.0 %	5.0 %	6.6 %
agency4	17.6 %	24.6 %	28 %	5.8 %	14.0 %	10.0 %

Table 2-7: Percentages of all agency variables in conglomerate agency variables, GeneHunter combinations

[247] 8-bit and 32-bit chromosomes were also tried; the former did not produce useful results while the latter did not improve noticeably over the 16-bit chromosomes, while needing more time.

Table 2-8 shows the combinations for the two GeneHunter agency conglomerates excluding the ratio of monitored to unmonitored debt. In *agency6* the reduction of the size and dividend signal variables to only one percent is noteworthy. Block ownership dominates in both versions, with the leverage, dividend signal, and market segment variables playing important roles.

	block ownership	market segment	size	leverage	dividend signal	monitored debt ratio
agency6	40.0 %	25.0 %	1.0 %	33.0 %	1.0 %	0.0 %
agency7	36.0 %	15.7 %	9.8 %	11.7 %	26.8 %	0.0 %

Table 2-8: Percentages of agency variables excluding the monitored debt ratio in conglomerate agency variables, GeneHunter combinations

Table 2-9 shows the correlations of all the agency conglomerates to each other. The first and second variables are highly correlated (almost 93 %). The correlations of the other variables to each other often reach fairly low levels. This is in part due to the dichotomous character of the conglomerates, but also shows that the mix of original agency variables does have an effect. Especially *agency3* strikes the eye with very low correlations, even a negative (but not significant one) to *agency7*. The variable *agency3* consists to almost 60 % of the leverage ratio.

	agency2	*agency3*	*agency4*	*agency5*	*agency6*	*agency7*
agency1	.9264 ***	.2354 ***	.4301 ***	.6080 ***	.5922 ***	.2859 ***
agency2	1.000	.1577 ***	.4695 ***	.6268 ***	.5796 ***	.3921 ***
agency3		1.000	.0517 *	.1656 ***	.3909 ***	-.0328
agency4			1.000	.0404	.4062 ***	.2692 ***
agency5				1.000	.5593 ***	.4384 ***
agency6					1.000	.2506 ***

N = 1119; *** = significant at 1 %-level (** = 5 %; * = 10 %)

Table 2-9: Correlations of the conglomerate agency measures, 1986-1992

Obviously, with a selection of variables so diversely mixed, it could well be possible that every hypothesis tested will neither be consistently rejected nor supported, due to a cacophony of results. On the other hand, fairly uniform results can be counted as especially strongly supported or rejected as the case may be.

All agency variables are operationalized so that low values stand for large agency problems, for consistency's sake. Low block ownership, low leverage, no dividend signal, small size or low monitored debt levels are examples where this concept intuitively applies. For the other variables this might seem to be a counterintuitive way of encoding them, with the zero value and not the one designating the assumed existence of agency problems in the firm.

Finally, since the target function calls for a maximization of the absolute correlations between agency variables and finance and performance variables, the combinations could be said to be artificially bent toward the results. Therefore these variables will be given less attention than those with the predetermined input proportions. The variables *agency1* and *agency5* with predetermined component constellations are correlated to about 60 %.

Table 2-10 gives a final overview over the agency variables, their interpretation, and the boundaries chosen to designate companies with or without agency problems. The first two, block ownership and size, stand for ownership control, the market segment and dividend signal encapsulate informational asymmetries, and the leverage and ratio of monitored to unmonitored debt are grouped under creditor control. These classifications are not exclusive; block owners will monitor the management by obtaining more information and reducing the asymmetry therein, and of course leverage works as a creditor control mechanism and an internal control.

variable	reason for influence	agency problems assumed if:
	information asymmetry	
market segment	Trade in the market segments entails varying demands on publicity, creating different levels of information asymmetry between the ownership and the management.	< 3 (not official continuous trade)
dividend signal	Raising dividends signals future prospects of the firm to the owners and reduces information asymmetry.[248]	= 0 (no signal in current or previous year)
	ownership control	
block owner-	Determines the monitoring possibilities	< 25 %

[248] Cf. Black (1976).

variable	reason for influence	agency problems assumed if:
	information asymmetry	
ship	of external owners	
size	As size increases, so does the public attention, effectively monitoring managers' actions. On the other hand managers prefer diversified companies in order to reduce their human capital risk.	< DM 100 million total assets
	internal and creditor control	
leverage	Diminishes the discretionary possibilities of the management by reducing cash flows and raising default risk[249] (internal control effect); high leverage gives creditors greater control (creditor control effect)	< ∅ leverage per year and sector
ratio of monitored to unmonitored debt	A high portion of external, monitored debt means that creditors have enough clout to control managerial activity (creditor control).	< 10 %
	agency conglomerates	
agency1	A predetermined mix of all agency variables above.	= 0
agency2	Like agency1, but a GeneHunter mix.	= 0
agency3	Like agency1, but a GeneHunter mix.	= 0
agency4	Like agency1, but a GeneHunter mix.	= 0
agency5	A predetermined mix of all agency variables above, except for the ratio of monitored to unmonitored debt.	= 0
agency6	Like agency5, but a GeneHunter mix.	= 0
agency7	Like agency5, but a GeneHunter mix.	= 0

Table 2-10: Agency variables in the analysis

249 Cf. Jensen (1986), pp. 323 ff.; Stulz (1990), pp. 3 ff.

Some of the agency variables are not dichotomous in their original form; the size variable, for example, is more or less continuous. Using the variables in this form allows multiple shades of agency problems to be represented. In the analyses, the logistic regressions will make use of the variables in that setup.

2.4 The Statistical Methods Used in the Analysis

2.4.1 T-Tests for Differences in Group Means

The agency variables can be used in a binary form to determine if companies have big or small agency problems. This subdivision of the sample being analyzed makes it possible to compare the average values of the financial, performance, or efficiency variables of the two groups to each other. For this t-tests for differences in group means are used.

The first thing to be determined when using t-tests for mean differences is if the samples being compared are independent of each other. This is the case when the same characteristic is being measured on different samples. An example is to compare the performance (same characteristic) of two groups of companies (different samples). Paired samples exist when different characteristics are compared for the same sample, for example, when the performance and efficiency (different characteristics) are compared for one group of companies (same sample).[250]

In this study, the same characteristic of different samples of companies will typically be compared, so that t-tests for independent groups are necessary. In the case of comparisons between owner-controlled and creditor-controlled firms, however, the groups will overlap slightly. Ownership control is for example determined by high block ownership and creditor control is a function of a high monitored debt ratio. Both characteristics can apply to one company, placing it in both the ownership control sample and the creditor control sample. As this setup still resembles the independent sample setup, in that the same characteristic is still compared for differing samples, the test for independent samples will be used here, too.

The null hypothesis is always that the difference in value of the characteristic between the groups is zero. The alternative hypothesis can be either one-sided, positing for example a positive difference, or a two-sided hypothesis positing a

250 Cf. Bleymüller/Gehlert/Gülicher (1988), pp. 115 f.

non-zero difference. The two-sided test is more conservative, i. e., it doesn't assign a given significance level to a difference as soon as a one-sided test does.[251]

In the case of equal standard deviations *s* for each sample, the test variable *z* for two samples x_1 and x_2 with the respective means $\overline{x}_1$ and $\overline{x}_2$, and *n* cases in total, is computed as:[252]

$$z = \frac{\overline{x}_1 - \overline{x}_2}{s \cdot \sqrt{\frac{n_1 + n_2}{n_1 \cdot n_2}}} \tag{2-3}$$

where the common standard deviation *s* is:

$$s = \sqrt{\frac{(n_1 - 1)s_1^2 + (n_2 - 1)s_2^2}{n_1 + n_2 - 2}} \tag{2-4}$$

If the standard deviations are different, the denominator of (2-3) must be adjusted accordingly:

$$z = \frac{\overline{x}_1 - \overline{x}_2}{\sqrt{\frac{s_1^2}{n_1} + \frac{s_2^2}{n_2}}} \tag{2-5}$$

The test variable *z* is computed using the means of each category x_1 and x_2, the estimated standard deviations s_1 and s_2 for the categories and the number of cases n_1 and n_2 in each category. The Levene statistic is used to determine if the standard deviations of the samples are equal or not.[253]

The t-test for mean differences assumes that the variables are distributed normally, which might not be the case for categories with less than 30 cases. When there are 30 cases or more in a group, the asymptotic normal distribution can be postulated for the group.[254]

The t-tests can be used to test for the separatory significance of each agency variable singly. It is only possible to jointly analyze the influence of the agency variables by aggregating the agency variables beforehand and using these conglomerate agency variables in the t-tests.

---

251 Cf. Werner (1989), p. 121.

252 Cf. Bleymüller/Gehlert/Gülicher (1988), pp. 109 ff.

253 Cf. SPSS Inc. (1991), pp. 266 f.

254 Cf. Bleymüller/Gehlert/Gülicher (1988), p. 78.

2.4.2 Logistic Regressions

Another parametric analysis that includes all relevant agency variables without making it necessary to conglomerate them beforehand is the logistic regression. In contrast to standard ordinary least square regressions, logistic regressions call for the use of a dichotomous dependent variable, which is a loss of information compared to the continuous financing variables available. The logistic function transforms variables with any scale into a zero-one dummy by estimating a sigmoid curve like the one sketched in Figure 2-12, and then rounding values greater than .5 up to 1, and the others down to 0. This final predictive character makes the logistic estimation more interesting than the normal ordinary least squares regression, although the loss in information due to the dichotomous nature of the dependent variable is regrettable. The classification does fit the two-category groups created with the agency variables, though.

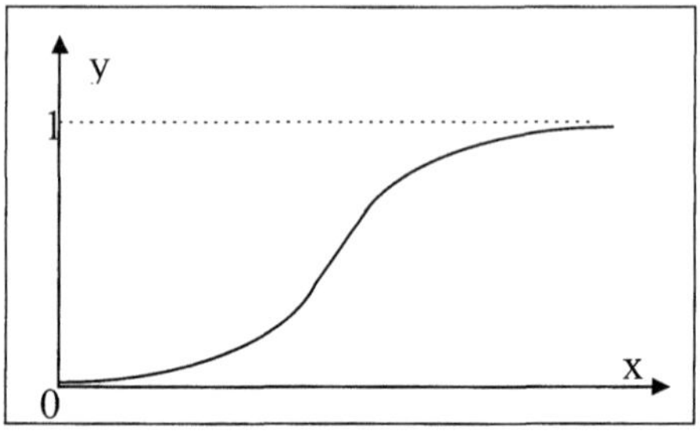

Figure 2-12: Sketch of a logistic function (before rounding)

The logistic regression is a fundamentally non-linear regression. The following basic equation for a logistic regression can be constructed, where the dependent variable *y* will be replaced by the dichotomous finance, performance, or efficiency measure to be analyzed:

$$Y_i = \text{round}\left(P\left(y_i = 1 \middle| \eta_i\right)\right) \qquad (2\text{-}6)$$

where:

Y_i = 1 if no agency problems are present
0 if agency problems are present

P = probability

η_i = $ß_{\text{BLOCK OWNERSHIP}, i} \cdot$ block ownership +
$ß_{\text{SIZE},i} \cdot$ size +
$ß_{\text{MARKET SEGMENT1},i} \cdot$ market segment dummy1 +
$ß_{\text{MARKET SEGMENT2},i} \cdot$ market segment dummy2 +
$ß_{\text{DIVIDEND},i} \cdot$ dividend signal dummy +

$ß_{LEVERAGE,i} \cdot$ leverage +

$ß_{MONITORED\ DEBT,i} \cdot$ monitored debt ratio

$ß_{BLOCK\ OWNERSHIP,i}$ etc. = coefficients.

As a result, the coefficient estimations with their respective significance tests will be given, along with an overall model log-likelihood measure. Multiplied by (-2), this measure follows a chi-square distribution which can be used to determine the significance of the overall model. The lower the modified likelihood, the more significant the regression is.[255] In addition, the correct classification percentage shall be given that compares the estimated classification to the real classification of the cases. It is here that very lopsided distributions of the cases can produce high classification scores by classifying all cases into the most strongly represented group. This implies that the agency variables have no import on the realization of the dependent variable. Such occurrences can be reduced by omitting the constant in the equation, as shown in (2-6). In addition, for lopsided groups it is important to compare the classification score to the random classification score that will strongly diverge from 50 %. If α is the proportion of one group in the whole sample, then the random classification percentage is $\alpha^2 + (1 - \alpha)^2$.[256]

[255] Cf. Krafft (1997), p. 632.

[256] Cf. Morrison (1969), p. 158.

3 Financial Behavior in the Industrial Firm

3.1 Capital Structure Theory on Perfect Markets

The neoclassical hypothesis of the irrelevance of capital structure in perfect markets[1] was the springboard for an intense discussion of the importance of capital structure which continues to this day.[2]

According to the hypothesis, capital structure has no influence on the value of a firm under these circumstances, and therefore, c. p. the firm values of leveraged and unleveraged firms must be equal. In addition to the perfect market conditions, one must assume that there is no default risk, allowing both private persons and companies unrestricted access to debt. Despite the homogeneous expectations of investors concerning future profits of the firms, these remain uncertain. Companies are finally grouped into risk categories, which allows the capital structure risk to be analyzed independently from the performance risk.

Modigliani/Miller (1958) construct three propositions:

1. The average cost of capital is a constant for all firms in the same risk class, independently of their respective financial structure.
2. For all firms in the same risk class, the relation between the yield on common stock and the financial structure (leverage) is a straight line, with the capitalization rate for a pure stream of equity for that class as the intercept, and a premium as the spread between the capitalization rate for a stream of equity for that class and the capitalization rate for pure streams as the slope.
3. The cut-off point for investment in a firm will be its capitalization rate for a pure stream of equity for that class, and therefore is completely unaffected by the security used to finance the investment.

If identical profit streams of companies in the same risk class are discounted at the same capitalization rate, then the market values will be identical, otherwise arbitrage is possible. In order for the arbitrage to work, the assumption of unlimited debt capacity of private persons is necessary.

As the perfect market and the assumptions for arbitrage are not given in reality, the propositions are not meant to be empirically tested, but provide a basis from which capital structure research can depart.

---

1 Cf. Modigliani/Miller (1958); Modigliani/Miller (1963).

2 For an overview, see Harris/Raviv (1992). Modigliani and Miller themselves evaluate the implications of their seminal research in Miller (1988) and Modigliani (1988).

3.2 Capital Structure Theory on Imperfect Markets[3]

The existence of imperfect markets has led to discussions concerning optimal leverage levels for companies and the reason for complex financial instruments.[4] On a perfect capital market, return demands of risk-bearing shareholders will be higher than those of non risk-bearing creditors. This suggests substituting equity with debt, ideally creating a completely debt-financed company. This behavior is not observed in reality, though. Assuming that return demands of shareholders and interest demands of creditors rise as leverage is increased, it can be shown that the total return of a company peaks at a leverage level below infinity (Figure 3-1). This is supported by the deduction of interest payments from pre-tax profits in Germany, causing an unequal treatment of returns to equity and to debt from the taxation point of view.[5]

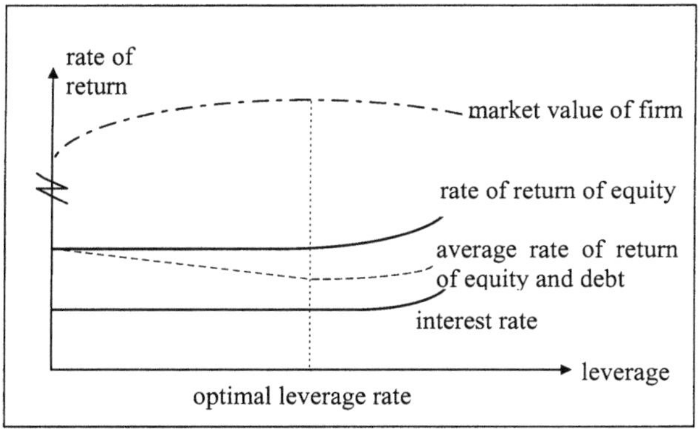

Figure 3-1: Graphical representation of the optimal leverage theory[6]

In most capital structure analyses today, information asymmetries are a key imperfection compared to perfect markets.[7] Managers in owner-controlled firms maximize the utility of the current ownership, or in manager-controlled firms due to asymmetric information follow the incentive structure of the pecking order hypothesis in order to maximize owner utility.[8] The pecking order theory of

---

[3] I am indebted to Sebastian Schneider for his invaluable comments regarding this chapter.

[4] Cf. Green (1984); Barnea/Haugen/Senbet (1980).

[5] Cf. Bieg (1997); Swoboda (1987); Drukarczyk (1981).

[6] Cf. Perridon/Steiner (1997), p. 487.

[7] Cf. e. g. Bradford (1987).

[8] Cf. Myers/Majluf (1984).

financial activity focuses on the interests of the current ownership and ranks the financing instruments by the relative level of wealth transfers induced by new financing actions.

In the agency theory, the information asymmetry allows managers to pursue other objectives than the owners wish them to. Since this theory is based on the divergence of managers' interests from the owners', I will refer to it as the managerial theory of financial behavior.[9] The managerial theory of financial behavior is a special case of the pecking order, as the asymmetric information, the sole condition for the pecking order theory, is expanded by the assumption of managers maximizing their own utility (risk-return profile), which has not been equalized to ownership utility in manager-controlled firms.[10] The managerialism hypothesis results from the level of control in the company. The human capital risks of the managers are negatively correlated to the resources under the manager's control. That is why a manager will choose the finance instrument for an investment in order to minimize the resources that will be transferred to the external financier as a compensation for receiving the investment outlay.

This will be contrasted in the following to the pecking order theory of the financial choices managers make when acting in the best interests of the owners, despite the information asymmetry.

3.2.1 Internal vs. External Funds

As long as the management of a company is solely acting in the interest of the ownership, assume that it will initially only realize investment projects with a positive net present value:[11]

$$NPV_I > 0 \qquad (3\text{-}1)$$

where: NPV_I = net present value of investment I.

Of all possible future states s that will affect the outcome of an investment, the critical state s_A identifies that state in which the ownership of a company is indifferent between investing or not. When internally financed, the value V of the growth possibilities, depending on the probability distribution of the separate states' happening, is:[12]

9 Cf. Griner/Gordon (1995); Bühner (1984), p. 812.

10 Cf. Garvey/Hanka (1996), pp. 5 ff.

11 One can argue in analogy for negative NPV investments with the same result.

12 Cf. Myers (1977), p. 151.

$$V(\text{Growth}) = \begin{cases} 0; s \leq s_A \\ \int_{s_A}^{\infty} q_s \cdot [V(s) - I] ds; s > s_A \end{cases} \tag{3-2}$$

with q_s as a discount factor depending on state s. Internally financing an investment costs the least by saving costs of issue in the case of equity or bonds or negotiation in the case of bank credit. These savings are attractive to managers either acting in their own or in the owners' interests. External funds always entail payment obligations, meaning the present value of the cash flows from a project must be large enough to fund all payment obligations (*P*) and the investment outlay:

$$V(\text{Growth}) = \begin{cases} 0; s \leq s_B \\ \int_{s_A}^{\infty} q_s \cdot [V(s) - I] ds \ - \ P; s > s_B \end{cases} \tag{3-3}$$

State s_B analogously to (3-2) describes the situation under asymmetric information and external finance in which the management is indifferent to investing or not. External financing entails a reduction in wealth to the amount of the cumulated present value of all originally profitable investments (the shaded triangle ABC in Figure 3-2) that are forgone if $s \in [s_A, s_B\rangle$. Without external finance, every state greater than s_A provides profitable investment opportunities for the owners, with external finance, this situation only occurs if state s_B is reached. In the pecking order theory, managers will prefer internal finance to external to avoid this loss.

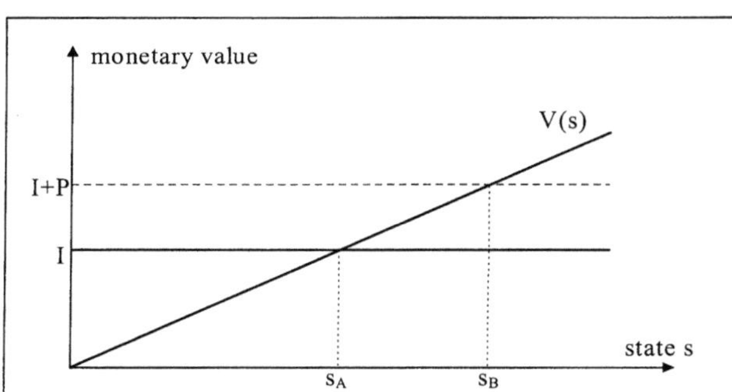

Figure 3-2: External financing under asymmetric information[13]

[13] Cf. Myers (1977), p. 153.

From the point of view of the agency theory, managers will additionally want to avoid the monitoring potential both external equity and debt finance introduce to the company. Owners, on the other hand, will also prefer internal to external equity financing, not only because of the cheaper cost of internal finance, but they also do not want the proportion of their ownership to decrease, causing them to lose control of company resources.[14] Retaining their ownership proportion is only possible at additional cost. External debt financing will finally be restricted by the convex relation of debt to the probability of bankruptcy and the rising interesest rates of increased leverage (Figure 3-1).[15] This speaks for internal financing as the preferred method of finance for managers and owners in the managerial hypothesis. So the preference for internal over external funds follows from both the managerial and pecking order hypotheses in the case of information asymmetry, regardless of the degree of managerial control in the company.[16]

However, internal means can also exceed the investment possibilities open to a firm. In this case, free cash flows can result.[17] Their allowance by the management is another source of agency problems. If there are no positive-NPV investments available, using the return demands of the ownership as a discount factor in the NPV calculations, then the best thing to do from the owners' point of view is to pay out the superfluous funds to the owners so that they can invest those funds more lucratively elsewhere. The dividend payout reduces the free cash flow to nil. From the management's point of view, this is not desirable, because internal funds provide the means of finance that least affect the control situation (or lack thereof) in a firm. Also, a manager could be reluctant to allow funds to leave his area of control, thereby diminishing his perceived power. Finally, the dividend raises associated with an additional payout can cause expectations about future profits to rise among investors, creating pressure on the management. Therefore, although the basic preference for internal funds is given in both owner- and manager-controlled firms, according to the agency theory, uncontrolled managers will favor free cash flow where owners do not.

3.2.2 Agency Costs of Debt and Equity

Once internal funds are exhausted, a financial bottleneck ensues. By financing the investment outlay *I* with external funds, investment projects that exceed in-

---

14 Cf. Amihud/Lev/Travlos (1990), pp. 603 f.

15 Cf. Stulz (1988), pp. 25 ff.

16 See though Bester/Scheepens (1996), who show that under certain circumstances, bank debt can be preferable to internal finance.

17 Jensen (1986). Free cash flows are defined as the cash flows remaining after investment outlays and dividends are subtracted from the cash flow.

ternal financial means can be funded. On the other hand, dividend or interest demands in the case of external equity and debt finance respectively reduce the value of the growth opportunities.[18] In addition, there are the assumed informational asymmetries between managers, shareholders, and the creditors. While the management can estimate the cost of capital using its insider information, outside shareholders and creditors must generally formulate their return demands on the basis of publicly available information that was possibly manipulated by the management. If the management can issue debt for a positive NPV investment below its correct risk-adjusted price, this increases the wealth of the current ownership. Managers can exploit this information asymmetry to the detriment of the creditors.[19] Owners will approve of the wealth transfer to equity (pecking order theory), while managers are intent on binding wealth in the company, minimizing repayment obligations (agency theory). The agency theory calls this loss of the creditors agency costs of debt, in addition to any monitoring or bonding costs or residual losses connected to debt-sided principal-agent relationships. The cost of nominally risk-free capital is not determined by the risk structure of a company, so the information asymmetry can only be exploited by issuing risky capital.

But equity financing causes agency problems, too.[20] Both managers and owners are risk averse, as otherwise neither convex indifference curves nor capital market theories hold. Managers will be much more risk averse than the shareholders, though. The latter are able to diversify their investment capital. They only must bear the systematic portion of the risk of a certain investment. Managers on the other hand enter their non-diversifiable human capital into the firm and must watch the total risk of the company. This implies a risk asymmetry in the owners' favor as opposed to the information asymmetry in the managers' favor. Managers will want to diversify the companies they control in order to reduce risk.[21] Investments for this purpose do not necessarily have positive NPVs. In owner-controlled firms, diversification normally is not important, as owners can more cheaply diversify on the capital markets.[22]

With the introduction of agency costs, another optimality criterion can be introduced to describe an optimal leverage theory, beside the one described on page 73. Issuing debt reduces the room for managerial discretion due to the introduction of amortization and continuous interest payments that must be met (cf. chapter 2.3.2.5). These marginal costs decline, the higher the leverage is in a company. Also, organized creditors such as banks can monitor the management

18 See Equation (3-3).

19 Cf. Stein (1995).

20 Cf. Jensen/Meckling (1977), p. 315 f.

21 Cf. Diamond (1984).

22 Cf. Stulz (1997), p. 12.

to a degree. On the other hand, as already described for the pecking order theory, the incentive of owners to transfer wealth from the creditors rises, the higher the leverage in the company is. These marginal agency costs of debt will rise with the increase in debt levels. In the managerial theory, the optimal trade-off is reached when the marginal costs of each cost category are equal (Figure 3-3).[23]

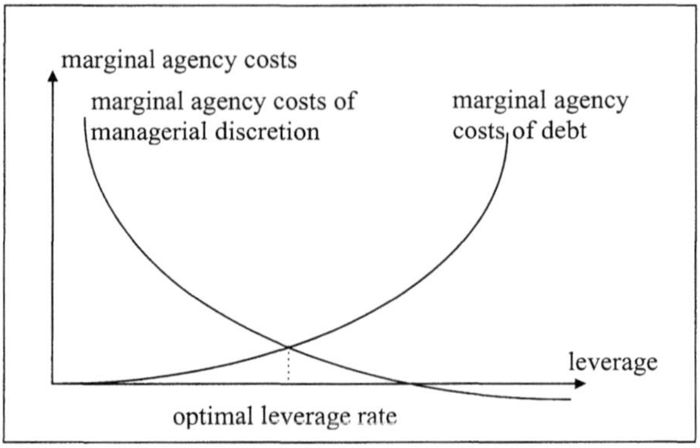

Figure 3-3: Graphical representation of the optimal leverage according to the managerial theory[24]

3.2.3 Investment and Firm Value

It is often overlooked that positive net present values ($\frac{dV_t}{dI_t} > 0$ where V = value of company and I = investment) are neither a necessary nor a sufficient criterion for an owner to agree to an investment. The reason for this is the substitutional relationship between the owners and creditors of a firm. The wealth effects from an investment consist of the sum of the changes in the market value of the equity and debt. Owner-controlled firms prefer investments that increase the value of equity:

$$\frac{dE_t}{dI_t} = \frac{dV_t}{dI_t} - \frac{dD_t}{dI_t} > 0 \tag{3-4}$$

where E_t represents the value of the equity and D_t the value of the debt at time t. The prospect of wealth transfers at the creditors' expense increase the propensity

23 For a discussion of the choice of debt or equity finance as a function of the riskiness of the investment see Swoboda (1985).

24 In contrast to Kim/Jung/Stulz (1996), p. 163.

of owners to invest.[25] This can even be possible if the investment has a negative NPV. The market value of debt can be written as a function of the corporate value and the corporate risk σ: $D_t = D(V_t, \sigma^2)$.[26] As decisions to invest change both the corporate value as well as the risk structure of a firm, their effect can be split into a direct effect, an indirect effect and a risk structural effect:[27]

$$\frac{dE_t}{dI_t} = \underbrace{\frac{dV_t}{dI_t}}_{\substack{\text{direct}\\\text{effect}}} - \underbrace{\frac{\delta D_t}{\delta V_t} \cdot \frac{dV_t}{dI_t}}_{\substack{\text{indirect}\\\text{effect}}} - \underbrace{\frac{\delta D_t}{\delta \sigma_t^2} \frac{d\sigma_t^2}{dI_t}}_{\substack{\text{risk structural}\\\text{effect}}} > 0 \tag{3-5}$$

The direct effect signifies the increase in the value of the firm V in the case of a positive NPV investment I. The indirect effect is the increase in the value of the debt due to the increase in the value of the firm, which can again be traced to the positive NPV investment. The increase in the value of the debt reduces the value of the equity, hence it is subtracted in (3-5). The risk structural effect is an increase in the value of the debt due to a decrease in the volatility of the firm. This is the case if the investment increases diversification. The risk structural effect, too, subtracts from the value of the equity. Issuing debt is equivalent to the owners' selling riskless bonds and simultaneously buying a put option on the company's assets.[28]

When considering positive NPV investments, the direct and indirect effects are always positive, as increases in the value of the firm reduce the default probability of debt, $\frac{\delta D_t}{\delta V_t} > 0$.[29] On the other hand, the risk structural effect will have a negative sign, due to option pricing considerations. Equity can be interpreted as a European call option on the company's assets.[30] The market value of the equity increases with higher volatility of the corporate value. Rational, diversified owners maximize their wealth if: $\frac{d\sigma_t^2}{dI_t} > 0$.[31] The creditors are the stillholders in this construction. The market value of the debt therefore is inversely pro-

25 Cf. Campbell/Kracaw (1990).

26 Cf. Myers (1984), pp. 575 ff.

27 Cf. Myers (1977), p. 165.

28 Cf. Brealey/Myers (1996), pp. 565 f.

29 To repeat for clarity: The positive indirect effect is subtracted in (3-5), reducing the value of the equity.

30 Cf. Merton (1974), pp. 449 ff. Also see Haugen/Senbet (1981).

31 Cf. Green/Talmor (1986).

portional to the company risk ($\frac{\delta D_t}{\delta \sigma_t^2} < 0$). Risky investments thus transfer wealth from the creditors to the owners. This risk structural effect is independent of the advantageousness of the investment. Negative NPV investments have negative direct and indirect effects. As manager-controlled firms invest risk adversely, the risk structural effect will be positive in this case and counteract the negative NPV: $\overbrace{\underbrace{\frac{\delta D_t}{\delta \sigma_t^2}}_{<0} \cdot \underbrace{\frac{d\sigma_t^2}{dI_t}}_{<0}}^{>0}$. At the same time this implies wealth transfers to the creditors at the owners' expense which causes agency costs of equity. Such risky, negative NPV investments thus are more probable for owner-controlled firms, because of the positive risk-structural effect (possibility of transferring wealth from creditors), while manager-controlled firms will more often forego positive NPV investments, again if that avoids higher risk (Table 3-1). In consequence the underinvestment problem described in the literature for manager-controlled firms[32] is offset by a potential overinvestment problem of owner-controlled firms.[33] Owners will avoid risk-reducing (diversifying) negative NPV projects that managers might prefer for that very risk reduction. They will also prefer risky investments that creditors would rather avoid.[34]

	ownership view		management view	
net present value	$\frac{dV_t}{dI_t} > 0$	$\frac{dV_t}{dI_t} < 0$	$\frac{dV_t}{dI_t} > 0$	$\frac{dV_t}{dI_t} < 0$
direct effect	+	–	+	–
indirect effect	–	+	–	+
risk structural effect	+	+	–	–

Table 3-1: Substitutional effects of risky investments on corporate value

32 Cf. Jensen/Meckling (1976); Wosnitza (1991). See also the game theoretical analysis in Bergman/Callen (1991) and Berkovitch/Kim (1990).

33 Cf. Cooney/Kalay (1993), p. 158; also Perotti/Spier (1993); Heinkel/Zechner (1990). Overinvestment by uncontrolled managers can occur when free cash flows are high. Cf. Stulz (1990).

34 Cf. Schmidt/Terberger (1996), pp. 414 f.

In Table 3-1, one can see that from the point of view of the owners, the choice of a positive NPV, risky investment (positive direct effect) causes a negative indirect effect and vice versa. The rise in volatility is seen as positive by the ownership and as negative by the management, independent of the sign of the net present value of the investment.

Modigliani and Miller's irrelevance theorem for perfect markets is superseded by the discussion above. This description shows that wealth transfers between financiers of a company that are seen as the reason for agency costs are not the result of the financing decision but already of the investment decision.[35] Investment and finance decisions may not be considered separately.[36] Investment decisions are rather the basis for finance decisions in the double sense that the expected present value and the risk of the investment both affect the wealth of the financier of the company, be it the ownership or creditors.[37] The financing decision determines the level of the wealth transfer and accordingly the order of preference of the financing instruments.

3.2.4 Debt versus Equity Finance

I showed above (3.2.1) that, with the exception of free cash flows, internal funds will be preferred to external financing both by the ownership and the management in the case of asymmetric information. It also became clear that wealth transfers are already initiated by the decision to invest, not by the choice of the method of finance (3.2.2 and 3.2.3). The method of external finance chosen only determines the absolute and relative level of these transfers between investor groups. That will be discussed in this section.

The priority ranking of the financial instruments is a result of the level of wealth transfers and can be explained with option pricing theory. As companies in all cases prefer internal to external finance, they will maintain a certain level of liquidity to continuously enable internal financing.[38] If the investment volume I exceeds that liquidity L, external funds will be necessary to the amount of $I - L$. The money may be provided by issuing equity or debt.

When assuming that the manager is maximizing the market value of the equity of the current ownership (pecking order hypothesis)[39] or that he is maximizing

---

35 Carpenter (1994), p. 22 comes to principally the same results. See Ravid (1988) and Darrough/Stoughton (1986) for a discussion of the interaction between investment and finance decisions.

36 Empirically shown for Germany by Frisse/Funke/Lankes (1991).

37 Cf. Milde (1995).

38 Cf. Devereux/Schiantarelli (1990).

39 Cf. Donaldson (1961).

the value of the investment remaining in the company and minimizing the outflows to external financiers (managerialism), I again assume that the manager will only invest if the value of the company increases through the investment.[40] In the case of equity financing this means that:[41]

$$L + a \leq L + a + b - \Delta E \tag{3-6}$$

The left term shows the wealth of the current ownership without the investment and therefore also without a seasoned issue. It consists of the sum of the liquidity *L* and the future value of assets *a* that the management can better quantify than external investors due to the information asymmetry. The right hand side shows the wealth of the current ownership in the case of investing via an equity issue. It contains the liquidity, the future value of the assets and the present value of the investment *b* minus the transfer of resources to the new shareholders ΔE. The investment will only take place if the present value of the investment exceeds the value of the transfer to the new investors, so if $b \geq \Delta E$.

Credit finance analogously takes place if the added value of the investment is greater than the resources transferred to the creditors in the light of the changed risk structure of the company, so if

$$L + a \leq L + a + b - \Delta D \tag{3-7}$$

and hence $b \geq \Delta D$. If a company can issue risk-free capital, the creditors cannot profit from a change in state. In that case all investments with a positive present value will be undertaken. The finance decision is governed by the comparison of ΔE and ΔD both for the pecking order and the managerialism. With option price theory one can show that $\Delta E \geq \Delta D$.

Issuing debt is akin to selling the total assets to the creditor. At the same time the owners receive a European call option on the total assets from the creditors. The strike price is the retirement price *P* of the debt and the time to maturity is *t* for the debt. Using the Black & Scholes model,[42] the value of the equity is:

$$E = V \cdot \Phi(d_1) - P \cdot e^{-r_F \cdot t} \cdot \Phi(d_2) \tag{3-8}$$

$$d_1 = \frac{\ln\frac{V}{P} + \left(r_F + 0.5 \cdot \sigma^2\right)t}{\sigma \cdot \sqrt{t}} \tag{3-9}$$

$$d_2 = d_1 - \sigma \cdot \sqrt{t}$$

with: E = market value of equity

V = market value of company

[40] One can argue in analogy for negative NPV investments with the same result.

[41] Cf. Myers/Majluf (1984), p. 207.

[42] Cf. Black/Scholes (1973).

σ	= standard deviation of corporate profits
r_F	= risk free interest rate
$\Phi(d)$	= cumulative standard normal density function
P	= retirement price of debt
t	= years to maturity of debt.

Assuming that the investment changes the risk structure and the corporate value, the effects of the investment on the wealth of the shareholders or creditors can be analyzed separately. The partial derivative of the market value of equity by the variance as an indicator of corporate risk illustrates the effect of a change in risk due to an investment:[43]

$$\frac{\delta E}{\delta \sigma^2} = P \cdot e^{-r_F \cdot t} \cdot \phi(d_1) \cdot \frac{\sqrt{t}}{\sigma} > 0 \qquad (3\text{-}10)$$

with: $\phi(d)$ = standard normal density function.

The value of the equity increases with the variance. If the investment raises the corporate value, as assumed here, the value of the equity also rises:[44]

$$\frac{\delta E}{\delta V} = \Phi(d_1) > 0 \qquad (3\text{-}11)$$

The market value of a corporation is the sum of the market values of equity and debt. The wealth of the creditors can therefore be written as:[45]

$$D = V \cdot \Phi(-d_1) + P \cdot e^{-r_F \cdot t} \cdot \Phi(d_2) \qquad (3\text{-}12)$$

The impact of corporate risk on the value of the debt is visible in the partial derivation of the value of debt by the variance:

$$\frac{\delta D}{\delta \sigma^2} = \overbrace{-\underbrace{P \cdot e^{-r_F \cdot t} \cdot \phi(d_1) \cdot \frac{\sqrt{t}}{\sigma}}_{>0}}^{<0} \qquad (3\text{-}13)$$

One sees that the value of debt falls when corporate risk rises. The value of debt increases with the corporate value, as:

$$\frac{\delta D}{\delta V} = \Phi(-d_1) = [1 - \Phi(d_1)] > 0 \qquad (3\text{-}14)$$

---

43 Merton (1974). The derivation by σ is called the option vega. Cf. Campell/Lo/MacKinlay (1997), pp. 353 f.

44 This is the option delta. Cf. Campell/Lo/MacKinlay (1997), p. 353.

45 $D = V - E$ and therefore $D = V - V \cdot N(d_1) + P \cdot e^{-r \cdot t} \cdot N(d_2)$.

By contrasting the various effects we can compare the wealth transfers to new creditors or owners (pecking order hypothesis) or their participation in the creation of value added by investing (managerialism). One has to be careful to look at the full owner or creditor groups though. The level of transfers can be determined as the new financiers are integrated into the old groups. Their gains in wealth determine the financing decisions.

The costs of the principal-agent relation are higher in equity financing than in debt financing, as the following terms are always true in the option pricing model:

$\frac{\delta E}{\delta V} \geq \frac{\delta D}{\delta V}$ and $\frac{\delta E}{\delta \sigma^2} > \frac{\delta D}{\delta \sigma^2}$. The first condition must always hold as d_1 in (3-11) can never be negative, and for all positive fractiles of the standard normal distribution like d_1, $\Phi(d_1) \geq 0.5$. $\Phi(-d_1)$ in (3-14) is accordingly $1 - \Phi(d_1) \leq 0.5$. The second inequality always holds as $\delta E/\delta\sigma^2$ is always positive and $\delta D/\delta\sigma^2$ is always negative.[46]

Therefore the wealth transfers are always greater in equity financing than in debt financing, i. e. $\Delta E \geq \Delta D$. Hence when assuming that the manager is maximizing the market value of the equity of the current ownership (pecking order hypothesis[47]) or that he is maximizing the value of the investment remaining in the company (managerialism), debt financing will always be preferred to new equity in both models, regardless of the control situation in the company.[48]

Owners were seen to possibly favor negative NPV investments if the wealth transfer from the creditors is sufficiently high. In the pecking order theory, the management will try to finance negative NPV investments with debt, in order to not harm owners by using their equity for this.[49] According to the managerialistic view, the uncontrolled manager is not maximizing the value of the firm. If a negative NPV investment contributes to in-company diversification, it can be appealing to the uncontrolled manager, too. But negative NPV projects that are financed with debt have disadvantages for the management that do not arise for him when using equity:

1. Repaying the debt reduces the funds available to a manager and increase the human capital risk that the investment was originally meant to reduce.

---

46 Issuing convertible bonds is a suggested solution to the wealth transfer problem. Cf. Fischer/Zechner (1990).

47 Cf. Donaldson (1961).

48 Cf. Fluck (1998). For this reason, more positive NPV investments are foregone in equity financing than with debt financing.

49 Naranayan (1988) argues that debt keeps unprofitable firms out of the market, giving it a further advantage over equity in the pecking order context.

2. The cost of capital rises with leverage because the risk of bankruptcy increases, especially as it is a negative NPV investment. This reduces the manager's discretionary freedom.
3. Positive NPVs of other investments must be partially transferred to the creditors.

Thus equity finance makes sense in a manager-controlled firm if the advantageousness of the investment is unsure or negative NPVs are expected. In this special case, rational owners will react negatively to issue announcements.[50]

One can assume that managers who can operate uncontrolled by the owners of a firm will try to choose instruments of finance that do not open up new monitoring possibilities in preference to those instruments that do. This will lead them to prefer internal to external finance and maintain a high level of free cash flows. If they must resort to external finance, short-term debt, which includes such forms as trade accounts payable, where there is no creditor interest in controlling the management, will be chosen before long-term debt.[51] External long-term debt in Germany usually consists of bank credit,[52] which is granted only if the creditor bank is given a detailed and comprehensive insight into the situation of the company.[53] Both are from the control point of view preferable to equity.[54] Equity issues that admit new owners follow in last place.

Current owners will not want equity issues that can diminish their influence or produce extra costs. While they favor internal finance, they wish to avoid unnecessary free cash flows, making this the second-least popular form of finance for the ownership. This leaves external debt as their preferred method of finance. It can be assumed that they, too will prefer the less monitored short-term debt to long-term debt from an agency standpoint.

---

50 In Germany, stock price reactions to issue announcements are typically positive. Cf. Padberg (1995); Brakmann (1993). This conforms to the managerial theory, because the management allows new monitoring potential into the firm. In the US, the stock market reactions are negative on average, which conforms to the pecking-order theory. Cf. Jung/Kim/Stulz (1996), p. 163. A major difference between the US and German stock markets is that in Germany, rights issues are the norm, which could affect the owners' perception of an issue announcement.

51 Krahnen (1988) relates maturity structure to sunk costs and recommends long-term debt for investments with high sunk costs under information asymmetry (managers acting in the owners' interests).

52 The importance of bank credit to German firms is assessed in Neuberger (1994) and Francfort/Rudolph (1992).

53 Especially in view of the German house bank system. Cf. Fischer (1990).

54 Williamson (1988) points out that governance by equity is much more flexible than governance by debt.

Equity is the least popular financial instrument for managers and owners. It remains to be clarified if owners are more or less averse to equity issues than managers are. Owners will either lose their previous level of block ownership through an issue, or have to expend further funds to buy new shares in proportion to their old ownership level.[55] For managers, this possibility of diluting current block owners' influence is something of a boon. It was also shown that managers prefer equity for negative NPV investments, contrary to owners. Therefore managers will find equity issues less undesirable than current owners.[56]

House banks, once established, will tend to be the first address for further debt, so I assume that creditors will generally favor long-term external debt before all other financial instruments. This will be followed by short-term debt. Equity, which introduces the possibility of new agency costs of debt, is less attractive than debt, but still preferable to free cash flows.

3.3 Empirical Analysis of the Financial Behavior of German Stock Corporations

3.3.1 Hypotheses

In this section, the hypotheses concerning the comparative financing behavior of companies with and without agency problems will be presented. The distinction between companies with and without agency problems will be made in the empirical analysis with the help of the agency variables discussed earlier (chapter 2.3.2). The hypotheses tested here are based on the managerial theory of financial behavior, in contrast to the pecking-order theory. Both were seen to predict very similar behavior.[57]

The first hypothesis concerns the difference between manager- and owner-controlled firms. Managers were seen in chapter 3.2.1 to prefer free cash flows to external funds, and in chapter 3.2.4 it was shown that they prefer short-term external debt to long-term external debt to external equity. Owners, on the other hand, will wish to avoid admitting new owners by way of capital issues, as maintaining previous ownership levels is costly, despite the rights offers common in Germany.[58] The desire to keep other controling interest groups out will

---

55 The former case applies to the opération blanche, in which some rights are sold in order to pay for the acquisition of new shares.

56 Girgensohn/Calmbach (1980) empirically confirm this for Germany for the period 1972-1977.

57 Cf. Shyam-Sunder/Myers (1994), p. 4.

58 Cf. the argumentation in Steiner/Schneider/Wolf (1998).

also lead them to prefer short-term debt to long-term debt. While they will be interested in using internal financing capabilities, they will not favor maintaining high levels of *free* cash flow, i. e., that cash flow that remains even after all investments and dividends have been paid.[59] The following Table 3-2 shows the orders of preference for the financial instruments by control group:[60]

preference for financial instrument	management control	ownership control
1.	free cash flow	short-term external debt
2.	short-term external debt	long-term external debt
3.	long-term external debt	free cash flow
4.	equity issue	equity issue

Table 3-2: Preferences for financial instruments, by management and ownership control

Equity issues thus are the least attractive alternative to either side. Since for large blockholders the prospect of the loss of controlling interest in a firm is a major threat, it is plausible to assume that equity issues will be even less popular in ownership-controlled firms than in management-controlled ones. This should produce negative differences, especially for groups where ownership control is at least in part defined by block ownership levels in excess of 25 % (i. e., when using block ownership or any of the agency conglomerates as grouping variables). Translated to differences between ownership control and management control in relative volume per financial instrument, this means that the following signs of the differences are to be expected and tested for:

The financial instruments in Table 3-3 are listed in the order of their signs, from positive to negative. This order will be preserved in the other tables, too. The differences in volume of each instrument by company do not require that companies in either control group average out to equal size in order to be comparable, if the financial activity is expressed in relative terms. Every financial activity variable of a company will be divided by the total fixed assets of that firm. This also means that the size variable can still be employed in this context as an agency variable. The hypothesis does, however, imply that the volume of investments is about equal for each control group.[61] Since short-term debt finance

59 Cf. Hackel/Livnat/Rai (1994).

60 Internal finance by normal cash flows is preferred by all and therefore not listed.

61 Over- and underinvestment problems are assumed to cancel each other out. A detailed analysis of investment behavior was not possible here, but constitutes an interesting

is a less organized activity, due to the many creditors involved (trade partners, government, banks), a zero was placed in parentheses behind the plus to signify that its resulting higher volatility could erase any significance in group differences.

financial instrument	expected sign of difference*
long-term external debt	+
short-term external debt	+ (o)
equity issue	–
free cash flow	–

* difference of ownership-controlled group to management-controlled group

Table 3-3: Hypothesis 1: Preferences for financial instruments, by management and ownership control

When comparing the management-controlled companies to creditor-controlled ones, it is entirely possible that increases long-term debt will be arranged with the same banks that already have a creditor stake in the company (especially house banks). This will make that form of debt most attractive to creditors, while short term debt follows. Equity issues do not bear the stigma they do for current shareholders, so they will not be as unpopular with creditors. The following tables result, with the signs in Table 3-5 defining the second hypothesis to be tested:

preference for financial instrument	management control	creditor control
1.	free cash flow	long-term external debt
2.	short-term external debt	short-term external debt
3.	long-term external debt	equity issue
4.	equity issue	free cash flow

Table 3-4: Preferences for financial instruments, by management and creditor control

starting point for further research. Preliminary tests point to a certain role of creditor control, particularly by banks, compared to managerial control. Ownership control was not a significant factor.

Matching up the orders of preference for financial instruments between owners and creditors gives an automatic third set of tables with a testable set of differences in financial activity. The creditor group values are subtracted from the ownership group values to create the respective signs of the differences in Table 3-7. I assume that the differences in equity and free cash flow finance will be more pronounced than those for the long- and especially short-term external debt. The short-term debt is more popular to owners who can attempt to transfer wealth from the creditors to themselves as seen in 3.2.4. For these financial instruments a reversal of the order in preference is more easily imaginable than for the other two. The volatility of short-term debt finance again is accounted for by adding a zero in parentheses for that financial instrument.

financial instrument	expected sign of difference*
long-term external debt	+
short-term external debt	o
equity issue	+
free cash flow	–

* difference of creditor-controlled group to management-controlled group

Table 3-5: Hypothesis 2: Preferences for financial instruments, by management and creditor control

preference for financial instrument	ownership control	creditor control
1.	short-term external debt	long-term external debt
2.	long-term external debt	short-term external debt
3.	free cash flow	equity issue
4.	equity issue	free cash flow

Table 3-6: Preferences for financial instruments, by ownership and creditor control

Table 3-6 shows that owners and creditors have similar, but not identical preferences. This makes the use of the conglomerate variables *agency1* through *agency4* less important than *agency5* to *agency7*, as the former include the creditor control variable 'ratio of monitored to unmonitored debt' together with the ownership control variables, which the latter do not.

financial instrument	expected sign of difference*
long-term external debt	–
short-term external debt	+ (o)
equity issue	–
free cash flow	+

* difference of ownership-controlled group to creditor-controlled group

Table 3-7: Hypothesis 3: Preferences for financial instruments, by management and creditor control

With regard to the sectors in the dataset, it is possible to formulate an additional hypothesis.[62] The sectors proxy in this case as indicators of the level of competition in the sales markets that the companies must face. One can introduce distinctions in the financial behavior of the management-controlled firms, due to the added control element that the competition on the sales markets brings to each company. The competition would align the financing behavior of otherwise management-controlled companies with that of the ownership-controlled companies.[63] The following hypothesis concerns the sectoral differences:

4. The differences between manager-controlled and owner-controlled companies will be more significant in sectors that are not subject to a high level of competition on the sales markets, and disappear in highly competitive sectors.

The ranking of the five sectors by their competitivity in chapter 2.3.2.6 gave the following order of sectors by amount of hypothesized agency problems, starting from the sector with the least assumed problems to the sector with the most: machinery, electronics, chemicals, food & beverages and in the last place the utilities sector, for which regulations are assumed to have stifled the market as a monitoring instance.[64]

The rankings that the first three hypotheses suggest for the affinities of each control group to each financial instrument can also be clarified in simple graphs.

62 On the importance of sectors, cf. Bowen/Daley/Huber (1982) and for Germany Schmidt (1976).

63 Cf. Neuberger (1989), pp. 177 ff.

64 Kovenock/Philipps (1995) suggest that regulated firms will have higher debt ratios in order to increase control via the interest payments, where product market monitoring fails. That hypothesis will not be tested here.

This is done in Figure 3-4, where the control group most partial to a financial instrument is listed at the top of each field for that respective instrument, with the others following below. Each control group has its own column, facilitating the recognition of its position in every subchart. Creditors like long-term debt and equity most, owners short-term debt, and managers free cash flow. Managers dislike long-term debt most of all groups, shareholders dislike issues of new equity, and creditors wish to avoid free cash flow most of all of the control groups, closely followed by the ownership.

Non-agency influences on capital decisions are excluded from this analysis. Taxes play an important role in the choice of financial instruments,[65] as does the default probability,[66] often represented by the volatility of stock returns.[67] Also, due to limitations of the data, it was not possible to include agency theoretic hypotheses related to the relation of bank control via equity and debt[68], the number of creditors[69], or special contracts such as bond warrants and convertible bonds.[70]

Developments over time will also not be studied in this section.[71] The overall development shows that the leverage for German companies is steadily rising,[72] but it is necessary to differentiate by financial instrument. The use of that amount of pension accruals that continually remains in the company as an internal finance instrument is gaining more and more popularity, while long-term external debt is being reduced.[73] This could be a sign of continued managerial control in firms, and waning creditor control.[74]

---

65 For Germany: Bieg (1997); for the US: Kim (1996); for the UK: Lasfer (1995).

66 Cf. Castanias (1983), Baxter (1967).

67 Cf. Jung/Kim/Stulz (1996), p. 170.

68 Cf. Bartoldy/Boyle/Stover (1996).

69 Cf. Bolton/Scharfstein (1996); Johnson (1997).

70 Cf. Stulz/Johnson (1985); Green (1984); Smith/Warner (1979).

71 Preliminary tests imply that no significant developments can be found in the time period studied. MacKie-Mason (1990) reaches a similar conclusion.

72 Cf. Albach (1975). Also see Francfort/Rudolph (1992).

73 Cf. Stehle (1994).

74 Cf. Fisher (1990) who notes a declining importance of house banks in Germany.

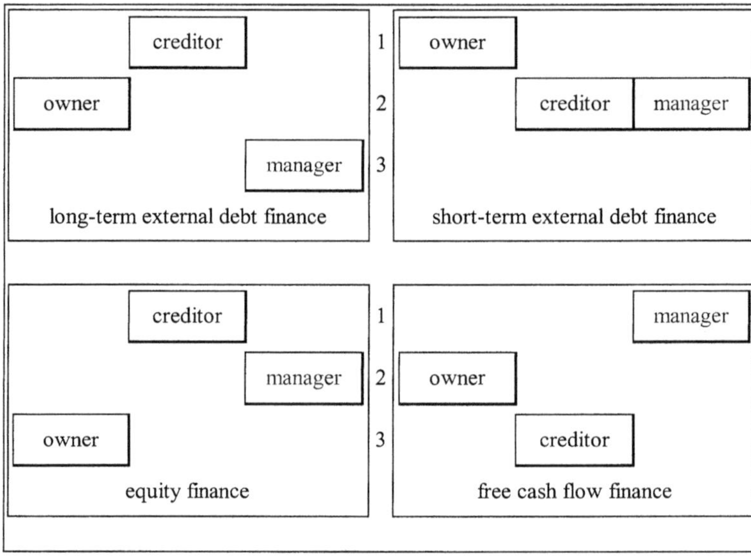

Figure 3-4: Graphical representation of the financial preferences by agency group according to hypotheses one to three

3.3.2 Previous Empirical Research

3.3.2.1 Research on Non-Agency Determinants of Capital Structure

The following tables list the most important studies for this analysis.[75] The papers are split into two groups. First there are those that study the effect of non-agency problems on capital structure, typically the debt ratio (cf. Table 3-8).[76,77] These include studies that measure the information asymmetry via firm specificity (Bradley/Jarrel/Kim 1984, Titman/Wessels 1988). R&D expenses are used as a proxy for company activity that cannot be evaluated by the ownership. Opler/Titman (1994) link the information asymmetry to the dividend signal, firm size and previous returns reasoning that managers with informational leads will time equity issues after phases of greater stock returns (timing model). Tax shields are also regularly included (Bradley/Jarrel/Kim 1984, Titman/Wessels 1988, Homifar/Zietz/Benkato 1994). The company risk or return volatility helps

75 Further references can be found in Wohlschieß (1997) and Harris/Raviv (1991).

76 The use of the debt ratio is criticized in Berens/Cuny (1995).

77 Note that in this analysis the financial flows are studied, not the capital structure.

explain capital structure in Marsh (1982), Titman/Wessels (1988), Chung (1993) and Homifar/Zietz/Benkato (1994). A current analysis of the German capital market is Wohlschieß (1996), who studies the debt ratio in relation to fundamental data with OLS regressions and the LISREL method.

author (year) dependent variables	independent variables	method country/years	results
Marsh (1982) • equity/debt issue probability	• size • firm risk • assets • capital market efficiency	event study with logit and probit GB 1959-70	equity classification: 62 % debt classification: 33 %
Bradley/Jarrel/Kim (1984) • long term debt ratio	• firm risk • non-debt tax shield • specificity	cross sectional OLS USA 1962-81	R^2 up to 58.6 %
Titman/Wessels (1988) • long/short term leverage • convertible bonds/debt	• fixed asset ratio • non-debt tax shield • growth • specificity • size • firm risk	LISREL USA 1974-82	inconclusive results
Chung (1993) • manager ownership • Tobin's Q • manager pay	• firm risk • growth • fixed asset ratio • size	OLS 3SLS USA 1987	R^2 up to 59% system-R^2 up to 65.4 %
Homaifar/Zietz/Benkato (1994) • debt ratio	• tax rate • non debt tax shield • size • growth opportunities • capital market effects • inflation • firm risk	pooled regression general autoregressive distributed lag model USA 1978-88	R^2 up to 91 %
Opler/Titman (1996) • equity, debt issues	• target debt ratio • company outlook • wealth transfer • information asymmetry • market outlook • size	OLS logit USA 1976-93	R^2 up to 20 % pseudo-R^2 up to 15 %

author (year) dependent variables	independent variables	method country/years	results
Wohlschieß (1996) • debt ratio	• size • security • growth opportunities • liquidity • quality • firm risk • asset specificity • age • sector	OLS correlations LISREL G 1980-92	R^2 up to 58.5 % adj. goodness of fit index up to 54.2 %

Table 3-8: Previous empirical studies of non-agency determinants of capital structure

3.3.2.2 Research on the Effects of Agency Problems between Owners and Managers on Financial Behavior

The second group of studies listed in Table 3-9 concentrates on agency problems and includes block or manager ownership in the study together other control variables. The analysis presented here belongs to this group, too. Most of the papers listed only analyze the debt ratio. None of the studies include short and long term debt, equity or internal financing simultaneously in their studies. Other variables included are the dividends and manager ownership, which are analyzed separately in ordinary least squares regressions (Crutchley/Hansen 1989) or in a three step least squares regression (Jensen/Solberg/Zorn 1992). In the latter study the dependent variable of one regression is entered as an independent variable in another function. Control variables include tax variables (Kim/Sorensen 1986), proxies for information asymmetry (Morck/Shleifer/Vishny 1988, Crutchley/Hansen 1989) and firm risk (Kim/Sorensen 1986, Friend/Lang 1988, Crutchley/Hansen 1989, Jensen/Solberg/Zorn 1992). The most comprehensive study as regards explanatory variables is Jung/Kim/Stulz (1996) for whom financial slack is an important variable, as well as macro-economic indicators.

author (year) dependent variables	independent variables	method country/per.	results
Kim/Sorensen (1986) • debt ratio	• block ownership • size • growth • firm risk • non debt tax shield	ANOVA OLS USA 1978-80	R^2 up to 18 %
Morck/Shleifer/Vishny (1988)	• block ownership	OLS	R^2 up to 64 %

author (year) dependent variables	independent variables	method country/per.	results
• Tobin's q • net cash flow/ tangible assets	• size • intangible assets • leverage • sector	USA 1980	
Friend/Hasbrouck (1988) • debt ratio	• block ownership • asset structure • return • risk • size	OLS USA 1983	R^2 up to 34.3 %
Friend/Lang (1988) • debt ratio	• block ownership • managerial ownership • assets • profitability • risk • size	OLS USA 1979-83	R^2 up to 35 %
Crutchley/Hansen (1989) • managerial ownership • ∅long term leverage • ∅dividends	• managerial ownership • firm risk • asset specificity • diversification • issue costs	OLS USA 1981-85	R^2 up to 46 %
Jensen/Solberg/Zorn (1992) • long term debt ratio • dividends/operating profits • managerial ownership	• firm risk • size • diversification • asset specificity • profitability • assets • growth	3SLS USA 1982, 1987	system-R^2 up to 30 %
Jung/Kim/Stulz (1996) • equity issues	• taxes • investment opportunities • leverage information asymmetry • bankruptcy cost • financial slack • liquidity • business climate • performance	logistic regression USA 1977-84	R^2 up to 41 %

Table 3-9: Previous empirical studies of agency determinants of the capital structure

Other papers (not listed in Table 3-9) include Balakrishnan/Fox (1993), who introduce asset specificity as a factor influencing capital structure, and Slovin/Sushka (1993), who study changes in firm value upon the exit of inside blockholders.

Another group of papers links management compensation to capital structure, such as Berkovitch/Israel/Spiegel (1996), John/John (1993), Mehran (1992), Brander/Poitevin (1992), Agrawal/Mandelker (1987), Grossman/Hart (1982); for Germany Wenger (1987). Capital structure as an instrument in takeover battles are discussed in Israel (1991) and Harris/Raviv (1988).

3.3.3 Empirical Results

3.3.3.1 Financial Behavior Variables in the Context of this Study

In the following analysis, four financial instruments will be scrutinized for differences in level between companies with different control groups. These are on the side of internal financial instuments:

- free cash flow

and on the external side

- long-term debt
- short-term debt, and
- equity.

The free cash flow[78] is the profit of the year plus non-liquid expenditures and earnings minus rises in fixed and financial assets and dividends. Long-term external debt includes bonds, long-term bank liabilities, liabilities toward relief funds (Unterstützungskassen), and other long-term external debt, but excludes pension accruals which are internal. Short-term external debt includes trade liabilities, acceptance commitments (Wechselverbindlichkeiten), short-term bank liabilities, cash deposits (erhaltene Anzahlungen), liabilities toward associated companies, and other short-term external debt.[79] The equity consists of the Grundkapital plus gesetzliche Rücklagen for 1987 and earlier, and the gezeichnetes Kapital plus Kapitalrücklage afterward. This ensures that only the external elements in this form of financing are included in the variable. The values for each financial instrument are divided by the fixed assets in order to exclude size effects at this level. The change of the value of the financing instrument, say

78 Cf. Jensen (1986).

79 Short-term liabilities also include long-term liabilities nearing maturity, which is not theoretically desirable. Cf. Leland/Toft (1996).

long term capital, to last year's, is in the numerator. The denominator contains last year's fixed capital. This gives the following variables for the study:

Variable	Calculation
d_l/fa	(Δ external long term debt) / lag(fixed assets)
d_s/fa	(Δ external short term debt) / lag(fixed assets)
e/fa	(Δ external equity) / lag(fixed assets)
fcf/fa	free cash flow / lag(fixed assets)

Table 3-10: Calculation of the financial instrument variables

3.3.3.2 Comprehensive Analysis

3.3.3.2.1 T-Tests for Differences in Mean Financial Behavior

To start off, the descriptives of the agency variables (Table 3-11) and the financial variables (Table 3-12) for the 1187 cases in the sample are presented. Companies in Germany are subject to high levels of block ownership, as the mean value of 63.4 % block ownership signifies. The size variable is the natural logarithm of the total assets. The dividend signal is very often set to one, with a mean value of .977, which should reduce the explanatory power of this variable. The ratio of monitored to unmonitored debt takes values between zero and one.

variable	**minim.**	**median**	**mean**	**maxim.**	**std. dev.**
block ownership	.000	.720	.634	.998	.295
size	9.214	12.877	12.953	17.831	1.780
market segment	1.000	3.000	2.532	3.000	.811
dividend signal	.000	1.000	.977	1.000	.149
leverage	.000	.460	.867	27.281	1.458
ratio of monitored to unmonitored debt	.000	.000	.432	1.000	.496

N = 1187

Table 3-11: Descriptives of the agency variables, 1986-1992

Table 3-12 shows that equity finance has the largest ratio, at .144 on average. This does not mean that equity is issued frequently, though. The median value of 0 confirms this. Instead, when equity is issued, this is done in large amounts. Short-term debt is the second most frequent financial form studied. Including internal long-term debt, such as pension accruals, could change that picture. Its standard deviation is fairly high, but that value is topped by the standard deviation for the free cash flow, which is 1.265, for a mean free cash flow ratio of .081. These standard deviations could impact the significance of group differences for these financial instruments.

The correlations of the agency variables amongst each other can tell if they are capturing the same or different aspects of agency problems. Using the original market segment variable, as done here, is not quite correct as the variable is only ordinally scaled.

variable	minim.	median	mean	maxim.	std. dev.
d_l/fa	-1.411	.000	.016	2.430	.135
d_s/fa	-3.657	.004	.136	6.688	.627
e/fa	-1.362	.000	.144	2.581	.326
fcf/fa	-7.203	.068	.081	8.270	1.265

N = 1187

Table 3-12: Descriptives of the finance measures, 1986-1992

Table 3-13 shows that most agency variables are significantly but not strongly correlated to each other. The highest correlation is between the company size and market segment it is traded in, at 36.46 %. The high correlation of size to the market segment is to be expected because of the legal requirements for market segment trading. The overall low correlations give a more realistic picture of the level of agency problems in a company, as the problems are not monocausal. Especially the dividend signal theoretically has a corrective function for the other variables describing information asymmetry. For this reason one might expect a negative correlation between the dividend signal and the block ownership, market segment and size variables. This is only the case for block ownership, though.

For the leverage and especially monitored debt ratio variables, there are negative correlations to the other agency variables. This sets the ownership-sided agency variables apart from the creditor-sided ones (although leverage belongs to both sides), and suggests that if one type of management control is already in place, the other is not needed or possibly even desired.

I initially use t-tests for differences in means between the agency groups to ascertain the discriminatory power of the financial behavior of firms regarding their agency problems. The datapoints for all seven years 1986-92 in the sample are analyzed together here, because the relative nature of the finance variables (ratios) cancels out any inflationary effects. The agency variables are either independent of inflation (e. g., the unchanging legal boundaries of block ownership), or chosen using psychological considerations (e. g., the size boundary from which point on companies are more closely scrutinized by the public). These variables, too, then, do not prohibit jointly analyzing the panel data.

	size	market segment	dividend signal	leverage	monitored debt ratio
block ownership	-.2670 ***	-.1528 ***	.0063	-.0079	-.1870 ***
size	1.0000	.3646 ***	.0757 ***	-.0440	-.1788 ***
market segment		1.0000	.0933 ***	-.1862 ***	-.1325 ***
dividend signal			1.0000	.0172	-.0152
leverage				1.0000	.2222 ***

N = 1187; *** = significant at 1 %-level (** = 5 %; * = 10 %)

Table 3-13: Correlations of the agency variables[80]

	d_l/fa	d_s/fa	e/fa	fcf/fa
expected sign	+	+ (o)	–	–
block ownership	-.0193	-.0214	-.1081 ***	.0701 **
size	-.0188	-.0342	-.0584 **	-.0981 ***
market segment	.0157	-.0592 **	.0207	-.0514 *
dividend signal	-.0172	.0126	-.0459	.0038
leverage	.1313 ***	.2140 ***	-.0714 **	.0096
expected sign	+	o	+	–
monitored debt ratio	.1130 ***	.0920 **	.0751 ***	-.0025

N = 1187; *** = significant at 1 %-level (** = 5 %; * = 10 %)

Table 3-14: Correlations between the agency and finance variables

80 The market segment variable is 3 for official continuous trade, 2 for official daily trade and 1 for non-official trade.

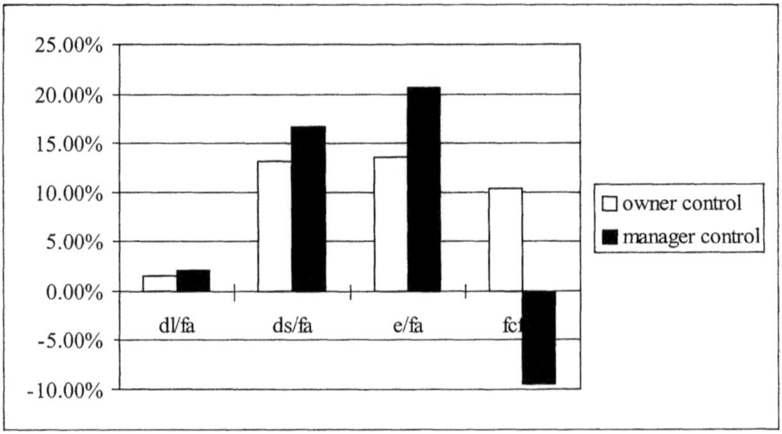

Figure 3-5: Average values for the financial activities by control group, using block ownership to distinguish

The first value in Table 3-15 (–.0049) e. g. means that the mean long term debt financing in relation to the fixed assets is –.0049 lower for firms with small agency problems (block ownership greater than 25 %) than for those with bigger agency problems. Figure 3-5 shows as an example the differences between the control groups when using block ownership to distinguish in graphical form. The values therefore are the same used to calculate the first row in Table 3-15. The financial instruments on the right, equity and free cash flow finance, show greater differences than the debt finance on the left.

High but insignificant mean differences come about if the finance variable has a high standard deviation. In interpreting the results, the major agency variables block ownership, *agency1* and *agency5* will be given somewhat more weight than the other variables. This is because block ownership is a central agency variable in research; the other two variables are the conglomerates with predetermined weights of the individual agency variables contained therein.

The signs in the third row of Table 3-15 give the expected signs if hypothesis one (comparison between owners and managers) is to hold; the signs in the second-to-last row refer to the second hypothesis (creditors and managers). For this hypothesis, the results from the leverage variable can also be used, as that variable has the dual role of denoting creditor monitoring and internal control via payment obligations. A hypothesis is ideally confirmed if all of the differences are significant and show the expected sign; as this is a very rare occurrence, I go by majorities under special consideration of the major agency variables block ownership, *agency1* and *agency5*, and also consider the signs of insignificant differences.

	d_l/fa		d_s/fa		e/fa		fcf/fa	
	diff	sig	diff	sig	diff	sig	diff	sig
expected sign	+		+ (o)		–		–	
block ownership	-.0049		-.0362		-.0705	**	.1983	*
size	.0041		.0202		-.0316		-.2015	*
market segment	.0030		-.0869		.0085		-.1574	
dividend signal	-.0156		.0532		-.1004		.0325	
leverage	.0431	***	.3980	***	-.0432	*	.0498	***
agency1	.0029		.0964	***	-.0697	*	.0683	
agency2	.0058		-.0335		-.0557		.1331	
agency3	.0346	***	.3583	***	-.0566	***	-.0292	
agency4	.0078		-.0281		-.0234		-.3274	**
agency5	-.0042		.0291		-.0792	**	.1916	
agency6	.0165	**	.1203	***	-.0246		-.1400	
agency7	-.0303		-.2748		-.1222		.2827	
expected sign	+		o		+		–	
monitored debt ratio	.0309	***	.1165	***	.0494	**	-.0063	

N = 1187; *** = significant at 1 %-level (** = 5 %; * = 10 %)

Table 3-15: T-tests for differences of means of finance measures for groups with and without agency problems, by agency variable, 1986-1992

Relatively few of the differences are significant. The long-term debt variable conforms to the hypothesis where the differences are significant and often when the difference is not significant, too. However, for the block ownership and agency5 variables, the signs are negative. Together with the often insignificant signs, I judge the first hypothesis not to hold for long-term external debt finance. For short-term external debt finance insignificant or positive differences are demanded, which is confirmed in all cases. Four differences, including the one obtained when using *agency1* as a group variable, are highly significant.

In the case of external equity finance the overall results for 1986-92 clearly favor the variant that owner-controlled firms will avoid that financial instrument even more than uncontrolled manager will. Almost all differences are negative, and five of them, including the three for all the major agency variables, are significant. The results for the free cash flow are much more mixed, with two significant positive differences and two significant negative ones. This does not allow the hypothesis to be confirmed for the free cash flow variable. Possibly this means that owners do tolerate and even demand free cash flow if they expect it to be used to finance future investments that were not incorporated in the calculation of the free cash flow.

The second hypothesis can be tested using the rows for leverage and especially the ratio of monitored to unmonitored debt in Table 3-15, referring to the expected signs just above the monitored debt ratio. More weight will be given to the monitored debt ratio results, if the two should differ, due to the dual character of the leverage variable. The significant sign of the difference in short-term debt financing does not jibe with the second hypothesis, as well as the insignificance of the difference in free cash flow, when going by the monitored debt ratio. The leverage variable only agrees with the hypothesis in long-term external debt financing. The equity finance is off (confirming the first hypothesis), but only with a 10 % level of significance. Giving preference to the monitored debt ratio, the second hypothesis is guardedly confirmed for the free cash flow, rejected for short-term debt, and accepted for the other two.

The third hypothesis is tested in Table 3-16. It compares financing behavior between creditor-controlled and owner-controlled firms. It is important to note that in this division of cases, some companies are classed into either group, due to a high ratio of monitored to unmonitored debt, and, say, high block ownership levels. For the first two hypotheses the groups were non-overlapping.

Except for the short-term debt, which has one significantly negative difference, the hypothesis is confirmed by the differences and there frequent significance. This means that creditors prefer long-term debt finance and equity issues compared to the shareholders of a company, and reject free cash flow more readily.

	d_l/fa		d_s/fa		e/fa		fcf/fa	
	diff	sig	diff	sig	diff	sig	diff	sig
expected sign	–		+ (o)		–		+	
block ownership	-1.81 %	*	-7.04 %	*	-3.63 %	**	2.67 %	
agency5	-1.78 %	*	-6.05 %		-3.51 %	*	1.98 %	

*** = significant at 1 %-level (** = 5 %; * = 10 %)

Table 3-16: T-tests for differences of means of the finance measures between owner-controlled and creditor-controlled companies, 1986-1992[81]

81 Differences are to the companies that count as monitored by creditors according to the ratio of monitored to unmonitored debt.

3.3.3.2.2 Logistic Regressions

The logistic regressions used allow the first two hypotheses to be tested. These regressions have the advantage of allowing the simultaneous inclusion of all agency variables in their un-conglomerate form. The separate agency variables without the monitored debt ratio are used to test the first hypothesis comparing management financial preferences to that of the ownership. The monitored debt ratio is creditor-oriented and thus is excluded from the model. The leverage variable which also contains an element of internal control is included here, however. It is also included in the model used to test the second hypothesis comparing management financial preferences to those of the creditors. The monitored debt ratio is the other variable used in this model for the second hypothesis.

A difficulty this procedure entails is that an agency variable, say, the dividend signal, might on its own have the correct sign, but lose it when used together with another variable, say, block ownership, which has the greater influence. This makes the use of conglomerate agency variables also worthwhile. Therefore, together with the unconglomerated models, the conglomerate variables *agency1* and *agency5* will additionally be used in logistic regressions to test the first hypothesis. The others are omitted to reduce the flood of results. *Agency1* contains a 15 % portion of the monitored debt ratio, which is only allowable if one assumes creditor control to not be too different from ownership control. As this is not a clear-cut decision at this point, the results from using *agency1* will be given less weight than those from using *agency5*.

No constant is used in the equation because its inclusion proved to cause high correct classification results by simply grouping all cases into the numerically stronger agency group, completely invalidating any informational content the agency variables might have had. This occurrence could be greatly reduced by omitting the constant. The comparison of the classification result to that achievable by random classification is suited to identify such situations.[82]

The dummy variables are computed from the finance variables by setting the dichotomous variable to one if the company's financing ratio was greater that the sector mean, and to zero otherwise. The utilization of sector averages makes it unnecessary to include sector dummies in the equation as independent variables.

Using long term debt finance as an example for all four models, the following equation for a logistic regression for this analysis can be constructed:

$$DL_i = \frac{e^{\eta}}{1+e^{\eta}} \qquad (3\text{-}15)$$

where:

---

[82] Cf. Krafft (1997), p. 632.

DL_i = dummy variable for long-term external debt finance ratio

η = $\beta_{BLOCK,i} \cdot$ block ownership +
$\beta_{SIZE,i} \cdot$ size +
$\beta_{MS1,i} \cdot$ market segment dummy1 +
$\beta_{MS2,i} \cdot$ market segment dummy2 +
$\beta_{DIV,i} \cdot$ dividend signal dummy +
$\beta_{LEV,i} \cdot$ leverage +
$\beta_{MON,i} \cdot$ monitored debt ratio

$\beta_{BLOCK,i}$ etc. = coefficients.

In addition, it is possible to join the four equations for the finance variables in seemingly unrelated regressions. This type of regression is necessary under two conditions. First, a set of equations does not contain dependent variables in one equation as an independent variable in at least one other equation, which would make a simultaneous set of equations.[83] Second, it is necessary that the error terms of the equations are correlated, making the equations only seemingly unrelated.[84] The seemingly unrelated regression technique (SURE) accounts for this correlation by using a generalized least squares estimation (GLS)[85] and avoids wasting important information. However, if the independent variables are identical, it can be shown that GLS and OLS regressions are also identical.[86] As in this study the independent variables are identical, it is sufficient to run simple logistic regressions over each financial form separately.[87]

Table 3-17 shows the coefficients, estimation log likelihood, and correct classification percentage for the three models that can be used to test the first hypothesis. The random classification row at the bottom of this and the following table shows the percentage of correct classifications that would result if a random classification were attempted. If α is the proportion of one group in the whole sample, then the random classification percentage is $\alpha^2 + (1 - \alpha)^2$.[88]

For the long-term external debt finance, negative signs abound, and only the coefficient for the leverage variable is significant and positive as demanded in the first hypothesis. The conglomerate agency variables in particular are strongly and significantly negative. For the short-term external debt finance, there is a mix of significantly positive and negative coefficients, where positive or insig-

---

83 Cf. Greene (1997), pp. 708 ff.

84 Cf. Greene (1997), pp. 674 ff.

85 Cf. Breslaw (1995), p. 197.

86 Cf. Greene (1997), p. 676.

87 Tests for the data showed that the differences to logistic regressions transformed into linear equations and thus able to be estimated as linear ordinary least squares regressions are minute.

88 Cf. Morrison (1969).

nificant ones are expected. The conglomerate agency variables again reject the first hypothesis. For equity finance, the negative signs, expected if current owners dislike allowing new shareholders to buy into a company, are very consistent and confirm the hypothesis. The signs of the coefficients for the free cash flow regression however reject the hypothesis again.

	dependent variable			
independent variables	d_l/fa	d_s/fa	e/fa	fcf/fa
expected sign	+	+ (o)	–	–
	model 1			
block ownership	-.9709 ***	-.9026 ***	-1.0681 ***	.3434 *
size	-.0215	.0513 *	.0411	-.0352
market segment 1	.1755	.3358 *	.2886	.5841 ***
market segment 2	-.4686	.4975	-.1522	.8510 ***
dividend signal	-.6006 *	-1.7976 ***	-1.5706 ***	.0627
leverage	.1144 **	.2968 ***	-.3020 ***	.0152
-2 log likelihood‡	1233.19 ***	1272.78 ***	1009.99 ***	1599.11 ***
% correct classification	77.76	74.64	83.74	59.48
	model 2			
agency1	-1.2589 ***	-1.1037 ***	-1.6752 ***	.3457 ***
-2 log likelihood‡	1279.22 ***	1347.67 ***	1086.73 ***	1591.35 ***
% correct classification	71.79	68.97	77.01	56.67
	model 3			
agency5	-1.3009 ***	-1.1270 ***	-1.7144 ***	.3411 ***
-2 log likelihood‡	1259.51 ***	1337.11 ***	1067.68 ***	1592.09 ***
% correct classification	73.16	69.83	78.03	56.67
% random classification	65.69	63.33	73.23	51.01

N = 1187; *** = significant on the 1 % level (** = 5 %; * = 10 %); ‡ = significance of model chi-square

Table 3-17: Coefficients and overall results of the logistic seemingly unrelated regressions on the finance dummy variables for the first hypothesis, 1986-1992[89]

89 The market segment dummy 1 is one for official continuous trade, the second dummy is one for official daily trade.

	dependent variable			
independent variables	d_l/fa	d_s/fa	e/fa	fcf/fa
expected sign	+	o	+	–
	model 4			
leverage	-.4337 ***	-.2205 ***	-1.2155 ***	.0978 **
monitored debt ratio	-.0907	.0129	-1.3880 ***	-.0479
-2 log likelihood‡	1556.24 ***	1618.45 ***	1227.18 ***	1638.13 **
% correct classification	71.69	54.25	78.94	57.20
% random classification	65.69	63.33	73.23	51.01

N = 1187; *** = significant on the 1 % level (** = 5 %; * = 10 %); ‡ = significance of model chi-square

Table 3-18: Coefficients and overall results of the logistic seemingly unrelated regressions on the finance dummy variables for the second hypothesis, 1986-1992

For the second hypothesis comparing the financial preferences of managers to creditors, Table 3-18 shows the results of the corresponding logistic regression using the leverage and monitored debt ratio variables as explanatory variables. It is easy to ascertain that none of the financial instruments conforms to the hypothesis. Only the coefficients for the monitored debt ratio are correct for the short-term debt and free cash flow (but not significant in the latter case, contrary to demand). For the short-term debt, the percentage of correct classification does not even reach that one a random classification would provide (54.25 % vs. 63.33 %). These results contrast with the acceptance of the second hypothesis for all instruments except the short-term debt using the t-tests for differences in group means.

Table 3-19 shows an overview over the results for the comprehensive analysis. Would only t-tests have been used, then all three hypotheses would have been accepted (the first conditionally, as shown by the parentheses). As it stands, this cannot be done for the first two, because the logistic regressions generally do not confirm any of the hypothesized relations.

The implication the results have is that manager-controlled firms do not differ significantly from either owner or creditor-controlled ones in financial behavior, although there is a tendency toward such a difference (again expressed by parentheses around the unchecked box). Shareholders do favor free cash flow more than creditors, and like avoid long-term external debt and new equity issues more than they. They are relatively indifferent to short-term external debt, which is less relevant in terms of admitting new principals to an existing control framework than long-term debt or new equity. It remains to be seen if separate sectoral analyses confirm these interim results.

hypothesis #	method	d_l/fa	d_s/fa	e/fa	fcf/fa	overall
1	t-tests	(☐)	☑	☑	(☐)	(☑)
	logistic regression	☐	☐	☑	☐	☐
overall		☐	(☐)	☑	☐	(☐)
2	t-tests	☑	☐	☑	☑	☑
	logistic regression	☐	☐	☐	☐	☐
overall		(☐)	☐	(☐)	(☐)	(☐)
3	t-tests	☑	☑	☑	☑	☑

Table 3-19: Overview over the validity of hypotheses one to three; 1986-1992[90]

3.3.3.3 Sectoral Analysis

3.3.3.3.1 Results for the Machinery Sector

The sectoral analysis is confined to the five sectors chemicals, machinery, electronics, food & beverages, and utilities, which have the largest group sizes (over 70 cases per sector). The advantage of this procedure is that potentially important sectoral differences are not glossed over as the comprehensive analysis could have done. Therefore the first three hypotheses will be tested on a sectoral basis, too.

This method also allows for the sector-specific hypothesis four to be tested. The fourth hypothesis states that differences in financial behavior between agency groups will disappear in highly competitive markets (sectors), due to the regulatory effect of the competition. Should this hypothesis be confirmed, it would shed some light on the mixed results for the first three hypotheses of the comprehensive analysis. These would then be due to the joint analysis of sectors for which the first three hypotheses hold, in accordance with the fourth hypothesis, and those for which according to the fourth hypothesis the first three do not hold.

---

90 A check marks a hypothesis that could not be rejected according to the model given at the top of the column.

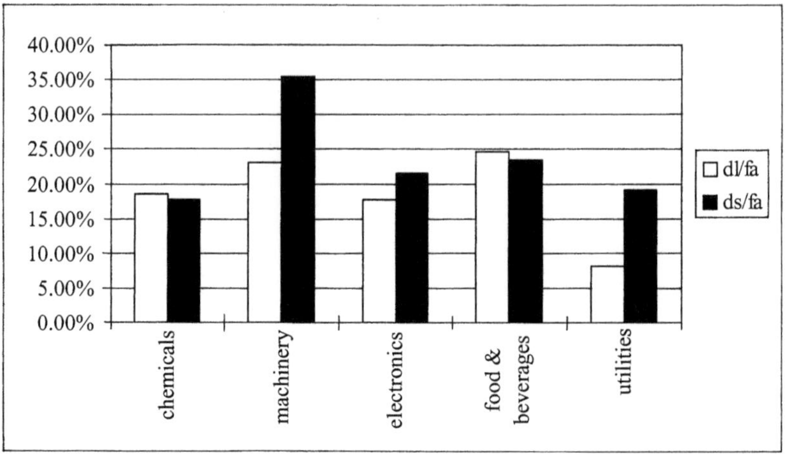

Figure 3-6: Average new long and short-term debt-to-asset ratios over all years, by sector

Figure 3-6 shows the external debt finance ratios for the five sectors in comparison. Sectoral differences are evident, especially with regard to the short-term debt finance in the machinery sector and the long-term debt finance in the utilities.[91] Other studies find regulated sectors to have high leverage ratios, [92] but this cannot be confirmed for the German sample (cf. Figure 3-7). The utilities in fact have the lowest debt ratios of all five sectors studied. For US firms, the high leverage is attributed to the attempt to force regulators to raise the regulated sales prices in order to mitigate the risk of bankruptcy the utilities drive up.[93] As bond issues are uncommon in Germany, this reasoning does not apply here. Instead, prospective or current creditor banks will catch any attempts to inflate the leverage.

91 The low debt finance activity speaks against the Kovenock/Phillips (1995) proposition that debt is raised in regulated firms to compensate for the missing product market control. Cf. footnote 64 above.

92 Cf. Bradley/Jarrell/Kim (1984); Taggart (1985). Neuberger (1989), p. 182, finds a high, but decreasing leverage for the utilities firms from 1979 to 1984.

93 Cf. Spiegel/Spulber (1994, 1997).

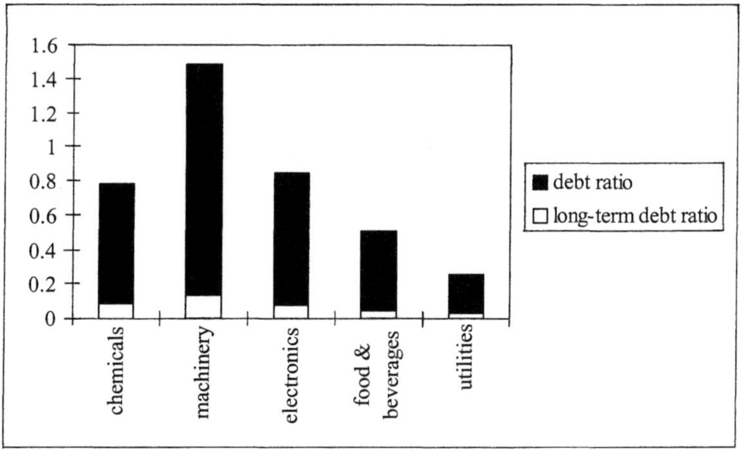

Figure 3-7: Debt ratios over all years, by sector

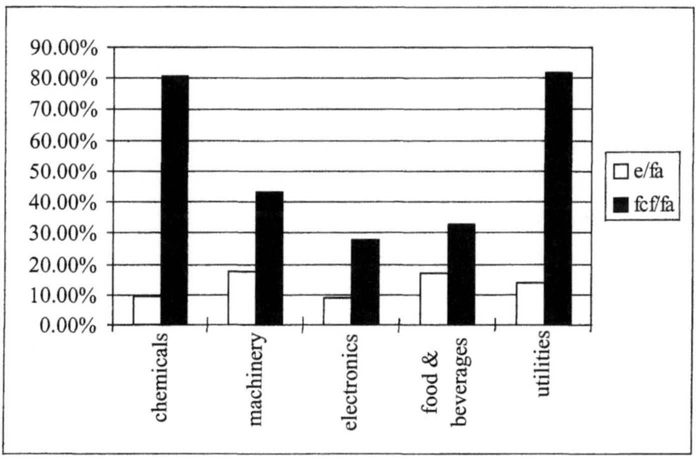

Figure 3-8: Average new equity and free cash flow-to-asset ratios over all years, by sector

Figure 3-8 repeats this depiction for the equity and free cash flow finance. Due to the different scale compared to Figure 3-6, the differences in equity finance seem even less important than they really are. The lowest ratio is 8.90 % (electronics), the highest 17.70 % (machinery), for a difference of 8.80 %. The free cash flow is very large in the utilities and chemical sectors. These are the least and third-least competitive sectors. The second least competitive sector is the food & beverages sector, for which the second best free cash flow ratio is evident.

Table 3-20 repeats the t-tests for differences in group means in the same manner as Table 3-15 above. It also includes companies for all seven years in the analysis, but only for the 130 cases of companies in the machinery sector. This is the sector that was ranked as the most competitive of the five being studied more closely. The results for the utility sector, the lowest-ranked sector, will be discussed next. The tables for the other sectoral analyses will be confined to the appendix and their content summarized here in the main body of the text, in order to avoid providing too much data and reducing the legibility of the analysis.

	d_l/fa		d_s/fa		e/fa		fcf/fa	
	diff	sig	diff	sig	diff	sig	diff	sig
expected sign	+		+ (o)		–		–	
block ownership	-.0207		.2598	**	.0232		.3875	
size	-.0328		.0919		.0093		-.4961	
market segment	-.0097		-.0090		.0877		.0404	
dividend signal	-.0803		.0989		-.0692		.8177	
leverage	-.0038		.5137	**	-.0678		.1969	
agency1	-.0397		.2598	**	-.0535		.9531	**
agency2	-.0376		.2616	**	-.0376		.9305	**
agency3	.0076		.6821	***	.0427		-.2643	
agency4	-.0084		.1555		.1300	**	-.5862	
agency5	-.0407		.2890	**	.0112		.5583	
agency6	.0013		.2637	*	.0874		-.0752	
agency7	-.0478		.2109		.0508		.5078	
expected sign	+		o		+		–	
monitored debt ratio	.0535	***	.0806		-.0450		-.0042	

N = 130; *** = significant at 1 %-level (** = 5 %; * = 10 %)

Table 3-20: T-tests for differences of means of finance measures for groups with and without agency problems, by agency variable, machinery sector

Table 3-20 again lists in the third row the signs expected for the differences according to the first hypothesis, comparing ownership-controlled financial behavior of managers to manager-controlled behavior. The second to last row gives the signs according to the second hypothesis, comparing creditor controlled financial behavior to manager control. The data necessary to test the third hypothesis that compares owner-controlled financial preferences to creditor-controlled ones is given in Table 3-21.

For long-term external finance, the first hypothesis that expects owners to favor it more than managers must be rejected. The differences are all insignificant with differences of often less than 5 % (.05) and mostly even negative. For the second financial instrument, the preference for short-term external debt in owner-controlled companies is clearly given, which supports the hypothesis. The notion that equity finance is equally acceptable to either control group is supported by all variables by insignificant differences, except *agency4*. For the free cash flow, negative signs are expected, but only occur for four agency variables, none of them a major one. The differences when using *agency1* and *agency2* are even significantly positive, rejecting hypothesis one. This means that of the four financial instruments studied, two support the first hypothesis (short-term debt and equity finance) and two reject it.

The second hypothesis can not only be checked using the results from the monitored debt ratio, at the bottom of Table 3-20, but also by the leverage variable which both denotes internal control via interest obligations and creditor importance. For the monitored debt ratio, the significant positive difference clearly supports the hypothesis, as do the results for the short-term external debt ratio. In the case of equity finance, negative signs turn up where positive ones are expected. The free cash flow differences also only guardedly confirm the second hypothesis, with a negative, but small difference for the monitored debt ratio confirming and the positive difference for leverage rejecting the hypothesis.

	d_l/fa		d_s/fa		e/fa		fcf/fa	
	diff	sig	diff	sig	diff	sig	diff	sig
expected sign	–		+ (o)		–		+	
block ownership	-2.56 %		0.85 %		2.24 %		6.44 %	
agency5	-2.87 %	*	2.92 %		2.35 %		10.48 %	

*** = significant at 1 %-level (** = 5 %; * = 10 %)

Table 3-21: T-tests for differences of means of the finance measures between owner-controlled and creditor-controlled companies, machinery sector[94]

In Table 3-21, the differences between the owner-controlled firms as defined by block ownership and alternatively *agency5* are compared to the creditor-controlled group of companies according to the ratio of unmonitored to monitored debt. The latter is subtracted from the former to achieve the differences

94 Differences are to the companies that count as monitored by creditors according to the ratio of monitored to unmonitored debt.

given. Apart from the equity finance variable, the hypothesis holds, although most of the differences are not significant. In the machinery sector, creditors prefer long-term external debt finance more than the other financial instruments, compared to shareholders.

	dependent variable			
independent variables	d_l/fa	d_s/fa	e/fa	fcf/fa
expected sign	+	+ (o)	–	–
	model 1			
block ownership	-1.0877	-.6075	-1.0463	1.0972 *
size	-.1582	-.0252	-.0229	-.0457
market segment 1	.0231	.4064	.6096	.5984
market segment 2	-7.0785	.0526	.2405	.7913
dividend signal	1.5316	-.2748	-1.0278	-.6779
leverage	-.0020	.0588	-.0570	-.0327
-2 log likelihood‡	133.865 ***	168.121 *	119.372 ***	173.097
% correct classification	76.92	63.85	82.31	56.15
	model 2			
agency1	-1.1607 ***	-.5849 ***	-1.4928 ***	-.1286
-2 log likelihood‡	141.946 ***	164.347 ***	126.088 ***	172.837
% correct classification	68.80	60.00	73.60	48.00
	model 3			
agency5	-1.3375 ***	-.5055 **	-1.5284 ***	-.0594
-2 log likelihood‡	136.531 ***	167.034 **	127.944 ***	173.198
% correct classification	73.40	55.20	72.40	44.80
% random classification	64.50	54.27	70.88	50.96

N = 130; *** = significant on the 1 % level (** = 5 %; * = 10 %); ‡ = significance of model chi-square

Table 3-22: Coefficients and overall results of the logistic seemingly unrelated regressions on the finance dummy variables for the first hypothesis, machinery sector[95]

The logistic regressions fairly consistently caused rejections of the hypotheses in the comprehensive analysis. It will be interesting to see their effect in the sec-

95 The market segment dummy 1 is one for official continuous trade, the second dummy is one for official daily trade.

toral analysis. Table 3-22 shows the results of regressions using the separate agency variables and the two major conglomerates *agency1* and *agency5*, and can be used to test the first hypothesis. Table 3-23 will be used to test the second hypothesis and regresses the finance variables on the leverage and monitored debt ratio variables. The third hypothesis cannot be tested with this method.

The estimations for the machinery sector produce fairly poor overall significance in the results, as the model chi-squares (χ^2) show. The lower the value [(-2) · log likelihood], the more significant the regression is. In the case of short-term external debt finance and especially free cash flow, the agency variables have little overall significance for the financial instrument.

The positive signs necessary to confirm the first hypothesis for the debt finance variables are not forthcoming in Table 3-22, in particular for the conglomerate variables, where the negative signs are significant, and signify that decreasing agency problems (unit values of the conglomerates, which are dummy variables) also cause the demand for external debt financing to decrease. The predominantly negative signs of for the equity finance on the other hand conform to expectations. The percentage of correct classifications lies only slightly over the random result, as is also the case for short-term debt finance, though.

The often negative but insignificant signs of the coefficients for the free cash flow could support the hypothesis, but the significantly positive sign for the block ownership explanatory variable and the fact that the random classification score of 50.96 % far exceeds the score of 44.80 % that the estimation achieves lead to a rejection of the hypothesis for this financial instrument. The low classification results mirror the weakly or insignificant model chi-squares.

	dependent variable			
independent variables	d_l/fa	d_s/fa	e/fa	fcf/fa
expected sign	+	o	+	–
	model 4			
leverage	-.3949 ***	-.0499	-.5070 ***	-.0155
monitored debt ratio	.2047	-.3553	-1.4867 *	-.8360 *
-2 log likelihood‡	163.472 ***	177.704	136.141 ***	174.915 *
% correct classification	63.08	56.92	77.69	60.00
% random classification	64.50	54.27	70.88	50.96

N = 130; *** = significant on the 1 % level (** = 5 %; * = 10 %); ‡ = significance of model chi-square

Table 3-23: Coefficients and overall results of the logistic seemingly unrelated regressions on the finance dummy variables for the second hypothesis, machinery sector

The regressions for the second hypothesis also show only partial confirmation for the expected coefficient signs. For the long-term external debt finance the significant coefficient for leverage has the wrong sign, and the classification score of 63 % does not beat the random one (64.5 %). The insignificant coefficients for the short-term external debt finance are expected, as are the negative signs for the free cash flow. The results of the equity estimation reject the hypothesis.

hypothesis #	method	d_l/fa	d_s/fa	e/fa	fcf/fa	overall
1	t-tests	☐	☑	☑	(☐)	(☑)
	logistic regression	☐	☐	☑	☐	☐
overall		☐	(☐)	☑	☐	(☐)
2	t-tests	☑	☑	☐	(☑)	☑
	logistic regression	☐	☑	☐	☑	(☐)
overall		(☐)	☑	☐	☑	(☑)
3	t-tests	☑	☑	☐	☑	☑

Table 3-24: Overview over the validity of hypotheses one to three; machinery sector[96]

The results for the machinery sector are somewhat mixed, with the first hypothesis (comparing owner and manager control) gaining the least support and the third (comparing ownership to creditor control) gaining the most. Table 3-24 makes the aggregation process followed to arrive at an overall decision for each of the first three hypotheses transparent. If the majority of acceptance or rejection decisions governs the overall decision as shown here, the first hypothesis is rejected, the second is accepted with reservations, and the third accepted.[97]

It is difficult to say that one of the financial instruments conforms to expectations more closely than others. Allowing a dislike of equity finance by current shareholders, compared to managers, to fulfill the first hypothesis, this hypothe-

96 A check marks a hypothesis that could not be rejected according to the model given at the top of the column.

97 If a hypothesis must be accepted for every financial instrument in order to not be rejected overall, then no hypothesis would hold, on account of the long-term debt and equity finance behavior of the firms. If one method accepted a hypothesis and the other rejected it, the result was marked as rejected, but in parentheses. The logistic regressions' frequent rejections of the hypotheses make this a common occurrence.

sis receives most support by that instrument. The second and third hypotheses are supported by the debt and free cash flow variables.

According to the fourth hypothesis, the frequently indistinguishable differences in financial behavior could be explained by the competitive forces machinery firms are subject to on their sales markets. These force managers to act in the interest of their principals. If that is so, then the differences in financial behavior should be very noticeable in the utilities sector. Therefore, that sector will be studied in detail next.

3.3.3.3.2 Results for the Utilities Sector

In this section, as usual first t-test for differences in group means will be discussed as presented in Table 3-25 and Table 3-26, followed by the analysis of the results produced by the alternate method of logistic regressions (Table 3-27 and Table 3-28). In many cases, the separate agency variables and conglomerates did not group the firms into the two categories as necessary, making it impossible to conduct the t-tests. Therefore, a number of lines in Table 3-25 are filled with the 'non applicable' (N/A) result.

Utilities companies typically have high investment expenses in the first years of their existance, which are then followed by a long period of only minor expenditures for upkeep and reinvestment. Including young companies and old companies in the same data sample could lead to a distortion of the results. The companies in this sample however all go back at least two years earlier (to 1984) than when the sample commences, which excludes this particular problem. All utilities companies studied here count as established firms.

Apart from the many non-applicable results, the differences in financial behavior are very small for the utilities firms, often less than 1 %, and only in two cases significant. This reduces the weight of the results. This is unfortunate, as the first hypothesis can be confirmed for all four finance instruments, going by the signs of the differences. The two significant results also have the correct signs. The second hypothesis can be confirmed for the first three instruments with regard to the monitored debt ratio, but the free cash flow difference has the wrong sign for either agency variable, the monitored debt ratio and leverage.

The same can be said for the third hypothesis, as shown in Table 3-26. The ownership control variables, block ownership and *agency5*, split the sample into identical groups, so that the results, too, are identical. The first three financial instruments perform as expected, although again with insignificant differences below 1 %, while the free cash flow is more acceptable to creditors than to owners, contrary to expectation.

	d_l/fa diff	sig	d_s/fa diff	sig	e/fa diff	sig	fcf/fa diff	sig
expected sign	+		+ (o)		–		–	
block ownership	.0020		.0170		-.0072		-.0431	
size	.0020		.0192		-.0606		-.1119	*
market segment	N/A		N/A		N/A		N/A	
dividend signal	.0020		.0135		.0100		.0168	
leverage	-.0132		-.0794		-.0349		.1104	
agency1	N/A		N/A		N/A		N/A	
agency2	N/A		N/A		N/A		N/A	
agency3	.0028		.0195		-.0398	**	-.0378	
agency4	N/A		N/A		N/A		N/A	
agency5	.0020		.0170		-.0072		-.0431	
agency6	.0020		.0133		-.0050		-.0525	
agency7	N/A		N/A		N/A		N/A	
expected sign	+		o		+		–	
monitored debt ratio	.0064		-.0036		.0075		.0481	

N = 99; *** = significant at 1 %-level (** = 5 %; * = 10 %)

Table 3-25: T-tests for differences of means of finance measures for groups with and without agency problems, by agency variable, utilities sector

	d_l/fa diff	sig	d_s/fa diff	sig	e/fa diff	sig	fcf/fa diff	sig
expected sign	–		+ (o)		–		+	
block ownership	-0.47 %		0.32 %		-0.58 %		-3.72 %	
agency5	-0.47 %		0.32 %		-0.58 %		-3.72 %	

*** = significant at 1 %-level (** = 5 %; * = 10 %)

Table 3-26: T-tests for differences of means of the finance measures between owner-controlled and creditor-controlled companies, utilities sector[98]

[98] Differences are to the companies that count as monitored by creditors according to the ratio of monitored to unmonitored debt. Block ownership and *agency5* produce the same groups.

The logistic regressions for the first hypothesis are reported in Table 3-27. For each financial instrument, three regressions were run; one using the ownership-related separate agency variables and one each for *agency1* and *agency5*. The regressions have higher overall significance levels than the machinery firms. The transformed log-likelihood levels are all below 100, with significance levels of 1 % or better.

	dependent variable			
independent variables	d_l/fa	d_s/fa	e/fa	fcf/fa
expected sign	+	+ (o)	–	–
model 1				
block ownership	-2.2127	3.7287	-1.3168	2.6782
size	1.5001 ***	.6894 *	.3412	-.6719 **
market segment 1	-30.4951	-14.8542 *	-4.3833	8.5899
market segment 2	-38.9175	-12.3811	-4.5409	16.0865
dividend signal	6.0316	-.9342	-.8101	.7673
leverage	1.8971	2.0850 **	-.9657	-.6756
-2 log likelihood‡	27.180 ***	69.228 ***	76.977 ***	72.925 ***
% correct classification	91.92	82.83	85.86	80.81
model 2				
agency1	-2.4314 ***	-1.4375 ***	-1.8036 ***	1.5040 ***
-2 log likelihood‡	55.586 ***	96.821 ***	80.689 ***	93.880 ***
% correct classification	91.92	80.81	85.86	81.82
model 3				
agency5	-2.3978 ***	-1.3993 ***	-1.8539 ***	1.5361 ***
-2 log likelihood‡	59.231 ***	99.679 ***	80.298 ***	93.812 ***
% correct classification	88.89	77.78	84.85	81.82
% random classification	85.14	68.98	75.72	70.25

N = 99; *** = significant on the 1 % level (** = 5 %; * = 10 %); ‡ = significance of model chi-square

Table 3-27: Coefficients and overall results of the logistic seemingly unrelated regressions on the finance dummy variables for the first hypothesis, utilities sector[99]

[99] The market segment dummy 1 is one for official continuous trade, the second dummy is one for official daily trade.

For the long-term external debt finance, the significantly positive size coefficient supports the first hypothesis, but the three major agency variables block ownership, *agency1* and *agency5* all have negative signs, and significant ones for the conglomerates. This leads to a rejection of the first hypothesis for this finance instrument, as is also the case for short-term external debt finance, for which the highest instance of significant coefficients can be found, where none were expected. The negative signs for the equity finance confirm the hypothesis for this instrument. For the free cash flow variable, again the size variable has a significant coefficient with the correct sign, as was the case for the long-term debt finance variable. But again the other variables, including the major ones, do not have the required negative sign. So the first hypothesis must be rejected again for this instrument.

	dependent variable			
independent variables	d_l/fa	d_s/fa	e/fa	fcf/fa
expected sign	+	o	+	–
	model 4			
leverage	-2.4911 ***	-.6848 *	-2.6379 ***	1.1617 ***
monitored debt ratio	.5195	-1.4742 *	-1.1164	1.0231
-2 log likelihood‡	105.043 ***	124.592 ***	95.143 ***	120.370 ***
% correct classification	72.73	71.72	78.79	81.82
% random classification	85.14	68.98	75.72	70.25

N = 99; *** = significant on the 1 % level (** = 5 %; * = 10 %); ‡ = significance of model chi-square

Table 3-28: Coefficients and results of the logistic seemingly unrelated regressions on the finance dummy variables for the second hypothesis, utilities sector

The results of the four logistic regressions to test the second hypothesis are in Table 3-28. All coefficients but the one for the monitored debt ration in the regression on the long-term debt finance have the wrong signs, or, in the case of short-term debt finance, are unexpectedly significant. This makes it easy to reject the second hypothesis when using logistic regressions. The t-tests for mean differences in Table 3-25 had supported the hypothesis.

For the utilities, the final overview over the hypothesis tests is given in Table 3-29. The t-tests give fairly strong support to all three hypotheses, which is interesting in view of the fourth hypothesis, which states exactly that for this sector with the least competitive pressure being analyzed more closely. However, the (usual) lack of support by the results of the logistic regressions leads to the conditional rejection of hypothesis one and two. The third hypothesis is accepted, which compares owner to creditor financial preferences. Again, the equity finance variables strongly supports the first hypothesis. The free cash flow variable of the utilities companies provides the least support for any hypothesis.

hypothesis #	method	d_l/fa	d_s/fa	e/fa	fcf/fa	overall
1	t-tests	☑	☑	☑	☑	☑
	logistic regression	☐	☐	☑	☐	☐
overall		(☐)	(☐)	☑	(☐)	(☐)
2	t-tests	☑	☑	☑	☐	(☑)
	logistic regression	☐	☐	☐	☐	☐
overall		(☐)	(☐)	(☐)	☐	(☐)
3	t-tests	☑	☑	☑	☐	☑

Table 3-29: Overview over the validity of hypotheses one to three; utilities sector[100]

3.3.3.3.3 Results for the Other Sectors and Overview of all Sectoral Results

hypothesis #	method	d_l/fa	d_s/fa	e/fa	fcf/fa	overall
1	t-tests	☑	(☑)	☑	(☑)	☑
	logistic regression	☑	(☐)	☑	(☐)	(☑)
overall		☑	(☐)	☑	(☐)	(☑)
2	t-tests	☑	☐	☐	☑	(☐)
	logistic regression	☐	☐	☐	☐	☐
overall		(☐)	☐	☐	(☐)	☐
3	t-tests	☑	☐	☐	☑	(☐)

Table 3-30: Overview over the validity of hypotheses one to three; chemicals sector[101]

[100] A check marks a hypothesis that could not be rejected according to the model given at the top of the column.

In this section, the overall results of the tables for the other three sectors, chemicals, electronics and food & beverages, that can be found in the appendix, will be briefly presented. They will not be discussed in as much detail as the machinery and utilities firms were. An overview over all sectors will enable a decision to be made on the validity of the fourth hypothesis, which suggests that the first three hypotheses will only be confirmed for the sectors not subject to strong competition. These would be the utilities and the food & beverages sectors.

For the chemicals sector, the results of the hypotheses tests are shown in Table 3-30. For the first hypothesis, the logistic regressions are only slightly less supportive than the t-tests for mean differences. Overall the results combine to weakly confirm the hypothesis comparing manager control to ownership control. The second hypotheses must be rejected with no support from the logistic regressions, and support from the t-tests for the long-term debt and free cash flow variables. These same instruments also conform to the third hypothesis, which overall is not enough to accept that hypothesis, either. The long-term debt finance instrument is most akin to expectations overall, while the equity variable as usual is strong in regard to the first hypothesis.

hypothesis #	method	d_l/fa	d_s/fa	e/fa	fcf/fa	overall
1	t-tests	☑	(☑)	☑	☑	☑
	logistic regression	☐	☐	☑	(☑)	☐
overall		(☐)	☐	☑	☑	(☐)
2	t-tests	☑	☑	(☐)	☑	☑
	logistic regression	☐	☐	☐	☑	☐
overall		(☐)	(☐)	☐	☑	(☐)
3	t-tests	☑	☐	☑	☑	☑

Table 3-31: Overview over the validity of hypotheses one to three; electronics sector[102]

In the electronics sector, the free cash flow shows the most support for the first three hypotheses. The equity variable supports the first and third hypothesis.

---

101 A check marks a hypothesis that could not be rejected according to the model given at the top of the column.

102 A check marks a hypothesis that could not be rejected according to the model given at the top of the column.

While the long-term external finance variable supports all three hypotheses in the t-tests, the logistic regressions do not confirm the first two hypotheses for this instrument and the short-term external finance. This leads to the conditional rejections of hypothesis one and two that can be seen in the far right column of Table 3-31.

hypothesis #	method	d_l/fa	d_s/fa	e/fa	fcf/fa	overall
1	t-tests	☑	☑	☑	☑	☑
	logistic regression	☐	☐	☑	☑	(☐)
overall		(☐)	(☐)	☑	☑	(☑)
2	t-tests	☑	(☐)	(☐)	☑	(☐)
	logistic regression	☐	☐	☐	☑	☐
overall		(☐)	☐	☐	☑	☐
3	t-tests	☑	☐	☑	☑	☑

Table 3-32: Overview over the validity of hypotheses one to three; food & beverages sector[103]

In the food & beverages sector, Table 3-32 shows that the first hypothesis comparing managerial to owner preferences in finance can be accepted with some reservations. Aside from the usual support from the equity variable, the results for the free cash flow are responsible for this. The latter variable conforms to all three hypothesized relations, as could also be observed for the electronics sector (Table 3-31).

Having completed a brief summary of the tabled data for the remaining three sectors in the appendix, these results can again be aggregated into an overall evaluation of the financial hypotheses in the sectoral analysis. This is done by taking the shaded overall results per sector and hypothesis from the sectoral tables and grouping them in similar fashion in Table 3-33. Using the same majority criteria, a final statement for the analysis in section 3.3.3.3 is possible. The table is constructed so that the results for a hypothesis can be read per sector or per financial instrument.

103 A check marks a hypothesis that could not be rejected according to the model given at the top of the column.

hypothesis #	sector	d_l/fa	d_s/fa	e/fa	fcf/fa	overall
1	machinery	☐	(☐)	☑	☐	(☐)
	electronics	(☐)	☐	☑	☑	(☐)
	chemicals	☑	(☐)	☑	(☐)	(☑)
	food & beverages	(☐)	(☐)	☑	☑	(☑)
	utilities	(☐)	(☐)	☑	(☐)	(☐)
overall		(☐)	(☐)	☑	(☑)	(☐)
2	machinery	(☐)	☑	☐	☑	(☑)
	electronics	(☐)	(☐)	☐	☑	(☐)
	chemicals	(☐)	☐	☐	(☐)	☐
	food & beverages	(☐)	☐	☐	☑	☐
	utilities	(☐)	(☐)	(☐)	☐	(☐)
overall		(☐)	(☐)	☐	(☑)	(☐)
3	machinery	☑	☑	☐	☑	☑
	electronics	☑	☐	☑	☑	☑
	chemicals	☑	☐	☐	☑	(☐)
	food & beverages	☑	☐	☑	☑	☑
	utilities	☑	☑	☑	☐	☑
overall		☑	(☐)	(☑)	☑	☑
4						☐

Table 3-33: Overview over the validity of hypotheses one to three, all sectors[104]

All three hypotheses receive support from the separate sectors, although it is often weak in the case of the first two hypotheses. This is due to the weak results in the logistic regressions, which subjected the agency variables to a joint scrutiny both in conglomerate and non-conglomerate form. Only the third hypothesis cannot be rejected in the overall view. This means that managerial financial behavior, when unchecked, does not significantly differ from owners' or creditors'

[104] A check marks a hypothesis that could not be rejected according to the model given at the top of the column.

preferences, although there is slight evidence for this. Owner and creditor interests do lie significantly far apart form each other to accept the third hypothesis. This means that manages prefer free cash flow and short-term debt, where creditors tend to long-term debt and equity issues.

Going by the financial instruments, the free cash flow variable most often conforms to expectations in the sectoral view, i. e., that unchecked managers prefer it more than the other control groups, and owners allow more free cash flow than creditors (third hypothesis). The equity form of finance is disliked by owners more than managers (first hypothesis), and there is some support that they also like it less than creditors do (third hypothesis). Long-term external debt is preferred by creditors in comparison with owners (third hypothesis), but otherwise debt finance plays an indifferent role in financial decisions based on agency considerations. This could be due to the importance of debt financing in German stock corporations, which does not allow financial decision makers to ignore it, even if they would like to.

The overview over the acceptance of the first three hypotheses for all sectors in Table 3-33 allows the fourth hypothesis to be tested, too. It states that the differences in financial behavior between agency groups are more pronounced in sectors where the added controlling force of fierce competition is lacking. In Table 3-33, the sectors are arranged in order of decreasing competitivity, as determined by 1992 sales per employee in chapter 2.3.2.6. Machinery firms are most subject to competition, utilities the least. Hypothesis 4 would require the most instances of accepted hypotheses to be found at the top of the subtable for each hypothesis. This is clearly not the case. The machinery firms show the most support, followed by the food & beverages sector and the electronics and utilities firms tied for third place. There is no apparent pattern in this result. Therefore, the fourth hypothesis must be rejected.

Because it was so apparent that the logistic regressions tended to reject the first two hypotheses in most cases, Table 3-34 shows for the interested the alternative result for the final sector overview that would have resulted, had only t-tests for mean differences been used. The separation of the results by financial instrument was omitted to save space. All three posited financial behavior patterns of uncontrolled managers, owners and creditors would have been confirmed, although in the case of the comparison of managers to creditors, this confirmation would have only been conditional. The fourth hypothesis would again have been rejected, with the chemicals firms showing the least support for the agency theory hypotheses, followed by the food & beverages sector. The machinery and electronics sectors were expected to exhibit that behavior.

hypothesis #	machinery	electronics	chemicals	food & beverages	utilities	overall
1	(☑)	☑	☑	☑	☑	☑
2	☑	☑	(☐)	(☐)	(☑)	(☑)
3	☑	☑	(☐)	☑	☑	☑
4						☐

Table 3-34: Alternative overview over the validity of hypotheses one to four; all sectors[105,106]

3.4 Summary of the Chapter

In this section, the financial behavior of companies was studied for differences by agency control group, distinguishing between manager control, ownership control and creditor control. The financial instruments were divided into the internal financial instrument of free cash flow (that cash flow which remains after all investment outlays have been paid for), and external finance instruments. The external instruments comprise equity issues and long- and short-term external debt. For each of the three relations, those between owners and managers, creditor and managers, and owners and creditors, a hypothesis was set up to comparatively rank the financial preferences of either group and deduce expected directions of influence of each control group on each financial instrument.

Tests of the hypotheses were conducted using two methods, t-tests for mean differences and logistic regressions. The t-tests were particularly suited to testing the individual influence of each agency variable, and their joint influence via conglomerate variables, while the logistic regressions computed the joint influence of the agency variables in their un-conglomerate form. The data sample from 1986 to 1992 with over 1100 cases was used in two fashions: first the total sample was analyzed with the t-tests and logistic regressions, using sector-based mean calculations to account for industry-wide characteristics. Then, the five sectors strongest in number were separately subjected to the same statistical tests. These sectors were the chemicals, machinery, electronics, food & beverages, and utilities firms. For these sectoral analyses, a fourth hypothesis was put forth that addressed the varying competitive conditions between the sectors/sales markets of the firms.

---

105 Using only the results from the t-tests for mean differences.

106 A check marks a hypothesis that could not be rejected according to the model given at the top of the column.

The sectoral results were aggregated by simple majorities to determine the validity of each of the first three hypotheses. In this summary, these aggregated sectoral results and the verdict from the comprehensive analysis will be combined to arrive at a final evaluation of the hypotheses. Table 3-35 shows the results by sample type and allows each financial instrument to be discussed separately.

hypothesis #	sample	d_l/fa	d_s/fa	e/fa	fcf/fa	overall
1	compre-hensive	☐	(☐)	☑	☐	(☐)
	sectoral	(☐)	(☐)	☑	(☑)	(☐)
overall		☐	(☐)	☑	(☐)	(☐)
2	compre-hensive	(☐)	☐	(☐)	(☐)	(☐)
	sectoral	(☐)	(☐)	☐	(☑)	(☐)
overall		(☐)	☐	☐	(☐)	(☐)
3	compre-hensive	☑	☑	☑	☑	☑
	sectoral	☑	(☐)	(☑)	☑	(☑)
overall		☑	(☑)	(☑)	☑	(☑)
4	sectoral					☐

Table 3-35: Overview over the validity of hypotheses one to four; all methods[107]

The first hypothesis treated differences in financial preferences between owners and uncontrolled managers. Only a dislike of owners for equity issues allowing new shareholders into a firm could be consistently confirmed.[108] In the second hypothesis, the differences between creditors and managers were inspected. There was only marginal support for the notion that creditors prefer long-term debt and dislike free cash flow, but not enough to accept those sub-hypotheses or the second hypothesis in full.

---

[107] A check marks a hypothesis that could not be rejected according to the model given at the top of the column.

[108] This contrasts somewhat with the positive stock market reactions new issue announcements produce in Germany. Cf. Padberg (1995). The positive returns probably can be traced to prospective new owners.

The third hypothesis came around full circle and compared ownership control with creditor control. This is the only hypothesis that receives conditional acceptance overall. The owners do not favor long-term debt as much as creditors do. Due to the insights creditors, especially house banks, receive into corporate workings, it is entirely understandable that a company in return has easier access to more debt. Owners, on the other hand, tolerate free cash flow more readily than creditors, which could be a sign that owners are more privy to future investment prospects requiring additional funds. In addition, owners are less partial to equity issues and equally or more interested in short-term debt than creditors, as hypothesized. These last two statements are only conditionally supported, though, leading to an only qualified acceptance of the third hypothesis in total.

In the fourth and final hypothesis, it was surmised that the varying levels of competition could affect financial choices. In sectors where the companies have to face stiff competition (machinery and electronics), this would force all control groups to follow the same financial policies, and cause the lack of distinctions found in the first three hypotheses. For the less competitive companies (food & beverages, utilities), the three hypotheses should be confirmed, though. This theory could not be corroborated in practice, leading to the rejection of the fourth hypothesis.

Figure 3-9 graphically displays the findings of this section, and is based on Figure 3-4. For each financial instrument, the control groups are listed from top to bottom in descending order of affinity to that instrument. Each control group has its own column, to make its identification easier. In addition to the information in Figure 3-4, bars are drawn in between control groups to show if there was full support (fat bars), medium support (normal bars), or little support (thin bars) for the ranking difference depicted. In the case of little support, marked by an empty box in parentheses in rows marked "overall" Table 3-35, the hypothesis is considered to be rejected.

At a glance one can see that the free cash flow variable received the most support, with all three relations (hypotheses) for that instrument finding some recognition. In the case of the equity finance, the shareholders are clearly set off from the other control groups in their dislike for it. To a lesser degree this is also true for short-term debt finance, which owners prefer more than others. The creditors show stronger preferences for the long-term debt finance than the other groups.

The investment side of corporate operations could not be analyzed here, but could contribute valuable additional insights into the financial side of decision making in the light of the agency theory. For example, a question that remains to be studied in detail is if investment volume depends on the control group of a company, i. e., if the under- or overinvestment problem can be observed in companies. Large differences in volume could affect the outcome of the hypotheses tested here. Additional information on control clauses, especially in credit contracts, would also be of special interest. House banks may have access to informal insights into companies, and further influence their policies through equity ownership.

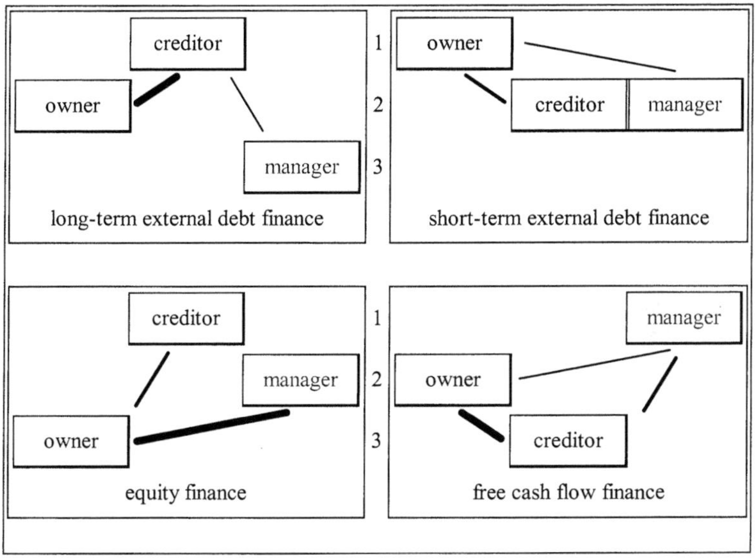

Figure 3-9: Graphical representation of the financial preferences by agency group as confirmed or rejected in the tests of hypotheses one to three[109]

Also, the riskiness of investment policies was seen to be theoretically related to the risk propensity of the control group, and could affect the financial mix used in investment funding and the return distributions resulting from these investments.[110] Capital structure itself is often related to performance.[111] In order to investigate return differences, the following chapter addresses the performance of the firms in the light of the agency theory.

---

109 Bold lines show confirmed relations.

110 Cf. Williams (1987). Preliminary test using standard deviations of the returns suggest that there are no significant differences in riskiness.

111 Cf. Aghion/Bolton (1989). Carleton/Silberman (1977) find little relationship between the two.

4 A Test of the Managerial Theory of Performance

4.1 Agency Theory and Performance

In chapter 2.2.2.2 above the agency problems were seen to produce three types of costs, the costs of monitoring, bonding, and the residual loss as the reduction of the firm value in comparison to its ideal value if the management were not consuming perks. The departure from the pure goal of profit maximization will conceivably affect suitably chosen performance measures (see chapter 4.3). Therefore agency costs provide the theoretical background for the following empirical analysis.[1]

4.1.1 The Overinvestment Problem and Free Cash Flows

Another fashion by which agency problems can affect the performance of a firm is of a more indirect nature, when the agency problems prevent an optimal investment policy to be pursued. This will keep the revenues from reaching their full profit-generating potential. Such a situation can for example arise when the management of a firm does not pay out extra profits to investors in the form of dividends but allows free cash flows to occur initially and later retains profits.[2] Ultimately the extra funds will be invested to cause the overinvestment problem. Free cash flows are defined in this context as those flows which remain after all lucrative investments have been funded and dividends paid.[3] They need not only negatively affect performance, but can also have a positive effect on future performance, by being held in order to finance future investments.[4]

The reasons for holding free cash flow are twofold. First, an uncontrolled management that wishes to preserve its freedom will try to find ways to prevent allowing principals additional insights into their dealings. The market valuation mechanism cannot take effect in this case.[5] External debt similarly introduces new creditors and causes interest payments which reduce cash flows, making debt also undesirable.[6] This goal can be achieved by funding projects with internal funds and avoiding raising external capital and means that cash flows will be retained if at all possible instead of paying them out to shareholders. The second

---

1 See also Bühner/Tuschke (1997), who link agency costs to the shareholder value concept.

2 Already noted by Berle (1954).

3 Cf. Jensen (1986).

4 Cf. Sloan (1992), who uses an unclear definition of free cash flow, though.

5 Cf. Easterbrook (1984).

6 Cf. Stulz (1990).

reason lies in the sense of power the management can enjoy if it presides over a large company.[7] This, too, will lead managers to reinvest profits in the company instead of increasing dividends. Building up reserves can have the added benefit of assuring current dividend levels in the future.[8]

After a company has invested in all the projects available with returns that promise to meet the return demands of the funding parties, any remaining funds should be paid out to the owners so they can find other companies with more lucrative projects in which to invest their money. This behavior can in a sense constitute a definition of the optimal firm size.[9] Any additional investments will by definition be into projects with less than the demanded return, and will cause the overall performance of the company to decline, too. As long as the overall performance does not drop lower than the minimum requirements of the shareholders, managers will not be reprimanded for such behavior.

4.1.2 The Underinvestment Problem, Agency Costs of Debt and Bank Control

It is also possible for the opposite effect to take place, that investments are not even expanded until all lucrative possibilities are exhausted, which is called the underinvestment problem.[10] This situation can occur if a company has a high leverage which leads to high interest payments.[11] Assume that a positive NPV project cannot be funded through available internal funds, making either a stock issue or debt issue necessary. If new debt that is issued must be risky and therefore costly due to the already high debt-equity ratio, an investment project that originally promises a positive net present value might still be foregone if its profits could in some states not exceed the interest payments the company must make.[12] Since the ownership and management will not have any advantage from the investment in that case, it might not be pursued, making this an agency problem between creditors and the management/ownership.[13] If available funds were paid out immediately, the downsized company would retain its high per-

---

7 Cf. Jensen (1986).

8 Cf. Lintner (1956).

9 The other being the point where marginal costs equal average total costs, cf. Schumann (1987), pp. 133 ff.

10 Cf. Myers (1977).

11 Zhang (1995) argues, though, that leverage is more effective than pure equity financing in reducing the underinvestment problem, if there is one large risk averse blockholder.

12 Cf. Stulz (1990).

13 To simplify things, the ownership and management are assumed to have identical interests here.

formance levels that relate the lower profits to the lower asset value. But since reducing the non-debt funding possibilities could lead to an exacerbated under-investment problem in the next period, it is unlikely that the now free cash flow will be paid out, causing the lower profit level to be related to the full asset value, and thus lower the company's performance.[14]

Managerial stock ownership as part of an incentive payment plan can also affect the performance of marketable debt, such as corporate bonds. At low levels of managerial ownership, managers can want to achieve ownership goals and follow a riskier investment policy than advocated by creditors (also see above chapter 3.2.4), but they reverse this trend at higher levels of ownership again, aligning their interests more closely with the creditors'.[15]

Another conflict between principals can arise through the involvement of German banks. They can at the same time be a creditor and hold shares of the same firm.[16] As creditors, they will not necessarily be interested in high performance.[17] Additionally, it is possible that banks that themselves suffer problems draw down the companies they are involved in.[18] But as simultaneous equity-holders this attitude might not apply any more. Banks can also hold seats in the supervisory board, which can greatly increase their influence as owners. In addition, banks can act as proxy voters for small investors, without necessarily representing the shareholders' interests.[19] Thus a purely equity-sided additional agency conflict between banks and small investors can arise from bank share-holding, too. Banks do not necessarily monitor companies in the way small investors would like, if they act more in the role of a creditor.[20]

---

14 These thoughts link the previous chapter concerning the capital structure to this chapter on performance. A study of the connection between capital structure and performance, albeit with few specific agency-theoretical elements, can be found in Schneider (1991).

15 Cf. Strock Bagnani et al. (1994).

16 Cf. Chirinko/Elston (1996).

17 Cf. Neuberger (1994), pp. 142 ff finds evidence that banks follow a risk-adverse credit granting policy.

18 For Japan, this was attested in Kang/Stulz (1996).

19 Cf. Gorton/Schmid (1996).

20 Cf. Edwards/Fischer (1994). Franks/Mayer (1997) find little evidence for an influence of bank ownership on performance and board turnover.

4.1.3 Managerialism and Performance

4.1.3.1 Growth Model

The managerial theory assumes like the agency theory in general that managers do not act in the ownership's best interests, but instead pursue other goals. Whereas the ownership is assumed to demand profit maximization, managers might be more interested in sales maximization (under condition that a certain profit level is maintained),[21] especially if their contracts are linked to sales numbers.[22] Other payment contracts not associated with profit maximization are also possible.[23] It can make sense for managers to maximize sales, as their reduction can lead to a loss of customers and image, and a resulting reduction of the future profit potential. Sales are also not unimportant for banks and capital markets.[24] Income smoothing is another possible intention that managers pursue, which conflicts with profit maximization.[25] Income smoothing can also be linked to the (unsystematic) risk of a firm (see chapter 2.2.2.3).[26]

It is also possible that managers strive to maximize growth, as many readily identify growth with success.[27] This pertains both to the personal view of the managers as well as to the criteria applied by other stakeholders in a firm.[28] Managers will combine this goal with the necessary condition of maintaining a certain level of job security. The job security is expressed as a target market valuation that prevents corporate raiders from attempting an unfriendly takeover. High market valuation calls for high profits. But as growth is the dominating factor, it is entirely possible that the growth rate chosen does not maximize profits.[29]

---

21 Cf. Baumol (1967).

22 Cf. Murphy (1985); Bühner (1984).

23 Cf. Jensen/Murphy (1990).

24 Cf. Baumol (1967).

25 Cf. Kamin/Ronen (1978); DeFond/Park (1996). An empirical test of income smoothing for the German market was conducted by Langendijk/van Praag (1996).

26 Cf. Amihud/Kamin/Ronen (1983).

27 Cf. Marris (1971). An empirical study of this hypothesis is given in Thonet/Poensgen (1979).

28 A recent application is in Kaplan (1997).

29 Cf. Marris (1968).

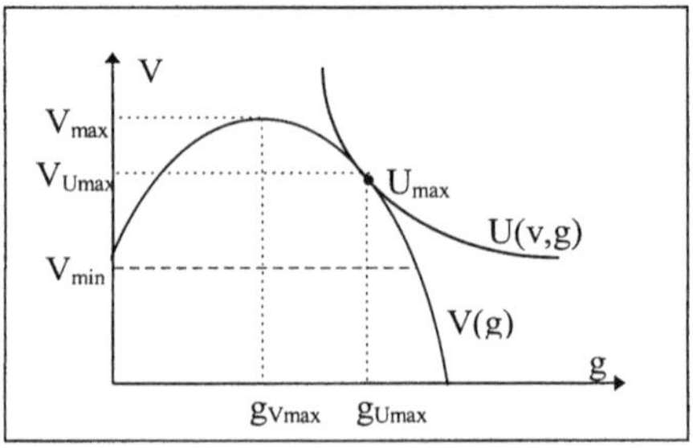

Figure 4-1: Growth model[30]

Figure 4-1 shows this model where the manager's utility U depends on growth g and the security v from takeovers of the company. The valuation curve V that potential raiders monitor depends on the growth rate chosen, and maximum growth does not produce maximum value. As long as the minimum valuation requirement is satisfied, the management will choose the growth rate g_{Umax} at the point where the utility indifference curve farthest away from the origin (with the highest utility) is brushed. The resulting valuation V_{Umax} is not the maximum.

4.1.3.2 Utility Model

Williamson describes three central elements that enhance a manager's utility, namely the increase in staff, increase in income and the achievement of a certain minimum profit to insure investments and satisfy shareholders.[31] The income increase can result both by working for bonuses or in the form of what here has been called consumption on the job or perquisites. The minimum profit also has the function of providing the manager with prestige and acclaim.

In a model similar to the growth model above (Figure 4-1), the utility model in Figure 4-2 shows that the function of the profit P dependent on staff expenditures s is maximized at a lower value of s than if the manager maximizes his utility U which is a function of discretionary profits P_d, staff expenditures and the manager's income c, which is set constant in the model.[32] There is a certain degree of substitutionality between the profits and the staff expenses, which both increase the manager's utility, but are contrary to each other once the staff expenses are increased past the profit maximizing level s_{Pmax}. At the utility maxi-

---

30 Cf. Marris (1968), p. 255.

31 Cf. Williamson (1963, 1969).

32 A non-constant, profit-linked income would move the utility indifference curve upwards and to the left, without reaching the profit maximum. Incentive-based compensation schedules will also affect performance. Cf. Chung/Pruitt (1996).

mizing point s_{Umax}, the staff expenses will be higher than if profits were maximized.

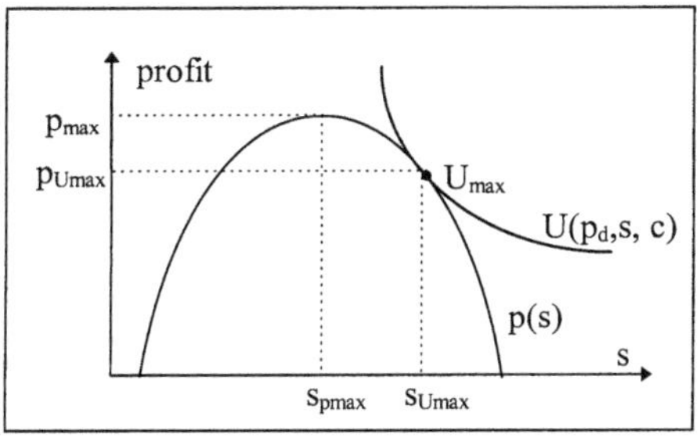

Figure 4-2: Utility model[33]

4.1.4 Market Forces and Competition

Aside from monitoring and bonding measures, competition on the sales market of a firm can be seen as another, external form of management control.[34] A company that cannot determine the sales prices but must accept the prices on the market will expand production to the point where the marginal revenue of the last item sold, i. e., its price, exactly matches the marginal cost of producing that item. Competitive firms will lower prices until they match their own average total costs.[35] Other companies whose average total costs lie higher must leave the market in the long term if they are not able to reduce costs. Competition thus has two effects on profits. The first is that profits will decrease in comparison to those possible in a monopolistic market, where prices are fixed in the Cournot point where marginal costs equal marginal revenues, and revenues are variable.[36] In return, though, increased competition forces the management to reduces costs in order to stay competitive. This includes reducing the agency costs such as the squandering of resources on the consumption of perks. The reduction of agency costs through competition occurs even if there is no owner willing or capable of monitoring the management.[37]

---

33 Cf. Williamson (1974), p. 33.

34 Cf. Stano (1976).

35 Cf. Schumann (1987), p. 139.

36 Cf. Schumann (1987), p. 250.

37 Cf. Qualls (1976).

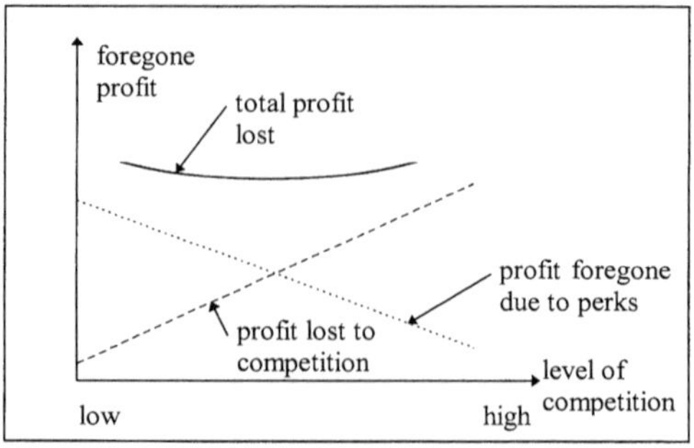

Figure 4-3: Profits lost to perks or competition

Expressed in terms of foregone profits, Figure 4-3 shows that as competition increases, the perks the management allows itself will decline which decreases the amount of profits foregone. At the same time any monopolistic profits will be eaten away by prices falling toward the level of average total costs. The two developments with opposite tendencies will cause minimal profit losses to be located somewhere in the middle between the extremes of perfect competition and a monopoly. There, too, maximum performance levels will be located.[38]

Another effect due to competition is depicted in Figure 4-4. Since the restraining force of prices falling from their monopolistic levels affects manager and owner-controlled firms alike, companies of both types will be forced to reduce costs in order to remain on the market. Assuming that managers run up higher costs (perquisites) in monopolistic structures, firms controlled by managers will be obliged to reduce their average total costs more than owner-controlled companies. All will have the common goal of reaching the benchmark lowest level of average total costs achieved by a competing company. It is therefore possible that the cost gap between owners and managers will decrease, as competition increases. For statistical purposes, the larger gap will be more easily identifiable, if all else is equal (in particular the variance in the costs). So performance differences can be more pronounced in monopolistic or quasi-monopolistic markets.

Beside the competition on the sales market, other market forces that can affect performance can be seen in the capital market and the market for corporate control.[39] Insufficiently high performance can cause the assets of a firm to be un-

---

38 See Jeger (1994) for further discussion on the reduction of abnormal profits due to competition.

39 An empirical test for this can be found in Zantout (1994).

dervalued by the capital market and call corporate raiders onto the scene (chapter 2.2.3.1.2.1).[40]

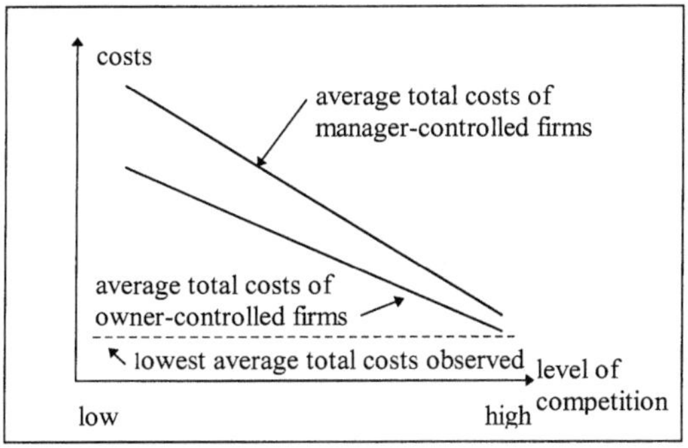

Figure 4-4: Development of costs due to agency problems by agency group

4.2 Classification of Performance Measures

4.2.1 Absolute vs. Relative Measures

The word performance can take on various meanings which all pertain to the evaluation of the success of a company. Performance can refer to absolute measures such as profits, but more commonly is connected with ratios that relate the actual measure of success to a benchmarking value. The word return is also often used in this context, but is more ambiguous than the word performance in its designation of an absolute or relative value.[41]

Relative measures always have the advantage of allowing comparisons to be made between companies that differ in some characteristic, by dividing the absolute measure of success by a suitable absolute measure for the said characteristic.[42] Often, the denominator will be a size measure. The comparison of companies can produce the paradox that the comparison is worthwhile only when the values differ; on the other hand, disparate values reduce the comparability.[43] Other comparisons are over time, where a value for a variable is divided by the

40 Cf. Fama/Jensen (1983).

41 In German, 'Erfolg' is used for absolute returns, while a relative return is called 'Rendite'.

42 See also Schierenbeck (1987), p. 559.

43 Cf. Leffson (1984).

value from a previous time period for that same variable; the third comparison can be between the actual and target performance of a firm.[44] Relative performance measures can be a disadvantage if there is no absolute benchmark they compare the companies to; saying that a company is better off than its competitors can be misleading if the companies are all performing very poorly on an absolute level. Therefore relative performance measures with absolute benchmarks will be preferred over purely absolute measures in this section.

4.2.2 Market vs. Book Performance

The relative success of a company can be determined by taking either a market or a book return measure and putting it into relation to the market values of the invested capital, i. e., the equity and/or debt, if available, or else the book values of these financial positions. Market-based return measures are increases in stock or bond prices, and then always include an element of time, and dividend payments.

Book measures of success in Germany usually center around the net profit of the year (Jahresüberschuß), but also can be determined at several earlier points in the calculation of that measure. The net profit consists of three elements, the operating result, the financial result and the extraordinary result.[45] The extraordinary result is often by far the smallest component and also the least representative of the company operations, so it will not be studied in greater detail. The calculation of the first two elements follows procedures such as those described below in Table 4-1 and Table 4-2.

The operating result takes the sales revenues plus internally produced and capitalized assets and inventory changes and subtracts from this gross performance measure the costs of the inputs materials, fixed assets and labor. The exact determination of the depreciation rate is left to the management's discretion and therefore is open to manipulation. Any interim result in the calculation of the operating result, such as the raw yield, has the disadvantage that major cost factors such as depreciation on tangible and intangible fixed assets are not included in the computation. This lack makes their use less advantageous than the operating result itself. The financial result takes earnings from profit and loss pooling agreements, financial investments and interest earnings and subtracts the cost of the financial input, which is the amortization of the financial assets and the interest payments.

---

44 Cf. Schierenbeck (1987), pp. 572 f.

45 Cf. Perridon/Steiner (1997), pp. 547 f.

	sales revenues
+	internally produced and capitalized assets inventory changes
=	gross performance
–	expenses for raw and production materials
=	raw yield
–	wages social insurance contributions
–	depreciation on tangible and intangible fixed assets
–	taxes
=	net operating result

Table 4-1: Calculation of the net operating result[46]

Taken alone, neither the operating result nor the financial result provide a full view of the revenues of a company. Therefore there is no reason to confine the profit measure to one of the above elements only (with the exception of the extraordinary result, as discussed). But the net profit of the year can be processed even further, as shown in Table 4-3, to produce the balance sheet income statement. It adds profits brought forward and withdrawals from capital or revenue reserves to the net profit of the year and subtracts transferals to earning reserves. In doing so, this procedure introduces data from other time periods into the profit measure, which is generally undesirable in this case. Also, the decision to withdraw or transfer profits from or to the reserves is not relevant for the purposes pursued here. It even opens further avenues for the manipulation of the profit measure by the management.[47] Therefore, using the balance sheet income is not advisable in this study, and the net profit of the year remains the book measure of profit of choice for this study. Another way of further processing the net profit of the year is shown below in 4.2.3.

---

46 Cf. Perridon/Steiner (1997), pp. 546 f.

47 Cf. Küting (1997). An empirical analysis of the performance accounting practices of German stock corporations is in Halbinger (1980).

	earnings from profit and loss pooling agreements
+	earnings from financial investments and affiliated companies interest earnings
–	amortization of financial assets interest payments
=	net financial result

Table 4-2: Calculation of the net financial result[48]

	net profit of the year
+	profits brought forward (– losses brought forward)
+	withdrawals from the capital or revenue reserves
–	transfers to earnings reserves
=	balance sheet income

Table 4-3: Calculation of the balance sheet income[49]

Finally, a joint commission of the Deutsche Vereinigung für Finanzanalysen und Anlagenberatung (DVFA) and Schmalenbach-Gesellschaft (SG) suggested several corrections to the profit calculation to increase the comparability and content of profit measures.[50] Fictitious taxes are excluded from the calculations, and investment bonuses are distributed over the useful period of the investment, instead of subtracting them from the net profit. This DVFA/SG profit measure makes comparisons between companies with and without losses brought forward more difficult, though. This also concerns comparisons over time for one company that has losses brought forward in some of the periods, but not in others.[51] Calculating the DVFA/SG profit measure requires a detailed analysis of

48 Cf. Perridon/Steiner (1997), p. 547.

49 Cf. Perridon/Steiner (1997), p. 545.

50 Cf. DVFA/SG (1990).

51 Cf. Perridon/Steiner (1997), p. 215.

the appendices to the annual statement, which often give unsatisfactory information and are not available in the dataset to be analyzed. Therefore the DVFA/SG result will not be used here.

The book measures of performance were seen to be more prone to managerial manipulation than market measures are, where pricing mechanisms are largely out of the control of the management of a company. This speaks for using market-based performance measures. Book-value measures, however, are widely used and accepted, for example the return on investment (net profit of the year divided by total capital).[52] Also, the utilization of disaggregate information (see 4.2.3) calls upon book values, and a direct comparison of the rejection or support of the agency theory-based hypotheses by the aggregate and disaggregate measures of success should provide interesting insights into the success of control mechanisms. Therefore measures from both categories, book and market measures, will be used here.

Other possible performance variables could be used if one assumes that the management is maximizing sales or book values of assets when left to its own devices. The variables to be analyzed in this case would be the growth rate of total assets (as a book measure) or the ratio of sales to total assets (as a sort of market valued measure).[53] This assumption is possible if the ownership judges manager performance by these values, even if that is not in the owners' best interests. As studies in this area are more or less based on subjective experience,[54] I do not adopt any of these variables for my approach.

4.2.3 Aggregate vs. Disaggregate Measures

The question of aggregation of a performance measure generally pertains to those calculated using book values. As was seen above in 4.2.2, a typical book measure of profit is the net profit of the year (Jahresüberschuß) in Germany. It processes the basic revenues such as the sales revenues or financial income and combines these with base costs such as depreciation or wages, and combines all these measures into one single number. This number is then put into the evaluation procedures for judging the corporate performance. Since only the one number is further used, the net profit of the year can be considered to be an aggregate profit measure. Placing the costs and revenues separately and distinctly into the further evaluation steps would constitute the opposite disaggregate way of proceeding.

---

52 Cf. Bühner/Weinberger (1991) link the return on equity to the market-to-book value of equity.

53 Cf. Baumol (1967), Marris (1968).

54 Cf. Ridder-Aab (1980), pp. 29 f.

Figure 4-5 below shows the steps taken in constructing the return on equity from expenses and revenues, by way of the return on investment. The lower part of the graph contains the elements of the net profit of the year as given above in Table 4-1 and Table 4-2. The net profit is then processed further, but differently than described in 4.2.2. Instead of adding and subtracting additional values to the net profit, it is divided by the sales to give a first relative success measure, the sales return. Multiplying the sales return with the capital turnover gives the net profit of the year divided by the capital, which is the return on investment (ROI). Dividing the ROI by the equity ratio gives the return on equity (ROE), which is at the top of the aggregate relative performance measures.[55]

Thus the top of Figure 4-5 contains relative and highly aggregated performance measures, the ROI and ROE. The values at the bottom of the figure are disaggregate and absolute. It is possible to judge the success of a company by values at either end of the figure, but only the aggregate measures toward the top will be referred to as performance measures, while the evaluation criteria for a company's success directly estimated from the disaggregate measures will be called efficiency measures. The companies' performance will be analyzed in this section of the study, while the efficiency, for whose determination special estimation techniques are necessary, is the subject of the following chapter 5.

Another aggregated performance measure is the return on capital (ROC), which differs from the ROI in that not only the net profit of the year, but also the interest payments are put in the numerator of the ratio, while the denominator contains the total capital in both cases. The ROI has the advantage of being separable into its two components, the sales return and the capital turnover. This allows structural differences in the performance of companies to be distinguished. One company may have a high ROI due to a high capital turnover rate, while the reason for another company's high ROI could lie in high sales returns.[56] The ROC in contrast factors the leverage into the ratio by not dismissing the interest payments on the company's debt. This improves the quality of a comparison of companies with different debt-equity ratios to each other. A disadvantage of the ROC lies in its inclusion of non-operating assets in the performance calculation.[57] Still, it is preferable to the ROI in this analysis.

---

55 Capital turnover = sales / total capital. Equity ratio = equity / total capital.

56 Cf. Perridon/Steiner (1997), pp. 558 ff.

57 Cf. Barber/Lyon (1996).

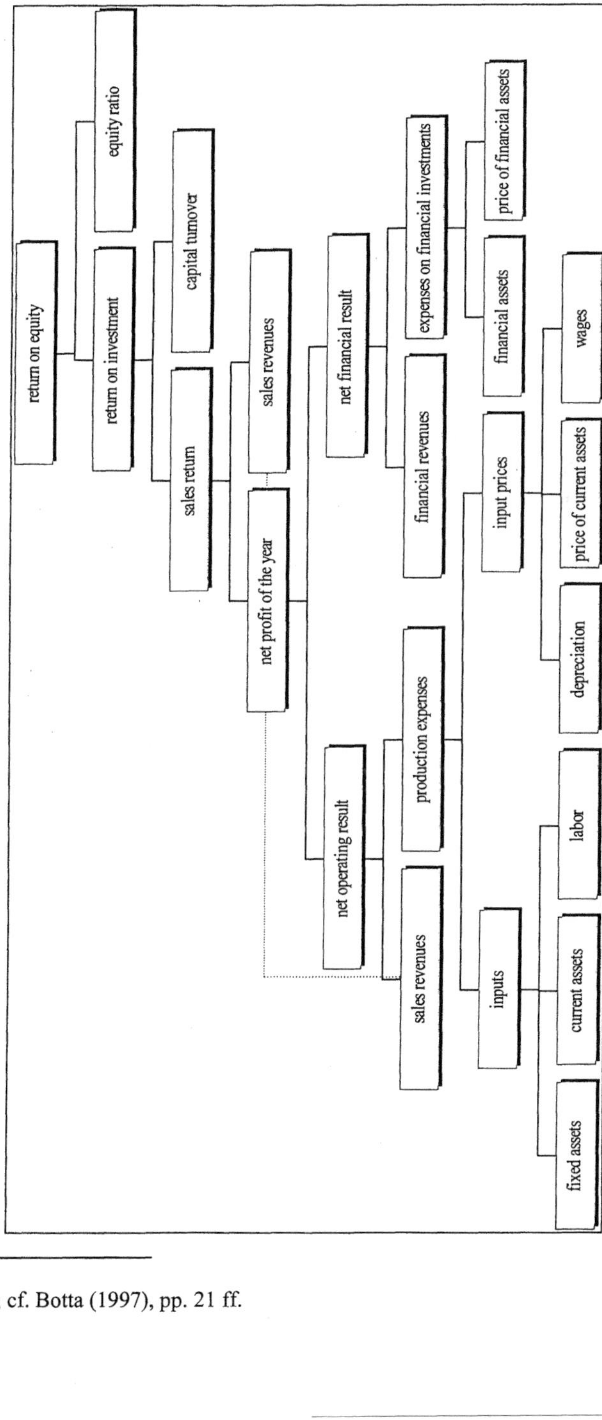

Figure 4-5: Return on Investment Diagram[58]

[58] Adapted; cf. Botta (1997), pp. 21 ff.

4.3 Empirical Analysis of the Performance of German Stock Corporations

4.3.1 Performance Measures in the Context of this Study

4.3.1.1 Return on Capital

In light of the considerations in 4.1, four measures of performance are chosen to be used in this study.[59] Two are book measures, namely the return on equity (ROE) shown above in Figure 4-5 and the return on capital (ROC). The ROC is preferable to the perhaps more common ROI in the context of this study because the advantage of being able to split the ROI into components is not the target pursued here. Instead, the greater comparability the ROC provides by accounting for the debt-equity ratio is a very desirable feature, as company groups are indeed to be compared. The return on capital for a company *i* in the year (period) *t* is calculated as

$$ROC_{i,t} = \frac{\text{net profit of the year}_{i,t} + \text{interest payments}_{i,t}}{\text{book value of total assets}_{i,t-1}} \tag{4-1}$$

As can be seen in Equation (4-1), the asset value in the denominator is taken from the end of the period preceding the one the ROC is observed for. The rational behind this procedure is that the profits and interest payments should be related to the capital that actually produced these flows. The same-period capital is not suitable in this regard, as it is a point value at the end of the profit flows in the numerator, and therefore did not contribute to their creation. Another possibility would be to take the average of the previous and current period capital values. This can be understood because the profits occurring at the beginning of the period are partly used to increase the capital stock which in turn produces more profits. It is lastly a matter of taste if one wishes to use this denominator or the one given in Equation (4-1).

4.3.1.2 Return on Equity

The ROE has its own merits due to two points, which make it worthwhile to be included in addition to the ROC. The first is the recent refocus of investor and research interests on what is now called shareholder value, i. e., basing the evaluation of a company on its success in increasing the wealth of its ownership.

---

59 Cf. Wittrock (1995); Steiner/Wittrock (1995) for a discussion of performance measurement for portfolios.

In the case of the stock corporation the ownership consists of shareholders. This approach acknowledges the participation and interests of other groups in corporate dealings and allots to these people, too, the right to demand the fulfillment of their interests. Stakeholders can be any individual or group affected by a company's activities.[60] Typical stakeholder groups are the workforce and the creditors of a company, or the government (as the tax authority).

The balance of shareholder and stakeholder interests can be based on economical or ethical reasons, neither of which can be discussed here in greater depth.[61] Econometrically speaking, stakeholder interests can be included in the shareholder wealth maximization demand as constraints. If stakeholders in one firm are simultaneously shareholders in another, though, the maximization of utility can be diluted by constraining shareholder utility. The efficient allocation of resources can suffer from this. Also, the shareholders are expressly acquiring the right to determine the company politics when they purchase voting stock, so the creditors' lack to do so can be interpreted as a conscious renunciation of such governance rights. Therefore, it is not necessary reintroduce such rights via a stakeholder approach.

From the ethical point of view, a company is part of society as a whole and the well-being of all elements in the society should be the top priority.[62] Running a company to maximize the utility of only part of the society seemingly does not jibe with this view. But the interests of the various groups do not conflict by necessity. Maximizing shareholder value can very well be in the best interests of the other stakeholders, whose main interest will be in the immediate and long-term well-being of the firm.[63] The reorientation toward shareholder value and the concurrent economic upswing in the US are more probably linked as cause and effect than as opposing forces.

The second reason justifying the additional inclusion of the ROE lies in the agency theory view that this analysis is taking. The main thrust of principal-agent theory defines the shareholders of a company as the principals and the management as the agent. The analysis of the effects and the resolution of conflicts between these two parties is the goal of this study. For this, the interests of the two parties must be carefully identified. In the case of the shareholders of a company, it is obvious that in order to judge the performance of their firm, they will choose to relate the absolute success of the company to their own invest-

---

60 Cf. Freeman (1984).

61 Cf. Osterloh/Löhr (1994). A detailed analysis of the stakeholder approach is in Eberhardt (1998).

62 See for example Dufrene/Wong (1996), with further references.

63 Cf. Dufrene/Wong (1996), p. 4. Capasso (1996) suggests viewing stakeholders as virtual shareholders who participate in the systemic goodwill that is part of the company value.

ment in that firm, and not to the total capital present in the firm. As an absolute success measure they will also choose one that falls to them to be paid out in dividends or reinvested in the company. The interest payment outflows are not of interest in that regard. As a result, the ROE is the book performance measure of choice for shareholders.

The leverage effect can cause the ROE and ROC to differ markedly, so using both measures will not necessarily cause a duplication of the results.[64] High debt-equity ratios lever the ROE up or down in comparison to the ROC, depending if the debit interest rate is greater or smaller than the ROC. As both the numerator and denominator are different between the two, as opposed to the ROI and ROE, where only the denominators are different, using the ROE and ROC should cover a larger spread of information than using the ROI.

The ROE is calculated as shown below in Equation (4-2). Here, too, as for the ROC, the equity value in the denominator is taken from the period immediately preceding the period being observed.

$$ROE_{i,t} = \frac{\text{net profit of the year}_{i,t}}{\text{book value of equity}_{i,t-1}} \qquad (4\text{-}2)$$

Both measures presented, the ROC and ROE, are based on book values. It is, however, also possible to express both in terms of market values. This could be done in the case of the ROE by replacing the net profit of the year by the stock return multiplied by the market value of the equity in *t-1* in the numerator and putting the market value of the equity in *t-1* in the denominator. As Equation (4-3) shows, the equity cancels out to leave the stock return plus dividend.

$$ROE_{i,t}(\text{market}) = \frac{(\text{stock return}_{i,t} + \text{div}_{i,t}) \cdot \text{equity(market)}_{i,t-1}}{\text{equity(market)}_{i,t-1}} = \text{stock return}_{i,t} + \text{div}_{i,t} \qquad (4\text{-}3)$$

The market valued ROC does not cancel out to such a simple measure, but it calculates in much the same way. Instead of using the stock return in its pure form as a market-based performance measure, an additional modification is introduced below.

64 The leverage effect states that ROE = ROC + (ROC – i) · L, where *i* is the debit interest rate and *L* is the debt-equity ratio (leverage). See Perridon/Steiner (1997), pp. 478 f.

4.3.1.3 Sharpe Ratio

Just as two book-value performance measures were chosen above, two market-value performance measures will be used to test the hypotheses formulated in 4.3.2. The first of these is the Sharpe ratio, defined for a company *i* as:[65]

$$\text{Sharpe ratio}_i = \frac{r_i - r_F}{\sigma_i} \tag{4-4}$$

where r_i is the stock return of a company i,[66] σ_i is its standard deviation, and r_F is the risk-free interest rate. The stock returns were calculated by dividing the last day quote of year *t* by the last day quote of year *t*-1 for dividend-adjusted quotes. The returns were then logarithmed. The standard deviation of the returns was calculated from the 12 monthly returns of the stock in each year. Weekly or daily values, although providing more datapoints, have the disadvantage of higher occurrences of infrequent trading, which usually reduces the standard deviation and gives the wrong picture of a stock's risk. The annualized quarterly interest rate for money was used for as the risk-free rate of return.[67] Toward the end of the time period analyzed, this rate rises sharply due to the German reunification in 1990.

The Sharpe ratio is a simple measure of success that belongs to the relative measures due to the time element the returns introduce by dividing the final share price from one year by the previous year's last quote (see 4.2.1).[68] It is the only measure used here that includes a risk measure, the standard deviation of the return. By putting the risk measure in the denominator, lower risk increases the performance measure. Low risk is thus seen as desirable by those who use this ratio. In chapter 2.2.2.3, it had been discussed that the owners of a firm could be interested in high-risk undertakings, or at least higher risk than managers would choose.

To determine the risk of an investment i, it would also be possible to use the Capital Asset Pricing Model (CAPM):[69]

$$E(r_i) = r_F + (E(r_M) - r_F) \cdot \beta_i \tag{4-5}$$

where $E(r_M)$ is the expected market index return[70] and

---

65 The choice of r_F follows Beiker (1993).

66 Compensating for dividend payments, new capital offers and changes to the face value of the shares.

67 The figures were taken from Deutsche Bundesbank (1986 – 1992).

68 Cf. Hodges/Taylor/Yoder (1997) also point out the importance of the investment horizon for the Sharpe ratio.

69 Cf. Sharpe (1964); Lintner (1965); Mossin (1966).

$$\beta_i = \frac{\sigma_{iM}}{\sigma_M^2} \tag{4-6}$$

which uses the covariance between the investment and the market index returns to risk-adjust the expected return of the investment.[71] The beta measures the sensitivity of the investment return to changes in the market index return. It is called the systematic risk of an investment, because it relates to the market index which is an endemic element of the model. The unsystematic risk is that which does not depend on the market fluctuations and incorporates investment-specific risk such as bad luck, changes in management, etc. Empirically, the beta is estimated via the market model

$$R_i = \alpha_i + r_M \cdot \beta_i \tag{4-7}$$

which gives an identical beta, apart from the fact that the market model uses historical data, while the CAPM refers to a future period, if the equality (4-8) holds.

$$\alpha_i = (1 - \beta_i) \cdot r_F \tag{4-8}$$

The CAPM can first be used to determine the abnormal return, which would be calculated from the above formula as

$$\text{abnormal return}_i = r_i - E(r_i) \tag{4-9}$$

The abnormal return provides an alternative market valued performance measure, that includes the risk of an investment through the estimation of the expected return $E(R_i)$. Another alternative is to calculate the Treynor measure:[72]

$$\text{Treynor measure}_i = \frac{r_i - r_F}{\beta_i} \tag{4-10}$$

The Treynor measure is identical to the Sharpe ratio except for the substitution of the risk measure in the denominator. Instead of the standard deviation, here only the investment's β is used. In the context of this study, however, it does not make sense to use the more refined Treynor measure. The reason for this lies in the nature of the agency problems of a firm, which can be classified as a firm-specific phenomenon. Agency problems do not by necessity arise in conjunction with the market index. This places the agency problems firmly in the sphere of

---

70 Cf. Steiner/Kleeberg (1991) on choosing the correct index.

71 See Barber/Lyon (1997) for an analysis of misspecifications when calculating abnormal returns using a reference portfolio.

72 Cf. Steiner/Bruns (1998), pp. 538 f.

unsystematic risk, which is only captured by the standard deviation of an investment's returns.[73]

The Sharpe ratio combines two elements, the first being the excess return of a stock or investment, expressed by the numerator of the ratio, $r_i - r_F$.[74] This simply shows how much higher the (risky) stock return is than the risk-free fixed interest rate. The second element is the risk measure in the denominator, the standard deviation of the stock return. Both of these elements can be affected by agency problems, allowing the Sharpe ratio to be affected in various ways. The hypotheses in 4.3.2 will address these possibilities.

4.3.1.4 Tobin's q

The fourth performance measure and second market-value based one to be used is Tobin's q, which relates the price for existing real capital to the price of newly produced (replacement) real capital.[75] In its original economic intention, the purpose of this measure is to gauge the demand for investment goods. If the price for existing real capital is sufficiently low, the demand for new real capital will decline. Aside from the economic interpretation of the measure, Tobin's q also is used in finance.[76] It can also be seen as a market-value based performance measure,[77] and its calculation is:[78]

$$\text{Tobin's } q_i = \frac{\text{market value of stock}_i + \text{market value of debt}_i}{\text{book value of stock}_i + \text{book value of debt}_i} \qquad (4\text{-}11)$$

All values used in Equation (4-11) are for a given year. In Germany, industrial bonds play a fairly small role in corporate finance. In addition, the trading volume and frequency is not that high, so the market pricing mechanism is not fully active. For these reasons, the book value of the debt will be substituted for the market value, making the market value of the equity the only market-valued element in the ratio. The end of year share quotes were used to determine the

---

73 It is recommended to use the Sharpe ratio for well diversified portfolios in order to reduce the unsystematic component in the risk measure.

74 See Bühner (1984) for an application of a performance measure incorporating risk.

75 Cf. Dichtl/Issing (1987), pp. 1838 f.

76 Cf. Gehrke (1994). pp. 24 ff.

77 It is also used as a predictor for future peformance, see Faught/Kale/Rebello (1996).

78 Cf. Morck/Shleifer/Vishny (1988), p. 296.

market value of the stock. The calculation of Tobin's q can be refined further, but that avenue will not be pursued here.[79]

The Sharpe ratio and Tobin's q provide an interesting set of market-value based performance measures.[80] If investors evaluate the external information used here in the same way to separate manager control from ownership control, then they will include this factor in their share pricing algorithm to discount the prices for manager-controlled firm shares. Since many agency factors are very stable, such as the level of block ownership or the market segment a share is traded in, changes in discounting will be a rare occurrence that will usually not influence the return generation process. As a result, the Sharpe ratios should not mirror differences in levels of agency problems. On the other hand, the posited lower overall price level would be very apparent in the values for Tobin's q, which should c. p. directly reflect a lower market price for management-controlled companies for assets with the same book value as a comparable ownership-controlled company. This way, the two measures complement each other.

	return on capital	Sharpe ratio	Tobin's q
return on equity	.7492 ***	.0731 **	.0386
return on capital	1.0000	.1125 ***	.0663 **
Sharpe ratio		1.0000	.1617 ***

N = 1119; *** = significant at 1 %-level (** = 5 %; * = 10 %)

Table 4-4: Correlations of the performance measures, 1986-1992

Table 4-4 shows the correlations for the four performance measures for the time period 1986-1992. The highest correlation, 75 %, is between the returns on equity and capital, the two book measures of performance. The other correlations are all significant except for the return on equity and Tobin's q. Here the correlation is below 4 %. The other correlation scores are also fairly low, though, all lying below 20 %. That is a good sign of sorts, as it confirms that the performance measures chosen are sufficiently varied to merit their joint inclusion.

---

79 See for example Badrinath/Kini (1994), p. 128. For a discussion of the computation of Tobin's q, see Lewellen/Badrinath (1997).

80 Book-to-market, which closely resembles Tobin's q, is often used not as a perfromanc measure but as an explanatory variable for stock returns. Cf. Fama/French (1995, 1992).

4.3.2 Hypotheses

In the context of the agency theory, several hypotheses can be postulated based on the various performance measures of companies. As regards the book performance measures, managers who are assumed to be able to operate under only weak control of the owners of a firm will try to hold certain return levels that avoid alarming the ownership but will not maximize performance in the sense of returns on capital or equity. Also, the higher risk involved in higher returns is a greater threat to managers who are invested in the company with all their human capital, part of which is non-transferable specific knowledge. Rational managers will also want to keep expectations of the stockholders for future returns from reaching too high levels, which can happen if the firm should currently achieve a high performance.[81] Since the main principals, the stockholders, will more closely watch the ROE than the ROC, it can be assumed that the return on equity of owner-controlled firms will be levered to higher rates than the return on capital, so differences in ROE will be greater.

As for the market-based performance measures, I assume that the investors will have discounted the stock prices of manager-controlled firms early on. This means that the Sharpe ratio of the shares should be equal in either group. Tobin's q, however, should mirror the discount by producing lower values for the manager-controlled companies. The central hypothesis is therefore formulated to state that:

1. Manager-controlled companies will perform more poorly than owner-controlled companies as regards the return on equity and Tobin's q. The difference should be less significant when using the return on capital as the performance measure, and non-existent when using the Sharpe ratio. The differences will also diminish in competitive sectors.

In view of the previous empirical results, it is very possible that this hypothesis could be rejected in the empirical section to come. This would mean that managers are either not acting in their own interests, but in the ownership's, or that the management's originally diverging interests have been successfully influenced by measures not captured here in order to equate them to the ownership's. Such measures could be in the form of performance-based incentive contracts. No significant differences in performance between the two types of companies, management and ownership-controlled, is the third possible outcome.

Managers and creditors are interested in maintaining a certain level of return, but neither has a reason to maximize performance, because neither profits from that state. Creditors cannot participate in returns that exceed the fixed interest payments they contractually agreed to receive. In the context of the agency theory,

---

81 The so-called ratchet effect. Cf. Milgrom/Roberts (1992), pp. 232 f.

the added effort of a manager to maximize performance is not compensated by higher utility in form of pay raises etc. after a certain point. Assuming, though, that the creditors' interest in a well-run company is still greater than the management's interests, the following second hypothesis is proposed.

2. Manager-controlled companies will slightly underperform creditor-controlled firms. The differences in performance will be most significant when using the return on capital as the performance measure, but non-existent when regarding the Sharpe ratios.

As for the performance measure used, the most interesting in this case is the return on capital from the point of view of the creditors, because it includes interest payments. The hypothesis specifies that the return on capital will increase more markedly in creditor-controlled firms than in manager-controlled firms, in analogy to what was stated in hypothesis one.

Due to the lower return demands of creditors, demanding high performance in general and high equity-based performance in particular is not as crucial to creditors as it is to the owners of a company. Creditors will, however, insist on a certain level for the return on capital. Closing the circle started by hypotheses one and two, the third hypothesis states that:

3. Creditor-controlled companies will underperform in comparison to ownership-controlled firms with regard to the equity-based return measures return on equity and Tobin's q. No difference will be detectable using the Sharpe ratio. Creditor-controlled firms will exhibit slightly higher returns on capital.

The development over time in the performance of the firms is the subject of the fourth hypothesis. If the management of a company puts less effort into steering the course of the company when it is uncontrolled, it can exploit the hidden action situation economic cycles provide. Downturns in the economic situation can be used to allow performance to decrease at a faster rate than warranted by circumstances, while managers blame the development entirely on the economy. The principals will not be able to verify the truth in the management's statements without almost perfect but extremely costly control possibilities. Similarly, economic upswings can lead to smaller performance increases in manager-controlled firms. The fact that the performance is rising at all can be used to stifle any criticisms.

Since owners demand high returns on equity, and not necessarily high returns on capital, this effect should be visible when comparing creditor-controlled and manager-controlled companies with regard to that performance measure. As for the Sharpe ratio, the fortuitous development that an economic upswing seemingly produces more or less affects all companies in the geographic or sector-specific region the upswing takes place in. Manager or owner control is not the key factor here, so the lucky breaks will be assumed to affect both types of companies equally. Lucky breaks that are by nature unexpected in a previous period will affect the excess return (the numerator in the Sharpe ratio) most of all the performance measures being used here, and vice versa for negative outside shocks.

4. Manager-controlled firms will increase performance at slower rates and decrease it at faster rates than owner-controlled companies. This effect will be least visible in the Sharpe ratio. For the return on capital measure, the hypothesis applies to the comparison between manager and creditor control.

The levels of competition and government regulation are more or less sectoral characteristics. For the competition characteristic, this is not quite true, as at the level of sectoral aggregation used here, companies selling different products are combined into one sector, although they are not competitors. But as a rough measure the sectors can still be used. In general, on uncompetitive markets the profits and with them the performance will be elevated, due to the exploitation of monopolistic or quasi-monopolistic market positions. This effect will be counterbalanced by increases in sloth and consumption on the job made possible by the lack of external control. Therefore, the sectors with medium levels of competition will be assumed to have a higher average performance than the very competitive or uncompetitive ones.[82] Again, these effect should not be visible in the Sharpe ratio, because such factors have already been incorporated in the share prices. This way, the Sharpe ratio acts as a norming factor. Differences in performance between the agency control groups should generally not appear using this measure. This leads to the following hypothesis five:[83]

5. Companies in slightly competitive sectors will perform better than companies in highly competitive or uncompetitive sectors, except when using the Sharpe ratio, where no difference is expected.

Sectoral competition acts as an outside control measure that can force certain levels of effectivity on the management in order to prevail. This will positively affect performance measures of manager-controlled companies.

On the other hand, competition is expected to reduce profit margins. Still, even in competitive markets a competent management will produce higher profits, and so cause higher performance. These gains could be smaller than the performance gains possible in uncompetitive markets, so a leveling of the differ-

---

82 See also Figure 4-3 above.

83 Jeger (1994) links competition and speed of performance adjustments.

ences should be apparent, the more competitive a sector is judged to be. Since no differences in performance are expected above as regards the Sharpe ratio, none are posited here, either. The following hypothesis treats the degree of competition in the sectors:

6. Manager-controlled firms will perform worse than owner-controlled companies in uncompetitive sectors, except for the Sharpe ratio, where performance should be equal. In highly competitive sectors the performance differences will be insignificant for all measures.

It is difficult to determine the competition the companies have to contend using just the data in the dataset, because a large portion of companies in Germany are not listed on the stock markets and thus are not included in this study. Therefore, sales and numbers of companies per sector are taken from statistical publications of the government, and the degree of competition established using those numbers is assumed to apply to the markets that the companies studied here are active in.[84]

The competitivity ranking of the five larger sectors in the database in chapter 2.3.2.6 gave the following order of sectors, starting from the sector with the highest degree of competition to the sector with the lowest: machinery, electronics, chemicals, food & beverages and in the last place the utilities sector, for which regulations are expected to have stifled the market as a monitoring instance.

No hypotheses are set up to test for differences in the risk of companies, as there is a nonlinearity assumed here depending on the degree of managerial participation in the firm. As in Germany data on managerial stakes in firms is unavailable and considered to fall under the laws of privacy, no meaningful results can be expected. Limited data on bank participation in the form of blockholders, supervisory board seats held by banks, and extent of proxy voting rights exercised by banks precludes a separate study of the effect of bank ownership on performance.[85]

---

84 See chapter 2.3.2.6. This implies that all companies in a sector are competing in the same relevant market, which is a bold assumption considering the geographical separation of markets for some goods and the variety of actual products being produced by companies in the same sector.

85 Chirinko/Elston (1996) find no relation between bank influence and performance in Germany for a small sample of firms before 1989.

4.3.3 Previous Empirical Research

Table 4-5 gives an overview over performance-related research on the basis of agency theory. In order to reduce the size of the table, only those studies were included that are similar to this analysis, with the exception of Morck/Shleifer/Vishny (1988) and Chen/Hexter/Hu (1993), who both use data on managerial ownership. Both papers find a nonlinear relationship between the level of managerial ownership and Tobin's q.

The influence of bank control, another test outside of the scope of this study, is tested by Cable (1985) and Gorton/Schmid (1996). Both find some support that bank control improves performance. More references can be found above in chapter 4.1.2.

author (year)	dependent variables	independent variables	method country/period	results
Monsen/Chiu/ Cooley (1968)	• return on equity	• block ownership • sector • size • year	ANOVA USA 1952-63	owner control ≻ manager control
Kamerschen (1968)	• return on equity	• block ownership • sector • size • concentration	correlations USA 1959-64	no difference
Hindley (1970)	• book to market price of equity	• block ownership • sector	OLS USA 1930/35/40	no difference
Larner (1970)	• return on equity	• block ownership • size • concentration • leverage	OLS USA 1956-62	owner control ≻ manager control
Radice (1971)	• return on equity	• block ownership • size • sector	OLS GB 1957-67	owner control ≻ manager control
Bouderaux (1973)	• return on equity	• block ownership • sector • size • risk	ANOVA USA 1952-63	owner control ≻ manager control
Palmer (1973)	• return on equity	• block ownership • size	ANOVA USA 1961-69	owner control ≻ manager control in monopolistic

author (year)	dependent variables	independent variables	method country/period	results
		• monopolistic power		markets
Sorensen (1974)	• return on equity	• block ownership • sector	ANOVA USA 1948-66	no difference
Ware (1975)	• return on equity	• block ownership	covariance analysis for food & beverages sector USA 1960-70	manager control ≻ owner control
Holl (1975)	• return on equity	• block ownership • sector • size	discriminant analysis GB 1948-60	owner control ≻ manager control
McEachern (1975)	• stock return	• block ownership	OLS USA 1963-72	owner/manager control ≻ owner control ≻ manager control
Kania/McKean (1976)	• return on equity • market return	• block ownership • sector • size	ANOVA USA 1963-72	owner control ≻ manager control
Qualls (1976)	• return on equity	• block ownership • concentration • monopolistic power	OLS USA 1961-69	owner control ≻ manager control
Holl (1977)	• market to book value of assets	• block ownership • size • market entry barriers	ANOVA USA 1962-72	owner control ≻ manager control
Thonet (1977)	• return on equity	• block ownership • size • monopolistic power	OLS G 1961, 1966, 1970	manager control ≻ owner control
Kamin/Ronen (1978)	• net operating income	• block ownership • market entry barriers	OLS USA 1965-69	manager-controlled companies smooth income more than owner-controlled companies
Thonet/	• return on	• block owner-	OLS	manager control

author (year)	dependent variables	independent variables	method country/period	results
Poensgen (1979)	equity	ship • size • monopolistic power	G 1961-70	≻ owner control
Bühner (1984)	• Jensen's α	• block ownership • diversification	OLS G 1966-81	owner control ≻ manager control
Cable (1985)	• net profit/total assets	• bank block ownership • bank supervisory board seats • ratio of monitored to unmonitored debt • concentration	OLS G 1974	bank control (weakly) improves performance
Kaulmann (1987)	• return on equity • return on investment	• block ownership • size • sector	OLS G, F, GB 1975-84	no difference
Morck/Shleifer/ Vishny (1988)	• Tobin's q	• management ownership • size • leverage • sector • intangible assets	piecewise OLS USA 1980	first positive, then negative (later again positive) relation
Murali/Welch (1989)	• return on equity • return on capital • market model beta • Sharpe ratio • Treynor measure • Jensen's α	• block ownership • size • firm-specific risk • intangible assets	OLS USA 1977-81	no difference
Zeckhauser/ Pound (1990)	• earning/price ratio	• block ownership • intangible assets	t-tests USA 1988	block ownership is effective in firms with low intangible assets
Chen/Hexter/ Hu (1993)	• Tobin's q	• management ownership	nonlinear regression	relation switches from positive to negative and

author (year)	dependent variables	independent variables	method country/period	results
			USA 1976/80/84	back to positive
Lipka (1995)	• return on equity • return on capital	• block ownership • size • sector • concentration • leverage • cost structure	OLS G 1982-88	no difference (return on equity) owner control ≻ manager control (return on capital)
Gorton/Schmid (1996)	• return on equity • return on capital	• block ownership of banks • size • sector • voting restrictions • foreign ownership	semiparametric estimation G 1974/85	bank control improves performance

Table 4-5: Previous empirical studies of agency determinants of performance

Book-to-market equity, a measure similar to Tobin's q, is used as a performance measure by Hindley (1970) and Hull (1977). The main performance measure is the return on equity, while market-valued performance measures are fairly rare (McEachern 1975, Kania/McKean 1976, Bühner 1984, Murali/Welch 1989). Size is generally used only as a control variable, not as an agency variable. Murali/Welch (1989) and Zeckhauser/Pound (1990) use the intangible assets and R&D expenses as a measure of asset specificity, which makes monitoring harder.

The results are mixed and find advantages for manager controlled firms (Ware 1975, Thonet 1977, Thonet/Poensgen 1979) or owner controlled firms (McEachern 1975, Holl 1977, Qualls 1976, Lipka 1995 et al.). Kamerschen (1978), Hindley (1970), Sorensen (1974), Kaulmann (1987) Murali/Welch (1989) and Lipka (1995) do not find any difference in performance.[86] There is a slight tendency toward owner-controlled companies showing better performance.

Studies for the German capital market are Thonet (1977), Thonet/Poensgen (1979), Bühner (1984), Cable (1985), Kaulmann (1987), Lipka (1995) and Gor-

[86] Picot (1991), p. 161, endnote 10 links this result to the fact that the ownership transferred the coordination rights to the management of its own free will and can recall those rights anytime. He does not see the need for disciplining instances in the form of ownership surrogates such as the market for managers.

ton/Schmid (1996). The results for Germany are especially inconclusive, possibly due to the different time periods tested.

4.3.4 Empirical Results

4.3.4.1 Comprehensive Analysis

4.3.4.1.1 Descriptives of the Variables

Table 4-6 below shows the descriptives of the performance variables for the time period to be analyzed, 1986-1992. The average return on equity of 7 % is slightly higher than the average return on capital (5 %), which is in accordance with theory. Shareholders bear greater risks of a company and are therefore entitled to a higher return. The on average negative Sharpe ratio is somewhat astounding, The high standard deviation of the variable, 4.27, for an average Sharpe ratio of -.68, could help explain this observation. Sharpe's ratio is not significantly negative. Temporal developments might also shed more light on this question (see Figure 4-7 below on p. 166). The average value for Tobin's q, 187 %, is very similar to studies for the US.[87] The value greater than 100 % signifies that the market value of fixed assets in place was higher than their book value in the seven years.[88]

variable	minim.	median	mean	maxim.	std. dev.
return on equity	-97.00 %	7.00 %	7.00 %	468.00 %	22.00 %
return on capital	-39.00 %	5.10 %	5.00 %	71.00 %	6.00 %
Sharpe ratio	-18.12	-.91	-.68	17.49	4.27
Tobin's q	68.00 %	159.00 %	187.00 %	496.00 %	82.00 %

N = 1119

Table 4-6: Descriptives of the performance measures, 1986-1992

87 Cf. Badrinath/Kini (1994), p. 129.

88 The net demand of companies for investment goods rose 3.6 % in the 80s, vs. 3.3 % in the 70s. Earlier and later years show much higher rates due to the "Wiederaufbau" and "Wirtschaftswunder" before 1970, and the reunification process in the 1990s. Cf. Institut der deutschen Wirtschaft (1996).

The descriptive statistics for the original agency variables are given below in Table 4-7. In the t-tests, they are used in dichotomous form to separate the companies into two groups by degree of agency problem, but in the logistic regressions the variables are used as is.[89] The importance of dividend signals for performance has already been detailed elsewhere (see chapter 2.3.2.2). Both the values for block ownership and ratio of monitored to unmonitored debt cover the entire range from zero to 100 %. The size and debt-equity ratios have fairly large standard deviations, showing that a diverse set of companies in regard to total assets and leverage are present in the data sample. There are about 160 companies per year.

variable	minim.	median	mean	maxim.	std. dev.
block ownership	0.00 %	71.00 %	63.00 %	100.00 %	29.00 %
size *)	9.21	12.85	12.97	17.83	1.80
market segment **)	1	3	2.47	3	.88
dividend signal ***)	0	1	0.98	1	.15
leverage	0	0.469	0.86	27.28	1.44
ratio monitored to unmonitored debt	0.00 %	0.00 %	43.00 %	100.00 %	50.00 %

N = 1119 *) logarithmed thousands of 1992 DM **) 1 = free trade; 2 = official daily trade 3 = official continuous trade ***) 1 if dividend hike occurred in current or previous year

Table 4-7: Descriptives of the agency variables, 1986-1992

4.3.4.1.2 T-Tests for Differences in Mean Performance

T-tests for differences in the mean performance values are the first statistical analyses run on the data. The tests use the dichotomous nature of the agency variables to divide the data into owner-controlled or manager-controlled, or in the case of the monitored debt ratio, creditor-controlled and manager-controlled. Due to the wealth of information the t-tests produce, again only the differences and significances thereof are listed below in Table 4-8. The differences are computed by subtracting the performance of the manager-controlled firms from that of the owner- or creditor-controlled companies, so that positive differences confirm the first two hypotheses. The first hypothesis states that owner-controlled firms should perform better than manager-controlled ones in return on equity and Tobin's q, with insignificant results expected for the return on capital and

[89] Except for the market segment variable, for which two dummies are created.

Sharpe ratio. The rows for the block ownership through leverage variables and the agency conglomerates in the Table 4-8 below can be used to test this hypothesis.

In general, significant results will be given greater weight than insignificant ones, and the major agency variables block ownership, *agency1* and *agency5* will also be given more attention. If few results are significant, I will also acknowledge a majority of correct signs in differences or coefficients as supportive of a hypothesis.[90]

	return on equity		return on capital		Sharpe ratio		Tobin's q	
	diff	sig	diff	sig	diff	sig	diff	sig
expected sign	+		+		o		+	
block ownership	.0290		-.0019		-.1079		.4230	***
size	.0215		.0098	*	-.1448		-.2954	***
market segment	-.0249		-.0032		.1185		.0286	
dividend signal	.0282		.0235	*	-.3739		.2482	**
leverage	-.0788	***	-.0262	***	.2402		-.4152	
monitored debt ratio	-.0074		.0024		-.0565		-.4036	
agency1	-.0086		-.0092		-.4555		.0468	
agency2	.0046		-.0056		-.2666		.0699	
agency3	-.0358	**	-.0188	***	.2850		-.3191	***
agency4	.0107		.0019		-.4388		-.1442	*
agency5	.0184		-.0019		-.0769		.3545	
agency6	-.0262	*	-.0120	**	-.0359		.0108	
agency7	.0393		.0151		.2202		.3857	***

*** = significant at 1 %-level (** = 5 %; * = 10 %)

Table 4-8: T-tests for differences of means of performance measures for groups with and without agency problems, by agency variable, 1986-1992

For the return on equity column, most differences are not significant, and those that are have negative signs. None of the differences of the key variables block ownership, *agency1* and *agency5* are significant, and the difference for *agency1*

90 For the hypotheses concerning the Sharpe ratio that call for insignificant results, the signs of the results will not be evaluated if they are insignificant.

is negative. All in all this rejects the first hypothesis for the return on equity. The results for the return on capital provide more significant differences than for the return on equity, where three of the five significant differences are negative. The signs of the differences using block ownership, *agency1* and *agency5* are also negative, again leading to a rejection of the hypothesis. No differences in the Sharpe ratio are significant, meaning that manager-controlled firms are no better and no worse at beating the fixed risk-free interest rates than owner-controlled firms after adjusting for risk. This directly supports the hypothesized insignificance of agency problems in regard to the Sharpe ratio. Finally, there is both significant support for and rejection of the first hypothesis when going by Tobin's q. The insignificant results have the positive sign that is demanded in the hypothesis, except for the leverage factor. So to sum up, the first hypothesis is rejected except for the addendum that the Sharpe ratio is not significantly different for either group of companies.

The ratio of monitored to unmonitored debt, and to a lesser extent, the leverage factor, can be used to test the second hypothesis, stating that the manager-controlled firms will underperform the creditor-controlled ones, especially with regard to the return on capital. In contrast to the other agency variables that separate owner-controlled companies from manager-controlled ones, this variable is used to split the companies into creditor-controlled and manager-controlled ones. The leverage variable is used for both of these purposes. Again, the calculation of the differences calls for positive signs if the hypothesis is valid. The hypothesis is rejected by all performance measures except the Sharpe ratio, with a majority of negative signs. For the Sharpe ratio the insignificant results was expected. The two significant differences in particular have negative signs.

The third hypothesis states that creditor control should be less effective than owner control with respect to the return on equity and Tobin's q, and more effective in generating return on capital. It is tested by comparing the average performance of the groups of companies that count as monitored by the ownership when using either block ownership or *agency5* to the performance of companies that count as monitored by creditors when using the ratio of monitored to unmonitored debt. The conglomerates *agency1* to *agency4* are not used to ascertain owner control, as they also contain the monitored debt ratio are not suitable for this hypothesis. The other agency variables are not used here to reduce the data flood.

	return on equity		return on capital		Sharpe ratio		Tobin's q	
	diff	sig	diff	sig	diff	sig	diff	sig
expected sign	+		–		o		+	
block ownership	0.76 %		-0.16 %		1.89		27.71 %	***
agency5	0.62 %		-0.15 %		2.33		26.57 %	***

*** = significant at 1 %-level (** = 5 %; * = 10 %)

Table 4-9: T-tests for differences of means of the performance measures between owner-controlled and creditor-controlled companies, 1986-1992[91]

In contrast to the results in Table 4-8, the groups so created can overlap. In Table 4-8, the block ownership variable for example splits the data into two groups, depending on if the ownership is greater/equal or less than 25 %. High block ownership means ownership control, low block ownership manager control. In Table 4-9, the high ownership companies are compared to those that count as creditor-controlled according to the monitored debt ratio. These are the companies with a ratio greater than 10 %. Obviously, there will be companies with high block ownership and high monitored debt ratio levels, causing the overlaps in the groups.

The signs in the first unshaded row of Table 4-9 show that the differences were calculated so that the third hypothesis is supported by positive differences for the return on equity and Tobin's q, and negative signs for the return on capital. The signs are correct for all three of these performance measures, and the differences using Tobin's q are even significant at the 1 % level. For the Sharpe ratio, the insignificant differences are on par with expectations, so on the whole the hypothesis is not rejected for the comprehensive data.

4.3.4.1.3 Logistic Regressions

While the t-tests either tested for the influence of each agency variable singly, or could only jointly account for all variables if they were previously aggregated into the agency conglomerates, the logistic regressions permit the agency variables to be simultaneously but separately entered in their original (non-dummy) form. Possible interaction between the agency variables is captured in this way. The regression model requires the dependent variables, in this case the performance variables, to be provided in a dichotomous form. In order to do this, sector-level means were calculated, and for all instances where the company's perform-

---

91 Differences are to the companies that count as monitored by creditors according to the ratio of monitored to unmonitored debt.

ance exceeded its sector mean, the dummy was set to one, and zero otherwise. Due to this calculation, sector dummies were not included in the functional description.[92] The creditor control variable monitored debt ratio was excluded in the first regression equation model which will be used to test the first hypothesis. The monitored debt ratio and the leverage are the independents in the second model, which tests the efficacy of creditor control.

In addition, the logistic regression was also run over the agency conglomerate variables. Since this additional aggregation of the agency variables is not strictly necessary when using the logistic regression methodology, only the two major agency conglomerates *agency1* and *agency5* that were not calculated with the aid of genetic algorithms were used. The conglomerates have the advantage of returning only one coefficient that can be directly compared to the sign expected.

In all regressions, no constant was included, which reduces the instances of simply classifying all cases into the stronger of the two groups, which would secure a classification score of above 50 %, but at the same time be a meaningless result. These instances still do occur, though, and are usually noticeable by significant model chi-squares, although none of the variables have significant coefficients. The lack of significant coefficients signifies that agency factors have no impact on performance levels.

The results of logistic regressions are shown in the same format as for the earlier analysis of financial structure. This operationalization of the variables mostly calls for positive signs of the coefficients, meaning that as the level of monitoring or control rises, the performance is expected to rise, too. The insignificant results that are expected for the Sharpe ratio are symbolized by the "o" in the row for the expected sign.

A large number of coefficients are significant for the returns on equity and capital, as well as Tobin's q, which conforms to the first hypothesis in the sense that agency problems affect performance, just as the lack of significance of most of the agency variables for the Sharpe ratio is expected. The dividend signal is closely linked to high performance, a plausible result even without an agency theoretic background. However, many of the significant coefficients are negative, especially for the book measures of performance. In addition, the first hypothesis calls for a decreased importance of agency variables for the return on capital. This is definitely not the case. The conglomerate variables, too, significantly support the negative relation of agency control and performance. This means that increasing the control over the management actually decreases especially the returns on equity and capital, and leads to a rejection of the first hy-

92 Tests run including the dummies gave no differences in signs or significance of the coefficients of the agency variables.

pothesis. The classification scores must be compared to the random classification benchmark, which lies at about 50 %. The results for the Sharpe ratio are poor according to this criterion, which is the expected outcome.

	dependent variable							
independent variables	return on equity		return on capital		Sharpe ratio		Tobin's q	
expected sign	+		+		o		+	
model 1								
block ownership	-.5565	***	-1.2354	***	.3303	*	.9118	***
size	-.0364		.0020		-.0018		-.1351	***
market segment 1	-.3967	**	-.6399	***	-.1282		.2018	
market segment 2	-.3881		-.4665	*	-.0517		-.0913	
dividend signal	1.2097	***	1.4769	***	-.1183		.8238	**
leverage	-.3013	***	-.3310	***	-.0704		-.4065	***
-2 log likelihood‡	1498.161	***	1472.089	***	1525.179		1407.853	***
% correct classification	58.00		61.04		52.80		63.63	
model 2								
leverage	-.3151	***	-.3240		-.0784	*	-.4108	***
monitored debt ratio	.2873	**	.6398		.0168		-.6274	***
-2 log likelihood‡	1510.868	***	1504.225	***	1529.399		1436.139	***
% correct classification	54.42		57.19		52.44		62.38	
model 3								
agency1	-.1978	***	-.1088	*	-.0691		-.5226	***
-2 log likelihood‡	1541.586	***	1548.328	*	1532.067		1485.632	***
% correct classification	53.71		52.82		51.18		59.96	
model 4								
agency5	-.1783	***	-.1060	*	-.0547		-.4531	***
-2 log likelihood‡	1543.340	***	1548.456	*	1532.503		1501.165	***
% correct classification	52.90		52.73		50.54		57.19	

N = 1119; *** = significant on the 1 % level (** = 5 %; * = 10 %); ‡ = significance of model chi-square

Table 4-10: Coefficients and overall results of the logistic regressions on the performance dummy variables, 1986-1992[93]

---

93 The market segment dummy 1 is one for official continuous trade, the second dummy is one for official daily trade.

The second hypothesis can be tested using the results from the second model, where again positive signs for the coefficients for the leverage ratio and especially the monitored debt ratio are expected. Five of the eight coefficients are negative, and the additional requirement that the return on capital show the most significant results is exactly reversed. This leads to a clear rejection of this hypothesis, too.

hypothesis #	method	return on equity	return on capital	Sharpe ratio	Tobin's q	overall
1	t-tests	☐	☐	☑	☐	☐
1	logistic regression	☐	☐	☐	☐	☐
overall		☐	☐	(☐)	☐	☐
2	t-tests	☐	☐	☑	☐	☐
2	logistic regression	☐	☐	☐	☐	☐
overall		☐	☐	(☐)	☐	☐
3	t-tests	☑	☑	☑	☑	☑

Table 4-11: Overview over the validity of hypotheses one to three; comprehensive tests 1986-1992[94]

Overall, Table 4-11 shows that the comprehensive analysis rejects both the first and second hypotheses, and confirms the third. The logistic regressions in particular do not support the hypotheses.

4.3.4.2 Yearly Analysis

To start off the analysis of the performance by years, Figure 4-6 and Figure 4-7 show graphically the development of the performance measures over time. Figure 4-6 shows that the return on equity and return on capital capture markedly different developments. Their correlation of almost 75 % given in Table 4-4 is high, given the course each variable takes over the years. The return on equity swings sharply while the return on capital stays inside a corridor of four to six percent. This demonstrates the nature of the net profit of the year as a residual

[94] A check marks a hypothesis that could not be rejected according to the model given at the top of the column.

profit measure that falls to the shareholders after all other obligations have been accounted for. In some years, this residual can be smaller, in others higher.

In addition, Figure 4-6 shows that the tenet that the return on equity should be higher than the return on capital holds in all years except 1992, where the return on equity continues a downward trend started in 1990 to dip below the return on capital.

Figure 4-6: Development of average returns on equity and capital over time

The other two performance measures are depicted in Figure 4-7. The average yearly Sharpe ratio figures range from – 4 to 3, which is due to marked performances of few companies (even after removing outliers). The unusual pattern coupled with the high variance of the variable could make the Sharpe ratio the hardest to explain of the performance measures by using agency variables. The average Tobin's q variables on the other hand lie for the most part between 150 % and 200 %.

Tobin's q is the performance variable most highly correlated with the Sharpe ratio (ca. 16 %), which becomes apparent when the patterns of the two variables are compared. Both have high values in 1986, then drop to low points in 1987. The next two years the measures increase, and then decrease again from 1990 on. The reason for this correlation lies in the use of market-valued equity in both measures.

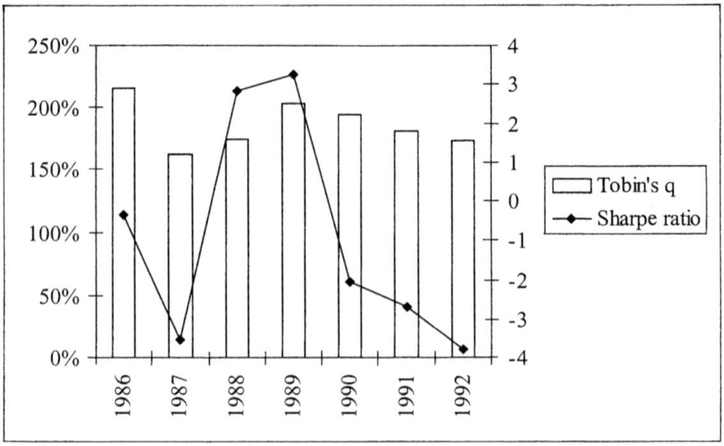

Figure 4-7: Development of average Sharpe ratios and values for Tobin's q over time[95]

4.3.4.2.1 T-Tests for Differences in Mean Performance

The t-tests for the years 1992, 1990 and 1988 are again shown inside the main body of the text, while the results for the other years can be found in the appendix, and will also partially be discussed and used in graphs here. A greater stress will be laid upon the results for the block ownership, *agency1* and *agency5* variables, as regards hypotheses concerning ownership control. The results for the first two hypotheses for 1992 are in Table 4-12. Unfortunately, the dividend signal does not split the data into two subsamples for this year.

The first hypothesis states that manager control is worse than owner control for the return on equity, Tobin's q and to a lesser degree return on capital. The hypothesis is tested by checking the differences for block ownership through leverage in the table, as well as the seven conglomerate variables. For the return on equity in 1992, the signs for the non-significant coefficient alternate between positive and negative, giving no real support for the hypothesis that ownership control produces a higher return on equity than manager control. The two conglomerate variables *agency6* and *agency7*, however, have significant positive differences, with 7.4 % and even 33.7 % higher returns on equity in owner-controlled firms. No signs are significant for the return on capital, which conforms to the hypothesis claiming that owners are evaluate companies by their return on equity more than their return on capital. For the Sharpe ratio, insignifi-

95 Left axis: Tobin's q; right axis: Sharpe ratio.

cant differences were demanded, and only the size and *agency4* variables have significant (negative) ones, which is contrary to the theory. The positive signs for the block ownership, *agency1* and *agency5* support the hypothesis for Tobin's q, but many other variables produce negative and for size and leverage significant differences. This means that on the whole the first hypothesis is rejected for the firms in 1992.

	return on equity		return on capital		Sharpe ratio		Tobin's q	
	diff	sig	diff	sig	diff	sig	diff	sig
expected sign	+		+		o		+	
block ownership	.0246		-.0192		-.5337		.4658	***
size	.0404		.0253		-1.5710	*	-.5023	*
market segment	.0539		.0145		-.3552		-.2275	
dividend signal[96]	N/A		N/A		N/A		N/A	
leverage	-.0463		-.0028		.0901		-.2948	**
monitored debt ratio	-.0612	**	-.0178		-.1440		-.3648	***
agency1	-.0329		-.0172		-2.1867		.2013	
agency2	.0046		-.0243		-1.2961		.0945	
agency3	-.0098		.0033		-.3427		-.2356	
agency4	.0351		.0138		-3.2267	***	-.5286	
agency5	.0461		-.0135		.0907		.3903	
agency6	.0736	*	.0213		-.4758		-.0133	
agency7	.3374	**	-.0048		3.4204		.7106	

*** = significant at 1 %-level (** = 5 %; * = 10 %)

Table 4-12: T-tests for differences of means of performance measures for groups with and without agency problems, by agency variable, 1992

The second hypothesis states that manager-control is worse than creditor control, especially as regards the return on capital. The hypothesis is tested using the agency variables monitored debt ratio and to a lesser extent the leverage ratio. Here an almost clean sweep of negative differences, over half of them significant, make it easy to reject the hypothesis that creditor control was effective in 1992.

---

96 The dividend signal is a constant for the companies in 1992.

	return on equity diff	sig	return on capital diff	sig	Sharpe ratio diff	sig	Tobin's q diff	sig
expected sign	+		+		o		+	
block ownership	-.0055		-.0147		1.3276	**	.6428	***
size	.0138		.0202	**	-.7886		-.3434	*
market segment	-.0067		-.0005		-.6686		-.0548	
dividend signal	.0699		.0514		-1.8574		-.2342	
leverage	-.0593	***	-.0163		1.4482	**	-.3766	***
monitored debt ratio	.0055		.0137	*	.4536		-.3722	***
agency1	-.0060		.0004		1.5567	**	.3492	
agency2	.0090		.0044		1.7046	**	.2922	*
agency3	.0092		.0072		.3862		.3035	
agency4	-.0459	***	-.0182	**	-.3945		-.2432	*
agency5	.0052		.0206		1.1978		.0121	
agency6	-.0145		-.0154		-.2250		.5659	***
agency7	-.0343	**	-.0150	*	-.1292		.2459	

*** = significant at 1 %-level (** = 5 %; * = 10 %)

Table 4-13: T-tests for differences of means of performance measures for groups with and without agency problems, by agency variable, 1990

In 1990, all significant differences in return on equity are negative, and two of the major variables, block ownership and *agency1*, have negative signs as well. The return on capital often shows fairly small differences of less than one percent, but two of the three significant differences are negative (*agency4* and *agency7*). This does not support the theory. The Sharpe ratios have four significant differences, all of which are positive. The theoretical considerations state, however, that the Sharpe ratio should be independent of agency influences. For Tobin's q, a mixed bag of signs of the significant results contradicts the three positive signs for the major agency variables. Block ownership does have an important effect on the performance measure, giving a q almost 65 % higher than manager-controlled q's. Still, for all performance measures the first hypothesis cannot be accepted as valid.

The second hypothesis produces three negative significant differences versus two positive significant ones, one of which is for the Sharpe ratio. The return on capital is significantly higher by 1.37 % when going by the monitored debt ratio. With only this single result speaking for the second hypothesis, this hypothesis, like already for 1992, is rejected for 1990.

	return on equity diff	sig	return on capital diff	sig	Sharpe ratio diff	sig	Tobin's q diff	sig
expected sign	+		+		o		+	
block ownership	-.0135		-.0088		-1.7013	**	.3854	***
size	.0060		-.0058		1.0333	*	-.2902	**
market segment	.0109		.0009		1.1395	*	.1150	
dividend signal	.0203		.0190		.3455		.2292	
leverage	-.0973	**	-.0378	***	.6049		-.4091	***
monitored debt ratio	-.0276		-.0002		-.2983		-.3980	***
agency1	-.0068		-.0068		-1.2657		-.0197	
agency2	-.0045		-.0033		-.9197		.0333	
agency3	-.0411	**	-.0223	*	-.5093		-.3663	***
agency4	.0084		-.0104		1.3461	*	-.0857	
agency5	-.0062		-.0061		-1.3025		.3477	***
agency6	-.0197		-.0095		-.4013		-.0038	
agency7	.0072		.0214		.4330		.4144	

*** = significant at 1 %-level (** = 5 %; * = 10 %)

Table 4-14: T-tests for differences of means of performance measures for groups with and without agency problems, by agency variable, 1988

The 1988 data produce very similar results, with negative differences in return on equity for the three major variables, and two significantly negative differences for this performance measure. The differences in return on capital are often below 1 %, which supports the first hypothesis, while the Sharpe ratios have many high differences, four of which significant. The block ownership variable produces a negative difference, the size, market segment and *agency4* positive ones. No significant differences are called for by the first hypothesis. Going by Tobin's q, the first hypothesis is confirmed for block ownership and *agency5*, but size, leverage and *agency3* reject the hypothesis with significantly negative signs. Again, the support is not enough to not reject the first hypothesis.

For the second hypothesis the usual clear rejection emerges due to almost completely negative and in half the cases significant differences in performance between creditor-controlled and manager-controlled firms.

The third hypothesis states that ownership control should be superior to creditor control with regard to the return on equity and Tobin's q, and vice versa for the return on capital. The groups compared are all companies with a high level of block ownership and those with a high ratio of monitored to unmonitored debt, and companies with a value of one for *agency5* and the high monitored debt ratio companies. These groups are not mutually exclusive, as opposed to the groups compared above. The results for the t-tests for differences of means start below in Table 4-15. The differences were again calculated so that positive signs for the return on equity as well as Tobin's q and a negative sign for the return on capital support the hypothesis.

	return on equity		return on capital		Sharpe ratio		Tobin's q	
	diff	sig	diff	sig	diff	sig	diff	sig
expected sign	+		–		o		+	
block ownership	3.91 %		0.87 %		0.0294		26.39 %	*
agency5	3.98 %		0.97 %		0.0928		24.50 %	*

*** = significant at 1 %-level (** = 5 %; * = 10 %)

Table 4-15: T-tests for differences of means of the performance measures between owner-controlled and creditor-controlled companies, 1992[97]

For 1992, no negative signs occur at all, but only the differences in Tobin's q are significant. The very small differences speak for the hypothesis in the case of the Sharpe ratio and to a degree for the return on capital, but not with regard to the return on equity. Still, the hypothesis can be considered to be supported.

	return on equity		return on capital		Sharpe ratio		Tobin's q	
	diff	sig	diff	sig	diff	sig	diff	sig
expected sign	+		–		o		+	
block ownership	-0.38 %		-0.95 %		-0.0784		29.11 %	**
agency5	-0.48 %		-0.94 %		-0.1111		27.42 %	**

*** = significant at 1 %-level (** = 5 %; * = 10 %)

Table 4-16: T-tests for differences of means of the performance measures between owner-controlled and creditor-controlled companies, 1990[98]

97 Differences are to the companies that count as monitored by creditors according to the ratio of monitored to unmonitored debt.

98 Differences are to the companies that count as monitored by creditors according to the ratio of monitored to unmonitored debt.

Negative signs for the return on equity do not support the third hypothesis for the 1990 data, but again the return on capital and especially Tobin's q confirm it. For 1988 the same can be said, with the added support of positive differences of around 1.5 % for the return on equity. So the hypothesis that owner control is better than creditor control is upheld for the three years presented here, even though the other two hypotheses in the ring of relationships owners-managers-creditors-owners were rejected. Considering the almost straight negative signs that signify higher performance levels for manager-controlled firms compared to creditor-controlled ones, a picture emerges that manager and owner control are equally beneficial to performance, while both dominate creditor control — with regard to the return on equity and Tobin's q, which are performance measures of lesser relevance for creditors (see Figure 4-8).

	return on equity		return on capital		Sharpe ratio		Tobin's q	
	diff	sig	diff	sig	diff	sig	diff	sig
expected sign	+		–		o		+	
block ownership	1.47 %		-0.09 %		-0.0152		27.72 %	***
agency5	1.55 %		-0.06 %		-0.0296		27.30 %	***

*** = significant at 1 %-level (** = 5 %; * = 10 %)

Table 4-17: T-tests for differences of means of the performance measures between owner-controlled and creditor-controlled companies, 1988[99]

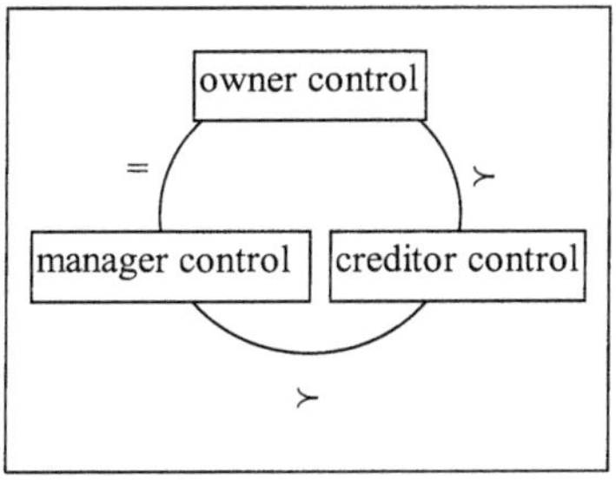

Figure 4-8: Ranking of the advantageousness of the three control groups regarding return on equity and Tobin's q for the years 1992, 1990 and 1988

99 Differences are to the companies that count as monitored by creditors according to the ratio of monitored to unmonitored debt.

The t-tests for the other years in the appendix also do not show consistent support for first two hypotheses. The second hypothesis is most easily rejected by a large majority of negative and often significant differences, even for the Sharpe ratio. The third hypothesis receives enough support to consider it accepted for all the yearly tests. Especially Tobin's q produces significant results in favor of the hypothesis. This confirms the structure suggested in Figure 4-8.

4.3.4.2.2 Logistic Regressions

The methodology used again allows for hypotheses one and two to be tested for. The only agency conglomerates reported on here are *agency1* and *agency5*, as this methodology mainly should test the joint explanatory power of the six agency variables. The single sign of the conglomerate variables does make interpretation easier, though. The agency variables are entered in their non-dichotomous form, so the two market segment dummies were used again. If the first dummy is one, the market segment is official continuous trade, if the second is one, the segment is official daily trade. Both dummies at zero means the company is in the free trade segment. The dividend signal is dichotomous in its original form.

The logit models reported for below in Table 4-18 and following were estimated without constants as before. The dependent performance variables are dummy variables, with a value of one if they are greater than the mean value of that performance measure for the sector the company belongs to, and zero otherwise. This means that positive coefficients support the theories stating that the lower the agency problems (= the higher the agency control and monitoring variables) are for a company, the higher the performance will be in that company.

The first hypothesis (owner control is better than manager control) demands positive coefficients for the block ownership through leverage variables and the agency conglomerates, *agency1* and *agency5*. The second hypothesis (creditor control is better than manager control) can be tested by checking the signs of the leverage and especially the monitored debt ratio coefficients. There the signs must again be positive, as also for the third hypothesis claiming the advantageousness of ownership control over creditor control. The interpretation for this is that when moving from owner-controlled companies to creditor-controlled ones, the positive signs show that performance increases. No significant coefficients are expected for the Sharpe ratio.

independent variables	dependent variable: return on equity	return on capital	Sharpe ratio	Tobin's q
expected sign	+	+	o	+
model 1				
block ownership	.0186	-1.7547 **	.2271	2.2930 **
size	-.0022	-.0327	-.2347	-.1613
market segment 1	.1111	-1.0151	.0088	-.3906
market segment 2	-.0475	-1.4352	.7653	-.4464
dividend signal	-.5590	2.7385	1.1565	-.0750
leverage	-.0692	-.1867	-.0017	-.1295
-2 log likelihood‡	133.136	131.810	88.800 ***	106.899 ***
% correct classification	63.73	62.75	83.65	74.51
model 2				
leverage	-.1681	-.0614	-.3652	-.3961 *
monitored debt ratio	-.6062	-.1027	-6.1839 **	-2.0605 *
-2 log likelihood‡	134.890 **	140.706	107.825 ***	121.185 ***
% correct classification	65.69	50.00	79.81	71.57
model 3				
agency1	-.6007 ***	.0417	-1.6339 ***	-.9904 ***
-2 log likelihood‡	133.115 ***	141.360	95.547 ***	120.462 ***
% correct classification	63.73	51.96	79.81	69.61
model 4				
agency5	-.5390 **	.0632	-1.5361 ***	-.9237 ***
-2 log likelihood‡	134.745 ***	141.307	100.743 ***	123.112 ***
% correct classification	60.78	51.96	75.96	66.67

N = 102; *** = significant on the 1 % level (** = 5 %; * = 10 %); ‡ = significance of model chi-square

Table 4-18: Coefficients and overall results of the logistic regressions on the performance dummy variables, 1992[100]

[100] The market segment dummy 1 is one for official continuous trade, the second dummy is one for official daily trade.

	dependent variable			
independent variables	return on equity	return on capital	Sharpe ratio	Tobin's q
expected sign	+	+	o	+
	model 1			
block ownership	-.9097	-2.1194 ***	1.5457 **	1.1574 *
size	-.0317	.0228	-.2482 **	-.2552 **
market segment 1	-.3939	-.5388	-.1016	.1954
market segment 2	-.1992	-.5869	-1.0452	-.4078
dividend signal	1.3318	1.8698	1.3952	2.2310
leverage	-.2764	-.1224	.1989	-.2445
-2 log likelihood‡	211.392	200.604 ***	173.900 ***	197.957 ***
% correct classification	58.23	65.82	69.28	66.46
	model 2			
leverage	-.3413 **	-.1584	-.1912	-.1561
monitored debt ratio	.4810	1.1729 **	-.3665	-1.2694 **
-2 log likelihood‡	213.275 *	211.490 **	207.764 **	205.235 ***
% correct classification	50.63	60.76	65.36	59.49
	model 3			
agency1	-.2007	.2296	-.6711 ***	-.3758 **
-2 log likelihood‡	217.632	217.202	197.608 ***	214.178 **
% correct classification	54.43	56.33	60.13	55.70
	model 4			
agency5	-.2007	-.2007	-.6599 ***	-.3169 *
-2 log likelihood‡	217.632	217.632	198.165 ***	215.563 *
% correct classification	54.43	54.43	59.48	56.13

N = 158; *** = significant on the 1 % level (** = 5 %; * = 10 %); ‡ = significance of model chi-square

Table 4-19: Coefficients and overall results of the logistic regressions on the performance dummy variables, 1990[101]

[101] The market segment dummy 1 is one for official continuous trade, the second dummy is one for official daily trade.

For 1992, only the lack of significant signs for the first model regression on the Sharpe ratio supports the first hypothesis, while for example a very significant positive coefficient for block ownership when regressed on Tobin's q is counteracted by straight negative signs for the other variables' coefficients. The negative coefficients persist when using the agency conglomerates, except for the regressions on the return on capital, which estimate positive, but non-significant coefficients. This is not enough to support the first hypothesis, though. The hypothesis is also rejected by the negative and highly significant signs for the conglomerate models with the Sharpe ratio as the dependent variable.

The classification benchmark scores lie between 50 and 55 %, except for the Sharpe ratio, for which the benchmark is 74 %. This means that the results for this variable are not too good when only few independent variables are used. The same is valid for the return on capital. For both of these variables the results were not expected to be significant for the first hypothesis models.

As for the second hypothesis, the same effects found with the t-tests are visible here, too, where the leverage and monitored debt ratio are simultaneously tested for. All eight coefficients for the four performance measures are negative, resulting in a definite rejection of the hypothesis that manager control is inferior to creditor control as far as performance is concerned. The classification result of 50 % for the return on capital is crushing.

The 1990 results paint much the same picture, with extremely high positive (but insignificant) coefficients for the dividend signal dummy. This fact seems to cause many negative signs for other coefficients, to counterbalance the impact of the dividend dummy variable. The agency conglomerate variables again reject the first hypothesis, especially with a view to the results of the regressions testing creditor control for the Sharpe ratio and Tobin's q, where significant negative coefficients occur. The signs of the monitored debt ratio are positive for both the return on equity and on capital, giving some support to the second hypothesis. This again is not enough to accept the hypothesis for 1990, though. The classification results again show a superiority of the first model with six independent variables, compared to the benchmark of 50 % (60 % for the Sharpe ratio).

Basically there is not enough consistent support for the first hypothesis with the first model, and even a clear rejection of it using the agency conglomerates (the significant positive signs for the Sharpe ratio are not postulated), and the second model only supports the second hypothesis with positive coefficients for the returns on equity and capital in the case of the monitored debt ratio variable.

The 1988 results follow the same pattern described for the other years and will not be detailed.

	dependent variable			
independent variables	return on equity	return on capital	Sharpe ratio	Tobin's q
expected sign	+	+	o	+
		model 1		
block ownership	-.5398	-1.4227 ***	-1.5438 *	.7790
size	-.0269	.0316	.1966 **	-.3029 ***
market segment 1	-.5495	-.6764	.2636	.5565
market segment 2	-.3048	.3279	-.1127	-.0018
dividend signal	1.3296	1.1731	.4509	2.4262 *
leverage	-.5255 ***	-.6590 ***	-.1824	-.5464 **
-2 log likelihood‡	237.127 *	225.928 ***	132.013 ***	199.859 ***
% correct classification	59.44	66.67	87.08	69.44
		model 2		
leverage	-.5296 ***	-.7302 ***	.6823 ***	-.5714 **
monitored debt ratio	.9828 *	1.2249 **	2.8875 ***	-2.6479 ***
-2 log likelihood‡	238.482 ***	231.842 ***	201.562 ***	208.871 ***
% correct classification	56.11	59.44	87.08	71.67
		model 3		
agency1	-.1268	-.2803 *	1.9169 ***	-.9207 ***
-2 log likelihood‡	248.900	246.460 *	149.982 ***	219.289 ***
% correct classification	51.67	56.11	87.08	67.22
		model 4		
agency5	-.1252	-.2768 *	1.8216 ***	-.8177 ***
-2 log likelihood‡	248.908	246.498 *	155.258 ***	224.867 ***
% correct classification	51.67	56.11	87.08	63.89

N = 180; *** = significant on the 1 % level (** = 5 %; * = 10 %); ‡ = significance of model chi-square

Table 4-20: Coefficients and overall results of the logistic regressions on the performance dummy variables, 1988[102]

[102] The market segment dummy 1 is one for official continuous trade, the second dummy is one for official daily trade.

The data for the other years is given in the appendix, and confirms the rejection of the first hypothesis for most performance measures. Only Tobin's q confirms the hypothesis regularly (1986, 1989, 1991) with generally positive coefficients. The second hypothesis receives support from the positive monitored debt ratio coefficients in 1986, 1987 and 1989; the leverage variable however consistently has a negative influence on performance.

4.3.4.2.3 Temporal Developments

The fourth hypothesis is time-related and states that the performance in manager-controlled firms will more quickly decrease and cling to poor levels than owner-controlled firms, if the general economy starts to sag and later rebounds. Figure 4-9 shows the development of the return on equity for the manager-controlled and owner-controlled firms, if block ownership is used to distinguish the two groups. Both follow a general downward trend, but especially the manager-controlled companies produce very volatile returns. In Figure 4-6 above one sees that this translates into an overall decline of the return on equity for the sample period. Therefore the slope for the manager-controlled firms should be steeper (more negative) than that for the owner-controlled firms. Simple ordinary least squares regressions using the years as independent variables gives a slope of -0.007 (significant) for owner-controlled firms and -0.011 for manager-controlled firms, confirming the hypothesis. The full results of the regressions are not reported here.

It is of course possible to repeat this regression test for the other performance measures and for other agency variables. Figure 4-10 and Figure 4-11 show the trends for the return on equity when using *agency1* and *agency5* respectively to determine the control group. For *agency1*, the slope for owner control is -0.005 and for manager control -0.010, and for *agency5* the numbers are -0.006 and -0.008, twice again confirming the fourth hypothesis for the return on equity.

For the return on capital, the hypothesis differentiates between the rate of change in performance between creditor-controlled and manager-controlled companies, as the owners of a company are not as interested in the return on capital as in the equity-based performance.

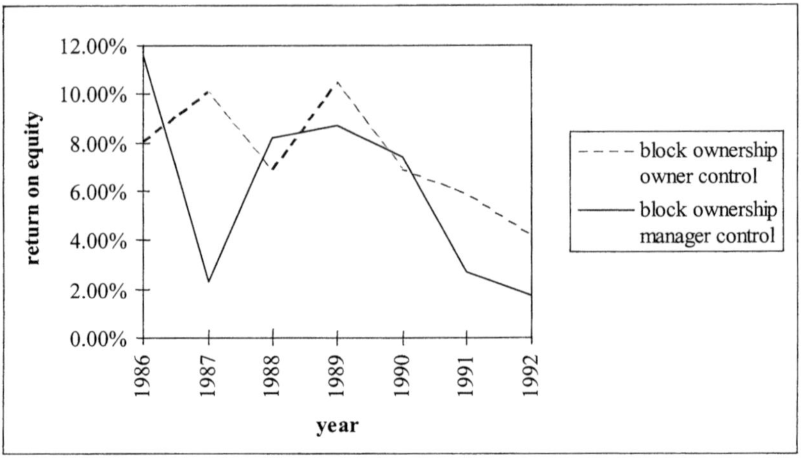

Figure 4-9: Development of return on equity over time, by agency group (using block ownership to distinguish)

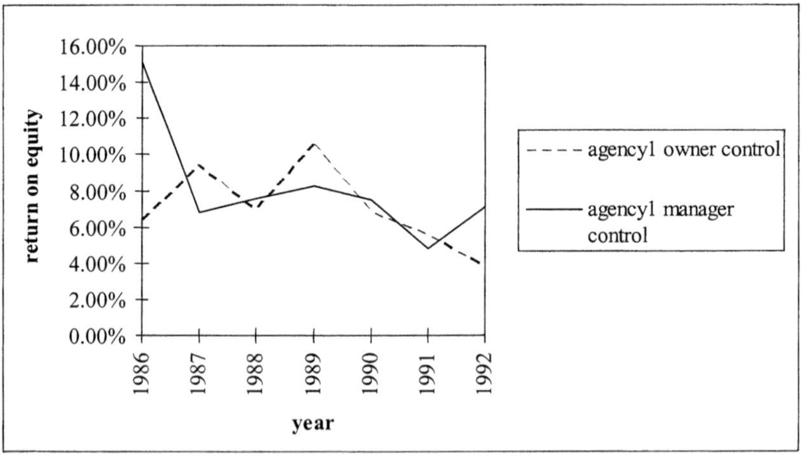

Figure 4-10: Development of return on equity over time, by agency group (using *agency1* to distinguish)

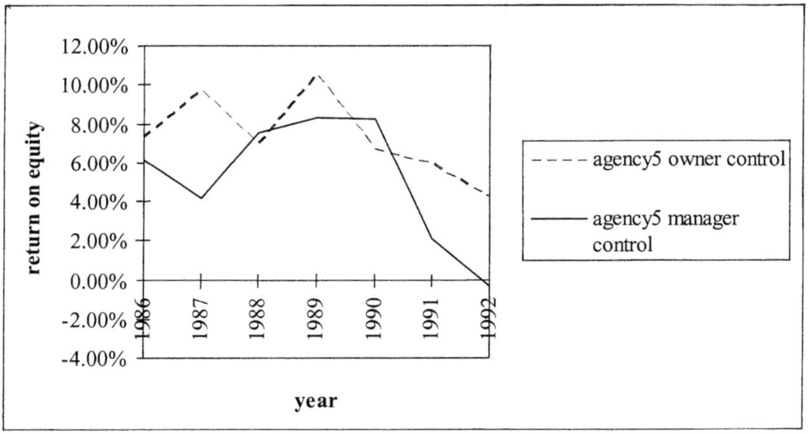

Figure 4-11: Development of return on equity over time, by agency group (using *agency5* to distinguish)

Figure 4-6 above shows that the return on capital overall shows more of a sideways movement. In Figure 4-12 one sees that this is due to companies under manager control, while creditor-controlled firms have more variance in the return on capital. Regressions on the return on capital that are constructed analogously to those above for the return on equity give insignificant slopes of -0.0009 and 0.0007 for creditor and manager control respectively. This means that the fourth hypothesis is rejected for the return on capital. A subdivision of the already short time span could be constructed to capture the phases where the creditor-driven return on capital increases (1986-1989) separately from the years where it decreases (1990-1992). It would show higher rates of change for creditor-controlled firms in either phase, again rejecting the hypothesis.

For the Sharpe ratio and Tobin's q, graphs of the development of the measures over time are only given here for the groups by block ownership, while the other graphs using *agency1* and *agency5* can be found in the appendix. The high volatility of the Sharpe ratio is visible in Figure 4-13 as well as Figure 4-7 above.[103] The manager-controlled firms' Sharpe ratios are slightly more volatile than the owner-controlled ones, but the insignificant slopes of -.476 and -.550 are both not significantly different from zero. This confirms the hypothesis, as do the similar results for using the two agency conglomerate variables to distinguish the control groups (not reported here).

---

[103] Note that the stock market crashed in October 1987.

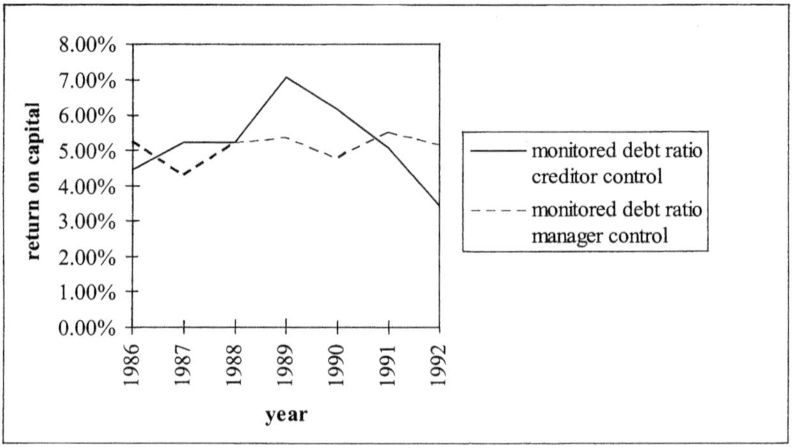

Figure 4-12: Development of return on capital over time, by agency group (using the ratio of monitored to unmonitored debt to distinguish)

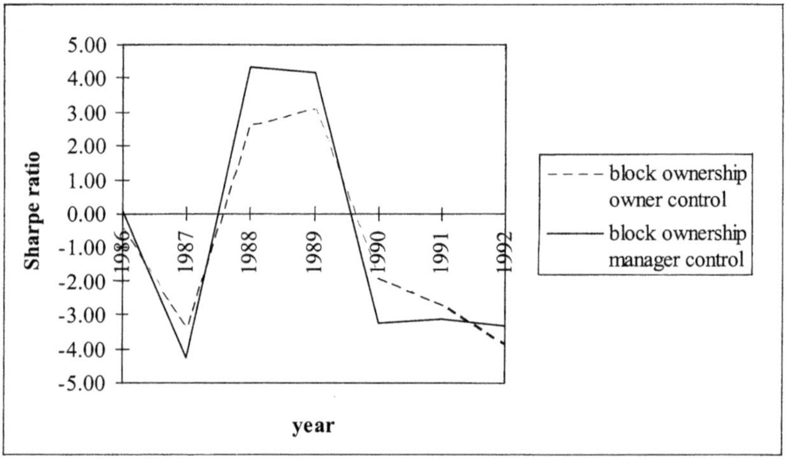

Figure 4-13: Development of Sharpe ratio over time, by agency group (using block ownership to distinguish)

Tobin's q declines slightly over time, with no big difference in slope to be expected between owner and manager-controlled companies. The ordinary least squares regressions confirm this with slopes of -0.019 and -0.073 giving only a slight and insignificant edge to the owner-controlled companies (first value). For the *agency1* conglomerate, the slopes of -0.016 (owner control) and -0.098 (manager control) and for *agency5* -0.019 (owner control) and -0.079 (manager control) repeat this almost imperceptible confirmation of hypothesis four.

Table 4-21 sums up the results that were obtained for the performance measures using the various methods. No performance level differences are apparent between managers and owners. Only Tobin's q shows some ability to differentiate by agency control group, but even this was not consistent. The owners do outperform the creditors going by Tobin's q, and the creditors ensure higher returns on capital (third hypothesis). The rate of change in performance does support the hypothesis that manager-controlled companies decrease in performance faster than companies controlled by the principals directly. The difference was always slight, though, and never enough to constitute significant differences that would confirm the first two hypotheses. Therefore, the confirmation of the fourth hypothesis is put in parentheses.

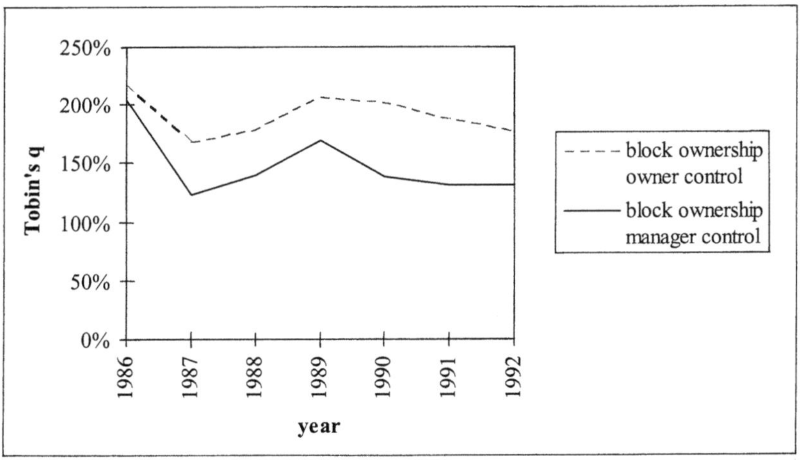

Figure 4-14: Development of Tobin's q over time, by agency group (using block ownership to distinguish)

hypothesis #	method	return on equity	return on capital	Sharpe ratio	Tobin's q	overall
1	t-tests	☐	☐	☐	(☑)	☐
	logistic regression	☐	☐	☐	(☑)	☐
overall		☐	☐	☐	(☑)	☐
2	t-tests	☐	☐	☐	☐	☐
	logistic regression	(☑)	(☑)	☐	☐	☐
overall		☐	☐	☐	☐	☐
3	t-tests	☐	☑	☑	☑	☑
4	OLS regression	☑	☐	☑	(☑)	(☑)

Table 4-21: Overview over the validity of hypotheses one to four; yearly tests 1986-1992[104]

4.3.4.3 Sectoral Analysis

4.3.4.3.1 T-Tests for Differences in Mean Performance

Since the comprehensive and yearly analyses above lump companies from all sectors together, it is possible that sectoral characteristics affected the results. Figure 4-15 and Figure 4-16 show that the differences in average performance levels are substantive, making sector-specific analyses worthwhile. Again, the five largest sectors in the sample are used for the analysis.

The return on equity is visibly higher and more volatile than the return on capital, by sectoral differentiation (Figure 4-15). These differences could prove to be related to differing agency levels by sector, and especially to differences in the competitive product market situation for each sector. Figure 4-16 paints a similar picture for the Sharpe ratio and Tobin's q, which show similar developments. It is interesting to note that the returns on equity and capital are the lowest for the food & beverages sector, while the Sharpe ratios and Tobin's q place that sector near the top of the five being studied here in more detail. This observation

104 A check marks a hypothesis that could not be rejected according to the model given at the top of the column.

follows the distinction between the book-valued and market-valued performance measures.

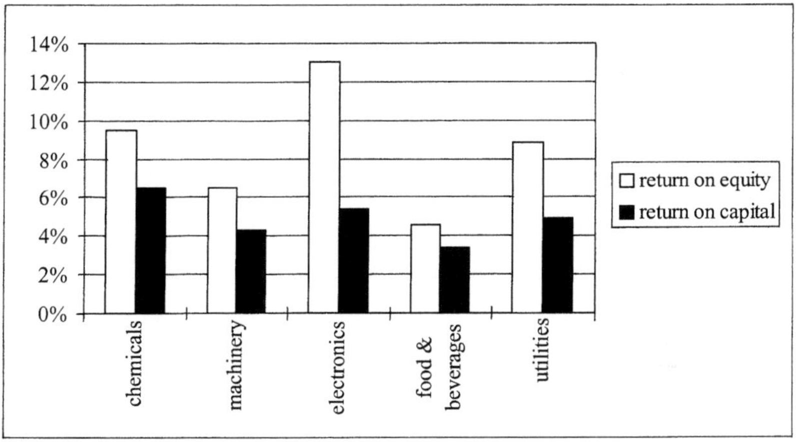

Figure 4-15: Average returns on equity and capital over all years, by sector

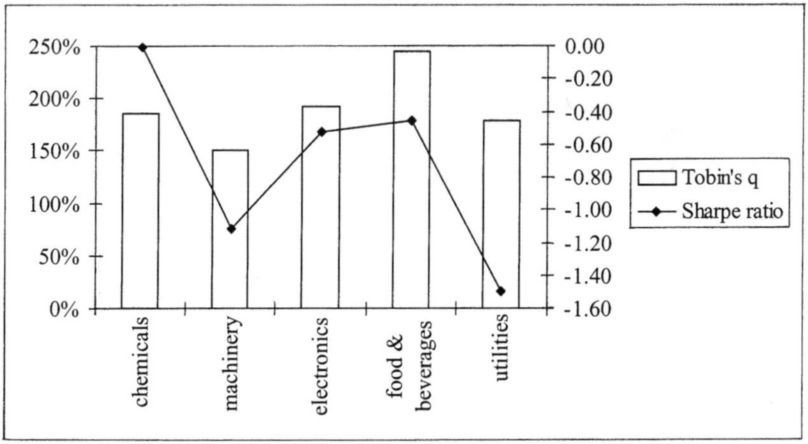

Figure 4-16: Average Sharpe ratios and values for Tobin's q over all years, by sector[105]

---

105 The right scale is for the Sharpe ratio.

As in the financial behavior analysis, the tables given here are again for the machinery sector in exemplary form, and in addition some data is presented here for the utilities sector. These two are at the opposite ends of the range of sectors ordered by level of competition on the product markets. The tables for the other sectors can be found in the appendix. The sector results can be used both to test the validity of the first three hypotheses, as well as to check the sector-specific hypotheses five and six. To start off, the first three hypotheses will be discussed below. The results can also directly be applied to the sixth hypothesis.

	return on equity		return on capital		Sharpe ratio		Tobin's q	
	diff	sig	diff	sig	diff	sig	diff	sig
expected sign	+		+		o		+	
block ownership	-.0008		-.0164		-.4288		-.3026	***
size	.0290		.0096		-1.3475		-.0583	
market segment	-.0542		-.0002		.1885		.0817	
dividend signal	-.0673		-.0266		-.1317		.3224	
leverage	-.1478	*	-.0476	**	-.2103		-.1772	**
monitored debt ratio	-.0114		-.0001		-.3922		-.0307	
agency1	-.0281		-.0298		-1.4461		-.1339	
agency2	-.0281		-.0298		-1.0193		-.1339	
agency3	-.1690	**	-.0507	***	-.2939		-.1926	**
agency4	.0191		.0023		-1.8295		-.1164	
agency5	.0062		-.0146		-.4360		-.2169	**
agency6	-.1786	**	-.0421	**	-.7535		-.2512	**
agency7	-.0580		-.0266		-.0239		.1027	

*** = significant at 1 %-level (** = 5 %; * = 10 %)

Table 4-22: T-tests for differences of means of performance measures for groups with and without agency problems, by agency variable, machinery sector 1986-1992

The results for the machinery sector in Table 4-22 show a large number of negative differences for the agency variables. All significant differences are negative, meaning that the first hypothesis does not apply to the machinery industry. Only the insignificant signs for the Sharpe ratio support that hypothesis. This could mean that the level of competition in that sector makes additional control through block owners or other measures superfluous. The second hypothesis, too, must be rejected, which is the same result as earlier.

The utilities companies, operating by contrast in a less competitive environment, produce a greater number of positive differences for the agency variables. The signs of the significant differences are about equally balanced. Unfortunately, for many of the agency conglomerates, including *agency1*, no groups were separated by those agency variables, giving the N/A (not applicable) result. But the two remaining main agency variables block ownership and *agency5* produce the same non-significant positive results for all but the Sharpe ratio. So here, where market control is lacking, the additional monitoring of block owners and the other measures apparently is both practiced and effective. This confirms hypothesis six somewhat, which states that manager-controlled firms will perform worse than owner-controlled companies in uncompetitive sectors, except for the Sharpe ratios, which should be equal. In highly competitive sectors the performance differences should be insignificant for all measures according to the hypothesis.

	return on equity		return on capital		Sharpe ratio		Tobin's q	
	diff	sig	diff	sig	diff	sig	diff	sig
expected sign	+		+		o		+	
block ownership	.0381		.0016		-2.8501		.4332	
size	-.0206		-.0350	***	-.5481		-.9250	***
market segment	.0129		.0089		-1.7700		.5130	***
dividend signal	.0137		.0263	*	-1.7203		-.0188	
leverage	.0009		-.0148		1.3582		-.4263	
monitored debt ratio	-.0242	***	.0085	*	1.1081		-.3242	*
agency1	N/A		N/A		N/A		N/A	
agency2	N/A		N/A		N/A		N/A	
agency3	-.0178	*	-.0265	***	.1999		-.6533	***
agency4	N/A		N/A		N/A		N/A	
agency5	.0381		.0016		-2.8501		.4332	
agency6	.0291	*	.0083		-2.7090		.4692	***
agency7	N/A		N/A		N/A		N/A	

*** = significant at 1 %-level (** = 5 %; * = 10 %)

Table 4-23: T-tests for differences of means of performance measures for groups with and without agency problems, by agency variable, utilities sector 1986-1992

The same cannot quite be said for the creditors, though. Although half of the differences here are positive, two of the three significant ones are negative. The positive one gives a .85 % edge to the creditor-controlled companies in the return on capital when using the monitored debt ratio as the agency variable, which is the most important of the performance measures for this hypothesis. Therefore the hypothesis can only be accepted with reservations.

The chemicals sector (the table for which is in the appendix) confirms the first hypothesis for the return on equity and Tobin's q due to positive and significant differences. The other major variables *agency1* and *agency5* however just as decidedly reject the hypothesis. The market segment and size variables produce several significantly positive signs, but those for leverage and other agency conglomerate variables are predominantly negative. So the hypothesis one is rejected here, as is the second hypothesis, for which almost all differences are negative. In the ranking by level of competition the chemicals firms come in third place.

The electronics companies, which come in second place by competitivity, show a predominance of positive signs, for Tobin's q even significant ones. That is the only performance measure for which significant signs occur. All in all the first hypothesis can count as not rejected. For the second hypothesis the familiar positive signs for the returns on equity and capital when going by the monitored debt ratio appear here, too. Most other signs are negative, and in the case of Tobin's q significant for the monitored debt ratio. This leads to a rejection of the second hypothesis.

For the food & beverages companies the many positive and often significant signs lead to an acceptance of the first hypothesis, which corroborates the assumption that non-market control mechanisms take effect if competition on the sales markets is lacking. The block ownership unfortunately does not subdivide the data when used alone, though. No differences are significant for the Sharpe ratio, which is exactly as hypothesized. For the return on capital, the significantly positive difference of 1.43 % confirms the second hypothesis, while the other results lean more toward a rejection (especially the strongly negative differences in Tobin's q).

The third hypothesis compares the monitoring effectivity of owners and creditors. These groups are not mutually exclusive, so the tests are not exact replicas of those above, except for other grouping criteria. The results in Table 4-24 for the machinery sector and Table 4-25 for the utilities show that the size and significance of the differences between these groups, too, rise in reverse proportion to the decrease in competition on the sales markets. For the machinery sector, the hypothesis cannot be rejected due to positive differences in return on equity and negative ones in return on capital. The negative signs in Tobin's q do not confirm the hypothesis, but are small and insignificant, which was usually not the case in earlier sections.

	return on equity diff	sig	return on capital diff	sig	Sharpe ratio diff	sig	Tobin's q diff	sig
expected sign	+		–		o		+	
block ownership	0.48 %		-0.26 %		0.0901		-3.60 %	
agency5	0.61 %		-0.27 %		0.0781		-2.73 %	

*** = significant at 1 %-level (** = 5 %; * = 10 %)

Table 4-24: T-tests for differences of means of the performance measures between owner-controlled and creditor-controlled companies, machinery sector 1986-1992[106]

The hypothesis can be again accepted for the utilities companies, this time with significant positive differences for both the return on equity and Tobin's q. This rise in significance again underlines the importance of the agency variables in the absence of market control, which is the subject of the sixth hypothesis. The return on capital shows the required negative signs.

	return on equity diff	sig	return on capital diff	sig	Sharpe ratio diff	sig	Tobin's q diff	sig
expected sign	+		–		o		+	
block ownership	1.87 %	***	-0.60 %		-0.8905		24.78 %	*
agency5	1.87 %	***	-0.60 %		-0.8905		24.78 %	*

*** = significant at 1 %-level (** = 5 %; * = 10 %)

Table 4-25: T-tests for differences of means of the performance measures between owner-controlled and creditor-controlled companies, utilities sector 1986-1992[107]

The results for the other three sectors presented in the appendix are as follows. For the chemicals sector, the signs are as expected except for the positive difference in return on capital. For the electronics and food & beverages sectors, the differences in return on equity have the wrong sign, the others are as hypothe-

106 Differences are to the companies that count as monitored by creditors according to the ratio of monitored to unmonitored debt.

107 Differences are to the companies that count as monitored by creditors according to the ratio of monitored to unmonitored debt.

sized, and in the case of Tobin's q, significant. The advantage of creditor control over ownership control for the return on capital is significant for the food & beverages sector, which was ranked as the second-least competitive. This again supports the sixth hypothesis that agency variables are important when competition is missing.

The fifth hypothesis states that companies in somewhat competitive sectors should show the highest performance levels, with the exception of the Sharpe ratio. In the tables below, the sectors are listed in the order of their average performance, with the expected ranking order given in the rightmost column. The electronics and chemicals will be counted as the sectors with some, but not fierce competition, while the machinery sector has to endure the most and the food & beverages and utilities the least competition.

sector	average return on equity	rank	sig[+]	rank by degree of competition in sales market
electronics	13.00 %	1		2
chemicals	9.50 %	2		3
utilities	8.90 %	3		5
machinery	6.50 %	4		1
food & beverages	4.60 %	5		4

[+]of difference to next sector; *** = significant at 1 %-level (** = 5 %; * = 10 %)

Table 4-26: Average values for return on equity for five sectors, over all years

Table 4-26 and Table 4-27 indeed do place the chemicals and electronics firms at the top of the ranking by return on equity and return on capital. The very competitive machinery companies come in between the utilities and food & beverages in return on equity and in last place for the return on capital. For the market-valued performance measures (Table 4-28 and Table 4-29), the food & beverages is at or near the top of the performance ranks. Otherwise the chemical and electronic firms do come in second and third place, still confirming the fifth hypothesis to a degree. This confirms on the whole what was already put to consideration above in 4.3.2, that increased inefficiency could diminish the high performance near-monopolistic structures made possible. The analysis of inefficiency alone in chapter 5 should shed some more light on this connection, by studying if inefficiency rises as competition declines.

sector	average return on capital	rank	sig⁺	rank by degree of competition in sales market
chemicals	6.50 %	1		3
electronics	5.40 %	2		2
utilities	4.90 %	3		5
machinery	4.30 %	4		1
food & beverages	3.40 %	5		4

+of difference to next sector; *** = significant at 1 %-level (** = 5 %; * = 10 %)

Table 4-27: Average values for return on capital for five sectors, over all years

sector	average Sharpe ratio	rank	sig⁺	rank by degree of competition in sales market
chemicals	-0.006	1		3
food & beverages	-0.457	2		4
electronics	-0.528	3		2
machinery	-1.117	4		1
utilities	-1.501	5		5

+of difference to next sector; *** = significant at 1 %-level (** = 5 %; * = 10 %)

Table 4-28: Average values for Sharpe ratio for five sectors, over all years

sector	average Tobin's q	rank	sig⁺	rank by degree of competition in sales market
food & beverages	244.2 %	1	***	4
electronics	192.6 %	2		2
chemicals	184.9 %	3		3
utilities	178.6 %	4	***	5
machinery	150.6 %	5		1

+of difference to next sector; *** = significant at 1 %-level (** = 5 %; * = 10 %)

Table 4-29: Average values for Tobin's q for five sectors, over all years

4.3.4.3.2 Logistic Regressions

The logistic regressions allow the agency variables to be jointly tested without having to resort to the conglomerates. With them, alternative tests can be run for the first two hypotheses. The signs for the coefficients to support the hypotheses are again given at the top of the tables. For the machinery sector, negative signs of the block ownership and leverage variables in Table 4-30 reject the first hypothesis. So, too, do the regressions of the agency conglomerate variables. The classifications must beat the benchmark of 50 % for all performance measures. That this low rate also applies for the Sharpe ratio speaks for the sector-specific analyses. The second hypothesis which is tested for using the model with the leverage and monitored debt ratio variables also gets cleanly rejected.

	dependent variable			
independent variables	return on equity	return on capital	Sharpe ratio	Tobin's q
expected sign	+	+	o	+
model 1				
block ownership	-1.2070 *	-1.9282 ***	1.1419 *	-1.6118 **
size	.0585	.1374 *	-.0253	-.1431
market segment 1	-.5859	-.4462	-.2619	.1959
market segment 2	-.0431	.0676	-.7912	.3793
dividend signal	1.3208	.5526	.1093	2.6731 *
leverage	-.9318 ***	-.5499 ***	-.1952	-.4755 **
-2 log likelihood‡	137.241 ***	143.473 ***	163.613	139.028 ***
% correct classification	69.92	64.23	58.20	68.29
model 2				
leverage	-.3842 ***	-.2574 **	-.0668	-.4598 ***
monitored debt ratio	-.4907	.2290	-.1866	-.2884
-2 log likelihood‡	150.763 ***	163.054 **	167.377	148.575 ***
% correct classification	57.72	51.22	47.54	61.79
model 3				
agency1	-.3977 **	-.0935	.0000	-.6791 ***
-2 log likelihood‡	166.366 **	170.280	169.128	158.852 ***
% correct classification	61.79	56.10	49.18	64.23

	dependent variable			
independent variables	return on equity	return on capital	Sharpe ratio	Tobin's q
expected sign	+	+	o	+
model 4				
agency5	-.4055 **	-.1201	.0000	-.8001 ***
-2 log likelihood‡	166.487 **	170.154	169.128	155.705 ***
% correct classification	60.98	56.91	49.18	66.67

N = 123; *** = significant on the 1 % level (** = 5 %; * = 10 %); ‡ = significance of model chi-square

Table 4-30: Coefficients and overall results of the logistic regressions on the performance dummy variables, machinery sector[108]

The data for the other sectors including the utilities is in the appendix. For the chemicals sector, the return on equity and Tobin's q give positive coefficients for block ownership (also for *agency5* for the return on equity), but the rest of the signs are more often negative than not for all models. This rejects both the first and the second hypotheses. A similar result also can be recorded for the electronics sector, while the second hypothesis receives some support from the less competitive food & beverages and utilities sectors. There, the monitored debt ratio has strong positive coefficients (close to three) for the return on capital as the dependent variable. This coefficient is the most important one for that hypothesis. The data for the food & beverages and utilities sectors do not support the first hypothesis. There are some positive coefficients for the food sector, but they are scattered.

Table 4-31 shows the overview of the hypothesis results for the five sectors, this time not differentiating by performance measure but by sector, which is more informative. The sectors are presented in descending order of competitivity, making it easy to ascertain at a glance that the first two hypotheses have more chances of not being rejected for the sectors with less competition on the sales market. This leads to a confirmation of the sixth hypothesis. The fifth hypothesis check is put in parentheses to account for the high market-valued performance the food & beverages sector showed, which was contrary to expectations.

108 The market segment dummy 1 is one for official continuous trade, the second dummy is one for official daily trade.

hypothesis #	method	machinery	electronics	chemicals	food & beverages	utilities	overall
1	t-tests	☐	☑	(☐)	☑	☑	☑
1	logistic regression	☐	☐	☐	☐	☐	☐
overall		☐	(☐)	☐	(☐)	(☐)	(☐)
2	t-tests	☐	☐	☐	(☑)	(☑)	(☐)
2	logistic regression	☐	☐	☐	(☑)	(☑)	(☐)
overall		☐	☐	☐	(☑)	(☑)	(☐)
3	t-tests	☑	☑	☑	☑	☑	☑
5	t-tests						(☑)
6	t-tests						☑

Table 4-31: Overview over the validity of hypotheses one to three, five and six; sectoral analyses[109]

Overall for the sectoral analysis, the first hypothesis of a superior performance for ownership-controlled firms over manager-controlled ones is rejected. There is also not enough support for the second hypothesis claiming superior performance for creditor-controlled companies over manager-controlled ones. Both rejection boxes are put in brackets, though, because there is some slight support for the hypotheses. The ownership-controlled firms do perform better than creditor-controlled ones, though (hypothesis three).

4.4 Summary of the Chapter

Agency problems are typically associated with decreases in corporate performance in the literature, although often the hypotheses were not validated in subsequent empirical analyses. In this section, four performance measures were selected to test six hypotheses. Two of them, the return on equity and the return on capital, are based on book valued data, while the other two, the Sharpe ratio and Tobin's q as a measure of the market value of assets to their book value, include market values in their calculation. The Sharpe ratio cancels market price levels out by using stock returns, whereas Tobin's q only uses the market value once

[109] A check marks a hypothesis that could not be rejected according to the model given at the top of the column. The sectors are given in descending order of the degree of competition on the sales markets of the sectors.

and so still mirrors price levels. The Sharpe ratio was expected not to be affected by agency problems, meaning that non-significant results when using it as the performance measure act as a calibrating mechanism for the tests. This result was generally achieved. The return on capital is included as a measure that is more important to creditors than to the ownership of a firm. All performance measures are at a high level of aggregation, as opposed to the concept of efficiency as used in the next section.

In this analysis, the central hypothesis to be tested was that managers, when able to act uncontrolled by the ownership of a firm, will only achieve an inferior performance to the one firms under ownership control produce. This effect should especially be visible in the return on equity and Tobin's q. In all three versions tested, for the comprehensive data, singly for the seven years in the sample, and by sector for the five most numerous sectors in the sample, this hypothesis was rejected. Both t-tests as well as logistic regressions on dichotomized performance levels were conducted. Tobin's q was the performance measure that most frequently uncovered differences in performance, which befits its status as a market-valued performance measure.

This result conforms to previous findings for the German market, and raises the question why the plausible hypothesis is so consistently rejected. A possible answer could lie in the aggregation of the performance measures. Especially the book measures are susceptible to manipulative measures in the accounting process which can be used to skew performance readings in the direction desired. If one assumes that the aggregate performance measures are more closely studied by investors than disaggregate numbers, then it makes immediate sense for unmonitored managers to apply their energy to maintaining certain performance levels.

If one rejects the agency theory and assumes that managers act in the best interests of the ownership, the result obtained is also easily understood. When able to exploit their inside knowledge of the company and competence unfettered by the less informed guidelines of the ownership, then the performance of manager-controlled firms can rise to high levels. Significant superiority of manager control was not apparent in the data, though. Instead, an overall equality of manager and ownership control is the most likely reality.

A similar result also was found for the second hypothesis, which asks if creditor control is more effective than manager control, especially with regard to the return on capital. This hypothesis, too, was rejected, and the results even suggest that the exact opposite state is true.

If this is the case, then the third hypothesis that claims that ownership control, too, is better than creditor control should hold. This hypothesis indeed was consistently not rejected by the data. Creditors with their lesser involvement in a company's dealings and especially lower information levels concerning that company are apparently not able to match the performance levels that owners or managers reach. They might not even be interested in doing so, as their interest and amortization demands for their loans can usually be met with non-maximal performance.

The fact that the sectoral breakdown tended to support the hypotheses somewhat while the comprehensive and yearly results did not might also be a sign that the mix of various sectors tends to wipe away differences that otherwise do appear. However, even the sectoral results did not support the first two hypotheses enough to accept them, confirming their overall rejection.

hypothesis #	compre-hensive	yearly	sectoral	overall
1	☐	☐	(☐)	☐
2	☐	☐	(☐)	☐
3	☑	☑	☑	☑
4		(☑)		(☑)
5			(☑)	(☑)
6			☑	☑

Table 4-32: Overview over the validity of the hypotheses; all methods[110]

The fourth hypothesis was time-related and called for a tendency of performance measures to cling to lower levels in manager-controlled companies over the course of time. This hypothesis was not rejected, due to slightly smaller negative slopes of regressions over the seven years. The differences in slope are too small to lay great store by this result.

On the other hand, the sector-related hypotheses found more support and give insights into the reasons for the rejection of the first hypothesis. The fifth hypothesis was formulated to say that both high and low levels of competition in the sales markets of companies are detrimental to performance. In the one case, cutthroat competition does not allow any one company or type of company to greatly outperform any other company, while in the other case unchecked sloth prohibits monopolistic or near-monopolistic companies from maximizing profits and performance. Indeed, the electronics and chemicals sectors exhibited the highest book performances, and were surpassed by the food & beverages sector

110 A check marks a hypothesis that could not be rejected according to the model given at the top of the column. The sectors are given in descending order of the degree of competition on the sales markets of the sectors.

with regard to the market performance measures. The electronics and chemicals firms came in second and third place. The food & beverages sector had been counted to the less competitive sectors, and indeed performed in last place by the book measures, so that result led to an only conditional acceptance of the fifth hypothesis.

The sixth hypothesis incorporated the high competition levels as external control mechanisms and stated that the other agency variables would only in their absence be of any importance. This was confirmed by the significant results for distinguishing performance levels by agency variables in the case of the utilities and food & beverages sectors (those facing the least competition), and the frequent rejection for the other three sectors. This means that the rejection of the first two hypotheses for the comprehensive and yearly samples could be due to the combination of companies facing varying levels of competition on the output markets, where the results of the more competitive sectors dominate those of the less competitive sectors. In addition, as the fifth hypothesis shows, the very competitive firms are not able to outdistance their competitors by far anyway.

An interesting question not studied here is if the lower performance levels of creditor-controlled firms are also associated with a corresponding lower variance in the performance of such firms.[111] This should be desirable to creditors who do not participate in profits elevated higher than those needed to satisfy their fixed claims and wish to minimize the default risk of the company.[112]

The analysis confirms the relevance of the agency theory for all sectors and companies, and speaks against the alternate suggestion made above to explain the rejection of the first hypotheses by rejecting the agency theory. It still is possible to assign a role to the manipulation of the book-value performance measures by uncontrolled managers.

---

111 Cf. Thonet/Poensgen (1979).

112 Tests were run calculating using only the standard deviations of the stock returns that are used in the denominator of the Sharpe ratio. Subsequent t-tests for differences in means consistently did not reject the null hypothesis that the means are equal for the creditor-specific agency variables. The often insignificant results for the Sharpe ratio between all agency categories stem both from insignificant differences in excess return and in standard deviations of the returns, i. e., the numerator and denominator separately produces similar results to the Sharpe ratio.

5 Agency Problems and Efficiency in the Firm

5.1 Efficiency and Production Theory

5.1.1 Efficiency

There are a number of terms used to describe the efficiency of a firm.[1] These include technical, allocative, and distributive efficiency, which describe different facets of the productive efficiency of a firm. Taken together, these efficiencies are those most easily affected by management decisions. For the efficiency due to managerial activity, the term x-efficiency is used.[2]

Also, the terms cost and profit efficiency will need to be defined and related to the x-efficiency. One can furthermore speak of information efficiency and risk efficiency in firm processes. Finally, economies of size and economies of scope are terms used to describe the efficiency of a firm.

As the efficiency of a company affects the profitability and return of a company, it is difficult to distinguish between these terms. I will use efficiency here when referring to the unaggregated measures that form the basis of the ROI diagram in chapter 4.2.3. These measures are at the bottom of the diagram. Performance measures refer to the aggregated ratios at the top of the diagram.

5.1.2 Types of Efficiency

5.1.2.1 X-Efficiency

Technical efficiency denotes that the maximum amount of outputs in the output set Y_m with m=1, ..., M is produced by the available inputs X_n with n=1, ..., N, or alternatively a given amount of outputs is being produced with a minimal amount of inputs. The first version of technical efficiency given describes output efficiency, the second input efficiency.

The physical amounts are not weighted with their variable monetary values at this point. Differences in prices for a good can differ over time or company. Not weighting the amounts in estimating technical efficiency means that the prices are implicitly seen as constant, i. e., prices do not affect technical efficiency. The

---

1 Cf. Førsund/Lovell/Schmidt (1980), pp. 6 f.

2 This term goes back to Leibenstein (1966).

technically most efficient company can at least in theory be determined by simply comparing the amounts of netputs used.[3] Technically efficient production however is not a sufficient criterion for a company that is pursuing specific profit or return goals. Such a company must optimize its production in view of output and input prices. Therefore the concept of efficiency must be expanded to include valued inputs and outputs.

Allocative efficiency includes variable input prices in the rationale, allowing costs to differ due to varying amounts and/or prices. It describes the choice of the input ratios of production factors in the case of their substitutionality. In order to achieve allocative efficiency, the use of one production factor is reduced in favor of an increase of an other or several other input factors until the marginal costs of the input factors are equal. Using different amounts of inputs changes the price to be paid for these inputs. Again, though, the output prices are assumed to be constant and therefore irrelevant. All improvements in profitability[4] are attributed to the changes in the input prices.

Distributive efficiency on the other hand assumes output prices to be variable. Therefore, the production of profitable outputs is increased by steering more inputs into those outputs' production (corporate distributive efficiency). On an economic level, one can also use labor or other input markets to shift workers or inputs from less profitable output production to more lucrative assignments in other companies (economic distributive efficiency). The criterion followed in this process is the equalization of the marginal profit of the outputs last sold.[5] The input prices are assumed to be constant.

output 1	x	output price 1	=	sales 1 −				
output 2	x	output price 2	=		+	sales 2 −	=	sales −
input 1	x	input price 1	=	costs 11 −	+	costs 21 −	=	costs 1 −
input 2	x	input price 2	=	costs 12	+	costs 22	=	costs 2
				= profit 1	+	= profit 2	=	= profits

Figure 5-1: Determinants of technical efficiency

3 A netput is defined here as either an input or an output and as a general term also allows for inputs to simultaneously be outputs.

4 Profits are taken as sales minus costs of a product.

5 Cf. Schumann (1987), pp. 203 ff.

In Figure 5-1 above technical efficiency is depicted for a two input, two output company. The gray shading shows which parameters are seen as variable and at what points the success of a measure is recorded. For the technical efficiency, the amounts of the inputs and outputs are variable and their totals are the measure of success. In the case of allocative efficiency (Figure 5-2), the input prices are assumed to be variable (by changing input amounts), shaded light gray. The marginal costs of the outputs are used to gauge the success of the measures taken to improve efficiency (shaded dark gray). They are not subdivided by output.

output 1	x	output price 1	=	sales 1 –	+		=	sales –
output 2	x	output price 2	=			sales 2 –		
input 1	x	input price 1	=	costs 11 –	+	costs 21 –	=	costs 1 –
input 2	x	input price 2	=	costs 12	+	costs 22	=	costs 2
				= profit 1	+	= profit 2	=	= profits

Figure 5-2: Determinants of allocative efficiency

In Figure 5-3, the same is shown for the distributive efficiency, where output prices vary with the output amounts and equal marginal profits for each output is the criterion for an optimal productive balance. The major difference between allocative and distributive efficiency as they are defined here is in the attribution of inefficiencies to using either the wrong amounts of the inputs (allocative efficiency) or the wrong amounts of the outputs (distributive efficiency), due to their respective prices.

output 1	x	output price 1	=	sales 1 –	+		=	sales –
output 2	x	output price 2	=			sales 2 –		
input 1	x	input price 1	=	costs 11 –	+	costs 21 –	=	costs 1 –
input 2	x	input price 2	=	costs 12	+	costs 22	=	costs 2
				= profit 1	+	= profit 2	=	= profits

Figure 5-3: Determinants of distributive efficiency

5.1.2.2 Cost and Profit Efficiency

Cost efficiency is spoken of when comparing the relative positions of companies on the basis of the costs they incur to produce the given output. **Profit efficiency** is used for the same purpose, but additionally includes the revenue side of a company's activity in its reasoning. These efficiencies are derived from production functions and need to be discussed in more detail below (5.1.3). Their relation to the x-efficiency measures will also be determined there.

5.1.2.3 Economies of Scale and Scope

The term **economies of scale**[6] can be used to describe the concept of an optimal firm size. The optimal size is reached when an increase in output amounts lowers the fixed costs per output unit just enough for the drop to be compensated exactly by the increase in variable unit costs incurred through the raise in output levels. An optimal output size exists if the cost function is curved like an S, with a decreasing, then increasing positive slope.[7]

Not only striving for the optimal size, but also the optimization of the output program improves structural efficiency. If producing single outputs in separate companies costs more than their joint production, one speaks of **economies of scope**. This would mean that specialization reduces efficiency. Whereas distributive efficiency concerns adjusting the amounts of outputs being produced, without changing the number of different output types under production, economies of scope are achieved by adjusting the number of output types.

5.1.2.4 Information and Risk Efficiency

The concept of **information efficiency** in a company arises from the possibility of informational asymmetries between the outside ownership and management of a company.[8] Increasing the efficiency, in particular by improving the informational level of the ownership of a company, is only possible at increased cost. Alternatively the owner can take control of the firm himself and thus achieve informational efficiency. That opposes the concept of division of labor, under which the manager is assumed to have been put in charge because he is more competent at leading the firm than the ownership.

---

6 Cf. Schumann (1987), pp. 229 ff.

7 Cf. Schumann (1987), pp. 153 ff.

8 Cf. Myers/Majluf (1984).

Other groups in a firm also can experience information asymmetries, such as the ownership/management in respect to the creditors, or the management as regards the employees.

Risk efficiency implies that the risks of a firm are assumed by those who are most willing/capable of bearing them. A risk averse person, such as a manager is usually assumed to be, will only want to assume more risk if his compensation is increased disproportionately to the increase in risk borne. Obviously, the risk functions of the participants (management, ownership, creditors) must be known, or at least their propensities to risk (risk averse, risk neutral, risk happy), in order to adequately determine the risk efficiency of a company. For this, the risk-based portion of the management's remuneration is also an important piece of information, but unfortunately this is not available for German top managers.

5.1.3 The Production Process

5.1.3.1 The Underlying Production Technology

When studying the aggregate performance of companies in the previous main chapter, it became clear that accounting policies make it possible to manipulate performance measures and thus produce better performance results than actually achieved. In this section I turn to the disaggregate accounting-based cost measures in order to determine if agency problems can be identified at this lower level of accounting. The assumption is that at this level, managers are not as well able to manipulate the numbers within the legally allowed leeway to produce desired results. This makes it necessary to discuss the productive process of a firm.

In a framework of a production function, the technology of a company can be denoted by all possible combinations between the inputs and outputs of that company, or its production possibilities.[9] Of course, most of these combinations that are called production points will be technically inefficient. A production function for an input vector and one output is defined in general form as $y = f(\mathbf{x})$, with y being the output and $\mathbf{x}$ the input vector. As y is the maximum output associated with $\mathbf{x}$, the production function constitutes a subset of the production possibilities.

The efficient border of the production points shows the geometric location of the production function. Figure 5-4 shows this for the one input, one output case. This subset determines the production function.

---

9 Cf. Fandel (1985), p. 57; Scheper (1981), p. 257.

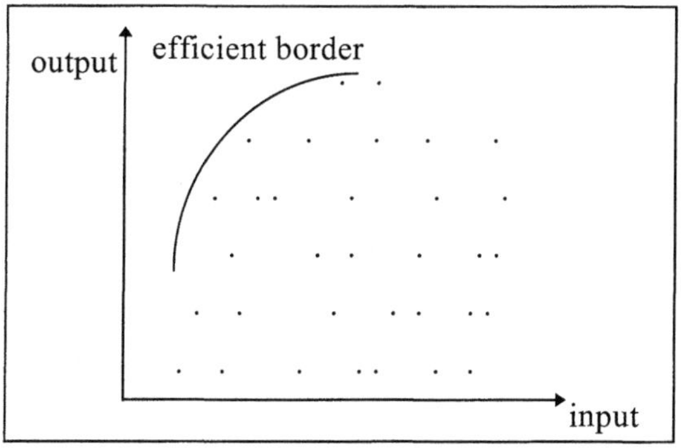

Figure 5-4: Technically efficient production set border for the one input, one output production function

The production function defines which product or output bundles can be produced with alternative factor input combinations.[10] As the production function gives the maximum output possible with a given factor combination, it is important to remember that it assumes technical output efficiency.

A company is only producing efficiently according to its production function if it is not only employing state of the art production techniques. It must also have an optimal organization, an excellent management, and optimally trained employees who are eager to work.

The input requirement set V(**y**) is used to denote all input levels that are capable of producing at least the output level given by an output vector **y**. It is an alternative way of describing the productive technology of a firm, as opposed to using the production function, and will be used below in the discussion of the duality between production and cost functions. V(**y**) is assumed to be nonempty and closed. This simply means that production is possible given the inputs available and that the boundaries of the production possibilities can be reached.

5.1.3.2 Costs and Profits

The cost function denotes the minimal costs of producing of a given output bundle with given factor prices. It assumes cost minimizing behavior on the side of the company, similar to the frontier concept of the production function. Defined on the disaggregate level, a cost function can be written as C = f(**w**, **y**),

---

10 Cf. Linde (1981), p. 276; Adam (1993), pp. 136 ff.

with C as the costs incurred by the company, **w** as the vector of wages for the inputs, and **y** as the output vector.

Figure 5-5 shows that the unit costs for the products of a firm can initially drop as input amounts are increased. An example for this is the division of labor. Later on, as input amounts increase, so do the unit costs.

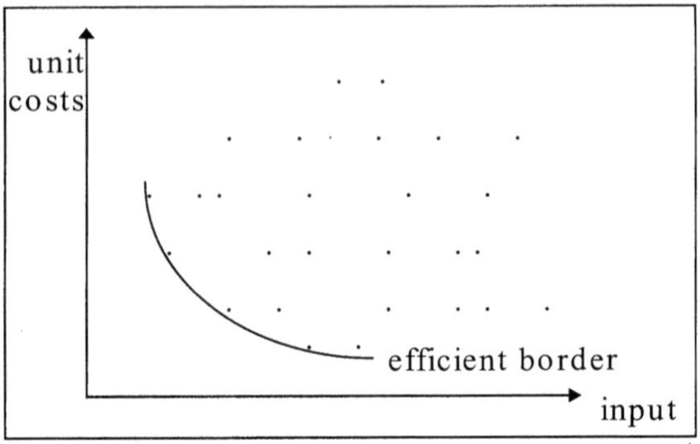

Figure 5-5: Cost-efficient production set border

Profits are defined as revenue minus costs. Thus, it becomes possible to include the revenue situation of a company into one's reckoning by studying profits and not only costs. A company that produces high costs in one field may just as well be earning its highest revenues in that same field, making the costly activity most profitable. Thus, the profit efficiency of a company seems to be a better measure of efficiency of a company than the cost efficiency. This will be further discussed below (5.1.4).

The types of efficiency discussed above, the x-efficiency and the scale and scope efficiencies, can all be related to the cost efficiency, as they all affect the costs of a company. Thus, these types of efficiency can be studied by analyzing the cost situation of a company.[11] Based on the cost function, and assuming a knowledge of prices and amounts of inputs and outputs, one can derive information on the technical, size and scope efficiencies as well as the allocative efficiency of a company (see Figure 5-6). Cost efficiency can be used as a comprehensive term for most of the types of efficiency mentioned above. Profit efficiency can be classed in the same manner as the profits are calculated using the costs.

---

[11] Cf. Ferrantino/Ferrier/Linvill (1995), p. 36.

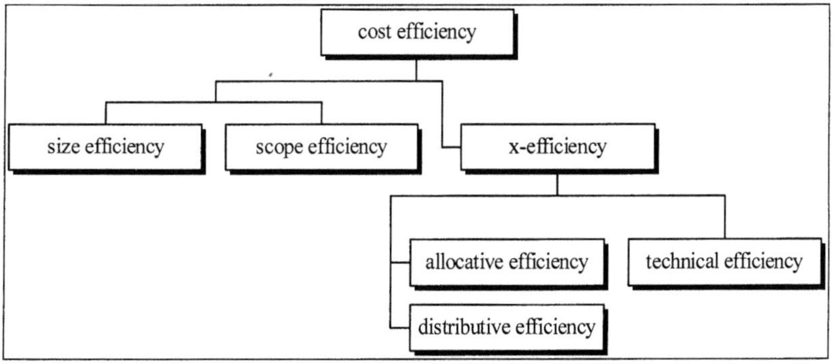

Figure 5-6: Systemization of cost efficiency measures

5.1.3.3 Duality between Production and Cost Functions

A production function relates the amounts of inputs to the amounts of outputs. These variables, linked to the concept of technical efficiency above, are often partially or completely unavailable to the economist and also of lesser importance, as the production function does not use netput prices.[12]

A cost function, on the other hand, replaces the input amounts with their costs, an economically relevant and available vector of variables. Therefore it is desirable to use a cost function in the place of a production function, should this be possible without a loss or distortion of the information contained in the production function.

To demonstrate the principle of duality, assume that the cost function describes a monotonously increasing homogeneous and convex curve. With the exception of the homogeneity, these are plausible assumptions. Homogeneity implies that $f(\lambda^{\alpha}x) = \lambda^{\alpha}f(x)$, with the most important variant being linear homogeneity, where $\alpha = 1$. That would mean that doubling the inputs ($\lambda = 2$) will double the outputs (Figure 5-7). For these functions, the ratio of partial derivatives is homogeneous to degree 0. Changing the input amounts in unison by a certain factor will not affect the marginal output. In consequence, the technical rate of substitution between the inputs is independent from the level of production, which is a desirable and realistic characteristic. A homothetic function is simply a monotonic transformation of a homogeneous function. Homogeneous, non-

---

12 Cf. Chambers (1988), p. 7.

homothetic functions are often used as a model to estimate empirical cost functions.

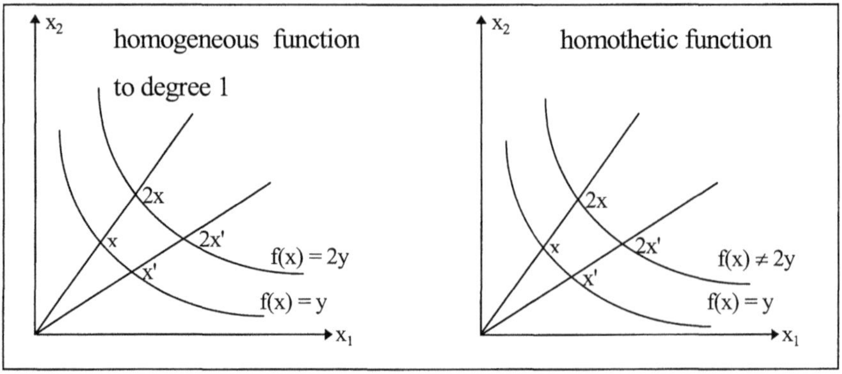

Figure 5-7: Isoquants of homogeneous and homothetic functions[13]

The cost function should represent a technology that itself is monotonous and convex or that has been transformed into such a curve. In this case all information from the production technology as contained in the production function is also depicted in the cost function.

To better understand this, I introduce the Weak Axiom of Cost Minimization (WACM),[14] and the concept of inner and outer input requirement sets.

WACM states that when taking all cost minimizing production points, there will be no other production points that produce the same amount or more of even one of the outputs at lesser cost. This can be expressed as $\mathbf{w}_t\mathbf{x}_t \leq \mathbf{w}_t\mathbf{x}_s$ for all $\mathbf{y}_s \geq \mathbf{y}_t$. If a set of data satisfies the WACM, that means it is possible to find a technology for which the observed choices are cost minimizing. Taking input requirement sets as technology defining sets, two appropriate input requirement sets can be constructed, the inner set VI($\mathbf{y}$) and the outer VO($\mathbf{y}$).

If the true production set Y is convex and monotonic, the inner requirement set VI can be marked by connecting the observed input requirement points (Figure 5-8). This is the smallest set that contains the observed values.

VO($\mathbf{y}$) is defined as all $\mathbf{x}$ for which $\mathbf{w}_t\mathbf{x} \geq \mathbf{w}_t\mathbf{x}_t$ for all t such that $\mathbf{y}_t \leq \mathbf{y}$. That means that it contains all $\mathbf{x}$ that will produce $\mathbf{y}$ or less at greater or equal cost as

---

13 Cf. Varian (1992), p. 18.

14 Cf. Varian (1984), p. 582.

the cost-minimizing $\mathbf{x}_t$, when applying the price vector $\mathbf{w}_t$ that corresponds to $\mathbf{x}_t$. It is possible to show that the outer bound VO($\mathbf{y}$) of the input requirement set V($\mathbf{y}$) contains V($\mathbf{y}$). VO($\mathbf{y}$) contains all input points that cost more than the actual (cost-minimizing) input combinations x_t observed. If there were an input combination that were cheaper, it would have been chosen instead. If VO($\mathbf{y}$) did not contain V($\mathbf{y}$), then there must be an $\mathbf{x}$ that is in V($\mathbf{y}$) but not in VO($\mathbf{y}$). That would mean there must be some t that fulfills the demand $\mathbf{y}_t \leq \mathbf{y}$, but for which $\mathbf{w}_t\mathbf{x} < \mathbf{w}_t\mathbf{x}_t$. But if $\mathbf{x}$ is in V($\mathbf{y}$), it can produce at least $\mathbf{y}_t$ units of output, although according to $\mathbf{w}_t\mathbf{x} < \mathbf{w}_t\mathbf{x}_t$, it costs less than $\mathbf{x}_t$. This contradicts the assumption that $\mathbf{x}_t$ is a cost-minimizing factor bundle (WACM). Figure 5-8 shows the two input requirement sets for two input combinations and two input price combinations, with their respective iso cost lines.[15]

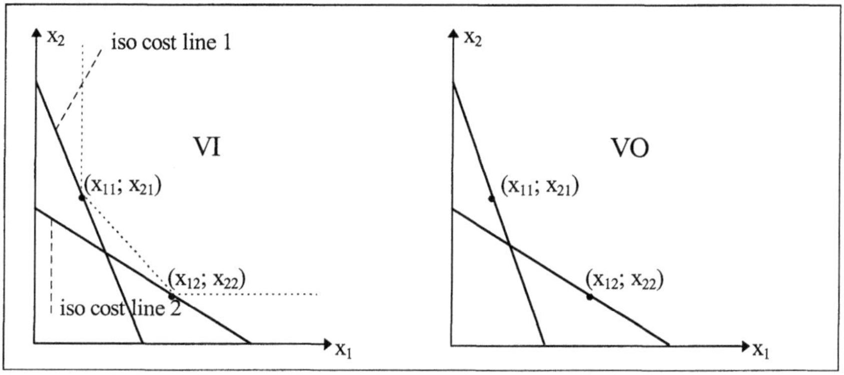

Figure 5-8: Inner (VI) and outer (VO) input requirement sets[16]

Duality exists if it can be shown that the cost function of a firm summarizes all the economically relevant aspects of the firm's technology. The firm's technology is characterized in this case by its input requirements, which is the alternative to describing the technology by giving its production function.

This means that:[17]

1. Given the cost function, one must be able to define the original input requirement set V($\mathbf{y}$).

---

[15] The iso cost line for a given input price combination shows the input combinations that produce the same costs. Cf. Chambers (1988), pp. 82 ff.

[16] Cf. Varian (1984), p. 592.

[17] Cf. Varian (1992), p. 84.

2. If the original technology is monotonic and convex, the technology constructed from the cost function must be identical to the original technology.

3. If the original technology were nonconvex or nonmonotonic, the constructed input requirement set should be a convexified, monotonized version of the original set, where the constructed technology has the same cost function as the original technology.

Ad 1. The natural generalization of the outer bound of the input requirement set VO(**y**) is V*(**y**), for whose **x** the following holds: **wx** ≥ **wx**(**w**,**y**) = C(**w**,**y**) for all **w** ≥ 0. V*(**y**) of course will also contain the original input requirement set V(**y**), because VO(**y**) already does. The cost function will only contain the economically relevant portions of V(**y**), but if the original technology is convex and monotonic, V*(**y**) will actually be equal to V(**y**). This is because in that case every point in V(**y**) will be a cost-minimizing factor demand for some price vector **w** > 0.[18]

Proof: V(**y**) has already been shown to be in V*(**y**). Now it must be only shown that if **x** is in V*(**y**), it must also be in V(**y**). If this were not the case, then by using the separating hyperplane theorem[19] there must be a vector **w*** > 0 such that **w*x** < **w*z** for all **z** in V(**y**). If **z*** were to minimize costs at the prices **w***, then **w*x** < **w*z*** = C(**w***,**y**). But if that were so, then **x** could not be in V*(**y**). q. e. d.

Ad 2. The assumption of monotonicity for the cost function can be accepted through plausibility reasoning: if **x** can produce **y**, and **x'** is greater than **x**, then **x'** can at least also produce **y**.

Assuming that the production set Y is convex, i. e., substituting one factor by another requires more and more of the other factor, the more that is substituted, is another plausible assumption. This in turn implies that the associated input requirement set V(**y**) is convex:

Proof: If (**y**,**x**) and (**y**,**x'**) are in Y, then (*l***y** + (1-*l*)**y**, *l***x** + (1-*l*)**x'**) are also in Y due to the convexity of Y. Hence if **x** and **x'** are in V(**y**), *l***x** + (1-*l*)**x'** is in V(**y**) and thus V(**y**) must also be convex. q. e. d.

Thus if the original technology is convex and monotonic, the cost function associated with the technology can be used to completely reconstruct the technology.

Ad 3. If V(**y**) is not convex, then the question arises how the associated cost function C(**w**,**y**) with its input requirement set V*(**y**) is related to a cost function

---

[18] For the description below cf. Varian (1984).

[19] The separating hyperplane theorem states that for two convex disjoint sets it is possible to find a hyperplane that separates the two sets.

C*(**w**,**y**) defined as min **wx** with **x** in V*(**y**). It can be shown that these are equal, due to their definitions.

Proof: C*(**w**,**y**) will be ≤ C(**w**,**y**), and V*(**y**) contains V(**y**). As from V*(**y**)'s definition **w'x'** ≥ C(**w'**,**y**), there cannot be a cost-minimizing bundle **x'** for prices **w'** in V*(**y**) that has the property **w'x'** = C*(**w'**,**y**) < C(**w'**,**y**).

So if the original technology is not convex, the cost function can still be used to reconstruct the original technology.

No information is lost by aligning the measurement of efficiency with the cost instead of the production function, if the duality principle holds between these two functions.[20] Another reason for estimating efficiency measures via the cost function is the possibility to easily incorporate outputs of different dimensions. This is especially important in multiproduct companies.

Gorman (1968) and McFadden (1978) first established the duality between production and profit functions, which can be explained in a similar fashion as the duality between production and cost functions and will not be expounded on here.

5.1.4 Production and Efficiency in the Context of this Study

In this chapter, the goal is to relate the informational inefficiency of the firms as captured in the agency variables (see chapter 2.3.2) to at least one of the x-efficiencies of a firm. This productive efficiency can take the form of the three x-efficiencies technical, allocative and distributive efficiency.

Using annual statements of German stock corporations as the source of data, initially only the positions given in the far right column of Figure 5-1 through Figure 5-3 above are available, i. e., the sales, the total costs of the input factors, and the total profits. It is not possible to measure the output in units, only in DM values. Therefore, the outputs used here will not be true unit outputs, but of necessity will be valued at their sales price.

Using annual statement data as planned in this analysis creates the problem of specifying technical efficiency. The only available data is the monetary worth of the inputs. What remains elusive is the required non-valued amount of inputs put into production (Figure 5-1). This rules out at least the separate analysis of the technical efficiency of the firms.

Taking the point of view of the distributive efficiency, using balance sheet data the necessary distinction between an industrial firm's outputs is not possible as

20 Cf. McFadden (1978), pp. 3 ff.; Shephard (1981) pp. 17 ff; Färe/Primont (1995), pp. 43 ff.

separate products cannot be accounted for. Instead, the sales constitute one (valued) output bundle. The price of the output is also not available. It is finally not possible to determine which input portions were used to produce which output. Hence, the distinction between "profit 1" and "profit 2" as given in Figure 5-3 is not possible and the distributive efficiency, which attributes inefficiency to separate outputs, cannot be the subject of analysis.

This leaves the allocative efficiency to be studied for its suitability. In order to estimate it, data is needed on the inputs, their prices and their costs (Figure 5-2), as inefficiencies are related to inputs in this context. Again, as for the technical efficiency the input amounts are unavailable when confined to annual statements. Any attempts to identify allocative inefficiency must fail as it is not possible to ascertain that it is not in fact technical inefficiency one has measured.

Therefore, assuming output prices and with them output amounts to be constants in a manager's reckoning, the joint analysis of the technical and allocative x-efficiency of industrial firms lies within the scope of this study, without a clear distinction being possible between the two. The allocative and distributive efficiencies are more or less two sides of the same medal, assigning inefficiency either to amounts of input or output, so it suffices to speak only of the technical and allocative inefficiencies from here on. Since the thrust of this study is to analyze the managerial influence on inefficiency, the failure to distinguish between technical and allocative inefficiency is not a major concern.

It is important to note, on the other hand, that one only sees the full picture of the situation of a company if one also regards the revenue side. As mentioned earlier, this is a strong argument for making the profit efficiency[21] the focus of the study.[22] But several reasons may speak against using the profit efficiency here: First, the profits of companies possibly are more volatile than the costs and make it harder to identify developments or patterns over time or in the cross section. From the purely empirical point of view, significant results are harder to obtain if the standard deviations of the variables studied rise in proportion to the means of the variables. Table 5-1 shows the descriptives of the costs and profits of the companies in the dataset used in this chapter.[23] The higher standard deviation to mean ratio actually cannot be confirmed here.

21 The profit efficiency would gauge the management's ability to maximize profits with a given set of inputs.

22 See also Berger/Mester (1997).

23 Negative costs result from negative equity return ratios coupled with low or zero other costs. I. e., increasing inputs reduces costs!

variable	mean	std. dev	minimum	maximum	valid N	std. dev./mean
cost	567134.35	1836099.85	-4530396	22384630	1669	3.237
profit	1184441.3	3766734.35	-7456198	47947469	1669	3.180
ln(cost)	11.66	2.00	2.12	17.05	1547	0.171
ln(profit)	12.34	2.05	1.17	17.69	1433	0.166

Table 5-1: Descriptives of costs and profits

The second reason not to include the profit efficiency in a central role in this study is that the types of outputs I am considering here are already valued in DM and thus the cost functions to be estimated are already one step closer to being profit functions than standard cost functions.

In addition, Table 5-2 shows the correlations between the costs and profits, as well as their logarithmed counterparts. The high correlations of over 75 % suggest that there is not too much difference between the two variables and thus the results from using either variable should be very similar.

From a purely empirical point of view, profits as the difference between two values, revenues and costs, can more easily become zero or less and therefore additional steps must be taken in order to still be able to logarithm the profits of all cases. In the interest of keeping the procedures as simple as possible, costs are preferable to profits.

	profit		ln(profit)
cost	.7537*** (1669)	ln(cost)	.8551*** (1311)

(Coefficient/(No. of Cases)); *** = significant at the 1 % level

Table 5-2: Correlations between costs and profits

Finally, the aggregated performance analysis presented in chapter 4 already did address the profitability of the companies, so studying the profit efficiency here might just duplicate the results found earlier.

By judging the efficiency of a company solely by its cost efficiency, I assume that input factor quality and prices may vary from one firm to the next, but that the output quality is equal and/or the prices for these products are constant, or that any differences are negligible. Insofar as output qualities are homogeneous and prices are dictated by the market, industrial firms must concentrate on improving their cost efficiency.

5.1.5 Classification of the Methods of Efficiency Measurement

It must be noted that all of the empirical methods which rely on real observations to derive an efficiency benchmark or frontier can in reality only provide best-practice frontiers and not theoretically obtainable frontiers. That means two things. First, the inefficiencies measured will generally be less than the actual inefficiency, as the inefficiency is only measured in relation to the best firms. These firms themselves will also be inefficient to a certain degree, though.

Secondly, the determination of efficiency using best-practice benchmarks remains a relative measure. That means that changes in inefficiency of a company might not be due to changes in the company's practice, but rather to a shift of the best practice frontier. Also, generally decreasing inefficiencies cannot simply be interpreted as improvements in efficiency, but mean that the field of companies is moving closer and closer together. Obviously, the field can expand again later on, for reasons that remain to be studied.

Various methods of empirically determining the efficiency of companies are possible as shown in Figure 5-9.[24] The initial distinction is between the parametric and non-parametric methods. The parametric methods employ a functional form to state the relationship in question, such as a cost function as discussed above. The shaded areas show the classification of the method that will be applied in this analysis.[25]

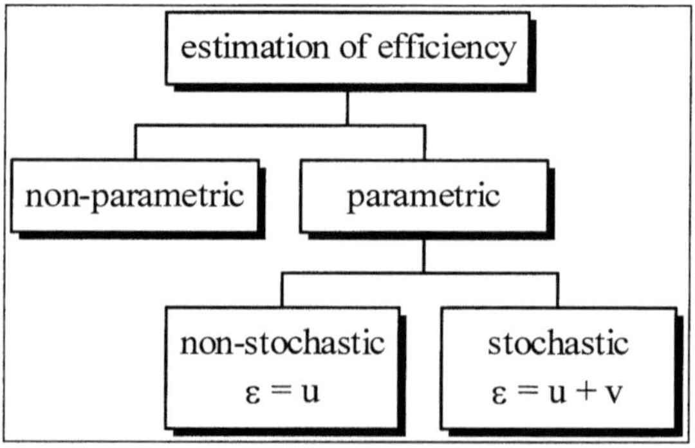

Figure 5-9: Classification of estimation methods

24 See also Førsund/Lovell/Schmidt (1980), pp. 7 f.

25 A test of the consistency of the results of various frontier efficiency methods is in Bauer/Berger/Ferrier/Humphrey (1998).

5.1.5.1 Non-Parametric Methods

The non-parametric methods can often be described as forms of linear programming, in which an envelope is drawn around the dataset according to varying algorithms. The distance of an actual datapoint to that envelope is interpreted as inefficiency. The envelope can be described as the efficient frontier of the observed technology.

Obviously, there are various methods of determining the distance to the envelope. Taking the shortest possible connection is one possibility, while the **data envelopment analysis** (DEA) method[26] measures the distance to the envelope along the ray drawn from the data point through the origin.[27] The DEA method will not be developed further here, Seiford/Thrall (1990) for example provide more details on the method.

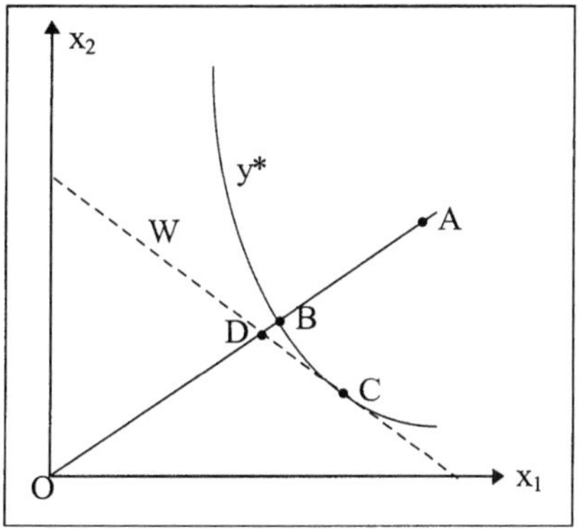

Figure 5-10: Technical and allocative efficiency[28]

The simplest non-parametric approach however is from Farrell (1957). For lack of a better name it is called **Farrell's method of efficiency measurement** and is depicted above in Figure 5-10. If a firm is producing at point A, then the ratio OB/OA can be interpreted as a measure of technical inefficiency. B is on the isoquant of production level y*. Assuming that W shows the ratio of the prices w_1 and w_2 of the inputs x_1 and x_2 to each other, OD/OB describes the allocative inefficiency. Production in D costs the same as in C, but is allocatively less ef-

---

26 Developed by Charnes/Cooper/Rhodes (1978).

27 Cf. Schefczyk (1996).

28 According to Farrell (1957).

ficient. The cost of D is less than the technically efficient but allocatively inefficient point B. OD/OA measures total inefficiency.

If one is able to derive the coordinates or values of the points B and D from an estimation, one is able to actually separately compute the two elements of the productive x-inefficiency, the technical and the allocative inefficiencies. This is possible by applying Shephard's Lemma[29] to the estimation. Shephard's Lemma states that the first partial derivatives of a cost function by the input prices (denoted by ∇_w) provide the coordinates x_C at C in Figure 5-10. This relationship is shown in equation (5-1).

$$x_C = \nabla_w C(\mathbf{y}^*, \mathbf{w}^*) \qquad (5\text{-}1)$$

The intersection of the line connecting A and the origin with the cost plane W gives the coordinates for D. B can be determined by exploiting the fact that it lies on the same line connecting A and the origin as D does, lies on the isoquant y^*, and by setting one input price w_N^B to 1, in order to reduce the unknown elements by one.[30] This is the equivalent of using relative prices.

Since the isoquant y^* is estimated using actual observations, the Farrell approach can be classed as a best-practice method of efficiency measurement.

Advantages of non-parametric methods are that no functional form must be specified,[31] which means that there is also no danger of the misspecification of the production function. In a similar vein, no distributional assumption must be made about the disturbance terms, which is necessary for parametric approaches. Also, no data on input prices is required.[32] A related advantage is that no restrictions are placed on the dimensions, or units of measurement, of the input factors. This makes it possible to employ actual input amounts in the analysis. Examples would be the number of screws used to assemble a cabinet, or the number of beds in a hospital. The available data already gives valued inputs, so this advantage cannot be used here. The returns to scale must generally be assumed to be constant, which can be restrictive.[33]

A disadvantage of the non-parametric class of efficiency determination is that it leaves no room for errors in measurement, or pure luck. This makes the non-parametric class very susceptible to outliers, in addition to their being non-averaging methods. Outliers cause the whole efficient frontier to move away

---

29 Cf. Shephard (1981).

30 Cf. Kopp/Diewert (1982).

31 Which can also be seen as a disadvantage.

32 Cf. Ferrantino/Ferrier/Linvill (1995), p. 37.

33 Cf. Førsund/Lovell/Schmidt (1980), p. 9.

from the bulk of the data to a normally unattainable distance, unless the outliers are corrected or removed.

The non-parametric methods in sum generally ignore input prices and thus measure technical efficiency.[34] As this efficiency is least interesting from the economic point of view, most empirical analyses will be found using some form of parametric efficiency estimation.

5.1.5.2 Parametric Methods

5.1.5.2.1 Non-Stochastic Methods

Parametric forms of efficiency estimation have the advantage that they allow for non-constant returns to scale. The fact that they allow a parametric characterization of frontier technology is often in itself seen as an advantage.

A disadvantage is that the number of efficient companies is often restricted by the approach itself. Efficiency estimates usually do not have any statistical properties, i. e., the significance of efficiency estimates cannot be tested.[35] The outlier problem of the non-parametric approaches persists, too. Still, this form of efficiency estimation will be used in the analysis.

The parametric method of efficiency estimation can be subdivided into two further categories, the non-stochastic and the stochastic methods. The non-stochastic or deterministic method takes the results from the estimation of the functional representation of the process being analyzed, such as the cost function, and interprets the error term ε as the inefficiency u.[36] The fact that the whole error term is interpreted as inefficiency makes the non-stochastic method of parametric efficiency measurement susceptible to the same criticism as the non-parametric methods, i. e., that it leaves no room for errors in measurement or luck, the elements the error term usually should capture.

A different type of a deterministic parametric approach is the **distribution-free approach**,[37] in which separate regressions are run for several periods, typically years. The companies' errors are then summed over all regressions. As the sum of all real errors is zero as the number of cases studied approaches infinity, any

---

34 Cf. Berger/Mester (1997), p. 905.

35 Cf. Førsund/Lovell/Schmidt (1980), p. 10.

36 Cf. e. g. Aigner/Chu (1968).

37 Cf. Berger (1993) who refers to Schmidt/Sickles (1984) as the ultimate source of this method to measure efficiency.

result deviating from zero can be interpreted as a non-error element, in this case, as (in)efficiency.

The **corrected ordinary least squares** (COLS) approach is another non-stochastic parametric method of inefficiency estimation.[38] A linear regression fitted on the data has the mean of the error term subtracted from the regression constant and added to the error in the case of a cost function. It is also possible to simply reduce the constant by the amount of the largest negative residual. The regression is thus pushed downward toward the efficient border and creates a frontier. If done following the first method described, some datapoints can still end up below the corrected position of the regression line. This is not possible when following the latter method. The opposite adjustment must be performed for production functions, where the efficient border is the upper boundary of the dataset.

Another deterministic parametric approach is the **thick frontier** method,[39] which requires the data to be split into several groups, usually quartiles, according to the average costs of the firms. Firms with the highest average cost are assumed to be the least efficient, and vice versa. A regression is run for the efficient group and its result forms the so-called thick frontier. Regressions for the other partitions, usually the lowest-efficiency group, can also be produced, and will provide different coefficients for each group.[40] These regression estimations do not contain information on inefficiency. The data from the non-thick-frontier datasets are then input into the thick frontier regression model. Differences in the error terms are assumed to be simply random errors, while the cost differences that the estimates provide are attributed to inefficiency, as well as differences in output quantities and input prices, and environmental variables.[41]

A disadvantage of the thick frontier method is that it is susceptible to the choice of the number of groups the data is divided into. Another difficult but central assumption is that low average-cost companies are automatically the most cost-efficient companies, which preempts the results of the analysis in a fashion. A high-cost company might be producing high revenues and thus also be (profit) efficient. Therefore, some researchers divide their data into size quintiles.[42]

---

38 Cf. Richmond (1974), Lovell (1993), pp. 21 f.

39 Cf. Berger/Humphrey (1991).

40 Cf. Lau/Yotopoulos (1971), Yotopoulos/Lau (1973), Trosper (1978).

41 Cf. Bauer/Hancock (1993), p. 292.

42 Cf. Berger/Humphrey (1991).

5.1.5.2.2 Stochastic Methods

The stochastic parametric methods of efficiency estimation can be divided into the fixed effects model and the random effects model, the latter of which is the method that will be used here.

The **fixed effects** or **within estimator**[43] model can be estimated by adding one dummy for each of the N firms involved to a regression through the origin, i. e., one without a constant, or by adding N-1 dummies to a model with a constant.[44] Either version avoids total collinearity of the independent variables which would make it impossible to estimate a regression model. The dummies will capture the inefficiency of each firm, while the interpretation of the error term remains unchanged in comparison with standard regressions. Assuming that the inefficiency is constant for each firm, this method can be applied to panel data. It must be noted that non-varying effects over time can also be captured by the model's dummies, so caution must be exercised.

The **random effects** model is very similar to the deterministic method which specifies a certain distribution for the error term of the regression. In order to account for the statistical noise that is missing in the deterministic models, the error term is split into two parts. One part is normally distributed with a mean of zero and captures the luck and errors in measurement that were lacking before. The other part follows the same one-sided distributions used in deterministic parametric models and stands for inefficiency. The two parts with their respective distributions are combined into one error term for the purposes of the estimation of the regression. The error term must be split up into its components in a second step.[45]

The first examples for this method of determination of inefficiency come from Aigner/Lovell/Schmidt (1977) and Meeusen/van den Broeck (1977). A popular method of estimating such a model is the maximum likelihood technique, which allows the distribution of the residual to be specified. If a normal distribution is specified, the maximum likelihood technique and the OLS regression deliver the same results.

A disadvantage with this fairly popular method of efficiency estimation is that it requires an assumption to be made concerning the distribution of the inefficiency part of the error term. Berger (1993) finds that for US banks, the distri-

---

43 Cf. Schmidt/Sickles (1984).

44 Cf. Greene (1993), pp. 84 f.

45 Cf. Jondrow/Lovell/Materov/Schmidt (1982).

bution of the inefficiency variable more closely follows a normal distribution than a one-sided distribution.[46]

5.2 Empirical Analysis of the Efficiency of German Stock Corporations

5.2.1 Hypotheses

In the context of the agency theory, several hypotheses can be postulated based on the cost efficiency of companies. Again, to test these hypotheses reference is made to the set of agency variables developed earlier (chapter 2.3.2). The hypotheses are very similar to those developed for the aggregated return analysis.

Assuming that managers who can operate uncontrolled by the owners of a firm will not exert as much effort to cut costs and improve profits above a certain safety level, the first and main hypothesis states that:

1. Manager-controlled companies will be less x-efficient than owner-controlled companies.

Should managers who are able to operate unhindered by the ownership be able to better exploit their informational advantages to the benefit of the company, the reverse observation could be possible. This would, in effect, reject the agency theory even while supporting the informational asymmetry assumption. This would mean that

a) the management is operating in the interest of the ownership, and that

b) owners meddling with the affairs of their companies' management tend to divert the companies from their optimal results.

There might also be additional agency factors omitted from the study. E. g., it was stated earlier that there is no data on performance-oriented payment agreements in the top levels of management in Germany. That could mean that some companies are being classed as management-controlled, while the management's interests are actually closely tied to the ownership's interests through the forms of compensation agreed upon in the managers' contracts. This, too, would cause no differences in the cost efficiency to be detectable.

The relation of creditor monitoring to manager control is slightly different. Both managers and creditors will be intent on maintaining a certain level of return, and thus of costs in the company, but are not interested in pushing returns as

46 This might simply be a demonstration of the fact that under certain circumstances, many distributions can be approximated by the normal distribution. Cf. Bleymüller/Gehlert/Gülicher (1988), pp. 65 ff.

high as possible. This is because creditors will not participate in higher returns, as they receive fixed interest payments. Managers wish to both avoid the high return volatility possibly associated with the higher returns and keep expectations of the stockholders for future returns from reaching too high levels. Assuming that creditors wish a company to maintain a higher level of returns than uncontrolled managers, the following should hold:

2.	Manager-controlled companies will operate slightly less x-efficiently than creditor-controlled firms.

Creditor control was discussed earlier as affecting the returns of a company by pushing toward slightly lower, but less volatile revenues. It is not clear if this effect should be visible on the efficiency level. Creditors will not necessarily break down a company's aggregate performance into such detail as the ownership or management will, due to the fact that as outsiders, they have less access to inside information (especially in the case of bond issue holders). The access they do have to a company's inside information can be available on a less frequent basis. Having lower return demands, creditors can more probably expect their demands to be met and the effort monitoring costs will not be as worthwhile as if they were demanding the higher returns that shareholders expect. Thus, the following hypothesis is proposed as a logical follow-on from hypotheses one and two. Less significant differences than those postulated in the other hypotheses should be expected.

3.	Creditor-controlled companies will operate less x-efficiently than ownership-controlled firms.

Considering the possibility of estimating the efficiency of the firms anew each year, it is also possible to postulate developments over time in the efficiency of the firms. It is possible that manager-controlled firms will be slower to adjust to increased competition. The efficiency of such firms might also decrease faster in times of economic upturn, assuming that such periods of prosperity lead to complacency. If efficiency gains go hand in hand with economic upswings instead of preceding them, decreases in efficiency would occur concurrently with economic downturns.[47]

4.	Manager-controlled firms will increase their x-efficiency at slower rates and decrease it at faster rates than owner-controlled companies.

As far as sectors are concerned, companies in different sectors will differ in their factor intensity, exposure to competition, and level of government regulation.

---

47 Cf. Tebroke/Wolf (1997).

Obviously, differences in cost efficiency can also be expected under these circumstances. From the agency point of view, the level of competition and the degree of government regulation appear most interesting. These factors determine the effectiveness of the sales markets as an external market-based control mechanism for the management that can either supplement or replace the measures the principals might take to align their management's interests with their own. For the degree of competition in each market the following hypothesis is formulated:

5. Firms in highly competitive markets will be more x-efficient than companies in less competitive markets.

In addition, a management uncontrolled by competition will be able to get by with more inefficiencies than one subject to this form of external control. Competition will force such companies to improve their cost efficiency in order to survive. That means that in uncompetitive sectors, the range of inefficiencies between owner and manager-controlled companies should be greater than in highly competitive sectors. The sixth hypothesis thus states:

6. In uncompetitive sectors, manager-controlled firms will have higher x-inefficiencies than owner-controlled companies. In highly competitive sectors this difference will be insignificant.

The ranking of the five sectors by their competitivity in chapter 2.3.2.6 gave the following order of sectors by amount of hypothesized agency problems, starting from the sector with the least assumed problems to the sector with the most: machinery, electronics, chemicals, food & beverages and in the last place the utilities sector, for which regulations are assumed to have stifled the market as a monitoring instance.

5.2.2 Previous Empirical Research

5.2.2.1 Research on Industrial and Agricultural Firms

The research already done for industrial firms differs from that presented here in that generally, production functions with exact amounts of inputs and outputs were available. Therefore, the estimation of production functions is fairly common. The data is usually only available for a small subset of firms of a very distinct type (cf. Table 5-3). Studies relying solely on Monte Carlo data, such as Aigner/Lovell/Schmidt (1977) and Olson/Schmidt/Waldman (1980), were omitted here.

author (year) function/estimation	industry, period, country	outputs	inputs
Aigner/Chu (1968) linear programming production function	metals industry 1957-58 USA	• value added	• labor • capital • technical efficiency
Ball/Chambers (1982) translog cost function	meat products industry 1954 USA	• industrial meat production index	• labor • capital • energy • intermediate materials • capital structure
Banker/Conrad/ Strauss (1986) translog cost function, DEA	hospitals 1978 North Carolina, USA	• patient days (patient below 14) • patient days (patient 14 – 65) • patient days (patient above 65)	• nursing • ancillary • administration • capital
Battese/Coelli (1988) stochastic frontier production function	dairy farms 1978-81 Australia	• returns	• fodder, seed in $AUS • capital
Battese/Coelli (1992) stochastic frontier production function	paddy farms 1975-85 India	• value of crops	• land • labor • bullock • costs
Cantner/Hanusch/ Westermann (1995) DEA	electricity utility industry 1983-92 Germany	• electricity	• labor • capital • purchased electricity
Cornwell/Schmidt/ Sickles (1990) GLS production function	airline industry 1970-81 USA	• ton miles	• capital • labor • energy • material input
Ferrantino/Ferrier/ Linvill (1995) Linear programming of cost and production functions	sugar factories 1981-86 India	• sugar • molasses	• roller area • knife sets • boiling capacity • generating capacity • agricultural sucrose • rated capacity • nonseasonal labor • seasonal labor

author (year) function/estimation	industry, period, country	outputs	inputs
Greene (1980) Cobb-Douglas cost and production functions, various estimation methods	Aigner/Chu (1968) data USA	• value added	• labor • fixed assets
Greene (1990) Cobb-Douglas cost functions	electric utility industry 1955 USA	• value added	• labor • fixed assets • fuel (utility industry)
Greene (1993) production and cost functions, various estimation methods	airline industry 1970-84 USA	aggregate of: • passenger service • charter service • freight • mail	• labor • fuel • fight equipment • ground property • materials
Hildebrand/Liu (1965) production function, simultaneous equation model	ten sectors 1957 USA	• value added	• capital • labor • technological change
Kneip/Simar (1995) production function	railway companies 1970-83 worldwide	• km covered • ratio of passenger trains • network density	• employees/km
Meeusen/van den Broeck (1977) production function	ten sectors 1962 France	• value added	• labor • capital
Pitt/Lee (1981) Cobb-Douglas production function	weaving industry 1972-73, 1975 Indonesia	• value added	• labor • capital
Reifschneider/ Stevenson (1991) stochastic frontier cost function	electric utility industry 1964-72 USA	• net generation	• labor • capital • fuel
Schalk/Untiedt/ Lüschow (1994) fixed effects and stochastic frontier production function	mining and processing sectors 1978-89 Germany	• real value added	• labor • capital

author (year) function/estimation	industry, period, country	outputs	inputs
Schmidt/Sickles (1984) production function	airline industry 1970-78 USA	• tons/miles	• capital • labor • energy • materials
Todd (1985) Farrell frontier	manufacturing industry 1970-80 Germany	• net output	• labor • capital

Table 5-3: Previous empirical studies of the efficiency of industrial and agricultural firms

The presentation of the studies will be grouped into those using non-parametric and parametric methods, and the parametric studies are further subdivided into those using cross-sectional and panel data. There are too few non-stochastic analyses of industrial firms to merit the distinction between stochastic and non-stochastic papers.

Non-parametric:

Cantner/Hanusch/Westermann study the inefficiency of electric utilities in Germany, which are government-regulated, using the DEA method. They find inefficiencies both due to government regulation and company-level factors.

Banker/Conrad/Strauss (1986) show the possibilities of the DEA function by applying it to hospitals, where the "output" is measured in patient days. They compare their results to a translog cost function. They find that the DEA estimates find more diverse behavior in the returns to scale than the translog function.

Todd (1985) computes the Farrell measures of inefficiency for West German industry sectors and compares the results to simple cross-sectional estimates of Cobb-Douglas production functions for two of the years included in the study. He finds little change in the ranking between more efficient and less efficient sectors.

Ferrantino/Ferrier/Linvill (1995) use a linear programming approach to estimate the inefficiency of sugar producers in India. Their inputs are broken down to such items as the number of knife sets employed in the production process.

Parametric:

Non-panel data:

The study of Aigner/Chu (1968) is quite interesting, despite its age, as it attempts to model the value added of the metals industry using labor and capital as inputs, as well as the technical efficiency within the firms. The model goes back to an earlier work by Hildebrand/Liu (1965). Aigner/Chu (1968) construct a two-equation simultaneously interdependent system of the value added and the labor demand using data aggregated on the state level. Additional explanatory variables include the speed of adjustment of the labor demand to its optimal rate. Their model can be classified as deterministic parametric in the context of Figure 5-9.

Hildebrand/Liu (1965) apply their model to ten separate sectors of the U. S. economy. They construct four different simultaneous equation models, with the value added, demand for production labor, and demand for non-production labor as the dependent variables of the three equations in each model. Each of the four models is applied to each sector separately.

An exemplary analysis of a translog cost function is provided by Ball/Chambers (1982). Using annual data from 1954–1976, they estimate a non-homothetic, non-neutral[48] translog cost function for the meat industry. There is no cross section implied, though, as the data used is aggregated to the sector level.

Meeusen and van den Broeck (1977), who started off the split-residual method of analysis, apply their technique to 10 French industry sectors in 1962 and estimate separate functions for each sector. They note that the error term remains fairly large, implying that any deterministic approach to inefficiency measurement could lead to gross mis-estimations of the inefficiency levels of the companies.

Panel data:

Battese/Coelli (1988, 1992) estimate stochastic frontier production models for dairy farms in Australia (1988) and paddy farms in India (1992). They use panel data and allow for firm effects to be time invariant in their earlier paper, and time dependent in their later study. An exponential dependency is modeled there. Including a time variable in the frontier specification produced time invariant technical inefficiencies.

Cornwell/Schmidt/Sickles (1990) also develop a panel estimation method which allows for cross-sectional and serial variations in the technical inefficiency. They do that by including the simple and squared time indexes in the model.

Greene's studies are most interesting as he provides the comparison between the results of various methods for measuring inefficiency. In his 1993 paper he also compares production and cost functions. His earlier papers use the same data as Aigner/Chu (1968), making his results eminently comparable to other studies.

---

48 Neutral cost function imply that technical change leaves the relative cost shares of the inputs undisturbed. Cf. Chambers (1988), p. 218.

Kneip/Simar (1995) also provide an analysis of panel data, estimating only the average inefficiency per firm due to the dearth of data they have available (17 railway companies over 14 years). Pitt/Lee (1981) even only estimate the average inefficiency of the whole sector they study, the Indonesian weaving industry.

Schalk/Untiedt/Lüschow provide one of the rare studies for the German market, comparing the fixed effects and stochastic frontier methods with each other for the mining and processing (verarbeitende Industrie) sectors.[49]

5.2.2.2 Research in Banking Firms

In the 1990s, a whole plethora of research has been published in the field of banking efficiency. With many bank products interpretable as monetary flows, the distinction between production and cost function blurs slightly, as the distinction between unvalued and valued netputs disappears.[50]

There are two concurring models for banking production, the most common one being the intermediation approach of dividing between inputs and outputs. Next to personnel and tangible assets deposits are seen as inputs. The underlying rationale is that money is taken in from others, banks and non banks, with the sole intention of loaning it out again. The loans then appear on the asset side of the balance sheet.

This approach does not acknowledge that it is an achievement in itself to offer a customer the possibility to deposit money to be used for monetary transactions or be disposed of later together with the interest earned. This separate action has to be accounted for separately, as seen in the market interest method used in bank controlling.[51] It is not important, and in most cases not attributable, for what purpose the deposits are actually used.

The less common model of production is the factor system of Deppe[52] that is known as the production approach. Labor and real capital as well as equity are input factors that are used to produce asset-side, liability-side and off-balance sheet products (pure services). Equity must underlie a bank's transactions to a certain degree, justifying the view that it is a production factor, and indeed often a bottleneck factor. The production approach takes into account that services are

---

49 The literature on efficiency is too large to summarize in total here. Reference to further, earlier studies can be found e. g. in Førsund/Lovell/Schmidt (1980), pp. 14 f.

50 Cf. Swank (1996) p. 157 on using the number of accounts as the unit measure of netputs.

51 Cf. Schierenbeck (1997); Breuer (1994).

52 Cf. Deppe (1978).

increasingly important in the German universal banking system, where banks offer such products as security transactions, investment consulting and insurance mediation. A recent example that uses a production approach similar to Deppe's to characterize banking production can be found in Tebroke/Wolf (1997).[53] Pulley/Braunstein (1992) use deposits as both inputs and outputs to account for their dual character.

Since very much has been published recently in the field of banking efficiency, especially for the US banking sector, it will not be possible to give a satisfactory overview over the extant literature in the framework of this study. Therefore, a selection of the papers with the greatest impact or prepared with German data will be presented below.

author (year) function/estimation	bank type, period, country	outputs	inputs
Bauer/Hancock (1993) thick frontier variant (free disposable hull) translog cost function	Federal Reserve check processing 1979-90 USA	• total checks processed	• labor • buildings • materials • transit
Berger (1993) distribution-free approach stochastic frontier translog cost function	commercial banks 1980-89 USA	• demand deposits • retail deposits • real estate loans • commercial and industrial loans • installment loans	• labor • physical capital • deposit interest • purchased funds interest
DeYoung (1998) thick frontier approach	national banks 1991-92 USA	• loans • transaction services • fee-based activities	• labor • physical capital • deposits

53 See Hughes/Mester (1993), p. 302, for a test concerning the nature of deposits. They are determined to be inputs, as increasing the use of other inputs should decrease the use of the deposits (partial derivative is negative).

author (year) function/estimation	bank type, period, country	outputs	inputs
Lang/Welzel (1996) fixed/random effects translog cost function	cooperative banks 1989-92 Germany	• short-term loans to non-banks • long-term loans to non-banks • loans to banks • bonds, cash, real estate • fees and commissions • revenue from commodity sales	• labor • physical capital • deposits
Lang/Welzel (1997) thick frontier translog cost function	universal banks 1992 Germany	• short-term loans to non-banks • long-term loans to non-banks • loans to banks • bonds, stocks, cash • fees and commissions	• labor • physical capital • deposits
Mester (1987) translog cost function	savings and loan banks 1982 USA	• mortgage loans • other loans • cash, securities, real estate investments	• labor • physical capital • passbook and demand deposits • high interest accounts
Pi/Timme (1993) stochastic frontier translog cost function	listed banks 1987-90 USA	• commercial and industrial loans • consumer loans • real estate loans • other bank output	• labor • physical capital • deposits
Sheldon (1994) Farrell measure of technical efficiency	universal banks 1988-91 Switzerland	• unsecured loans • non-mortgage loans • mortgage loans • money market investments • securities • real estate • commissions	• labor • physical capital • deposits
Swank (1996) translog cost function	all banks 1982, 1989 Netherlands	• loans • demand deposits • savings deposits • branches	• constant prices assumed

author (year) function/estimation	bank type, period, country	outputs	inputs
Tebroke/Wolf (1997) stochastic frontier translog cost function	universal banks 1991-95 Germany	• loans to non banks • bonds and other securities • savings deposits, certificated liabilities • demand and time deposits • interbank assets and liabilities • commissions and other services	• labor • physical capital • equity
Westermann/Pröll/ Cantner (1996) DEA	Sparkassen 1995 Germany	• deposits • credits • securities	• labor: consultants • labor: tellers • space • technical equipment

Table 5-4: Previous empirical studies of the efficiency of bank firms

One of the most interesting papers from the point of view of the analysis presented here must be DeYoung (1998). The x-efficiency of banks with regard to management competence is tested there, and the assumption that the two are positively linked is confirmed. The management quality is determined by way of bank exam ratings. Simple accounting benchmarks however produce the opposite result, showing that these measures cannot be used to represent efficiency.

Another important study is from Pi/Timme (1993), who test for differences in banking efficiency by control type of the banks. The classification variables are the ownership percentage of the chief executive officers (CEOs) and the joining of the positions of CEO and Chairman of the Board. The product of the two variables is included as well. Pi/Timme (1993) use the translog cost function as the model of productive process. They take the return on assets as an alternative measure of performance. This means they check the efficiency using a disaggregate cost side-only measure and an aggregated profit-based measure.

They find that linking the positions of CEO and chairman of the board is detrimental to performance, with larger differences in returns on assets than in costs, implying that CEO-chairman banks produce higher costs but even higher revenues than non-chairman-CEO banks. Non-chairman-CEO banks show a positive relationship between performance and ownership, whereas a negative or insignificant relationship could be found for chairman-CEO banks. The ownership by institutions or large block holders and the proportion of inside board members seems to be unrelated to performance.

Berger (1993) gives an important application of the distribution-free approach to the banking industry. He tests the distribution of the resulting errors to see if they conform with the typical distributional assumptions made for inefficiency terms. He must reject the hypothesis of one-sided distributions, finding that the errors most closely conform to a normal distribution.

Bauer/Hancock (1993) present an application of the thick frontier method of estimation, applied to a service of the Federal Reserve, check processing. They also run a split-residual translog cost function regression, which can be seen as a sort of benchmark to compare the results of other methods by. DeYoung (1998) provides the most recent example for a thick frontier analysis.

Mester (1987) is provided as an example of early research published in the field. Mester estimates a translog cost function with a SURE model using share equations for the outputs. These were derived by applying Shephard's Lemma to the cost function.

Sheldon (1994) is one of the few examples of the application of the Farrell measure of technical efficiency to the banking sector. His paper is also noteworthy as it is an analysis of the Swiss banking market.[54] Swank (1996) provides an analysis of the Dutch banking industry. His paper, too, is noteworthy, because it employs the production approach of bank production, as opposed to the much more common intermediation approach. Lacking trustworthy information on input costs, he is forced to assume them to be constant for all banks and therefore can omit them from his cost function specification.

The two studies from Lang/Welzel (1996, 1997) represent only some of the research the two have published concerning efficiency in the German banking system. Their 1996 paper studies a panel of what might be called German cooperative banks (Kreditgenossenschaften) using fixed and random effects models, while their 1997 publication provides a thick frontier analysis of about one third of the German banks in 1992. They conclude that internal inefficiency is a much graver problem than inefficiency due to not having the optimal size.

Another analysis for the German banking market is that of Westermann/Pröll/Cantner (1996), which applies detailed DEA analyses to two Bavarian Sparkassen (savings and loan banks).

Finally, Tebroke/Wolf (1997) provide an example for a production approach view of the production function, i. e., they see deposits as an output (service). Based on a stochastic frontier translog cost function they study the efficiency of 510 German banks in separate regressions for the years 1991, 1993 and 1995, studying the x-efficiency and size efficiency of the three bank groups private

---

[54] An analysis using a translog cost function and Data Envelopment Analysis for the Swiss banking sector can be found in Sheldon (1993).

banks, Sparkassen and Genossenschaftsbanken. X-inefficiencies are not size-related, speaking against mergers and acquisitions as a means for quickly improving efficiency.

5.2.3 The Dataset

	1986	1987	1988	1989	1990	1991	1992	Row Total
1. Chemicals	13	8	10	11	12	12	7	73
2. Plastics, Rubber	2	1	1	1	1	1	0	7
3. Mining, Ceramics	8	9	7	8	6	8	3	49
4. Metallurgy	5	5	5	6	2	3	1	27
5. Machinery	18	23	25	25	24	23	14	152
6. Automotive	5	2	2	1	1	1	0	12
7. Electronics, Precision Mechanics	10	9	11	13	11	10	6	70
8. Wood, Paper, Printing	5	2	4	4	4	4	1	24
9. Leather, Fabrics and Apparel	4	4	4	5	5	6	5	33
10.Food & Beverages*	23	21	24	21	20	19	10	138
11.Construction	2	4	4	4	4	4	4	26
12.Trade	4	5	5	5	4	5	3	31
13.Utilities	12	14	11	12	11	9	11	80
14.Holdings, Participation Acquisition,[55] Property Management	2	3	5	5	5	4	4	28
15.Others, including diversified companies	12	13	17	18	16	15	7	98
Column Total	125	123	135	139	126	123	77	848
Total in %	14.7	14.5	15.9	16.4	14.9	14.5	9.1	100.0

Table 5-5: Sectors in Dataset for the Efficiency Analysis, by Year[56]

55 Cf. Horn (1994), pp. 93 ff.

56 Cf. Table 2-3. Shaded sectors are used in the sectoral analysis.

The dataset that was used until now cannot be analyzed here in its entirety as the employee figures are not available for all the companies. This information is necessary to calculate the cost of the input "labor" per unit, i. e., per employee. For the period 1986 to 1992, this information is available for about 80 % of the firms in the dataset during that period (848 datapoints).

There are only a few sectors[57] with enough companies to provide for the necessary degrees of freedom and sufficient intra-sectoral diversification to allow for sector-specific measurement of efficiency. These are the chemical, machinery, electronics, food & beverages and the utilities, with over 50 observations for the seven years (shaded in Table 5-5).[58] Therefore, aside from an overall estimate of efficiency over all seven years available, I will also separately analyze and compare the efficiency of the five sectors mentioned, over all the years.

Single-year estimates of the efficiency are also possible due to there usually being over 120 observations available in each year, excluding 1992, for which there are only 77 cases.

5.2.4 Theoretical and Econometric Considerations

5.2.4.1 Using Translog Functional Form to Estimate the Efficiency Measures

After deciding to use the random effects, stochastic-parametric approach, one is confronted with the task of specifying a production function. From a theoretical point of view, general models are to be preferred over special ones.

One of the most common transformations of economic variables is to take the natural logarithm of the variable. This suggests a first decision to study the natural logarithm of an arbitrary function f(x). The function in the context of efficiency estimation can be a cost, profit or a production function. In this analysis cost functions will be used.

Using the Taylor expansion,[59] in a second decision this function shall be expanded around $x_0 = \{1, 1, ..., 1\}$. This vector is chosen because its logarithm is the zero vector, which is a common point to expand around.

---

57 The sector classification follows the framework used by the Statistisches Bundesamt. If the classification was unclear, information on the company activity from Hoppenstedt & Co. (1986-1991) was additionally taken into consideration.

58 50 observations is given as a minimum to achieve asymptotic characteristics. Cf. Urban (1993), pp. 1, 13; Aldrich/Nelson (1984). Normal distributions of data are already assumed for 30 cases. Cf. Bleymüller/Gehlert/Gülicher (1988) p. 78.

59 Cf. Opitz (1995), p. 537.

In general terms, if a function f can be differentiated as often as wanted in an interval I containing point x (as is done here, x_0 is often set to 0), then the nth-order Taylor series expansion at the point x_0 is:

$$f_n(x) \cong \sum_{i=0}^{n} \frac{f^{(i)}(x_0)}{i!}(x - x_0)^i \quad (5\text{-}2)$$

So if $x_0 = 0$, the second order expansion is $f(0) + x \cdot f'(0) + x^2 \cdot f''(0)/2$. If the series converges for all x, the expansion can be used instead of f(x).[60]

The desired second order Taylor expansion for the logarithm of the function f(x), using as the final specification the logarithmic notation of the arguments x_i and x_j, gives the following result:[61]

$$\ln f(x) \cong \ln f(x_0) + \Sigma(\delta \ln f(x_0)/\delta \ln x_i) \ln x_i + \tfrac{1}{2} \Sigma\Sigma (\delta^2 \ln f(x_0)/\delta \ln x_i\, \delta \ln x_j) \ln x_i \ln x_j \quad (5\text{-}3)$$

The derivatives of $f(x_0)$ in (5-3) can be understood as coefficients. Replacing them with appropriate symbols gives:

$$\ln f(x) \cong \beta_0 \qquad + \Sigma\, \beta_i \ln x_i \qquad + \tfrac{1}{2} \Sigma\Sigma\, \beta_{ij} \ln x_i \ln x_j \quad (5\text{-}4)$$

This is the transcendental logarithmic (translog) function, a second-order approximation to the logarithm of an arbitrary f(x) in the neighborhood of $\ln(x_1) = \{0,\dots 0\}$.

Due to their general nature, translog or other flexible functions[62] are often used to model production, profit or cost functions.[63] These functional forms include more restrictive functions such as the Cobb-Douglas or the constant elasticities of substitution (CES)[64] function as special cases.[65] Simple functions are not well able to describe complex production processes. Many researchers prefer the translog function especially to depict multiple product companies.[66]

---

60 Cf. Binmore (1977) p. 145.

61 Cf. Chambers (1988), p. 167.

62 E. g. the Fourier-flexible form is used in Berger/Mester (1997) to achieve an even better adaptation specifically to the U.S. data.

63 See Guilkey/Lovell (1980) on the flexibility of the translog functional form.

64 Cf. Kmenta (1967).

65 The translog function which was developed as a second order Taylor series expansion around the zero vector might not correctly approximate the underlying function for large input spans, or for variables with values far removed from the expansion point chosen. For this reason, Swank (1996) recommends trying even more flexible methods than the translog cost function, such as the Fourier transformation. He also notes that the translog function cannot accommodate zero output observations.

66 See though McAllister/McManus(1993); Swank (1996).

A translog cost function of the type that will be used here, with M outputs $\mathbf{y}_m$ and N inputs $\mathbf{x}_n$ that can be procured at the cost of $\mathbf{w}_n$, can be written as:

$$\begin{aligned}\ln C &= \alpha + \sum_{m=1}^{M}\beta_m \cdot \ln y_m + 0{,}5 \cdot \sum_{l=1}^{M}\sum_{m=1}^{M}\beta_{lm}\cdot \ln y_l \cdot \ln y_m \\ &+ \sum_{n=1}^{N}\gamma_n \cdot \ln w_n + 0{,}5\cdot \sum_{n=1}^{N}\sum_{p=1}^{N}\gamma_{np}\cdot \ln w_n \cdot \ln w_p \\ &+ \sum_{m=1}^{M}\sum_{n=1}^{N}\delta_{mn}\cdot \ln y_m \cdot \ln w_n\end{aligned} \tag{5-5}$$

This is a non-homothetic function, for which linear homogeneity in the input prices can be specified if the following restrictions on the coefficients are introduced:[67]

$$\begin{aligned}&\sum_{n=1}^{N}\gamma_n = 1 \\ &\sum_{n=1}^{N}\gamma_{np} = 0; p = 1,\ldots,N \\ &\sum_{n=1}^{N}\delta_{mn} = 0; m = 1,\ldots,M\end{aligned} \tag{5-6}$$

The linear homogeneity in the input prices is an important characteristic because it ensures that the duality between production and cost functions applies, as developed above for homogeneous functions (5.1.3.3). The symmetry of the translog cost function can be ensured by setting the following restrictions:[68]

$$\begin{aligned}&\beta_{lm} = \beta_{ml}; m,l = 1,\ldots,M \\ &\gamma_{np} = \gamma_{pn}; n,p = 1,\ldots,N\end{aligned} \tag{5-7}$$

In theory, all relevant production factors x_n (with their prices w_n) and outputs y_m must be included in the functional approach. Only those factors may be omitted that are constant over all observations. In the empirical analysis only the most important production factors can be included. This is because firstly the data often doesn't allow a more detailed look. Secondly, the danger of multicollinearity rises with the number of variables, and the degrees of freedom are reduced. That can lead to statistical results with a low significance and high standard errors. Finally, the empirical content of the model decreases with rising numbers of

---

67 Cf. Diewert/Wales (1987), p. 46.

68 See Diewert/Wales (1987), pp. 44 f.

variables and reduces the possibility of falsification of the model. On the other hand, factors relevant for the production or costs but not included in the model can bias all parameter estimates.[69]

The functional description given by Equation (5-5) was designed for cross-sectional data. In this analysis, it can be used to estimate seven cost functions, one for each of the years in the dataset. In this way, temporal developments in the efficiency of the companies can be observed. Such differences can be expected due to economic cycles, or increasing/decreasing competition among the companies, forcing them to reduce costs or mitigating that force, respectively.

The function for panel data will have the following form, which is identical to Equation (5-5) except for the last line which is added:

$$\begin{aligned}
\ln C \; = \; & \alpha + \sum_{m=1}^{M} \beta_m \cdot \ln y_m + 0.5 \cdot \sum_{l=1}^{M} \sum_{m=1}^{M} \beta_{lm} \cdot \ln y_l \cdot \ln y_m \\
& + \sum_{n=1}^{N} \gamma_n \cdot \ln w_n + 0.5 \cdot \sum_{n=1}^{N} \sum_{p=1}^{N} \gamma_{np} \cdot \ln w_n \cdot \ln w_p \\
& + \sum_{m=1}^{M} \sum_{n=1}^{N} \delta_{mn} \cdot \ln y_m \cdot \ln w_n \\
& + \theta_t \cdot t + 0.5 \cdot \theta_{tt} \cdot t^2 + \sum_{n=1}^{N} \theta_{nt} \ln w_n \cdot t
\end{aligned} \qquad (5\text{-}8)$$

The inclusion of the time index t to the second power makes it possible to twice partially differentiate the equation by *t*. The multiplication of the time index with $\ln w_n$ accounts for the importance that the variability of the input prices over time is given. It is possible to either leave that element out of the function or further expand the equation by multiplying the time index with each of the output variables, but neither approach will be pursued here.[70] If companies from more than one sector are used as inputs, sector dummies must be added to the equation.

In addition to the homogeneity restrictions in (5-6), the following restriction must be added to keep the required linear homogeneity of the input prices:

$$\sum_{n=1}^{N} \theta_{nt} = 0; n = 1,\ldots,N \qquad (5\text{-}9)$$

---

69 The error terms that capture differences between the econometric estimation and reality do not only reflect errors in measurement and random shocks, but also such errors in specification.

70 Schalk/Untiedt/Lüschow (1994, p.13) omit time variables from their estimation because the multicollinearity prohibited the results from being economically interpretable.

Should it appear that the differences for each company in its efficiency over time are not too great, a panel estimation over all years can be attempted. The panel estimation assumes there is one level of inefficiency for each company during the whole time period and thus precludes the study of temporal effects. This method offers two advantages, though: First, the estimates per company will be more stable, as for most companies several observations will contribute to the estimation and thus increase the stability of the results.

Secondly, the increased number of observations will allow the data to be split "lengthwise" along the time series to estimate the efficiency of various sectors separately. While the inclusion of dummy variables for the sectors in equation (5-8) above already introduces a means of comparing the results of the total panel estimation on a sectoral basis, it can be noted that the assumption of a common production function for all the sectors in the dataset is heroic. On the other hand, this can be made more acceptable by defining an underlying production function that uses very general input and output classifications, such as fixed assets and labor on the input and sales on the output side. Accordingly, that is what will be done here for the production function behind the cost function used here.

5.2.4.2 Operationalization of Efficiency Measures

The x-inefficiency can be calculated using the difference between actual costs C_i and forecast costs $\hat{C}_i$. For a given output bundle, the cost deviation of a bank *i* can be calculated either as an absolute value ΔC_i:

$$\Delta C_i = C_i - \hat{C}_i \qquad (5\text{-}10)$$

or as a relative value via the difference of the logarithms:

$$\varepsilon_i = \ln C_i - \ln \hat{C}_i \qquad (5\text{-}11)$$

which leads to:

$$e^{\varepsilon_i} = e^{(\ln C_i - \ln \hat{C}_i)} = \frac{C_i}{\hat{C}_i}$$
$$\frac{C_i}{\hat{C}_i} - 1 = e^{\varepsilon_i} - 1 \quad \geq \varepsilon_i \qquad (5\text{-}12)$$

In a deterministic model the ΔC_i or $e^{\varepsilon i} - 1$ are directly taken to be inefficiencies. This means that possible specification errors, measurement errors or outside shocks that the company cannot influence are interpreted as management-induced inefficiency. This is a highly questionable practice that has lead to the development of stochastic models (see 5.1.5).[71]

In order to separate errors in measurement and estimation and random shocks outside of a company's influence from inefficiency, stochastic models define the residual as consisting of a part *u* with a one-sided distribution, $u \geq 0$, as the measure for inefficiency and a symmetrically distributed stochastic component *v*. This error term includes random deviations from the best practice results over time and/or other companies. The component *u* goes back to influences directly under control of the company and represent the x-inefficiency of that company.

In order to depict the x-inefficiency, I compute a ratio *xineff* as the ratio of the actual costs *C* to the estimated costs, $\hat{C}$. Taking:

$$\begin{aligned} &\ln C_i - \ln \hat{C}_i = E(u_i|\varepsilon_i) \\ &e^{\ln C_i^{\circ} - \ln \hat{C}_i} = \frac{C_i}{\hat{C}_i} = e^{E(u_i|\varepsilon_i)} \end{aligned} \tag{5-13}$$

I define:

$$\text{xineff} := \frac{C}{\hat{C}} - 1 = e^{E(u_i|\varepsilon_i)} - 1 \qquad \text{with xineff} \geq 0 \text{ as } E(u_i|\varepsilon_i) \geq 0 \tag{5-14}$$

5.2.4.3 The Stochastic Frontier Approach

5.2.4.3.1 Inefficiency in the Regression Residual

In a deterministic model errors in specification, errors in measurement or outside shocks that a company cannot control are all interpreted as inefficiencies. Discontentment with that state of affairs led to the development of the stochastic frontier approach or composed error model that will be used here. The stochastic models distinguish between measurement errors and other random shocks and the inefficiency proper by redefining the regression residual. Under its new definition, the residual contains two components; the first being the symmetrically distributed, mean zero residual, called *v*. It also contains a component with a one-sided distribution *u*, $u \geq 0$, which is used to capture the inefficiency. Typical distributions are the half-normal or truncated normal distribution,[72] an expo-

---

[71] The first stochastic frontier models, also known as composed error models, were presented in Aigner/Lovell/Schmidt (1977) and Meeusen/van den Broeck (1977).

[72] The half-normal distribution is a normal distribution truncated at $\mu = 0$, making it a special case of the truncated normal distribution. See Greene (1993), p. 78.

nential or a gamma[73] distribution.[74] Thus *u* represents an influence that can be affected by the company's actions, while *v* cannot. The production function underlying the cost function can be reformulated as

$$y = \hat{f}(x) + \varepsilon \quad \text{where } \varepsilon = v - u,\ u \geq 0 \tag{5-15}$$

or

$$y = \hat{f}(X) \cdot e^{\varepsilon} \quad \text{where } e^{\varepsilon} = e^{v-u}, u \geq 0 \tag{5-16}$$

Given a constant input level, *u* represents the absolute (5-15) or relative (5-16) deviation of the actual output level from the one the production function would predict for the given input level.

The interpretation of (5-16) as a relative measure of inefficiency can be explained by considering the case of $v = 0$, i. e., the standard residual is zero. That corresponds to its mean value. An efficient company, meaning with a value of zero for *u*, will have a residual term of $e^0 = 1$, meaning the production is multiplied by 100 % to arrive at the production level of a company with zero inefficiency. An inefficient company, say with a value for *u* of -.2, will have a relative efficiency of $e^{-.2}$, or 81.87 % again assuming $v = 0$. As can be seen, the absolute value of *u* (-.2) and the value of the relative inefficiency (.1813 %) are similar in size, so the unmodified *u* can already be seen as a rough estimate of relative inefficiency.

The same can be said for the dual cost function, where the inefficiency *u* is positive and is added, not subtracted from *v*. It captures costs incurred over and above those that can be expected due to the production technology the cost function represents. Again, an absolute (5-17) or relative (5-18) version can be given:

$$C = \hat{f}(y, w) + \varepsilon \quad \text{where } \varepsilon = v + u,\ u \geq 0 \tag{5-17}$$

or

$$C = \hat{f}(y, w) \cdot e^{\varepsilon}, \text{ where } e^{\varepsilon} = e^{v+u},\ u \geq 0 \tag{5-18}$$

The relative version of the function is especially interesting in view of a common transformation researchers apply to functions, taking the logarithm of it. That transforms (5-18) into:

$$\ln(C) = \ln(\hat{f}(y, w)) + \varepsilon \quad \text{where } \varepsilon = v + u, u \geq 0 \tag{5-19}$$

---

[73] Cf. Ritter/Simar (1994), who state that the shape parameters of a gamma distribution are difficult to estimate correctly unless there are several thousand observations.

[74] Cf. Stevenson (1980).

This has the advantage of providing an additive error term.

It remains to be clarified how the two components u and v can be separated from ε, the only observable error term. This can be done by considering the standard errors of the two error components. The sum of the variances of the error components is the total residual variance.[75]

$$\sigma_\varepsilon^2 = \sigma_u^2 + \sigma_v^2 \tag{5-20}$$

The ratio of the two partial error standard deviations will be called λ.

$$\lambda = \frac{\sigma_u}{\sigma_v} \tag{5-21}$$

If λ is large, this means that the standard deviation of the inefficiency dominates. The stochastic frontier methodology described below uses σ_ε and λ to determine the company-level inefficiency u_i.[76, 77]

5.2.4.3.2 Econometric Description of the Panel Frontier Cost Function

The Stochastic Frontier Approach assumes that deviations from a cost frontier will be due to random errors or inefficiency. In general notation, the functional form can be written as[78]

$$\ln C_i = \ln C(\mathbf{y}_i, \mathbf{w}_i, \mathbf{q}_i, \mathbf{B}) + u_i + v_i \tag{5-22}$$

with C_i as the actual cost of the company, $\mathbf{y}_i$ the output vector, $\mathbf{w}_i$ the input price vector, $\mathbf{q}_i$ the quality vector for the outputs, and $\mathbf{B}$ the parameter vector. As mentioned above, u_i is the individual inefficiency term for each company and v_i the residual.

The Stochastic Frontier Approach prespecifies the distribution of the error components. The true error component v is assumed to be iid and normally distributed with a mean of zero. The distributional assumptions for u can vary, however. It can be assumed to follow truncated normal, half normal, gamma or ex-

---

75 Cf. Greene (1997) pp. 949 ff.

76 From (5-20) and (5-21), $\sigma_u^2 = \sigma_\varepsilon^2 \cdot \frac{\lambda^2}{1+\lambda^2}$ and $\sigma_v^2 = \sigma_\varepsilon^2 \cdot \frac{1}{1+\lambda^2}$ follows.

77 For convenience, the index ε will generally be omitted from σ_ε from now on.

78 Cf. Mester (1994), p. 6.

ponential distributions.[79] For any of these choices, *u* is always assumed to be independent of *v*.

In this analysis I will assume that *u* follows a half-normal distribution, i. e., a normal distribution truncated at its mean of zero. The distribution function for such a variable in general can be given by:[80]

$$f(u) = \begin{cases} 0 & \text{if } u < 0 \\ \dfrac{1}{\left(\displaystyle\int_0^{\infty} \frac{1}{\sigma \cdot \sqrt{2\pi}} \cdot e^{-\frac{1}{2}\left(\frac{u-\mu}{\sigma}\right)^2} du\right)} \cdot \dfrac{1}{\sigma} \cdot \dfrac{1}{\sqrt{2\pi}} \cdot e^{-\frac{1}{2\sigma}\left(\frac{u-\mu}{\sigma}\right)^2} & \text{if } u \geq 0 \end{cases} \tag{5-23}$$

or simplified using $\phi(\cdot)$ for the standard normal density function and $\Phi(\cdot)$ for the standard normal cumulative distribution function,[81]

$$f(u) = \frac{\frac{1}{\sigma}\phi\left(\frac{u-\mu}{\sigma}\right)}{1-\Phi\left(\frac{u-\mu}{\sigma}\right)} \qquad \text{for } u \geq 0 \tag{5-24}$$

Starting with a general notation, the mean of this truncated normal distribution of the variable *u*, E(*u*), is given by:[82]

$$E(u) = \mu + \sigma \cdot \frac{\phi\left(\frac{u_{lower} - \mu}{\sigma}\right) - \phi\left(\frac{u_{upper} - \mu}{\sigma}\right)}{\Phi\left(\frac{u_{upper} - \mu}{\sigma}\right) - \Phi\left(\frac{u_{lower} - \mu}{\sigma}\right)} \tag{5-25}$$

With $u_{lower} = 0$ and $u_{upper} = \infty$, the mean inefficiency *u* is given by[83]

---

79 Cf. Stevenson (1980); Aigner/Lovell/Schmidt (1977); Meeusen/van den Broeck (1977); Greene (1990).

80 Cf. Hartung (1986), p. 150; Stevenson (1980), p. 59.

81 Cf. Greene (1997), p. 950.

82 As in Hartung (1986), p. 149.

83 Using the equality $\phi\left(\frac{-\mu}{\sigma}\right) = \phi\left(\frac{\mu}{\sigma}\right)$.

$$E(u) = \mu + \sigma \cdot \frac{\phi\left(\frac{\mu}{\sigma}\right)}{\Phi\left(\frac{\mu}{\sigma}\right)} \tag{5-26}$$

which also holds when overlaid by the normally distributed, mean zero v with the standard deviation of σ. For the assumptions of $u_{lower} = 0$ and $u_{upper} = \infty$, and now $\mu = 0$ in addition, equation (5-25) can be simplified to:[84]

$$E(u) = \sigma \cdot \frac{0.3989 - 0}{1 - 0.5} = \sigma \cdot \sqrt{\frac{2}{\pi}} \tag{5-27}$$

It is now necessary to determine the value of u_i conditional on the ε_{it}, or $(u_i|\varepsilon_{it})$. Starting out with estimates for μ and σ:[85]

$$\tilde{\mu}_i = \frac{\lambda^2 \cdot \sum_{t=1}^{T} \varepsilon_{it}}{1 + \lambda^2 \cdot T} \tag{5-28}$$

and

$$\tilde{\sigma}_i^2 = \frac{\sigma^2 \cdot \frac{\lambda^2}{1+\lambda^2}}{1+\lambda^2 T} \tag{5-29}$$

$(u_i|\varepsilon_{it})$ can be calculated following equation (5-26) as:[86]

$$E(u_i|\varepsilon_{i1},\ldots,\varepsilon_{iT}) = \frac{\lambda^2 \cdot \sum_{t=1}^{T} \varepsilon_{it}}{1+\lambda^2 \cdot T} + \sqrt{\frac{\sigma^2 \cdot \frac{\lambda^2}{1+\lambda^2}}{1+\lambda^2 \cdot T}} \cdot \frac{\phi\left(\frac{\lambda^2 \cdot \sum_{t=1}^{T} \varepsilon_{it}}{1+\lambda^2 \cdot T} \Big/ \sqrt{\frac{\sigma^2 \cdot \frac{\lambda^2}{1+\lambda^2}}{1+\lambda^2 \cdot T}}\right)}{\Phi\left(\frac{\lambda^2 \cdot \sum_{t=1}^{T} \varepsilon_{it}}{1+\lambda^2 \cdot T} \Big/ \sqrt{\frac{\sigma^2 \cdot \frac{\lambda^2}{1+\lambda^2}}{1+\lambda^2 \cdot T}}\right)} \tag{5-30}$$

From the econometric point of view, it is preferable to have several observations per company for a smaller number of companies than single observations for a

---

84 $\mu_u = 0$ is due to the assumption of a half-normal distribution for u.

85 Cf. Battese/Coelli (1988), p. 391, for a production function with $\varepsilon = v - u$.

86 Cf. Jondrow/Lovell/Materov/Schmidt (1982) for a production function. Before that, only average inefficiencies over a number of firms, but not firm-specific inefficiencies could be estimated.

great number of companies.[87] This bears the great advantage over the cross-sectional estimation model described below in that the estimators derived here are consistent, i. e., as the number of observations approaches infinity, the value of the estimate converges on the true value.[88]

In the case of a panel of data with a total of N companies i over T_i years, the loglikelihood function for a function that must be optimized can be written as follows. The function is assumed to have a split residual, $\varepsilon = u + v$, with u following the half-normal and v the normal mean zero distribution:[89]

$$\begin{aligned} \ln L = & \\ & \sum_{i=1}^{N}\left\{-\frac{1}{2}\cdot\left[T_i\cdot\ln 2\pi-\ln 2+T_i\cdot\ln\frac{\sigma^2}{1+\lambda^2}+\ln(1+\lambda^2\cdot T_i)-2\cdot\ln\Phi\left(\mu\cdot\frac{\sqrt{1+\lambda^2}}{\sigma}\right)\right]\right\} \\ & +\sum_{i=1}^{N}-\frac{1}{2}\cdot\left\{\frac{-\lambda^2}{1+\lambda^2\cdot T_i}\cdot\left[\sum_{t=1}^{T}(\mu-\varepsilon_{it})\cdot\frac{\sqrt{1+\lambda^2}}{\sigma}\right]^2+\sum_{t=1}^{T}\left[(\mu-\varepsilon_{it})\cdot\frac{\sqrt{1+\lambda^2}}{\sigma}\right]^2\right\} \qquad (5\text{-}31) \\ & +\sum_{i=1}^{N}\ln\Phi\left\{\sqrt{\frac{\lambda^2}{1+\lambda^2\cdot T_i}}\cdot\frac{\sqrt{1+\lambda^2}}{\sigma}\cdot\left[\sum_{t=1}^{T}\varepsilon_{it}+T_i\cdot\mu\cdot\frac{1}{\lambda^2}\right]\right\} \end{aligned}$$

Assuming that u_i has a mean $\mu_u = 0$, equation (5-31) reduces to:

$$\begin{aligned} \ln L = & -\frac{N}{2}\cdot\left[T_i\cdot\ln 2\pi+\ln 2+T_i\cdot\ln\frac{\sigma^2}{1+\lambda^2}+\ln(1+\lambda^2\cdot T_i)\right] \\ & +\sum_{i=1}^{N}-\frac{1}{2}\cdot\left\{\frac{-\lambda^2}{1+\lambda^2\cdot T_i}\cdot\frac{1+\lambda^2}{\sigma^2}\cdot\left[\sum_{t=1}^{T}\varepsilon_{it}\cdot\right]^2+\frac{1+\lambda^2}{\sigma^2}\sum_{t=1}^{T}[\varepsilon_{it}]^2\right\} \qquad (5\text{-}32) \\ & +\sum_{i=1}^{N}\ln\Phi\left\{\frac{\lambda^2}{1+\lambda^2\cdot T_i}\cdot\frac{\sqrt{1+\lambda^2}}{\sigma}\cdot\sum_{t=1}^{T}\varepsilon_{it}\right\} \end{aligned}$$

The ε_{it} denote deviations of the actual costs from the estimated costs of the company i in the year t. Assuming further that the inefficiency portion of ε_{it} is constant over time, I write ε_{it} as:

$$\varepsilon_{it} = u_i + v_{it} \qquad (5\text{-}33)$$

---

[87] Cf. Greene (1993), pp. 82 ff. For a mean T_i observations per company the result is $(T_i)^{0.5}$ times better than for one observation per company (p. 84).

[88] Cf. Greene (1993), p. 85.

[89] Cf. Greene (1993), p. 86 for a production function and $\varepsilon = v - |u|$. The necessary modifications for a cost function are given on p. 107.

The actual cost function specification and the distributional equation (5-32) are iteratively optimized together in a maximum likelihood process.[90] The procedure determines the values of σ and λ that make the observed distribution most probable, given the prespecified distributions the residual components are determined to be following. From the estimates of σ and λ, equations (5-20) and (5-21) can be used to determine the estimates of σ_u and σ_v. With that information, for every company the conditional means of u_i, given ε_i, can be calculated using equation (5-30).

The means of $(u_i|\varepsilon_i)$ determined according to (5-30) are the company-level inefficiencies that are the real objective of this exercise. Once they are determined, it is possible to test for differences in the levels of the conditional inefficiencies $(u_i|\varepsilon_i)$ between companies that are assumed to have agency problems and those that are assumed not to.

5.2.4.3.3 Econometric Description of the Cross-Sectional Frontier Cost Function

It is also possible to perform the same estimations, described above for panel data, for cross-sectional data. This can generally be described as a simplification achieved by setting the number of observations per company, *T*, to one.

The mean μ of the residual can be estimated by applying this adaptation to equations (5-28) and (5-29) as:[91]

$$\tilde{\mu} = \frac{\varepsilon_i \sigma_u^2}{\sigma^2} = \varepsilon_i \cdot \frac{\lambda^2}{1+\lambda^2} \tag{5-34}$$

and σ^2 as

$$\tilde{\sigma}^2 = \frac{\sigma_u^2 \sigma_v^2}{\sigma^2} = \frac{\lambda^2}{(1+\lambda^2)^2} \tag{5-35}$$

Substituting these values into (5-24) gives the distribution of u_i conditional of ε_i:

---

90 The calculations were performed with the statistical software packages Gauss from Aptech and Jon Breslaw's GaussX from Econotron. I would like to thank Jon Breslaw for his valuable tips.

91 Cf. Jondrow et al. (1982) for a production function.

$$f(u_i|\varepsilon_i)=\frac{\frac{\sigma}{\sigma_u\sigma_v}\phi\left(\frac{\sigma}{\sigma_u\sigma_v}(u_i|\varepsilon_i)-\frac{\varepsilon_i\lambda}{\sigma}\right)}{1-\Phi\left(-\frac{\varepsilon_i\lambda}{\sigma}\right)} \quad \text{for } (u_i|\varepsilon_i)\geq 0 \tag{5-36}$$

Again following (5-26), the mean of this conditional distribution is:

$$E(u_i|\varepsilon_i)=\varepsilon_i\cdot\frac{\lambda^2}{1+\lambda^2}+\sigma\cdot\frac{\lambda}{1+\lambda^2}\cdot\left[\frac{\phi\left(\varepsilon_i\cdot\frac{\lambda^2}{1+\lambda^2}\Big/\sigma\cdot\frac{\lambda}{1+\lambda^2}\right)}{\Phi\left(\varepsilon_i\cdot\frac{\lambda^2}{1+\lambda^2}\Big/\sigma\cdot\frac{\lambda}{1+\lambda^2}\right)}\right]$$

$$=\varepsilon_i\cdot\frac{\lambda^2}{1+\lambda^2}+\sigma\cdot\frac{\lambda}{1+\lambda^2}\cdot\left[\frac{\phi\left(\frac{\varepsilon_i\cdot\lambda}{\sigma}\right)}{\Phi\left(\frac{\varepsilon_i\cdot\lambda}{\sigma}\right)}\right] \quad \text{for} \tag{5-37}$$

$$=\left(\sigma\cdot\frac{\lambda}{1+\lambda^2}\right)\cdot\left[\frac{\phi\left(\frac{\varepsilon_i\cdot\lambda}{\sigma}\right)}{\Phi\left(\frac{\varepsilon_i\cdot\lambda}{\sigma}\right)}+\frac{\varepsilon_i\cdot\lambda}{\sigma}\right]$$

$(u_i|\varepsilon_i)\geq 0$

or, using s_u and s_v:

$$E(u_i|\varepsilon_i)=\frac{\sigma_u\sigma_v}{\sigma}\left[\frac{\phi\left(\frac{\varepsilon_i\lambda}{\sigma}\right)}{\Phi\left(\frac{\varepsilon_i\lambda}{\sigma}\right)}+\frac{\varepsilon_i\lambda}{\sigma}\right] \quad \text{for } (u_i|\varepsilon_i)\geq 0 \tag{5-38}$$

Equation (5-38) can be estimated using the empirical results for σ_u and σ_v. The estimator for $E(u_i|\varepsilon_i)$ is unbiased but inconsistent, meaning that as the number of observations N approaches infinity, the estimate does not converge on the true value.[92]

Using the prespecified density functions for u and v, it is possible to use maximum likelihood techniques to estimate the parameters of the best practice fron-

92 Cf. Greene (1993), p. 83.

tier function.[93] For a cross sectional analysis, with N companies included in the estimation, $\mu = 0$, setting T to 1, and pulling some elements together, the log-likelihood function of the model (5-32) simplifies to:[94]

$$\ln L = -\frac{N}{2}\cdot\left\{\ln 2\pi + \ln 2 + \ln\left[\frac{\sigma^2}{1+\lambda^2}\cdot\left(1+\lambda^2\right)\right]\right\} + \sum_{i=1}^{N} -\frac{1}{2}\cdot\left\{\frac{-\lambda^2}{1+\lambda^2}\cdot\frac{1+\lambda^2}{\sigma^2}\cdot\left[\varepsilon_i\right]^2 + \frac{1+\lambda^2}{\sigma^2}\cdot\left[\varepsilon_i\right]^2\right\} + \sum_{i=1}^{N}\ln\Phi\left\{\frac{\lambda}{\sqrt{1+\lambda^2}}\cdot\frac{\sqrt{1+\lambda^2}}{\sigma}\cdot\varepsilon_i\right\} \tag{5-39}$$

$$\ln L = -N\cdot\ln\sqrt{2\pi} - N\cdot\ln\sqrt{2} - N\cdot\ln\sigma + \sum_{i=1}^{N} -\frac{1}{2}\cdot\left\{-\lambda^2\cdot\frac{\varepsilon_i^2}{\sigma^2} + \left(1+\lambda^2\right)\frac{\varepsilon_i^2}{\sigma^2}\right\} + \sum_{i=1}^{N}\ln\Phi\left\{\frac{\varepsilon_i\cdot\lambda}{\sigma}\right\} \tag{5-40}$$

$$\ln L = -N\cdot\ln 2\sqrt{\pi} - N\cdot\ln\sigma - \frac{1}{2\cdot\sigma^2}\cdot\sum_{i=1}^{N}\varepsilon_i^2 + \sum_{i=1}^{N}\ln\Phi\left\{\frac{\varepsilon_i\cdot\lambda}{\sigma}\right\} \tag{5-41}$$

Again, as specified above in equations (5-19) through (5-21), $\varepsilon_i = u_i + v_i$, $\sigma^2 = \sigma_u^2 + \sigma_v^2$, and $\lambda = \sigma_u / \sigma_v$.

5.2.4.3.4 Determination of the Variables in the Cost Function

Two variants of the Stochastic Frontier Approach were presented above, the cost function for panel and for cross-sectional data. Both will be applied in the following empirical analysis.

In the previous chapter 4 I studied the aggregate performance of the firms. As investors are most likely to judge a firm by its aggregate performance, managers who can act uncontrolled might employ the legal leeway they have in accounting procedures to ensure that their companies' performance registers at least as well as that of owner-controlled firms. If that should be so, then it should be

93 The maximum likelihood method of estimation is described in Koutsoyiannis (1981), pp. 473 ff.

94 Cf. Mester (1994), p. 6.

possible to find inefficiencies in manager-controlled firms on the disaggregate level, as inefficiency there is beyond the interest of the investors.

The most basic level of the firm is the cost level, which is why that will be pursued in detail below. Above it was discussed that using panel data is most interesting from an econometric point of view. However, the panel data model presented has the drawback of assuming the efficiency levels of the firms to remain constant throughout the time period studied. For a two or three year period, this can be entirely plausible. As the dataset available covers seven years, it seems questionable if this is indeed the case here.

Therefore, in order to shed light on this question, the cross-sectional model specification will initially be applied to each of the seven years in the database. The number of cases per year is unfortunately not enough to allow an individual cost function to be estimated for each sector, or even for the largest sector in the database. Sectoral differences will be accounted for by entering sectoral dummies into the model. As there are 15 sectors in the dataset (see Table 5-5),[95] 14 dummies will be necessary. If all dummies are equal to zero, the firm is a holding.

Despite the use of the dummies, it is a fairly bold assumption that it is possible to estimate one cost function for companies of the myriad sectors in Germany. While this of course cannot be totally denied, the nature of the cost function applied here is so general that if it is at all possible to combine the sectors, this general definition of the function must contain that possibility in itself.

The first output y_1 consists obviously of the sales to which are added the self-constructed assets. The self-constructed assets surely are additional cost drivers, meriting their inclusion, but they do not constitute a separate output category. This assumes implicitly that the self-constructed assets in some way resemble the sales outputs so that their combination is not too extraordinary.

Financial capital-related accounting positions[96] are used symmetrically to provide an input and an output. As the output y_2, the interest and earnings from affiliated companies and profit-sharing agreements outside of the industrial company, are seen as an output, similar to those of a banking production function.[97] This output mirrors the calculation algorithm for the determination of the net profit of the year shown above in Tables 4-1 and 4-2, where the major compo-

---

95 One of which is the holdall for all companies not classifiable into the 14 other sectors.

96 As opposed to the real capital of a firm.

97 One can even discuss for this output if it is valued in DM or if the DM is actually the original unit measure.

nents of the net profit are the operating and financial results.[98] With companies in Germany such as Siemens heavily invested in the financial realm, this output is important for the study of German industrial companies.

In addition, though, the financial capital itself can be interpreted as an input (x_3, whose price will be abbreviated with w_3) in the productive process of a firm, where the production concept is expanded to include the financial dealings. Just as capital on the right side of the balance sheet is used to buy fixed assets that are recorded on the left side of the balance sheet and used to produce outputs, this same capital can also be used for investments in other companies or in financial securities. In this case, it is necessary to assign a price to the financial capital input.

The immediate price that can be assigned to financial capital consists of the sum of the interest payments and the amortization on financial capital (see Table 4-2). But it is also possible to consider an opportunity price stating the profit foregone because the financial input was not used for the opportunity purpose. The opportunity purpose in this case would be the investment of the capital in the company's own production process, making the company's stock return an opportunity price. This approach will be taken in this analysis, as using stock returns favors a market valuation over the book values that amortization and interest payments constitute. The actual return serves as a simple forecast of the expected return which investors could demand.

The annual return is calculated as the product of the 12 monthly returns of the stocks in each year. Higher frequency returns are not used as many German stocks are infrequently traded, reducing the quality of the return data. One feature of this choice of price is that it allows for negative prices. This implies that the company is not creating costs by increasing its input x_3, but actually reducing them, even when substitutional effects are disregarded. This could impact the interpretation of the estimation results and the well behavior of the cost function. A drawback of using this opportunity price lies in the fact that the income the financial capital produces, even though it might be generated in a different firm, will be factored into investors' share price calculations to a certain extent. This reduces the opportunity characteristic of the stock return.

Discussion of the first two inputs x_1 and x_2, as well as their respective prices w_1 and w_2, was put off until here in order to treat the two variables based on financial assets, y_2 and w_3, together. Employee figures constitute the input factor labor (x_1) and are used to determine the corresponding input price w_1. This is achieved by dividing each company's labor costs by the number of employees in the firm, for every year. The labor costs are calculated under inclusion of the social contributions the employer must pay. Social costs constitute a significant portion of

98 Again omitting the extraordinary result, the third component.

labor costs in Germany. Employee figures for about 80 % of the companies in the complete dataset from 1986 to 1992 are on hand. Only companies with employee numbers are used in this part of the study.

The final input factor used is very straightforward: the fixed assets of the firm. For this factor x_2, the DM value of the assets can be read from the balance sheet, which is the multiplication of the input units by their price. Dividing this by the joint depreciation of material and immaterial fixed assets (i. e., their costs) one derives the price per input unit of the fixed assets in percent, w_2.

These two outputs and three inputs constitute the elements in the cost functions used here. One can question if more inputs or outputs are necessary. For example, many studies use materials and other current assets as an input in their production function. As the number of companies available for this analysis is not terribly high, it is incumbent to restrict the number of coefficients to be estimated to allow enough degrees of freedom to remain for the models using only part of the data, such as the cross-sectional model described here. Since German companies are special in their high degree of financial involvement in each other, it is important to include financial variables in the model in order to capture the idiosyncrasy of the country. Also, using the financial input in lieu of the current assets secures the symmetry of the financial capital in its role of providing revenue but also being an input with an assigned cost factor.

category	abbreviation	variable
dependent	C	costs
output	y_1	sales and self-constructed assets
	y_2	interest earnings and earnings from affiliated companies
	x_1	labor
input	x_2	tangible and intangible fixed assets
	x_3	financial capital
	w_1	salary/wage rate plus social costs
input	w_2	depreciation rate on tangible and intangible fixed assets
price	w_3	cost of financial assets (via stock return as opportunity earning)

Table 5-6: Central variables in the cost function model[99]

99 Sector dummies and a time index variable are added as necessary.

Figure 5-11 shows that the value of the financial assets surpassed that of the fixed assets in 1990, which underlines the importance of the financial assets for German firms. The financial assets and the current assets are highly correlated (90.66 %), making the inclusion of both variables simultaneously problematic. Therefore, the current assets are omitted from the model.

The estimates of the companies' inefficiencies using production models based on the variables given above can then be tested to see if they actually are stable and statistically indistinguishable from one another over the years. For this, it will also be important to include key economic ratios that describe the overall economic development in Germany over the time period involved, 1986 – 1992.

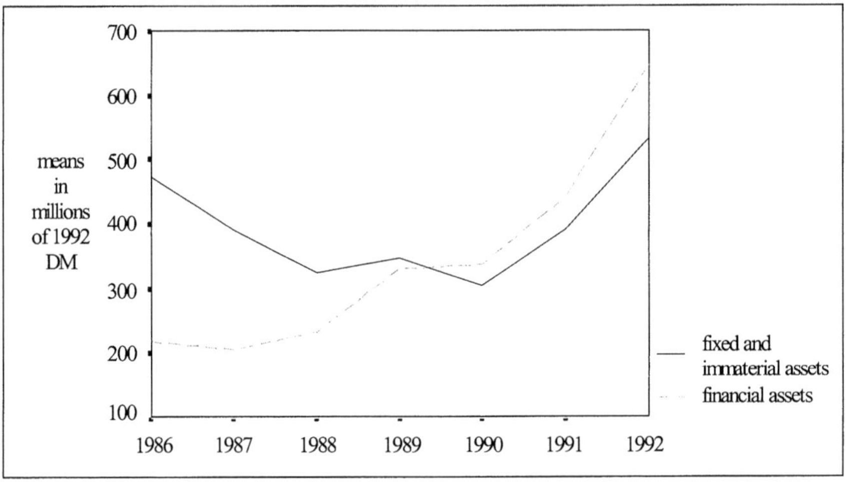

Figure 5-11: Development of the mean values of the fixed and financial assets over time

The results form these test will shed some light on the question which model's results should be weighted more heavily, those from the cross-sectional studies or the panel model. The panel model will then be estimated in two different variants. First, a true overall model including all the datapoints available which have employee figures (848) will be estimated. It will of course also make use of the dummy variables for the sectors, just as for the cross-sectional model. In addition, the factor time must be included in the model itself, to account for any temporal influences unrelated to corporate efficiency.

The second panel data model will be used to conduct estimations of cost functions for separate sectors. There are five sectors in the dataset that are represented in strong enough numbers to allow for this procedure. As with the time factor, these models will especially help answer the question if it is at all permissible to include all sectors in one estimation, or if they are best treated separately. Also, the different levels of government regulation visible in some of the sectors will allow to test for differences in efficiency due to lack of market control on the sales side.

Possible differences in the results here in comparison to the aggregate performance analysis can be due to two reasons. First, they can stem from the postulated attempts of an unmonitored management to present their companies to the investors in a good light, using accounting rules to create good results for those performance ratios that investors judge companies by.

Second, it is conceivable that incongruous results can be traced to the fact that the analysis on an aggregate level used performance measures that incorporate both the cost and profit sides of a company's activities. The cost functions estimated on the disaggregate level of course only see half of that picture, the cost side. Companies with good performance ratios but poor ratings in the cost analysis might be producing such high earnings that higher costs are overcompensated.

5.2.4.4 Tests and Properties of the Cost Function

Once the cost function is estimated, one must test the resulting function for its well behavior and significance.

The significance of a function estimated in with maximum likelihood procedures can be determined by the likelihood ratio test.[100] This test compares the additional explanatory power the full regression models provides in contrast to an unrestricted model consisting solely of the constant term.[101] The ratio of the two likelihoods for each estimated model,

$$\hat{LR} = \frac{\hat{L}_R}{\hat{L}_U} \tag{5-42}$$

with the indexes R = restricted and U = unrestricted is chi-square-distributed when transformed following:

$$\hat{L} = -2 \cdot \ln(\hat{LR}) \tag{5-43}$$

This value can be tested for significance at standard levels using the critical values of the chi-square distribution. Due to the many right-hand side variables

---

[100] Cf. Greene (1997), pp. 161 f.

[101] See Breslaw (1995), pp. 206 f.

added to the constant in a second-order translog cost function, it is very probable that the likelihood ratio tests in all cases will confirm the significance of the full translog model.

A cost function can be evaluated for its well behavior by testing its curvature properties. This means that the slope and concavity of each function must be analyzed and evaluated.

The following properties characterize a cost function:[102]

1. Nondecreasing in input prices **w**.
2. Nondecreasing in outputs **y**.
3. Homogeneous of degree 1 in **w**.
4. Concave and continuous in **w**.

Ad 1) For the input prices, costs are assumed to increase on the margin. If **w'** ≥ **w**, then for the cost function C the following must hold: C(**w'**,**y**) ≥ C(**w**,**y**).

Proof: If **x** and **x'** are the cost minimizing factor bundles associated with the input prices **w** and **w'**, then **wx** ≤ **wx'** and **wx'** ≤ **w'x'** by definition, remembering that **w** ≤ **w'**. The two equalities can be combined to **wx** ≤ **w'x'**. q. e. d.

Ad 2) The same as said in Ad 1) applies to the outputs by analogy. For **y'** ≥ **y**, it is necessary that C(**w**,**y'**) ≥ C(**w**,**y**). This means that the gradient G of a function F with G = $\{F_1, F_2, ..., F_n\}$, i. e., G is the vector of first partial derivatives, must be nonnegative for both the outputs and input prices. The gradient is evaluated at each point of the dataset and the number of offenses against the assumption of nonegative marginal costs in each input price or output is counted. The result throws a first spotlight on the goodness of the estimation in comparison to its theoretical background.

Ad 3) Homogeneity of the cost function to degree one implies that increasing the input price vector **w** by a certain percentage means that the costs c will rise by that same percentage.

Proof: Assuming again that **x** is the cost-minimizing factor bundle for the price vector **w**, then linear homogeneity means that input prices **w** increased by the positive scalar *l* will still have **x** as the cost-minimizing input bundle. If not, then one can imagine an **x'** such that *l***wx'** ≤ *l***wx**. Dividing by *l* gives **wx'** ≤ **wx**, which in fact contradicts the definition of **x**. q. e. d.

This third characteristic of a cost function need not be tested for, after estimating the cost function, if certain restrictions are imposed on the estimation process to ensure that the results will be linearly homogeneous. The relevant restrictions

102 Cf. Varian (1992), p. 72; Chambers (1988), p. 52.

are listed in Equation (5-6) and for panel data additionally in Equation (5-9) above and will be used in the manner described.[103]

Ad 4) In addition, the cost function must be concave in its input prices. Figure 5-12 shows the meaning of this condition in graphical form. If w_j associated with input j is the price being examined, then at point B the cost-minimizing point is given for the concrete price w_j^1. The associated costs are $\mathbf{w}^1\mathbf{x}^1$. Increasing the price of input j to w_j^2 and keeping the amount of input j fixed at x^1 would give costs C. Substitution, however, causes costs to rise at a slower rate, which satisfies the concavity condition. So, in effect, concavity is a direct result of the concept of substitution of inputs.

Concavity means that if **wx** and **w'x'** are two cost-minimizing price-factor combinations, and **w''** is defined as $l\mathbf{w} + (1-l)\mathbf{w}'$ for a $0 \leq l \leq 1$, then $C(\mathbf{w}'',\mathbf{y}) = \mathbf{w}''\mathbf{x}'' = l\mathbf{w}\mathbf{x}'' + (1-l)\mathbf{w}'\mathbf{x}''$. Since **x''** need not be the cheapest factor amount to produce **y** at either price **w** or price **w'**, one can write $\mathbf{w}\mathbf{x}'' \geq C(\mathbf{w},\mathbf{y})$ and $\mathbf{w}'\mathbf{x}'' \geq C(\mathbf{w}',\mathbf{y})$. Then $C(\mathbf{w}'',\mathbf{y}) \geq lC(\mathbf{w},\mathbf{y}) + (1-l)C(\mathbf{w}'\mathbf{y})$ follows. q. e. d.

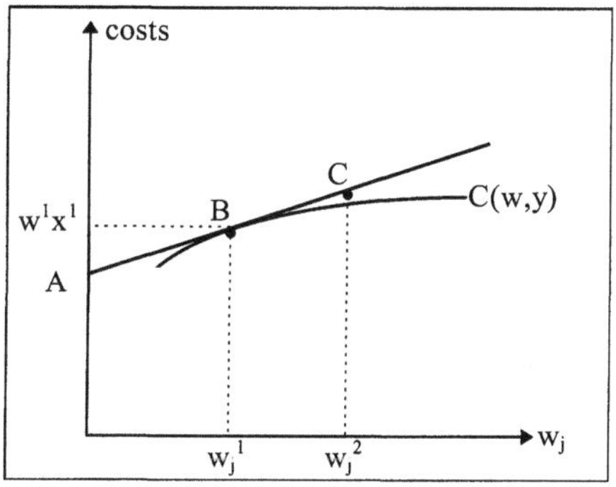

Figure 5-12: Concavity of the cost function[104]

There are four different ways of testing for the concavity, each of which will be presented below. For the concavity condition to be true, the Hessian matrix of the function must be negative semidefinite.[105] This can be tested in two ways.

---

[103] Forcing all the properties of a cost function as given above to apply by including them as restrictions in the estimation destroys the flexibility of the cost function and therefore is not attempted. See Diewert/Wales (1987), p. 48.

[104] Cf. Chambers (1988), p. 53.

[105] This is incidentally the sufficient condition for a (local) maximum, which of course can only occur in a strictly concave section of a function. Whereas the concavity applies to a

The first way is to determine the eigenvalues of the main minors of the Hessian matrix of second-order derivatives for the input prices. If the eigenvalues are less or equal to zero, the function is negative semidefinite.[106] The Hessian matrix H is the symmetric matrix of the second partial derivatives F_{ij} of a function F,

$$H = \begin{Bmatrix} F_{11} & \cdots & F_{1j} & \cdots & F_{1n} \\ \vdots & & \vdots & & \vdots \\ F_{i1} & \cdots & F_{ij} & \cdots & F_{in} \\ \vdots & & \vdots & & \vdots \\ F_{n1} & \cdots & F_{nj} & \cdots & F_{nn} \end{Bmatrix} \tag{5-44}$$

An eigenvalue or characteristic value *eval* of a matrix H is defined as the number for which[107]

$$H \cdot \mathbf{evec} = \text{eval} \cdot \mathbf{evec} \tag{5-45}$$

Instead of calculating the eigenvalues of each point in the definition space of the cost function, the datapoints from each company are used. The vector **evec** is replaced in this case with the right-hand side variables of the case (firm) in point, thus producing a firm-specific eigenvalue for each input price. In order to test for concavity in the input prices only, the main minors for each input price are taken from the Hessian. The main minors are the square matrices starting at the top left of the Hessian and having the diagonal element of the relevant input price as their bottom right element. If the price of input one is the third element in the matrix,

$$H_3 = \begin{Bmatrix} F_{11} & F_{12} & F_{13} \\ F_{21} & F_{22} & F_{23} \\ F_{31} & F_{32} & F_{33} \end{Bmatrix} \tag{5-46}$$

is its main subminor. If all the eigenvalues of the main submatrices for the input prices are less or equal to zero, the function is concave in these prices.

A disadvantage of this method of determination of concavity is that values of widely varying magnitude on the gradient level of calculations can produce

definition space, an optimum refers to a single point. Nonetheless the concavity is tested for here by evaluating it at each case in the dataset. These cases, should the function prove to be concave at their points, are not (necessarily) optima. This is because the concavity in the other right-hand side variables is not tested and the gradients are tested for positivity, not equality to zero (the necessary condition for an optimum), when evaluating the monotonicity of the function.

106 Cf. Opitz (1995), p. 372.

107 Cf. Opitz (1995), p. 353. Generally **evec** can be any vector for which the equation can be solved. Such an **evec** is called an eigenvector (or characteristic vector).

useless results.[108] In these cases, the negative semidefinity of the Hessian can alternatively be examined via the determinants of the main minors of the Hessian matrix. This constitutes the second method for testing the concavity of a function.

The determinant of a matrix is a single number derived from that matrix. It is calculated as the sum of all products consisting of one element from each row and one element from each column. The sign of each product is determined by the number of inversions in the indices of the elements. An inversion is given when the first index of a matrix element is higher than the second element. The sign is negative for an uneven number of inversions (including one).[109] Determinants can only be calculated for square matrices. For a matrix $X = \begin{Bmatrix} 3 & 5 \\ 4 & 2 \end{Bmatrix}$, the possible products are $x_{11} \cdot x_{22}$ and $x_{12} \cdot x_{21}$. Since there is one inversion in the second product (x_{21}), that product gets a negative sign, and the determinant is calculated as $x_{11} \cdot x_{22} - x_{12} \cdot x_{21}$, or $3 \cdot 2 - 4 \cdot 5 = -14$.

A visualization of the determinant of X is sketched below in Figure 5-13. Two vectors consisting of the columns of X can be drawn in a graph emanating from the origin. By mirroring the vectors horizontally and then vertically a parallelogram is formed. The area of the parallelogram thus formed is the absolute value of the determinant of X, in this case, 14. Two vectors that are linearly dependent, meaning they would lie one on top of the other in the graph, do not open any space between them. This means that the determinant of such a matrix is zero.

In order to verify the concavity in the input prices, the determinants of the main subminors for the input prices of the Hessian matrix are calculated for every point in the dataset. Their values must alternate in sign, beginning with a negative one.[110]

It is also possible to employ a third, albeit auxiliary, criterion to evaluate the concavity of the cost function. This can be achieved by checking for negative own price elasticities of the inputs. While a price elasticity for inputs x_i and their prices w_i is defined as[111]

---

108 Cf. Aptech Systems (1994), p. 1226.

109 Cf. Henderson/Quandt (1983), pp. 378 f.

110 Cf. Opitz (1995), pp. 374, 586.

111 Cf. Schumann (1987), pp. 44 ff.

$$\eta_{i,j} = \frac{\partial x_i}{\partial w_j} \cdot \frac{w_j}{x_i}, \tag{5-47}$$

the own price elasticity η_{ii} is given for input x_i and its own price w_i. It describes by how many percent the demand for an input changes if its own price is raised on the margin. For most goods, the demand should drop, leading to the negative sign. This method of checking for concavity often leads to less violations of that condition.[112] Inspection of equation (5-47) shows that a negative sign can usually only be produced by the derivative of the demand function, as both the price and the amount of x_i are constrained to positive values.[113]

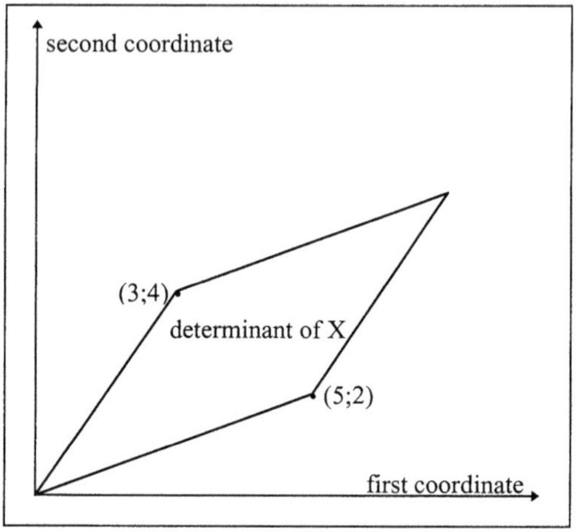

Figure 5-13: Graphical demonstration of the determinant of a matrix[114]

Finally, the fourth and surest way of assuring the concavity of the cost function is simply to impose that restriction on the estimation procedure itself.[115] This can lead to coefficient estimates that differ widely from those an unrestricted estimation would produce,[116] making this solution of the concavity problem perhaps the least attractive one. It will not be pursued further in this study, whereas

---

112 Cf. Lang/Welzel (1994), p. 14.

113 For the second input, financial assets, however, the opportunity price (stock return) does produce negative values.

114 Cf. Greene (1997), p. 24.

115 Cf. Jorgensen/Fraumeni (1981).

116 Cf. Diewert/Wales (1987), p. 48.

the eigenvalues of the Hessian will be used by preference, replaced by the determinants if the eigenvalues if the eigenvalues don't compute. The own price elasticities will also always be given.

5.2.5 Empirical Results

5.2.5.1 Cross-Sectional Cost Functions

5.2.5.1.1 Model Description

The cost function used in the cross sectional models (for single years) is a translog version similar to the base function given in equation (5-5) for two outputs y_1 and y_2; and three inputs x_1 to x_3, given below in Table 5-7 together with the input prices w_1 to w_3.

The financial output for 1992 dwarfs the sales numbers for that year, by a factor of almost 50 on the mean. The financial capital ranges from 0 DM to 18,151 million DM, with predominantly negative prices (stock returns). That means that companies were acting rationally to invest capital as much as possible outside of their companies, as the opportunity price was negative and they thus avoided greater losses. The depreciation rates for tangible and intangible fixed assets goes from less than 9 % to over 180 %, which is 20 times higher. This wide range shows that the rates can be selected to fit the current needs of the companies, which can be very disparate. This could affect the quality of the estimates.

The resulting transcendental logarithmic model developed from a second-order Taylor approximation[117] for the cross section of the data using the two outputs and three inputs given in Table 5-7 is based on Equation (5-5). Equation (5-48) differs from (5-5) in the fact that sector dummies were added at the end of the equation.[118]

---

117 See also Greene (1997), pp. 49 f.

118 It is necessary to provide starting values for the iteratively estimated maximum likelihood regression of the equation. I used the coefficients from an iterative non-linear regression of the functions, which in turn was given the coefficients of a linear ordinary least-squares regression as starting values.

$$
\begin{aligned}
\ln C = {} & \alpha + \sum_{m=1}^{2}\beta_m \cdot \ln y_m + 0{,}5 \cdot \sum_{l=1}^{2}\sum_{m=1}^{2}\beta_{lm} \cdot \ln y_l \cdot \ln y_m \\
& + \sum_{n=1}^{3}\gamma_n \cdot \ln w_n + 0{,}5 \cdot \sum_{n=1}^{3}\sum_{p=1}^{3}\gamma_{np} \cdot \ln w_n \cdot \ln w_p \\
& + \sum_{m=1}^{2}\sum_{n=1}^{3}\delta_{mn} \cdot \ln y_m \cdot \ln w_n \\
& + \sum_{s=1}^{14}\zeta_s \cdot \text{sector}_s
\end{aligned}
\qquad (5\text{-}48)
$$

variable		minim.	median	mean	maxim.	std. dev.
	total assets*)	13.08	485.57	2213.28	55437.0	6643.73
C	costs*)	2.13	151.82	657.07	18979.40	2263.19
y_1	sales and self-constructed assets*)	2.45	515.51	2009.05	43755.00	5436.23
y_2	interest earnings and earnings from affiliated companies**)	62.00	17032.00	98323.26	2714000.3	332966.58
x_1	labor***)	21	1629	6811.688	184800	22742.91
x_2	tangible and intangible fixed assets**)	1597.00	87883.00	532024.52	9573277.0	1446006.4
x_3	financial capital**)	.00	101834.00	646865.22	18151000.	2183726.1
w_1	salary/wage rate plus social costs**)	35.05	82.22	82.89	146.17	22.55
w_2	depreciation rate on tangible and intangible fixed assets****)	.087	.229	.288	1.816	.249
w_3	cost of financial assets (via stock return as opportunity earning*****)	-1.221	-.034	-.125	.487	.280

N = 77 *) millions of DM **) thousands of DM ***) no. of employees
****) 1 = 100 % *****) ln(return + 1)

Table 5-7: Netputs and 1992 summary statistics of the cross sectional cost function data

5.2.5.1.2 Estimation Results

As there are 7 separate yearly regressions, it would be too much to reproduce every single maximum likelihood regression result here in the body of the text. Instead, the 1992, 1990, and 1988 results will be shown Table 5-8 in full, while the other results are provided in the appendix. The overview over the central results given in the text pertains to all of the regressions.

	1992		1990		1988	
coeff.	value	std. error	value	std. error	value	std. error
α	14.822451	0.118381 ***	1.030977	0.095000 ***	7.420939	0.079424 ***
β_1	-0.252406	0.008972 ***	-0.652026	0.007253 ***	-1.508001	0.004552 ***
β_2	-0.607689	0.012526 ***	1.420394	0.010191 ***	1.599276	0.009085 ***
γ_1	-0.131658	0.026961 ***	1.089874	0.021757 ***	2.385620	0.014221 ***
γ_2	4.877990	0.082441 ***	-0.251757	0.063979 ***	2.489134	0.034766 ***
γ_3	-3.746332	0.088788 ***	0.161883	0.069480 **	-3.874754	0.037004 ***
β_{11}	0.066644	0.000690 ***	0.080376	0.000563 ***	0.099575	0.000340 ***
β_{12}	0.046717	0.000929 ***	-0.074517	0.000773 ***	-0.106528	0.000500 ***
β_{22}	-0.033343	0.001292 ***	0.084789	0.001100 ***	0.111181	0.000656 ***
γ_{11}	0.014341	0.006322 **	-0.374531	0.005070 ***	-1.604596	0.003936 ***
γ_{12}	-0.412243	0.018770 ***	0.112060	0.014725 ***	-0.195092	0.011543 ***
γ_{13}	0.397903	0.020055 ***	0.262471	0.015800 ***	1.799688	0.010714 ***
γ_{22}	0.157823	0.050356 ***	0.000638	0.005277	0.132767	0.031226 ***
γ_{23}	-3.010441	0.613843 ***	0.189898	0.789160	0.311863	0.211341
γ_{33}	1.116098	0.617687 *	-0.055127	0.788192	-2.822256	0.186179 ***
δ_{11}	-0.076074	0.002042 ***	0.202997	0.001665 ***	0.379286	0.001398 ***
δ_{12}	-0.051948	0.006235 ***	-0.059127	0.005033 ***	-0.120815	0.003342 ***
δ_{13}	0.128022	0.006720 ***	-0.143870	0.005457 ***	-0.258470	0.003462 ***
δ_{21}	0.016964	0.002833 ***	-0.207938	0.002335 ***	-0.195957	0.001367 ***
δ_{22}	-0.224542	0.008718 ***	0.088685	0.007334 ***	0.052618	0.006058 ***
δ_{23}	0.207578	0.009398 ***	0.119253	0.007883 ***	0.143339	0.006350 ***
ζ_1	-0.276689	0.123000 **	0.183897	0.096443 *	-0.162150	0.065942 **
ζ_2	29.616658	0.123040 ***	0.837024	0.096485 ***	0.825393	0.069732 ***
ζ_3	0.651799	0.123034 ***	0.744945	0.096551 ***	0.461551	0.069758 ***
ζ_4	2.425369	0.123038 ***	0.428025	0.096484 ***	0.311335	0.085414 ***
ζ_5	0.540275	0.122901 ***	0.906107	0.096450 ***	0.653603	0.059308 ***
ζ_6	0.884090	0.123039 ***	0.443266	0.096488 ***	0.816380	0.109808 ***
ζ_7	0.198933	0.123021	0.842558	0.096509 ***	0.557591	0.104191 ***
ζ_8	1.488658	0.123039 ***	0.220669	0.096501 *	0.415103	0.103735 ***
ζ_9	0.048297	0.123023	0.386609	0.096482 ***	0.173106	0.080593 **
ζ_{10}	-0.406441	0.122983 ***	0.160993	0.097687	0.123374	0.106572 ***
ζ_{11}	0.446512	0.123027 ***	0.568429	0.096490 ***	0.366992	0.066163 ***
ζ_{12}	-0.368685	0.123033 ***	0.758978	0.096485 ***	0.552517	0.059126 ***
ζ_{13}	-0.250032	0.122910 **	0.632286	0.096820 ***	0.668713	0.071622 ***

	1992		1990		1988	
coeff.	value	std. error	value	std. error	value	std. error
ζ_{14}	0.153814	0.122998	0.387120	0.096414 ***	0.452842	0.075700 ***
λ	0.394004	0.122189 ***	0.591988	0.097968 ***	0.804473	0.301555 ***
σ	0.649778	0.126731 ***	0.559361	0.042925 ***	0.494727	0.039947 ***

N = 77/126/135; *** = significant at the 1 % level (** = 5 %; * = 10 %)

Table 5-8: Results of the cross-sectional maximum likelihood regressions for 1992, 1990, and 1988

One sees that a great number of the coefficients are significant at high levels, a not completely predictable result as it was questionable if the addition of simple sector dummies alone would be enough to allow a common cost function to be estimated for companies with widely differing products and production methods.

In most years the coefficients for the sales output $\ln y_1$ are negative (except 1987 and 1989), which does not mean that the slope of the functions in $\ln y_1$ is negative though, as $\ln y_1$ appears in many other variables, too. The coefficients of $\ln y_1^2$ for example are mostly positive. The slope characteristics are discussed in 5.2.5.1.3.

The values for λ, the ratio of the standard deviation of the inefficiency component of the composite error term to the standard deviation of the actual error in the error term, decline over time, while the standard deviation of the overall error tends to increase. A more detailed discussion of the temporal effects visible is in 5.2.5.1.5 below. The standard deviations of the error terms are very high, reaching 64.98 % in 1992. This can be due to the diversity of the companies in each regression, which cannot be sufficiently captured by the simple dummy variables for the sectors. Variations in the datapoints' positions that remain unexplainable by the model specifications are relegated to the error term.

The γ_{ij} coefficients for the combination variables $\ln(w_i)\cdot\ln(w_j)$ are the least significant of all coefficients, when neither i nor $j = 1$, i. e., the wages variable is not involved. This could be a sign that the price variables for fixed assets, the depreciation rate, and for financial assets, the (opportunity price) stock return, are not quite adequate.

Most of the sector dummy coefficients are highly significant, which indicates that there are substantial differences between the sectors.

5.2.5.1.3 Tests of the Properties of the Functions

Since it can be done in brief here, the results of the likelihood ratio tests for all of the seven yearly functions are given below in Table 5-9. As can be seen, the results are overwhelmingly significant, due to the many variables in the equation. This was already surmised above in section 5.2.4.4.

year	test statistic	sig.
1986	348822251.4556	***
1987	282672952.8570	***
1988	364291421.5504	***
1989	411377493.9939	***
1990	325360949.7629	***
1991	319839137.7728	***
1992	205959279.9096	***

Table 5-9: Results of the likelihood ratio tests for the seven yearly regressions[119]

The results of the test for well behavior of the cost functions for each year are presented below. The sales output (output number 1) shows no infringements of the monotony demand except for less than one percent of the firms in 1988. The second output, the financial gains, is less well behaved and exhibits monotonicity errors between 2.88 % and 27.27 % of the time.

This result, however, is far better than the monotonicity errors exhibited by the input prices. Most of the time, over 50 % of the cases are in error, i. e., they have a negative slope. This goes especially for input price 2, which only in 1992 has a negative slope for less than 70 % of the cases. Interestingly, in that year the other two inputs have their highest count of errors in monotony (93.51 %).

The poor result except for 1986 for the first input, labor, is difficult to interpret, as it implies that in many cases, the costs decrease with rising wage rates. If rising employment numbers necessitate rising wages for the employees, in order to attract the additional labor, then the wage rates can be seen as a proxy for company size. Companies below the optimal size could in fact experience decreasing overall costs as they approach their optimal size.

Alternatively, and perhaps mathematically more likely, decreasing employment numbers will drive the wage rate per employee up if all else is equal, as the rate is calculated as the total wages paid divided by the number of employees. In the worst case, inaccurate data could cause the observed effect. With all DM values expressed in terms of 1992 DM, the inflation rate chosen to inflate all pre-1992 numbers will also be of a certain import. Should wages rise more slowly than the consumer price index used here, their inflated 1992 DM values will be too high in the years 1986 through 1991. This can evoke the effect that high wage rates seem to coincide with falling costs.

[119] There were 36 degrees of freedom for each test. *** = significant at the 1 % level.

violation of property	% errors 1986	1987	1988	1989	1990	1991	1992
monotony of output 1	0.00	0.00	0.74	0.00	0.00	0.00	0.00
monotony of output 2	7.20	10.57	4.44	2.88	6.35	17.07	27.27
monotony of input price 1	1.60	52.85	81.48	58.99	55.56	64.23	93.51
monotony of input price 2	80.80	73.98	99.26	99.28	87.30	82.93	55.84
monotony of input price 3	79.20	75.61	31.11	2.88	36.51	52.03	93.51
elasticity of input price 1	8.00	47.15	61.48	41.01	34.92	52.04	44.16
elasticity of input price 2	19.20	26.02	0.74	2.16	0.00	6.50	2.60
elasticity of input price 3	4.80	24.39	19.26	0.72	3.17	17.89	17.75
concavity of the input prices	100.00	100.00	74.81	80.58	100.00	99.19	100.00

Table 5-10: Results of the tests of the properties of the yearly estimates of the cost functions[120]

Another important point can be seen in the possibility factor substitution. At the aggregated level used in this study, the input factors employed can be substituted for one another if desired. Should wage rates rise, the company management will strive to replace costly labor with cheaper capital. Substitution in excess of that necessary is possible if future wage hike are being anticipated or the exact degree of substitution is unknown to the management.

Finally, a point can also be made with reference to the fairly strong position of the labor unions in Germany. Should they have been able to secure high wage rates during years of general downsizing and cost reduction, the observed results will indeed mirror the actual development of the companies.

In fact, the correlation between the (natural logarithms of) the labor and the wage variables is significant at -24.14 %. This invalidates the first theory above and supports the various possibilities sketched to explain why rising wage rates and dropping costs can occur simultaneously. It is not possible to say which of the explanations presented is relevant.

The second input price is the depreciation rate of the fixed material and immaterial assets. It also displays errors in monotony well over 50 % of the time. Negative values mean that the more expensive a fixed asset unit is, the lower the costs are. As the choice of the depreciation rate is a managerial decision inside of certain legal bounds, this variable might not reflect the true price of the assets.

120 For all years except 1990, the concavity was tested via the eigenvalues of the Hessian matrix. For 1990, the determinants of the subminors of the Hessian were used.

The third input price variable, the price for financial investments, is somewhat different from the other input price variables. The stock return of the company is used as the price of the financial assets. In this sense it is an opportunity price which shows what might have been earned with the money had it been invested in the company and not somewhere else. Since stock returns can very well be negative seen over one year, this means that it is possible for the unit price of financial assets to become negative.[121] In other words, it does not cost anything to invest the financial capital elsewhere, but it is even rewarded.

The results for this input price are almost as bad as for the other input prices, though. In 1988 the lowest rate of 2.88 % errors in monotony is recorded, otherwise the rate lies over 30 %. Possibly negative input prices cause more positive slopes than usual for the positive input prices.

The tests for concavity of the cost function in the input prices are most aptly performed using the eigenvalues of the Hessian matrix, and where these did not calculate, the determinants of the Hessian's subminors.[122] As Table 5-10 shows, the results for this method of testing are, in a nutshell, disastrous. The lowest rate for errors in concavity are recorded in 1988 with a sizable 74.81 % cases of positive elasticities. In four of the years, concavity cannot be reported even for a single company.

This poor showing apparently is not uncommon, however. The few studies that report tests of any kind encounter similar problems.[123] One might assume that other studies have do not report on the behavior of their estimated functions have similar problems. The alternative method of checking the own price elasticities of the demand functions[124] provides a more varied view of the situation.

The elasticity of the wage rate is the worst, with up to 61.48 % of the cases exhibiting positive own price elasticities. For the other two variables, elasticity errors are rather more uncommon and reach a maximum of 26 % for the depreciation rates. The positive own price elasticity for labor contradicts somewhat the correlation test which was reported above for the monotonicity. There, the correlation of the employees to the wage rate was significantly negative, while here the derivative of the labor demand function is often positive.

In sum it can be said that the cost functions estimated do not conform very well to the theoretical demands made on them. They only represent coarse adapta-

---

[121] This does not conflict with the nondecreasing characteristic of the cost function in input prices, as if $w_3' \geq w_3$, $C(\mathbf{w}',y) \geq C(\mathbf{w},y)$.

[122] As was the case for 1990.

[123] Cf. Lang/Welzel (1984); Evans/Heckman (1984), Diewert/Wales (1987).

[124] Cf. Lang/Welzel (1984).

tions of the true functions. Using different variables or operationalizations thereof might sometimes be a solution (e. g., for the price of fixed assets), whereas in for other variables this does not seem to be feasible (wages). Errors in measurement are of course always possible, but the quality of the data is deemed to be good enough to rule out this explanation on a general basis. As other studies encounter the same obstacles or ignore the issue altogether, I content myself here to continue the analyses notwithstanding.

5.2.5.1.4 T-Tests for Differences in Mean Inefficiency

Below, from Table 5-11 to Table 5-15 the results of the efficiency tests for the years 1992, 1990 and 1988 are given. The overall mean x-inefficiency value of *xineff* for each year is given at the top of each table to give a benchmark by which to quickly judge the situation of the companies in a particular category. For each agency variable, the tables list the average group inefficiency for the companies with large agency problems in the first row and those with low agency problems in the second. The difference between these two average values of *xineff* is given in the right panel together with the corresponding z-level and the significance of the difference.

Obviously, the large number of agency measures will tend to dilute, not emphasize, the results in many cases. Various variables will provide conflicting results, which can be traced to the different aspects of agency problem control each variable incorporates. As has been said before, special note will be given to the following variables: block ownership as a major and uncontested measure of the monitoring possibilities of the ownership, and *agency1* and *agency5* as the standard agency conglomerate variables. The variables leverage and monitored debt ratio are separated by a line from the other agency variables because they capture debt-side agency problems. Of course, the leverage also denotes internal control, so it shouldn't be taken to exclusively signify creditor control.

For the majority of the hypotheses that suppose firms with agency problems to be less efficient than those without or with a low level of such problems, this means that in order for the hypotheses to be accepted, the sign of the difference between the two groups needs to be negative.

For the year **1992**, in many cases few companies fall into the large agency problem category. For these companies, the standard deviation of the x-inefficiency variable is also much smaller. This could mean that the results could partly be attributed to a very few companies without the added security of the effect of portfolios to diversify away other influences that are not of interest here. The t-tests were shown in chapter 2.4.1 to account for the number of cases in each subsample, though.

mean(xineff) overall: **24.53 %**

variable	mean(xineff)	std. dev.	N	diff	z	sig
block own-	24.17 %	2.29 %	4	-1.48 %	-0.9738	
ership	22.70 %	7.33 %	54			
size	20.39 %	4.49 %	12	4.91 %	2.68488	***
	25.30 %	10.42 %	65			
market	24.39 %	8.72 %	21	0.20 %	0.08632	
segment	24.59 %	10.35 %	56			
dividend	25.58 %	14.62 %	5	-1.12 %	-0.1689	
signal	24.46 %	9.61 %	72			
leverage	22.01 %	5.85 %	45	6.15 %	2.2098	**
	28.16 %	13.73 %	27			
monitored	22.00 %	6.21 %	40	5.27 %	2.35396	**
debt ratio	27.27 %	12.22 %	37			
agency1	19.63 %	3.08 %	5	3.47 %	2.03487	**
	23.10 %	7.31 %	53			
agency2	22.05 %	2.74 %	5	0.82 %	0.51671	
	22.87 %	7.38 %	53			
agency3	21.46 %	5.58 %	35	3.36 %	1.64825	*
	24.83 %	8.67 %	23			
agency4	18.63 %	2.83 %	6	4.64 %	3.02174	***
	23.28 %	7.29 %	52			
agency5	23.75 %	2.48 %	4	-1.02 %	-0.6419	
	22.73 %	7.33 %	54			
agency6	21.52 %	3.96 %	12	1.61 %	0.9973	
	23.13 %	7.70 %	46			
agency7	24.41 %	3.03 %	2	-1.67 %	-0.7135	
	22.74 %	7.20 %	56			

for each variable: first row = large agency problems, second row = low agency problems;
*** = significant at the 1 % level (** = 5 %; * = 10 %)

Table 5-11: T-tests for differences of means of *xineff* by agency variable, 1992

Of the main variables *block*, *agency1* and *agency5*, both *block* and *agency5* show the expected negative sign in Table 5-11, meaning that for these category variables, the inefficiency of the agency problem-ridden companies was greater than that of the other firms. Those differences in means are not significant, though, whereas the positive sign for *agency1* is significant. All the other significant results (size, leverage, monitored debt ratio, *agency3* and *agency4*) also all exhibit positive differences.

The x-inefficiency going by the agency conglomerates 5 through 7 slightly favors the low agency-problem firms, although not significantly so. These conglomerate variables were created under exclusion of the monitored debt ratio, meaning that all forms of management control are considered except the creditor-sided monitoring.[125] So the combination of a level of control for all agency variables and the exclusion of creditor influence might reduce agency problems. Therefore, for 1992 the hypothesis 1 cannot be totally rejected, which states that manager-controlled firms operate less efficiently than owner-controlled firms. It is, however, unlikely.

The differences by creditor control variables both have positive and significant signs, which clearly rejects the second hypothesis that gives creditor-controlled firms an efficient edge over the manger-controlled ones. Should this result repeat itself for other cost functions, the role of creditor monitoring will have to be rethought.

The third hypothesis that pits owners and creditors against each other states that the creditor-controlled firms will operate less efficiently than the owner-controlled firms. Table 5-12 shows the results of the corresponding t-tests.

variable	mean(xineff)	std. dev.	N	diff	z	sig
block ownership	22.70%	7.33%	54	-4.57%	-2.03901	**
creditor	27.27%	12.22%	37			
agency5	22.73%	7.33%	54	-4.54%	-2.02497	**
creditor	27.27%	12.22%	37			

first row = ownership control according to the variable given, second row = creditor control; *** = significant at the 1 % level (** = 5 %; * = 10 %)

Table 5-12: T-tests for differences of means of *xineff* between owner-controlled and creditor-controlled companies, 1992

Only the monitored debt ratio was used to represent creditor control, again to avoid the difficulties the leverage variable entails. Two versions of ownership control are used; first, the block ownership variable and second, the conglomerate *agency5*. This variable is the non-GeneHunter mix of all agency variables, excluding the monitored debt ratio. The strongest element in *agency5* is block ownership (40 %), so the variables block ownership and *agency5* are not too dissimilar.[126]

[125] Again, the leverage variable does capture this somewhat.

[126] Due to too small group sizes, the classification was not made according to the rule "creditor-controlled *and* not owner-controlled" etc., which would have been the correcter way of forming the groups. This way it is possible for firms to be simultaneously classified into both groups.

mean(xineff) overall: **26.20 %**

variable	mean(xineff)	std. dev.	N	diff	z	sig
block own-	23.69 %	10.85 %	9	2.59 %	0.70157	
ership	26.28 %	7.26 %	90			
size	26.65 %	10.67 %	27	-0.57 %	-0.23293	
	26.08 %	13.07 %	99			
market	25.29 %	10.80 %	35	1.25 %	0.57462	
segment	26.55 %	11.39 %	91			
dividend	25.31 %	11.81 %	10	0.97 %	0.25262	
signal	26.28 %	8.95 %	116			
leverage	24.93 %	10.23 %	68	2.75 %	1.43186	
	27.68 %	10.49 %	51			
monitored	26.01 %	11.02 %	55	0.33 %	0.17527	
debt ratio	26.34 %	9.67 %	71			
agency1	21.23 %	11.75 %	11	5.42 %	1.5009	
	26.65 %	6.58 %	88			
agency2	22.19 %	10.80 %	10	4.29 %	1.2337	
	26.48 %	6.01 %	89			
agency3	24.26 %	10.86 %	53	3.83 %	1.9508	*
	28.10 %	8.67 %	46			
agency4	24.83 %	12.10 %	14	1.42 %	0.42417	
	26.24 %	7.76 %	85			
agency5	24.69 %	10.94 %	9	1.49 %	0.39924	
	26.18 %	7.83 %	90			
agency6	24.27 %	10.79 %	23	2.31 %	0.96519	
	26.58 %	7.21 %	76			
agency7	24.96 %	11.33 %	7	1.16 %	0.26476	
	26.13 %	9.22 %	92			

for each variable: first row = large agency problems, second row = low agency problems;
*** = significant at the 1 % level (** = 5 %; * = 10 %)

Table 5-13: T-tests for differences of means of *xineff* by agency variable, 1990

In both cases, clear advantages for ownership control are apparent. Owner-controlled firms operated on average over 4.5 % more efficiently than those classed as creditor-controlled. This confirms hypothesis three for the year 1992.

The results for **1990** are quickly discussed, as no difference in inefficiency except for that according to *agency3* is significant, and all differences except for that measured using the size variable are positive.

This result leads to a rejection of the hypotheses one and two, speaking against a relevance of both agency problems and problems due to information asymmetry in a company. The third hypothesis comparing owner-control to creditor-control is tested in Table 5-14. It is confirmed by the slightest of margins, of course without a significant difference.

variable	mean(xineff)	std. dev.	N	diff	z	sig
block ownership	26.28%	7.26%	90	-0.06%	-0.04591	
creditor	26.34%	9.67%	71			
agency5	26.18%	7.83%	90	-0.16%	-0.11548	
creditor	26.34%	9.67%	71			

first row = ownership control according to the variable given, second row = creditor control; *** = significant at the 1 % level (** = 5 %; * = 10 %)

Table 5-14: T-tests for differences of means of *xineff* between owner-controlled and creditor-controlled companies, 1990

In return, the 1988 results featured in Table 5-15 show a majority of negative signs, albeit none of them significant. Relatively high standard deviations are the reason for this. Accepting the results as meaningful despite the lacking significance confirms the hypotheses one and two, that manager-controlled firms are less cost-efficient than both owner-controlled and creditor-controlled ones.

mean(xineff) overall: **27.56 %**

variable	mean(xineff)	std. dev.	N	diff	z	sig
block own-	27.56 %	11.22 %	10	-3.29 %	-0.90431	
ership	24.27 %	8.04 %	102			
size	28.15 %	11.25 %	39	0.70 %	0.30841	
	28.85 %	13.60 %	96			
market	28.10 %	11.37 %	41	-1.89 %	-0.89411	
segment	26.21 %	11.19 %	94			
dividend	29.24 %	13.33 %	30	-1.45 %	-0.54903	
signal	27.79 %	10.71 %	105			
leverage	27.03 %	10.13 %	76	-0.91 %	-0.54954	
	26.12 %	8.57 %	53			

mean(xineff) overall: **27.56 %**

variable	mean(xineff)	std. dev.	N	diff	z	sig
monitored	27.49 %	11.41 %	64	-1.01 %	-0.57962	
debt ratio	26.48 %	8.40 %	71			
agency1	28.53 %	13.25 %	13	-1.45 %	-0.38029	
	27.08 %	9.94 %	98			
agency2	27.90 %	11.38 %	12	-1.43 %	-0.41526	
	26.47 %	10.38 %	99			
agency3	27.96 %	11.31 %	61	-1.69 %	-0.89562	
	26.27 %	8.55 %	50			
agency4	29.67 %	13.59 %	16	-0.80 %	-0.22151	
	28.86 %	12.21 %	95			
agency5	27.62 %	11.06 %	14	-2.21 %	-0.71664	
	25.42 %	8.56 %	97			
agency6	28.15 %	11.50 %	23	-2.46 %	-0.96177	
	25.69 %	8.29 %	88			
agency7	28.35 %	11.80 %	12	0.75 %	0.20556	
	29.11 %	13.22 %	99			

for each variable: first row = large agency problems, second row = low agency problems;
*** = significant at the 1 % level (** = 5 %; * = 10 %)

Table 5-15: T-tests for differences of means of *xineff* by agency variable, 1988

The third hypothesis also can be confirmed for 1988, meaning that the ownership control produces greater cost efficiency than creditor control. Using the variable block ownership to define owner control even gives a result that is significant at the 10 %-level.

variable	mean(xineff)	std. dev.	N	diff	z	sig
block ownership	24.27%	8.04%	102	-2.21%	-1.73595	*
creditor	26.48%	8.40%	71			
agency5	25.42%	8.56%	97	-1.07%	-0.80706	
creditor	26.48%	8.40%	71			

first row = ownership control according to the variable given, second row = creditor control;
*** = significant at the 1 % level (** = 5 %; * = 10 %)

Table 5-16: T-tests for differences of means of *xineff* between owner-controlled and creditor-controlled companies, 1988

The tables for the remaining four years 1986, 1987, 1989 and 1991 can be found in the appendix. Summarizing their results by hypothesis and confining the discussion to the major agency variables, the first hypothesis is only rejected in 1986 going by the block ownership and in 1991 when using *agency1*. This means that except for the 1990, the first hypothesis that manager-controlled companies are less x-efficient than ownership-controlled ones can be accepted. The second hypothesis is not rejected for 1986, the only other year for which this cannot be done apart from 1988. The third hypothesis claiming that owner-controlled firms will be more x-efficient than creditor-controlled ones is only rejected for 1986, resulting in six out of seven years in which the hypothesis cannot be rejected.

5.2.5.1.5 Temporal Developments in Inefficiency

As can be seen in Figure 5-14 below, there is a definite downwards trend in the average inefficiency of the German industrial firms studied over the observed period. This does not necessarily mean that the firms became absolutely more efficient, but that the group of firms as a whole moved closer together, reducing the distances between firms. The firms might even have become absolutely less efficient while their relative efficiency increased.

A linear trend was overlaid as an interrupted line in the chart, with the corresponding functional description added at the bottom right in the chart. On average, the relative inefficiency of the firms declined by 1.2 % per year during the observation period with a corresponding R^2 of 74.86 %.

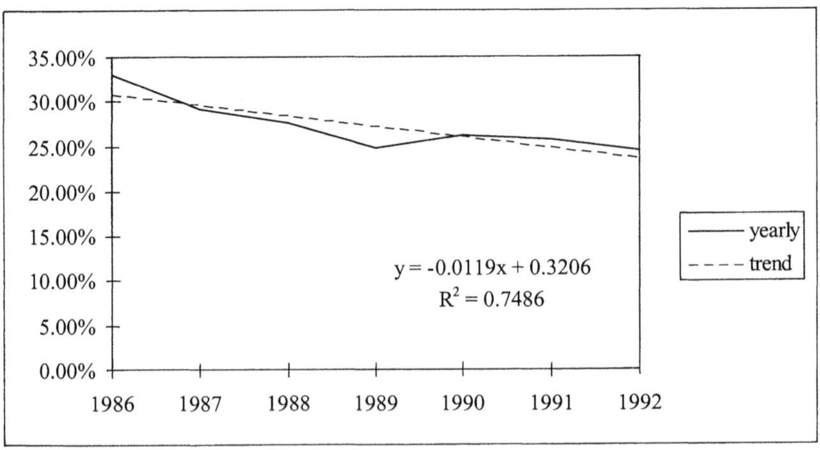

Figure 5-14: Development of *xineff* over time

This result means that the comprehensive regression over all years which assumes constant inefficiency levels for each company over time might not be ideally suited to the data. Should the tests of the subgroups in the yearly analyses show that the groups' inefficiencies remain constant in relation to each other, signifying that there is no temporal effect on group-level efficiency induced through agency problems, then this deficiency is of little import. Therefore, the comprehensive model with fixed inefficiency levels over time will be estimated later, despite its shortcomings. In the meantime, the temporal developments will be studied more closely.

In Figure 5-15, the development of *xineff* (average overall value per year), σ and λ is shown in one graph in order to be able to compare the changes in the values estimated over the years. The axis for *xineff* and σ which are shown as bars is on the left, the one for λ is on the right. λ and σ show opposing tendencies, so in a year when σ is lower, λ is a bit higher.

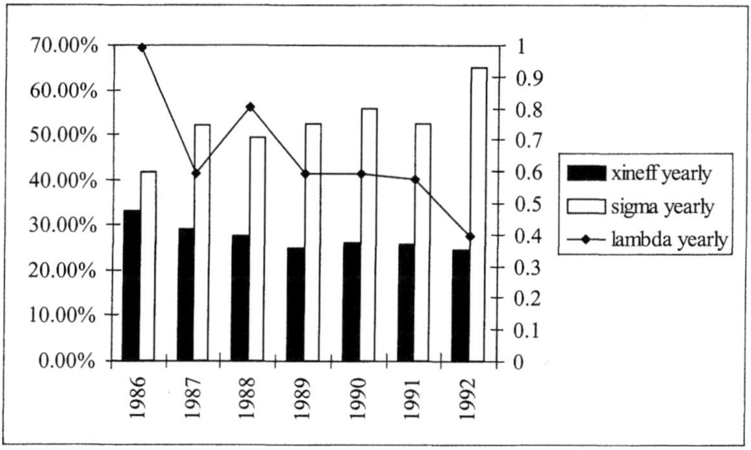

Figure 5-15: Comparison of the development of *xineff*, σ and λ over time[127]

With λ as the quotient between the standard deviation of the inefficiency and that of the true error, this means that the true error component is to a greater degree responsible for changes in the volatility of the composed error term than the inefficiency. It also implies that the standard deviation of the inefficiency does

[127] The right scale is for the values of λ.

not change as much over time. The development of *xineff*, while declining, in fact does not mirror the development of σ that strongly.

Going by the major agency variables block ownership, *agency1* and *agency5*, Figure 5-16 to Figure 5-18 show the development of the variable *xineff* over time, separated by managerial or ownership control over the firm. These figures allow the fourth hypothesis to be tested. In that hypothesis it is postulated that the x-inefficiency in companies controlled by managers will increase more rapidly and decrease more slowly than the x-inefficiency in owner-controlled firms.

The development using block ownership as the agency variable is depicted in Figure 5-16. This rendition has the added advantage of conveying at a glance the superior efficiency of owner-controlled companies. Only in 1986 and 1990 are the manager-controlled firms more efficient.

The trends exhibited by the two groups are very similar and it becomes clear that only one half of hypothesis four can be tested, i. e., if there are differences in the rates of decline in inefficiency, because the general trend in this and the other figures is downward. There are not enough years to split the data into parts with rising and parts with falling efficiency.

Regressions through each group give slopes of -0.0115 and -0.0128 for manager and owner-controlled companies, respectively. That is a difference of 11.3 % in favor of the owner-controlled firms, which is slight. If a similar result should be found for the other agency variables, the hypothesis, or its testable half, can be said to be valid.

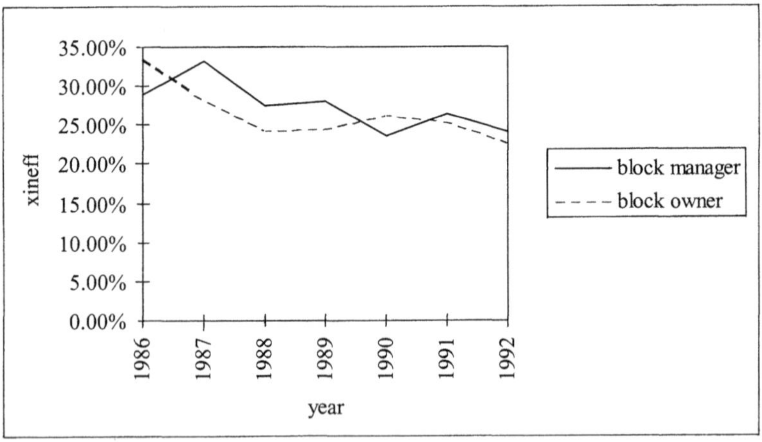

Figure 5-16: Comparison of the development of *xineff* over time, by managerial and ownership control (using block ownership to distinguish)

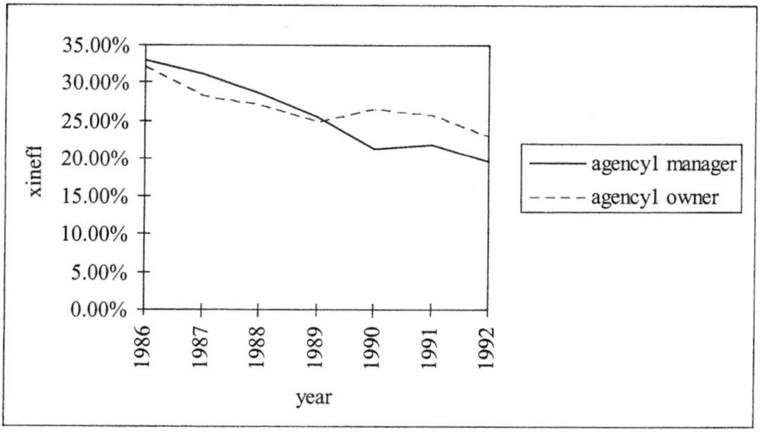

Figure 5-17: Comparison of the development of *xineff* over time, by managerial and ownership control (using *agency1* to distinguish)

The slopes of the two *xineff* lines that result when using agency1 to distinguish between groups are -0.0236 for manager-controlled firms and -0.0117 for the owner controlled firms. The difference between the two amounts to 101.7 % and is in favor of the manager-controlled firms. This clearly rejects hypothesis four.

Figure 5-18 below shows the development using *agency5*. Here, the slope values produced by linear regression are -0.0137 and -0.0119, again for manager and owner-controlled firms, respectively. The relative difference is 15.1 % in favor of the management-controlled firms, again rejecting hypothesis four.

The other agency conglomerate variables except for *agency7* provide similar results, with the x-inefficiency in manager-controlled companies decreasing faster than that of owner-controlled ones (not shown here). For all variables, the slope is generally negative over the full time period studied, meaning that the obverse hypothesis, that manager-controlled companies increase their cost-inefficiency faster than the owner-controlled firms, cannot be evaluated. The variables market segment and dividend signal are the only single agency variables where the negative slope is greater for the owner-controlled firms. This results in an overall rejection of hypothesis four. The results from many of the other variables show, similar to Figure 5-17, a result of this observation that one could deduce as a logical consequence: Toward the end of the observation period, the manager-controlled firms often decrease their inefficiency to a level below that of the owner-controlled firms.

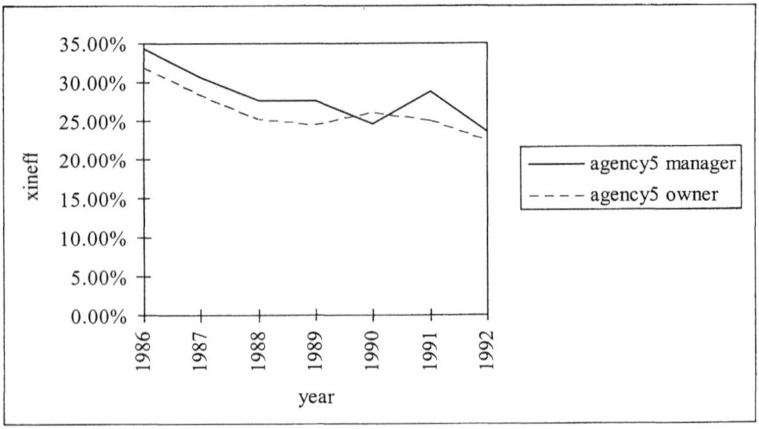

Figure 5-18: Comparison of the development of xineff over time, by managerial and ownership control (using *agency5* to distinguish)

5.2.5.1.6 Logistic Regressions

The logistic regressions again provide the possibility of testing the hypotheses with the joint inclusion of the un-conglomerated agency variables. The regressions allow for hypotheses one and two to be tested. The only agency conglomerates reported on here are *agency1* and *agency5*, as the main focus of this methodology is to test for the joint explanatory power of the agency variables in their original form. Therefore, the agency variables are again used in their non-dichotomous form, and so two market segment dummies were created to account for the three market segment classifications used. If the first dummy is one, the market segment is official continuous trade, if the second is one, the segment is official daily trade. Both dummies at zero means the company is in the free trade segment. The dividend signal remains dichotomous, as it had no other operationalization.

The logit models reported for below in Table 5-17 were as in the earlier sections estimated without constants, as their inclusion often led to an optimization of the predictions by classifying all cases into the stronger group. The log likelihood values are chi^2-distributed and the significance values provided for them refer to the improvement the full model provides over a flat 50 % probability for each case to belong to either group of high or low x-inefficiency companies.

	1986	1987	1988	1989	1990	1991	1992
expected sign	–	–	–	–	–	–	–
			model 1				
block ownership	.2334	-.5506	-.0929	-.7790	.8288	-.2679	3.1432
size	-.1105	.0401	.0343	-.0899	-.0741	.0370	1.2154 *
market seg. 1	.6537	-.5503	.5181	.5834	1.6048 *	.3003	-3.352
market seg. 2	.2566	-.7989	8.1706	9.7412	1.6197	1.8110 *	-6.342
dividend sig.	.9830	.5419	-1.3610	.0648	-1.7975	-1.4818	-19.697 *
leverage	-.1843	-.1786	.1150	.1599	.2367	.1198	.1516
-2 log likelihood‡	163.816	145.633	138.190 **	119.076 ***	109.058 **	106.052 **	17.190 ***
% correct classifications	62.30	53.27	62.73	74.31	68.54	70.11	96.00
			model 2				
leverage	-.0878	-.0401	-.1688	-.3364	-.2463	.0822	-.1733
monitored debt ratio	-.1182	.0428	-.3720	-.9297	.2330	-.7880 *	-1.3329
-2 log likelihood‡	170.406	166.285	175.410	166.717 ***	163.118	158.495	91.776 **
% correct classifications	51.61	50.00	55.81	67.69	52.10	55.56	81.94
			model 3				
agency1	-.1054	.0000	-.3808 *	-.8812 ***	-.4978 **	-.6931 ***	-2.7081 ***
-2 log likelihood‡	168.812	148.333	148.897 *	133.604 ***	118.453 *	111.433 ***	25.217 ***
% correct classifications	52.46	51.40	59.09	67.89	58.43	65.52	90.00
			model 4				
agency5	-.1596	-.0206	-.3469 *	-.8615 ***	-.5839 **	-.7492 ***	-2.6852 ***
-2 log likelihood‡	168.410	148.323	149.559 *	133.972 ***	116.759 **	109.991 ***	26.472 ***
% correct classifications	54.92	52.34	57.27	67.89	61.80	67.82	88.00

*** = significant at the 1 % level (** = 5 %; * = 10 %); ‡ = significance of model chi-square

Table 5-17: Coefficients and overall results of the logistic regressions on the *xineff* dummy variable, by year[128]

The dependent dummy variable created from *xineff* for each company was set to 1 if *xineff* was greater than the mean value of the inefficiency of all companies in the same sector, and zero otherwise. This means that negative coefficients support the theories stating that the lower the agency problems (= the higher the

[128] The market segment dummy 1 is one for official continuous trade, the second dummy is one for official daily trade.

agency control variables) are for a company, the lower the x-inefficiency will be in that company. For the first hypothesis (owner control is better than manager control), the block ownership, *agency1*, *agency5* and size variables are of interest, followed by the market segment and dividend signal variables, which strictly depict the informational asymmetry in a company, and the leverage. The second hypothesis (creditor control is better than manager control) can be tested by checking the signs of the leverage and especially the monitored debt ratio coefficients in the second regression model. There the signs must be negative.

Negative signs are the case for four of the seven block ownership coefficients, but none are significant. Of the four significant coefficients for all yearly regressions using the first model, only one has a negative sign. These coefficients seem to be more randomly significant than interpretably so, though. The agency conglomerate variables, however, come out strongly in support of the first hypothesis, with almost straight negative coefficients and high levels of significance. So the first hypothesis is not rejected, but only barely so.

The second hypothesis claiming the superiority of creditor control over manager control receives more consistent support and cannot be rejected. The results from the second model using only the leverage and the monitored debt ratio have few significant coefficients, though. The classification results for all models peak at 96 % but dip as low as 50 %. A random classification would result in less than 60 % hits except for 1992, where the score is 88.72 %. This means that the models with only one or two agency variables did not do so well in 1986/87 and 1992. All in all, about 70 % of the models show significant improvements in the log likelihood. This supports the view that agency problems do affect the x-inefficiency of firms.

In order to provide a quick overview of the results of the hypothesis tests for all the yearly inefficiency estimates, the following Table 5-18 shows the groups being compared for differences in *xineff* for each hypothesis one through three, and a check if the hypothesis can be said to be confirmed. A confirmation is usually recorded if the sign of the difference is as postulated, as most differences are not significant. Only the major agency variables are processed here, and simple majorities are used to evaluate the overall columns and rows added for convenience. For the second hypothesis, however, the monitored debt ratio would have been weighted more heavily than the leverage, had it been necessary.

The results are fairly consistent, confirming hypotheses one and three and rejecting hypothesis number two in the overall view. The logistic regressions tend to support the t-test results for the first hypothesis, but differ several times for the second hypothesis. The results mean that for the cross-sectional regressions, one can say that manager-controlled firms are less x-efficient than owner-controlled firms. Also, creditor-controlled firms are less x-efficient than owner-controlled firms. No difference in efficiency is detectable between manager-controlled and creditor-controlled firms, however. The fourth hypothesis can only be evaluated at the overall level. In view of the major agency variables block ownership, *agency1* and *agency5*, the hypothesis was rejected two out of three times, and also for the majority of the other variables. One should keep in mind that the GeneHunter conglomerate variables not listed in the table do not necessarily always support the overall hypothesis evaluations given here, though.

hypothesis #	variable	1986	1987	1988	1989	1990	1991	1992	overall
1	block ownership	☐	☑	☑	☑	☐	☑	☑	☑
	agency1	☑	☑	☑	☑	☐	☐	☐	(☑)
	agency5	☑	☑	☑	☑	☐	☑	☑	☑
	logistic	(☐)	(☑)	☑	☑	(☐)	☑	☑	☑
overall		(☑)	☑	☑	☑	☐	☑	☑	☑
2	leverage	☑	☐	☑	☐	☐	☐	☐	☐
	monitored debt ratio	☑	☐	☑	☐	☐	☐	☐	☐
	logistic	☑	☐	☑	☑	☐	☑	☑	☑
overall		☑	☐	☑	☐	☐	☐	☐	☐
3	block ownership	☐	☑	☑	☑	☑	☑	☑	☑
	agency5	☐	☑	☑	☑	☑	☑	☑	☑
overall		☐	☑	☑	☑	☑	☑	☑	☑
4	overall								☐

Table 5-18: Overview over the validity of hypotheses one through four, yearly regressions[129]

[129] T-tests for group differences by the variable given or logistic regressions. A check marks a hypothesis that could not be rejected according to the model given at the top of the column. N/A = not applicable, used where the agency variable does not subdivide the sample into two groups. For hypothesis three, the monitored debt ratio was used to identify creditor-controlled firms.

5.2.5.2 Panel Model Overall Cost Function

5.2.5.2.1 Model Description

The summary statistics for the overall panel regression are given in Table 5-19. A total of 848 cases could be included over all seven years, with an average of about 121 companies per year. All DM values are expressed in terms of 1992 DM. The opportunity price of the financial assets, w_3, takes a very negative minimum value. The maximum depreciation rate, while correct, also constitutes a number which could be called an outlier. The case was not removed from the dataset, however.

variable		min.	median	mean	maxim.	std. dev.
	total assets*)	8.33	351.10	1613.32	55437.00	4835.70
C	costs*)	.79	134.20	593.88	24521.33	1914.94
y_1	sales and self-constructed assets*)	1.84	450.60	1739.76	47640.59	5055.33
y_2	interest earnings and earnings from affiliated companies**)	2.270	8398.502	57660.273	2714000.3	197899.85
x_1	labor***)	19	1409.5	6011.397	206200	19087.38
x_2	tangible and intangible fixed assets**)	43.08	74476.73	422879.14	12258782.	1262581.1
x_3	financial capital**)	.00	40627.33	352390.20	18151000.	1259306.1
w_1	salary/wage rate plus social costs**)	34.18	74.93	76.28	146.17	19.31
w_2	depreciation rate on tangible and intangible fixed assets****)	.025	.275	.332	20.298	.721
w_3	cost of financial assets (via stock return as opportunity earning*****)	-1.22	.051	.063	1.513	.334

N = 848 *) millions of 1992 DM **) thousands of 1992 DM ***) no. of employees ****) 1 = 100 % *****) ln(return + 1)

Table 5-19: Netputs and summary statistics of the panel cost function data

The functional form chosen for this section of the analyses is given in Equation (5-49), which follows Equation (5-8) above except for the addition of the sectoral dummies in the last line. The time variable used is a simple index, i. e., companies in 1986 have a value for t of 1 and 1992 companies a value of 7.

$$\begin{aligned}\ln C &= \alpha + \sum_{m=1}^{2} \beta_m \cdot \ln y_m + 0.5 \cdot \sum_{l=1}^{2}\sum_{m=1}^{2} \beta_{lm} \cdot \ln y_l \cdot \ln y_m \\ &+ \sum_{n=1}^{3} \gamma_n \cdot \ln w_n + 0.5 \cdot \sum_{n=1}^{3}\sum_{p=1}^{3} \gamma_{np} \cdot \ln w_n \cdot \ln w_p \\ &+ \sum_{m=1}^{2}\sum_{n=1}^{3} \delta_{mn} \cdot \ln y_m \cdot \ln w_n \\ &+ \theta_t \cdot t + 0.5 \cdot \theta_{tt} \cdot t^2 + \sum_{n=1}^{3} \theta_{nt} \ln w_n \cdot t \\ &+ \sum_{s=1}^{14} \zeta_s \cdot \text{sector}_s\end{aligned} \tag{5-49}$$

5.2.5.2.2 Estimation Results

The panel data estimation requires a different loglikelihood function to be implemented. The cross-sectional regressions were based on Equation (5-48) which was derived from the Equation (5-32), used here. The different estimation kernel, together with the slightly altered functional form, reduces the comparability of the two types of estimation (cross-section and panel, cf. Table 5-8) somewhat. The same restrictions, given in 5.2.4.1, were again applied to the estimation. The results of the estimation are given in Table 5-20.

coefficient	**value**	**std. error**
α	4.349066	9.931416
β_1	-1.236317	0.765587
β_2	1.398096	1.110269
γ_1	1.566099	2.305781
γ_2	0.432708	6.807091
γ_3	-0.998806	7.245066
β_{11}	0.094597	0.058488
β_{12}	-0.079670	0.083631
β_{22}	0.086041	0.118325
γ_{11}	-0.787233	0.537123
γ_{12}	0.038845	1.578875
γ_{13}	0.748387	1.675239
γ_{22}	-0.039123	4.112610
γ_{23}	-0.924004	107.666603

coefficient	value	std. error
γ_{33}	0.313480	107.550468
δ_{11}	0.323929	0.177689 *
δ_{12}	-0.023947	0.525255
δ_{13}	-0.299982	0.559755
δ_{21}	-0.225370	0.256339
δ_{22}	-0.010405	0.753176
δ_{23}	0.235774	0.807305
θ_t	0.111310	2.560534
θ_{tt}	0.008553	0.530412
θ_{1t}	-0.052180	0.590541
θ_{2t}	-0.007101	1.748974
θ_{3t}	0.059281	1.884827
ζ_1	-0.137503	9.998478
ζ_2	0.710624	9.999991
ζ_3	0.466307	9.999161
ζ_4	0.332587	9.999860
ζ_5	0.629392	9.994748
ζ_6	0.267133	9.999900
ζ_7	0.572105	9.999992
ζ_8	0.254791	9.999903
ζ_9	0.186664	9.999376
ζ_{10}	-0.092190	9.998534
ζ_{11}	0.335924	9.999112
ζ_{12}	0.537094	9.999926
ζ_{13}	0.186217	9.996312
ζ_{14}	0.317085	9.999967
λ	0.410077	8.242725
σ	0.515224	9.797207

N = 848; *** = significant at the 1 % level (** = 5 %; * = 10 %)

Table 5-20: Results of the overall maximum likelihood panel regression

The first thing that becomes apparent is that the number of significant coefficients has dropped markedly. Only the coefficient for $\ln y_1 \cdot \ln w_1$, δ_{11}, is significant, and that only at the 10 % level. This contrasts seemingly with the consistency for the coefficients the addition of more cases for one company entails.[130]

[130] Cf. Greene (1993), pp. 82 ff.

In fact, these results show the true import of using translog cost functions which implies high levels of multicollinearity in the independent variables that was not that apparent in the cross-sectional regressions.

In addition, the multicollinearity makes it questionable if the coefficients can be interpreted at all. For this reason, some researchers completely omit time index variables from all their models.[131]

Unfortunately, the estimates for the λ and the σ for this estimation are also far from being significant. While the comprehensive estimate for σ, 51.52 %, lies near the mean of the yearly values, Figure 5-19 shows that the comprehensive λ is lower than most of the yearly estimates for λ. This means that the comprehensive estimate for *xineff* will be lower than the average over the years.

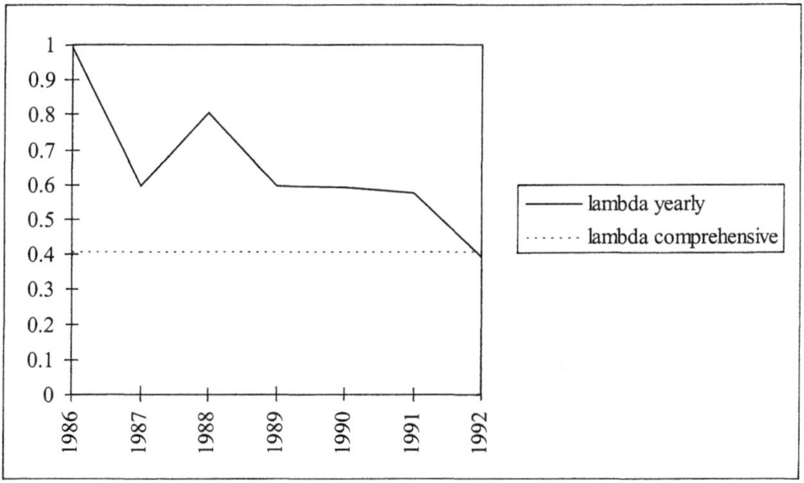

Figure 5-19: Comparison of the development of the yearly values for λ and the comprehensive value

The coefficient for the sales variable is negative. This again does not immediately imply that the costs drop when sales are increased. The monotony test in the following section 5.2.5.2.3 will show if this is truly the case. In general, the coefficients for variables that include either the sales output or the wage unit price (i. e., all coefficients with a one in the index) perform the best, without approaching significance, though (except δ_{11}, as mentioned). The coefficients γ_{23}

---

131 Cf. Schalk/Untiedt/Lüschow (1994), p. 13.

and γ_{33}, which respectively belong to the variables $\ln w_2 \cdot \ln w_3$ and $\ln w_3^2$, fare the worst of all. The sector dummies prove to be far from significant.

The newly added time variables unfortunately are not significant, which is disappointing. Should this observation be valid despite the multicollinearity, this would speak against any development in time of x-inefficiency, even though the cross-sectional regressions seemed to contradict that view, as a downward trend of decreasing cost inefficiency was noticeable there.

5.2.5.2.3 Tests of the Properties of the Function

likelihood ratio test statistic	sig.
1920639856352.7061	***

Table 5-21: Results of the likelihood ratio tests for the comprehensive panel regression[132]

violation of property	% errors
monotony of output 1	0.00
monotony of output 2	8.84
monotony of input price 1	22.52
monotony of input price 2	82.78
monotony of input price 3	59.08
elasticity of input price 1	29.72
elasticity of input price 2	5.54
elasticity of input price 3	5.54
concavity of the input prices	100.00

Table 5-22: Results of the tests of the properties of the comprehensive panel estimate of the cost function[133]

Again, the likelihood ratio test shows that the estimated function is significant (see Table 5-21). The value is largest for this estimation because the number of

---

132 There were 41 degrees of freedom for the test. *** = significant at the 1 % level.

133 The concavity was tested via the determinants of the subminors of the Hessian matrix.

additional variables, 41, was the greatest in this case, through the inclusion of time variables and sector dummies.

The tests of the well behavior of the overall panel cost function are given in Table 5-22. Both output variables perform very well as regards monotony, and despite the negative coefficient of the simple sales output variable $\ln y_1$, there are no actual negative slopes for this variable for any firm in the sample.

The percentages of monotony errors in the input prices mirror somewhat those of the cross-sectional tests reported in Table 5-10 above. Over one-fifth of the wage variable w_1 values violates the monotony requirement. The depreciation variable as the price for the fixed assets, w_2, surprisingly has more errors than the price for financial assets, w_3, which can even assume negative values. Just like the price for financial assets, the depreciation is expressed as a percentage, so neither had to be adjusted for inflation. The fixed assets used to calculate the depreciation rate were purchased in various years, meaning their book values actually are DM values from varying years. The inability to accurately portray these underlying DM values might explain the many errors to a degree. Even more important is the susceptibility of depreciation to managerial decisions that can be motivated by a myriad of reasons, and would tend to reduce the informational content of depreciation numbers.

The percentage of own elasticity errors as a criterion for concavity in the input prices is fairly low, especially for the two inputs fixed assets and financial assets. All numbers lie within the ranges defined by the results in Table 5-10. The direct test of the own elasticity unfortunately again produces a 100 % error rate.

5.2.5.2.4 T-Tests for Differences in Mean Inefficiency

As became apparent above by the low estimate for λ in the comprehensive regression, the overall inefficiency of 25.18 % lies near the lower end of the range of inefficiencies estimated in the yearly regressions (Figure 5-20). The inefficiency levels from the yearly regressions were only lower in 1989 and 1992.

The yearly results were determined using a different model than the comprehensive estimation, with variables added for time effects, be they learning effects, cyclical influences or changes in the competitive situation of the firms. Additional variables usually lead to a reduction of the error term. The error term contains the inefficiency component, so a reduced error term will tend to produce reduced inefficiency estimates. Therefore the comprehensive average inefficiency term *xineff* of 25.18 % (the lower, interrupted horizontal line) is slightly lower than the average of the seven yearly inefficiency estimates, 27.28 % (the higher, dotted horizontal line).

Figure 5-20: Comparison of yearly and comprehensive inefficiency estimates

The comprehensive estimate proved very sensitive to changes in the starting parameters chosen for the iterative optimization process. Choosing only slightly different parameters led to different, but plausible, results. Here, for consistency, the same starting parameters were used as in the sectoral estimates that also contain panel data.

The tests of the hypotheses one and two are shown in Table 5-23. Here, the value "N", in the fourth column, represents the number of companies in each group, not the number of companies multiplied by the number of years for each company. One sees that the groups are unequally loaded. Very often, but not always, the number of companies with a high level of agency problems is much smaller than the number of low-problem companies. Apart from one result, that for *agency3*, no difference in inefficiency is significant.

As regards the first hypothesis, that manager-controlled firms are less efficient than owner-controlled companies, Table 5-23 shows that the central agency variables *block*, *agency1* and *agency5* all support the hypothesis, while almost all other variables reject it. Again only one of the differences is significant. Together this leads to a tentative acceptance of the first hypothesis.

The second hypothesis, that manager-controlled firms are also less efficient than creditor-controlled ones, can be confirmed using the monitored debt ratio as the indicator variable. The creditor-controlled firms operated 2.02 % more efficiently than the manager-controlled firms. The leverage variable, however, rejects the hypothesis, showing a 4.16 % difference in efficiency in favor of the manager-controlled firms.

mean(xineff) overall: **25.18 %**

variable	mean(xineff)	std. dev.	N	diff	z	sig
block	29.63 %	23.88 %	12	-4.34 %	-0.61329	
own-ership	25.29 %	18.96 %	139			
size	24.68 %	19.26 %	41	0.66 %	0.1934	
	25.33 %	18.61 %	140			
market	22.59 %	15.81 %	55	3.72 %	1.34578	
segment	26.32 %	19.79 %	126			
dividend	20.73 %	17.37 %	24	5.13 %	1.33212	
signal	25.86 %	18.86 %	157			
leverage	23.77 %	15.90 %	107	4.16 %	1.29434	
	27.94 %	22.95 %	66			
monitored	26.17 %	18.67 %	93	-2.02 %	-0.72612	
debt ratio	24.15 %	18.80 %	88			
agency1	26.38 %	23.18 %	19	-0.70 %	-0.12593	
	25.67 %	18.82 %	131			
agency2	26.77 %	23.75 %	18	-1.14 %	-0.19545	
	25.63 %	18.76 %	132			
agency3	23.00 %	15.63 %	92	7.15 %	2.04425	**
	30.15 %	23.56 %	58			
agency4	22.23 %	15.50 %	24	4.20 %	1.1579	
	26.44 %	19.96 %	126			
agency5	30.11 %	24.05 %	16	-4.86 %	-0.78059	
	25.25 %	18.74 %	134			
agency6	23.74 %	18.02 %	39	2.73 %	0.79223	
	26.47 %	19.80 %	111			
agency7	22.91 %	20.05 %	11	3.08 %	0.49233	
	25.99 %	19.33 %	139			

for each variable: first row = large agency problems, second row = low agency problems; N = number of companies in group, *** = significant at the 1 % level (** = 5 %; * = 10 %)

Table 5-23: T-tests for differences of means of *xineff* by agency variable for the comprehensive panel regression

variable	mean(xineff)	std. dev.	N	diff	z	sig
block ownership	25.29%	18.96%	139	1.15%	0.44641	
creditor	24.15%	18.80%	88			
agency5	25.25%	18.74%	134	1.10%	0.42707	
creditor	24.15%	18.80%	88			

first row = ownership control according to the variable given, second row = creditor control; *** = significant at the 1 % level (** = 5 %; * = 10 %)

Table 5-24: T-tests for differences of means of *xineff* between owner-controlled and creditor-controlled companies, overall panel regression

The third hypothesis concerning the superiority of ownership control over creditor control as measured by the monitored debt ratio must be rejected. Creditor-controlled firms are 1.1 % or 1.15 % more efficient than owner-controlled firms in the overall panel view, at non-significant levels.

5.2.5.2.5 Logistic Regressions

The results of the logistic regressions over all the data are given in Table 5-25. All regressions are strongly significant, with the regulatory power of block ownership in evidence. This supports the hypothesis one that ownership control reduces x-inefficiency compared to manager control. Most other agency variables pertaining to the first hypothesis however show positive signs, which does not support the hypothesis. These other variable coefficients are also not significant, though. The agency conglomerates significantly support the first hypothesis. Their classification scores lie only slightly below the 67 % that the six agency variables together achieved. The generally high correct classification results underline the importance of agency problem control for x-efficiency improvement. A random classification would achieve a score of about 54 %. In view of the significant support for the first hypothesis provided by the agency conglomerates, hypothesis one is not rejected overall. The presence of monitoring debt and a high debt-equity ratio also reduces x-inefficiency, which clearly supports the second hypothesis.

Table 5-26 gives a final overview over the results of the hypothesis tests for the comprehensive panel cost function. The same comments on the procedure in constructing the table apply as given above for Table 5-18, except of course that the time-related hypothesis four cannot be evaluated here. The first and second hypotheses are not rejected using the comprehensive panel cost function, while the third hypothesis is rejected for both ownership control variables used. In the case of the second hypothesis, the monitored debt ratio variable was weighted more heavily than the leverage variable when marking the hypothesis as overall not rejected.

comprehensive regression	
model 1	
block ownership	-.9464
size	.0303
market segment 1	.2850
market segment 2	.7431
dividend signal	-.6311
leverage	-.0084
-2 log likelihood‡	174.482 **
% correct classifications	67.15
model 2	
leverage	-.0556
monitored debt ratio	-.7014 *
-2 log likelihood‡	232.148 **
% correct classifications	60.69
model 3	
agency1	-.6690 ***
-2 log likelihood‡	176.79 ***
% correct classifications	64.23
model 4	
agency5	-.6567 ***
-2 log likelihood‡	177.34 ***
% correct classifications	63.50

N = 181; *** = significant at the 1 % level (** = 5 %; * = 10 %); ‡ = significance of model chi-square

Table 5-25: Coefficients and overall results of the logistic regressions on the *xineff* dummy variable, comprehensive regression[134]

hypothesis #	variable/model	overall panel
1	block ownership	☑
	agency1	☑
	agency5	☑
	logistic	☑
overall		☑
2	leverage	☐
	monitored debt ratio	☑

[134] The market segment dummy 1 is one for official continuous trade, the second dummy is one for official daily trade.

hypothesis #	variable/model	overall panel
	logistic	☑
	overall	☑
3	block ownership	☐
	agency5	☐
	overall	☐

Table 5-26: Overview over the validity of hypotheses one, two and three; comprehensive panel regression[135]

5.2.5.3 Panel Model Sectoral Cost Functions

5.2.5.3.1 Model Description

The hypotheses one through three can also be tested per sector using the panel data. This is possible by running separate regressions over every single sector of sufficient size in the dataset, or by analyzing the results from the overall regression by sector. Both approaches will be pursued here and the results compared.

The fifth and sixth hypotheses will also be tested for the five sectors with the most companies in the dataset.[136] The fifth hypothesis (see 5.2.1) states that firms in highly competitive sectors will be more cost efficient than those in more regulated sectors. The sixth expects greater differences in x-inefficiency to be found in sectors with little competition.

This section bases on the same model used above for the comprehensive panel estimation. Due to the small number of firms per sector, it is not possible to estimate separate yearly regressions. Therefore the cost function to be estimated given in Equation (5-50) is identical to Equation (5-49) except for the omission of the sector dummies, which of course are not necessary here. It pertains to a panel of data and again includes the time factor in form of a simple time index variable, the square of that variable, and the wage rate variables respectively multiplied by the time index.

---

[135] T-tests for group differences by the variable given or logistic regressions. A check marks a hypothesis that could not be rejected according to the model given at the top of the column. N/A = not applicable, used where the agency variable does not subdivide the sample into two groups. For hypothesis three, the monitored debt ratio was used to identify creditor-controlled firms.

[136] Chemicals, machinery, electronics, food & beverages and utilities firms.

$$
\begin{aligned}
\ln C = {} & \alpha + \sum_{m=1}^{2} \beta_m \cdot \ln y_m + 0.5 \cdot \sum_{l=1}^{2} \sum_{m=1}^{2} \beta_{lm} \cdot \ln y_l \cdot \ln y_m \\
& + \sum_{n=1}^{3} \gamma_n \cdot \ln w_n + 0.5 \cdot \sum_{n=1}^{3} \sum_{p=1}^{3} \gamma_{np} \cdot \ln w_n \cdot \ln w_p \\
& + \sum_{m=1}^{2} \sum_{n=1}^{3} \delta_{mn} \cdot \ln y_m \cdot \ln w_n \\
& + \theta_t \cdot t + 0.5 \cdot \theta_{tt} \cdot t^2 + \sum_{n=1}^{3} \theta_{nt} \ln w_n \cdot t
\end{aligned}
\qquad (5\text{-}50)
$$

variable	**minim.**	**median**	**mean**	**maxim.**	**std. dev.**
total assets*)	27.54	294.01	638.87	4891.34	960.33
C costs*)	16.39	145.96	287.75	1968.16	369.31
y_1 sales and self-constructed assets*)	16.92	374.57	715.26	3962.95	885.70
y_2 interest earnings and earnings from affiliated companies**)	.01	2.96	19.36	293.13	43.73
x_1 labor***)	135	1854	3532.45	20103	4497.02
x_2 tangible and intangible fixed assets**)	3678.34	44769.12	117779.70	824583.93	187556.27
x_3 financial capital**)	18.162	15885.775	105440.29	1386495.4	235520.69
w_1 salary/wage rate plus social costs**)	49.22	73.98	72.96	101.95	8.46
w_2 depreciation rate on tangible and intangible fixed assets****)	.096	.284	.301	1.139	.133
w_3 cost of financial assets (via stock return as opportunity earning*****)	-.996	.012	-.019	1.067	.411

N = 152 *) millions of DM **) thousands of DM ***) no. of employees
****) 1 = 100 % *****) ln(return + 1)

Table 5-27: Netputs and summary statistics of the panel cost function data for the machinery sector

Alternatively, the inefficiency estimates from the overall panel estimation in 5.2.5.1.6 can be grouped by sector to provide another take on the sectoral differences. The separate regressions however can be assumed to be more accurate in that they are able to more closely model the single sector than the overall regression with one dummy variable for each sector can do. The separate regressions in effect are based on separate production functions for each sector which is definitely closer to reality. The smaller number of cases per regression makes the results more susceptible to single companies' idiosyncrasies, which reduces the importance of the single-sector regressions slightly.

As with the yearly cross sectional regressions above, the descriptive results of the sectoral analyses will partially be removed to the appendix to avoid overcrowding the main text.

Table 5-27 shows as an example the summary statistics of the netputs for the machinery sector, one of the sectors with the most companies in Germany. The average total assets of the companies are worth 639 million DM, with 3532 employees. There are 152 cases in the dataset over all seven years, giving an average of only about 22 machinery-building companies per year. The values for the interest earnings are very low in comparison with the levels the other sectors attain.

Figure 5-21 below shows that there are distinctive size differences between the five sectors that will be further studied, both when measured by total assets (millions of DM) and by employee figures. The companies in the machinery and food & beverages sectors are on average the smallest, while the electronics firms (which include Siemens AG) are the largest on average. There are many breweries in the food & beverages sector, which generally have a rather small firm size. The utilities sector is noteworthy for the small number of employees it has in relation to its total assets.

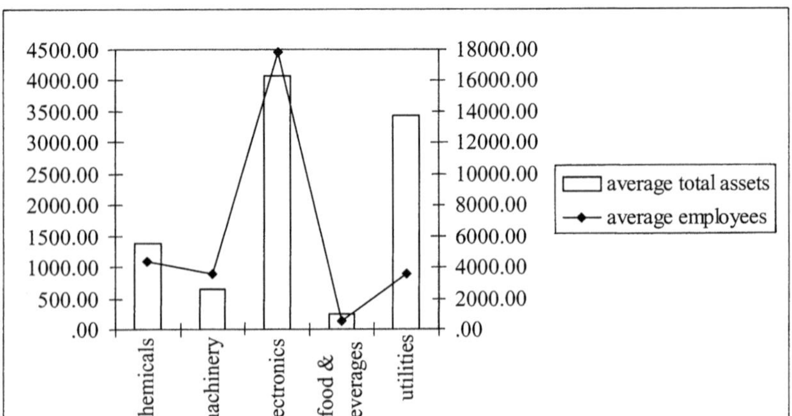

total assets in millions of DM (left axis)

Figure 5-21: Average total assets and employees over all years, per sector

Figure 5-22 shows the average total assets and the costs for the sectors in graphical format. One can see that there are big differences in the relation of the values. Costs make up about half the total assets for the machinery sector, while the ratio for the utilities is much lower.

These ratios are presented in Table 5-28. As a rough measure of inefficiency, and disregarding sectoral peculiarities that could account for differences, one would rank the utilities as the most efficient, with a cost/asset ratio of only 19 %. These are followed by the food sector, then chemicals, electronics and machinery in the last place with a ratio of over 41 %. It remains to be seen if this preliminary ranking holds for the maximum-likelihood cost function estimates.

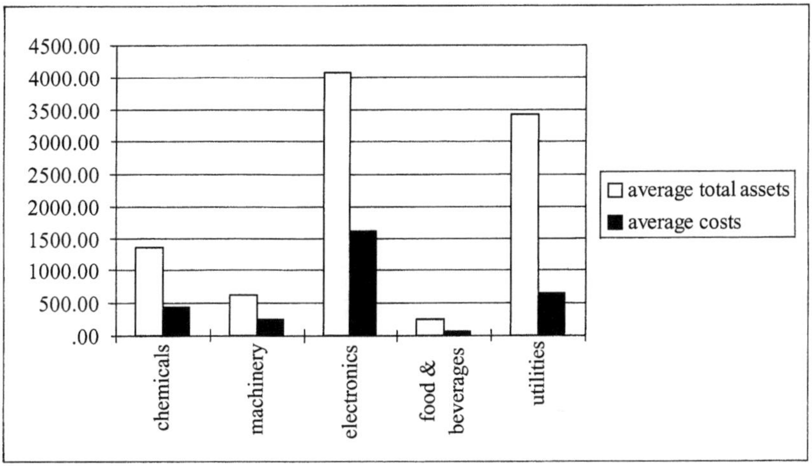

Figure 5-22: Average total assets and costs over all years, per sector (in millions of DM)

sector	cost/assets	rank
utilities	19.02 %	1
food & beverages	26.76 %	2
chemicals	31.74 %	3
electronics	39.49 %	4
machinery	41.03 %	5

Table 5-28: Cost/asset ratios for five sectors

5.2.5.3.2 Estimation Results

	chemicals 1986-92		machinery 1986-92		electronics 1986-92	
coefficient	**value**	**std. error**	**value**	**std. error**	**value**	**std. error**
α	-23.26656	9.999067 ***	-9.798051	9.837176	12.239181	10.133757
β_1	2.766258	0.748498 ***	-0.264826	0.765493	0.599866	0.754473
β_2	-3.296705	1.074967 ***	0.565787	1.201151	0.022277	1.154911
γ_1	12.291340	2.312147 ***	6.620018	2.296440 ***	-4.086297	2.392087 *
γ_2	0.326158	7.080121	-0.018020	7.168522	3.284410	8.365480
γ_3	-11.61750	7.424935	-5.601998	7.594681	1.801887	8.659426
β_{11}	-0.088883	0.055210	0.136736	0.059822 **	-0.097045	0.054845 **
β_{12}	0.028588	0.078846	-0.024907	0.091807	0.013290	0.082728
β_{22}	0.036175	0.109256	-0.003592	0.139830	0.061477	0.117392
γ_{11}	-3.275566	0.533642 ***	-1.210444	0.542412 **	0.524291	0.559206
γ_{12}	0.071715	1.679465	-0.115740	1.673900	-0.407256	1.972434
γ_{13}	3.203851	1.759674 *	1.326184	1.767299	-0.117035	2.046695
γ_{22}	-0.147486	4.473609	0.031145	3.680157	-0.002078	0.782686
γ_{23}	-2.269513	74.860307	-2.180063	217.61362	-1.413014	140.89463
γ_{33}	-0.670840	74.679663	0.405079	218.70134	0.087318	143.26344
δ_{11}	-0.265010	0.173164	-0.049355	0.178634	0.236819	0.177518
δ_{12}	0.136241	0.526441	0.068519	0.558188	-0.152673	0.629498
δ_{13}	0.128769	0.553055	-0.019164	0.591302	-0.084147	0.651710
δ_{21}	0.607405	0.246601 **	-0.066250	0.279922	-0.095311	0.270720
δ_{22}	-0.257436	0.778645	-0.019477	0.870060	0.079668	0.975937
δ_{23}	-0.349968	0.815382	0.085727	0.921374	0.015643	1.010503
θ_t	-0.016531	2.542428	-0.252156	2.523689	0.463420	2.616996
θ_{tt}	-0.002887	0.513219	0.001357	0.528376	0.029937	0.549798
θ_{1t}	0.004390	0.588650	0.054328	0.586905	-0.183803	0.611907
θ_{2t}	0.003868	1.741976	0.000787	1.815303	-0.036327	2.151400
θ_{3t}	-0.008258	1.856461	-0.055115	1.920749	0.220131	2.229845
λ	0.600435	9.652004	0.201959	9.916222	0.168879	11.341634
σ	0.358639	6.279522	0.226927	9.401725	0.439398	10.113871

	food & beverages 1986-92		utilities 1986-92	
coefficient	**value**	**std. error**	**value**	**std. error**
α	120.82175	9.770160 ***	-10.14850	9.998632
β_1	8.066066	0.814950 ***	-2.424398	0.718974 ***
β_2	-1.573263	1.291481	3.695394	0.968644

	food & beverages 1986-92		utilities 1986-92	
coefficient	value	std. error	value	std. error
γ_1	-70.90055	2.237410 ***	6.180767	2.194582 ***
γ_2	8.581827	8.575817	-0.395758	4.821374
γ_3	63.318725	8.989139 ***	-4.785009	5.278629
β_{11}	-1.557300	0.068819 ***	-0.050767	0.051381
β_{12}	0.496489	0.106303 ***	0.040544	0.069231
β_{22}	-0.028184	0.166241	-0.155220	0.092442 *
γ_{11}	13.756007	0.520256 ***	-3.154220	0.481878 ***
γ_{12}	-0.684576	1.966018	-0.364563	1.071174
γ_{13}	-13.07143	2.047343 ***	3.518782	1.173487 ***
γ_{22}	0.427836	6.872491	-0.177780	2.267596
γ_{23}	4.044160	102.59834	-5.417422	59.290045
γ_{33}	6.021876	102.24355	0.761905	59.296319
δ_{11}	1.511008	0.186570 ***	0.874808	0.157787 ***
δ_{12}	-0.558644	0.714087	0.032025	0.345595
δ_{13}	-0.952364	0.749142	-0.906832	0.378640 **
δ_{21}	-0.862025	0.295473 ***	-0.550091	0.211968 ***
δ_{22}	0.173093	1.139626	0.118525	0.470284
δ_{23}	0.688933	1.196632	0.431566	0.514022
θ_t	0.844627	2.654122	-0.724564	2.604252
θ_{tt}	-0.025167	0.572864	0.001312	0.525557
θ_{1t}	-0.127248	0.605975	0.143586	0.566844
θ_{2t}	0.108205	2.378971	-0.049266	1.337547
θ_{3t}	0.019043	2.497687	-0.094321	1.443809
λ	0.560606	10.023156	0.616814	6.096301
σ	0.612207	11.444778	0.296372	8.851854

N = 73/152/70/138/80; *** = significant at the 1 % level (** = 5 %; * = 10 %)

Table 5-29: Results of the separate maximum likelihood panel regressions for five sectors

The results of all the sectoral estimations are presented below in Table 5-29. A larger number of coefficients are significant in comparison to the overall results in Table 5-20, and with lower error probabilities. The electronics sector has only two significant coefficients, both again for variables including the sales (output 1) or the wage rate (input price 1). The three significant coefficients for the machinery sector also follow this pattern.

For these two sectors, as well as the others, the coefficients for the variables lnw2·lnw3 and lnw3·lnw3 have extremely high standard errors. The other sectors have many more highly significant coefficients than the electronics and machinery sectors, again mostly for variables comprised of the sales output or wage rate input. This repeated observation makes a strong case for the importance of these two factors for the cost function estimation.

The results in Table 5-29 clearly show that the standard deviations of the error terms are markedly smaller when each sector is taken by itself than when all sectors are incorporated in one regression.[137] The food & beverage sector with a value for σ of 61.22 % is the exception to this observation, while the other values range from 22.7 % to 43.9 %, compared to the 51.5 % of the overall regression. Figure 5-23 below shows the comparison of the σ estimates in graphical form. It makes immediate sense that the overall estimation will produce a higher σ due to the many sectors the estimation must fit into one mold.

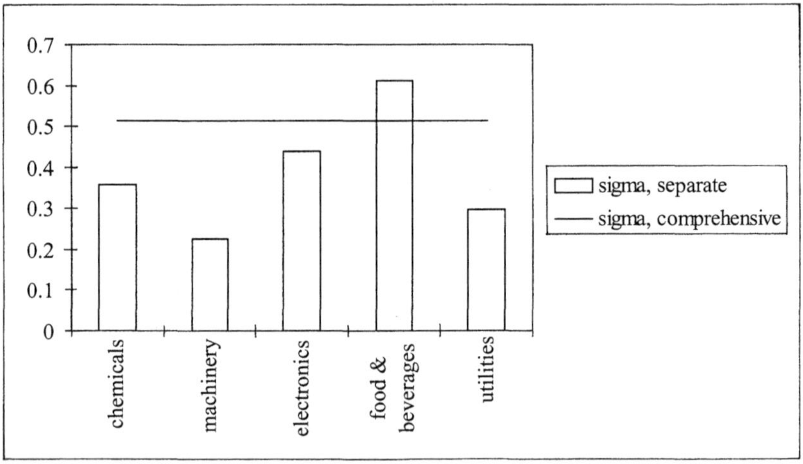

Figure 5-23: Comparison of estimates for σ, sectoral and comprehensive regressions

Both the λ and the σ estimates in all cases have very high standard errors, rendering them insignificant. This generally observed fact for the regressions presented in this efficiency study could have to do with the iteration algorithm used.[138] In the estimation process it proved to be less susceptible to converging

---

[137] Although it is important to remember that not all sectors are analyzed separately here.

[138] In most estimations only the Berndt-Hall-Hall-Hausman algorithm produced plausible results. Cf. Breslaw (1995).

on local optima than other algorithms and so produced the only plausible results.[139]

The λ estimates for the sector regressions roughly average out to the comprehensive estimate (not shown here). This means that the higher variance of the error term observed for the overall panel regression should be equally due to higher variances of both of the true error term and of the inefficiency error component estimated in the overall regression.

5.2.5.3.3 Tests of the Properties of the Functions

The results of the likelihood ratio tests for the five sectoral regressions are shown below in Table 5-30. Again, the tests produce overwhelmingly significant results which do not need to be discussed further.

sector	test statistic	sig.
chemicals	13201434212.0946	***
electronics	16584527549.5856	***
machinery	27117938284.2532	***
food & beverages	19451670013.7476	***
utilities	11568781672.6804	***

Table 5-30: Results of the likelihood ratio tests for the sectoral regressions[140]

The results of the tests for well behavior of the five functions are shown in Table 5-31. The positive monotony of the sales output (y_1) is surprisingly not given in over one third of the cases for the food & beverages sector. The other sectors show the usual excellent result for this output.

The test of the monotony of the second output, interest earnings, produces more varied results. The values for the chemicals, electronics and food & beverages sectors are not too high, whereas for the machinery and utilities sectors far more than half of the cases do not fulfill the condition of a positive gradient.

The monotony test of the input prices are very mixed and again rather unsatisfactory. None of the input prices has less than 50 % errors in the utilities sector. The third input price, the price for holding financial assets, fares best of all in-

139 The algorithm also produces exact maximum likelihood estimates of the standard errors. Cf. Breslaw (1995), p. 137.

140 There were 27 degrees of freedom for each test. *** = significant at the 1 % level.

puts and the wage rate the worst. The elasticity errors are similarly varied, ranging from zero % errors to over 94 %, while the direct concavity tests give the usual over 95 % error rates. So again the quality of the regressions is not the best and could impact on the validity of the results presented.

violation of property	chemicals	electronics	% errors machinery	food & beverages	utilities
monotony of output 1	0.00	5.71	0.00	34.78	0.00
monotony of output 2	8.22	14.29	77.63	23.19	63.75
monotony of input price 1	36.99	4.29	30.92	44.93	77.50
monotony of input price 2	78.08	57.14	50.00	13.77	61.25
monotony of input price 3	83.56	87.14	57.89	26.81	55.00
elasticity of input price 1	50.68	94.29	13.82	55.07	61.25
elasticity of input price 2	9.59	24.29	45.39	86.23	27.50
elasticity of input price 3	9.59	0.00	20.39	73.19	17.50
concavity of the input prices	97.26	100.00	100.00	96.38	100.00

Table 5-31: Results of the tests of the properties of the sectoral estimates of the cost functions[141]

5.2.5.3.4 T-Tests for Differences in Mean Inefficiency

The average values of *xineff* taken from the separate sectoral regressions are shown in Figure 5-24 below, with the overall average inefficiency from the comprehensive regression added again for comparison. The comprehensive value for *xineff* is not markedly higher than the separate sector averages, in fact, it is slightly lower.

The electronics and food & beverages firms emerge as efficient over and above the average efficiency for the full data set. It is important to remember that the comprehensive regression contained more sectors than the five studied separately here, so the overall average inefficiency result of 25.18 % of the comprehensive regression need not be the average, or in view of the high σ estimate for the overall regression, above the average of the five sectors shown.

[141] For the chemicals, food & beverage and utilities sectors, the concavity was tested via the eigenvalues of the Hessian matrix. For the electronics and machinery firms, the determinants of the subminors of the Hessian were used.

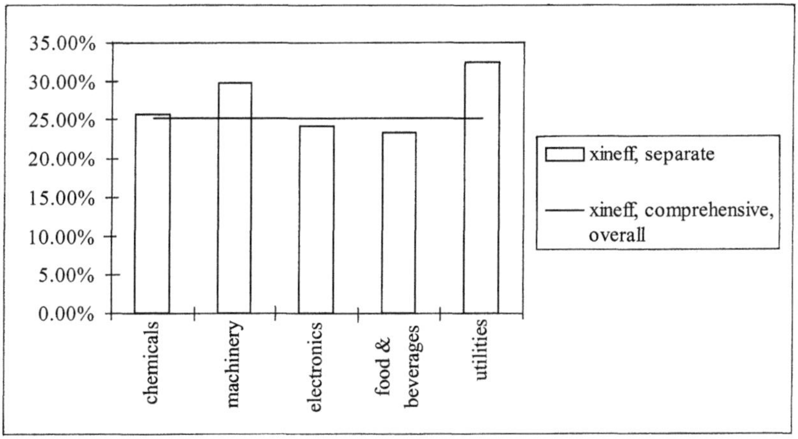

Figure 5-24: Comparison of the average *xineff*, by sector, separate regressions to the overall average *xineff*

Table 5-32 compares the ranking that the average *xineff* values produce to the off-the-cuff ranking the comparison of cost/total asset ratios provided earlier. The most remarkable observation that can be made is that the utilities sector, which has the lowest cost/asset ratio, emerges in the last place as regards the x-inefficiency estimates. The other sectors more or less hold their relative positions: only the chemicals and the electronics sectors trade places.

This result means that firms in the utilities sector have fairly low costs in relation to their total assets, but that a large portion of these costs cannot be explained by the outputs produced or the input prices. Inefficiency costs constitute a far greater portion of the utilities' cost structure than for the other sectors. Also, one sees that data that is processed at a too aggregated level can, but must not, be misleading and hide important information.

sector	average *xineff*	rank	sig[+]	rank by degree of competition in sales market	rank by cost/asset ratio
food & beverages	23.33 %	1		4	2
electronics	24.18 %	2		2	4
chemicals	25.76 %	3		3	3
machinery	29.74 %	4		1	5
utilities	32.44 %	5		5	1

[+]of difference to next sector; *** = significant at the 1 % level (** = 5 %; * = 10 %)

Table 5-32: Average values for *xineff* for five sectors

The t-tests for the five chosen sectors will be run both over the results from the separate regressions (5.2.5.3.4.1) and additionally over the results from the comprehensive panel regression presented above (5.2.5.3.4.2). Differences can be expected due to the fact that the comprehensive regression, with its mélange of firms from various sectors, for which one common production function is supposed, could produce low inefficiencies for one or more sectors which are close to the common frontier. Other sectors, which taken into a regression by themselves would of course have frontier firms, could end up far removed from the common frontier. The dummy variables which were introduced to counter this effect might not compensate fully for the disparity. In separate regressions for each sector the frontier of the function will of course always be defined by the companies in that sector alone.

5.2.5.3.4.1 T-Tests for the Separate Sectoral Estimates

In the full body of the text I will include detailed results for only the machinery and the chemicals sectors, while the data on the other sectors can be found in the appendix or in part here in graphical format.

Table 5-33 shows the t-tests for differences in the means of *xineff* for the **machinery** sector by the agency variables. There are only 26 firms in this sector, which still constitutes the largest sector in the data set. Lacking data on block ownership further reduces the number of firms in block ownership and by consequence in the conglomerate agency variable groups. Unfortunately, some of the conglomerate agency variables also group all cases into the low agency-problem category (second row for the variable). Other lopsided groupings (e. g., only one firm with low block ownership) make it difficult to distinguish between firm-specific results and true agency-related phenomena. The desired diversification effect that was created in the earlier steps of this analysis could not be achieved here. This especially affects the core variables block ownership, *agency1* and *agency5*, which are the most interesting agency variables. Note also in this context that up to seven cases in one group can even constitute data from one single company, with one case for every year from 1986 to 1992.

With this in mind, the hypothesis of higher inefficiency in manager-controlled firms is soundly rebutted for the machinery industry. For all agency variables except the dividend variable, the companies with agency problems are comparatively much more efficient, and to significant degrees. For three variables, no result at all is possible due to empty groups. The *block* and *agency5* variables, two of the three which are given extra attention, subdivide the data sample in exactly the same way, duplicating the results obtained.

This rejection of the hypothesis can be due to the competitive situation in the machinery industry, where many small firms compete for market share. The sales per employee for the machinery sector are the lowest of all five sectors.

mean(xineff) overall: **29.74 %**

variable	mean(xineff)	std. dev.	N	diff	z	sig
block own-	1.08 %		1	23.38 %	2.65311	***
ership	24.46 %	35.25 %	16			
size	5.77 %	10.34 %	4	28.33 %	2.37749	**
	34.10 %	50.35 %	22			
market	23.23 %	31.37 %	10	10.59 %	0.61846	
segment	33.81 %	55.81 %	16			
dividend	40.50 %	45.71 %	3	-12.16 %	-0.43019	
signal	28.34 %	48.48 %	23			
leverage	9.97 %	17.74 %	17	57.11 %	2.65248	***
	67.08 %	63.29 %	9			
monitored	7.77 %	19.36 %	10	35.70 %	2.37906	**
debt ratio	43.47 %	54.81 %	16			
agency1			0	23.09 %	N/A	N/A
	23.09 %	34.60 %	17			
agency2			0	23.09 %	N/A	N/A
	23.09 %	34.60 %	17			
agency3	10.24 %	19.34 %	11	36.39 %	1.87578	*
	46.64 %	45.33 %	6			
agency4	0.36 %	0.13 %	2	25.75 %	2.78271	***
	26.12 %	35.84 %	15			
agency5	1.08 %		1	23.38 %	2.65311	***
	24.46 %	35.25 %	16			
agency6	16.08 %	30.96 %	4	9.16 %	0.49512	
	25.24 %	36.54 %	13			
agency7			0	23.09%	N/A	N/A
	23.09 %	34.60 %	17			

N =26; for each variable: first row = large agency problems, second row = low agency problems; *** = significant at the 1 % level (** = 5 %; * = 10 %)

Table 5-33: T-tests for differences of means of xineff by agency variable over the machinery industry (separate regression)

mean(xineff) overall: **25.76 %**

variable	mean(xineff)	std. dev.	N	diff	z	sig
block own-	21.70 %	6.34 %	5	3.74 %	0.77311	
ership	25.44 %	13.60 %	12			
size	21.21 %	11.28 %	4	5.69 %	0.87966	
	26.90 %	12.67 %	16			
market	17.87 %	9.57 %	4	9.86 %	1.72962	*
segment	27.74 %	12.40 %	16			
dividend	26.69 %	12.17 %	2	-1.03 %	-0.11258	
signal	25.66 %	12.71 %	18			
leverage	21.76 %	12.50 %	12	6.61 %	1.29208	
	28.37 %	8.89 %	6			
monitored	23.43 %	11.87 %	10	4.67 %	0.83956	
debt ratio	28.10 %	12.98 %	10			
agency1	18.59 %	8.99 %	3	6.98 %	1.1366	
	25.57 %	12.29 %	14			
agency2	18.16 %	7.39 %	4	8.08 %	1.59408	
	26.24 %	12.52 %	13			
agency3	22.14 %	13.03 %	11	6.23 %	1.16548	
	28.37 %	8.89 %	6			
agency4	18.21 %	11.69 %	3	7.44 %	0.99763	
	25.65 %	11.88 %	14			
agency5	21.70 %	6.34 %	5	3.74 %	0.77311	
	25.44 %	13.60 %	12			
agency6	18.89 %	7.88 %	6	8.42 %	1.67062	*
	27.31 %	12.88 %	11			
agency7	17.47 %	0.86 %	2	7.78 %	2.39618	**
	25.26 %	12.36 %	15			

N =20; for each variable: first row = large agency problems, second row = low agency problems; *** = significant at the 1 % level (** = 5 %; * = 10 %)

Table 5-34: T-tests for differences of means of xineff by agency variable over the chemicals industry (separate regression)

The significance of some of the results is due to the small group sizes with as little as zero % standard deviation for the one-case groups. This improves the test statistic greatly, which divides by the standard deviations, but since the standard deviation for such small group numbers is unreliable, the test statistic subsequently is, too.

Also the second hypothesis that posits a higher inefficiency for manager-controlled firms compared to creditor-controlled firms is significantly rejected. The levels of inefficiency measured are somewhat astounding (67 % for highly leveraged firms), for single-sector data which was corrected for outliers.

Because of the very uneven groupings in the machinery sector, the results of another sector, in this case the **chemicals** sector, is shown here in the body of the text in addition to the machinery sector results. Here too, though, the groupings of the 20 chemicals firms remain somewhat lopsided.

For the chemicals industry, too, the hypothesis one concerning superior cost efficiency of owner-controlled firms does not hold; for three of the variables (market segment variable, *agency6* and *agency7*) the comparisons are significant. Only the dividend signal variable, the variable most strongly intended to be used in conjunction with other variables, allows an advantage of the owner-controlled firms. Again, block ownership and *agency5* produce identical results. Also the second hypothesis concerning the variables leverage and monitored debt ratio must be rejected for the chemicals sector, although the differences in inefficiency are not significant.

The remaining separate estimation sectoral results in the appendix support the results given here for the most part. Hypothesis one is rejected (only *agency4* supports it), while hypothesis two is confirmed by the monitored debt ratio grouping in the **electronics** sector. For that variable, the difference in inefficiency of 17.88 % is significant at the 10 % level.

The **food & beverages** sector produces very mixed results, with the core variables divided evenly between rejecting and accepting the first hypothesis. Block ownership does not subdivide the dataset and thus is useless, *agency1* rejects and *agency5* does not reject the hypothesis. The second hypothesis is accepted according to the monitored debt ratio result, with manager-controlled firms 7.56 % more inefficient than creditor controlled ones (not significant).

The **utilities** sector with 15 firms finally and unfortunately produces almost completely useless results because the agency variables mostly do not split the sample into two groups and so make comparisons impossible. No statement can be made as to the accuracy of hypothesis one. The most even split into groups is 10–4 (with one missing value). This is for the leverage variable, which together with the monitored debt ratio rejects the second hypothesis. A redefinition of the agency variable split rates where not warranted by legal rulings for the utilities sector alone does not make sense as it would reduce the comparability of the results; an overall redefinition for all regressions would just recreate the same problem elsewhere.

The tests for the third hypothesis are shown below in Table 5-35 for the machinery industry and Table 5-36 for the chemicals companies. In both tables the groupings by block ownership and *agency5* provide identical results because they create the same subgroups for the sample. Block ownership is the main component of the *agency5* conglomerate variable.

variable	mean(xineff)	std. dev.	N	diff	z	sig
block ownership	24.46 %	35.25 %	16	-19.01 %	-1.16688	
creditor	43.47 %	54.81 %	16			
agency5	24.46 %	35.25 %	16	-19.01 %	-1.16688	
creditor	43.47 %	54.81 %	16			

first row = ownership control according to the variable given, second row = creditor control; *** = significant at the 1 % level (** = 5 %; * = 10 %)

Table 5-35: T-tests for differences of means of *xineff* between owner-controlled and creditor-controlled companies, separate regression for the machinery sector

For both sectors, the owner-controlled firms fare better than the creditor-controlled ones. This means that the third hypothesis cannot be rejected. As usual, the results are insignificant, due to the high standard deviations in the estimates, even in the case of the machinery sector, where the difference in x-inefficiency is 19 %.

variable	mean(xineff)	std. dev.	N	diff	z	sig
block ownership	25.44 %	13.60 %	12	-2.66 %	-0.46799	
creditor	28.10 %	12.98 %	10			
agency5	25.44 %	13.60 %	12	-2.66 %	-0.46799	
creditor	28.10 %	12.98 %	10			

first row = ownership control according to the variable given, second row = creditor control; *** = significant at the 1 % level (** = 5 %; * = 10 %)

Table 5-36: T-tests for differences of means of *xineff* between owner-controlled and creditor-controlled companies, separate regression for the chemicals sector

The results for the other sectors, placed in the appendix, give a mixed picture. For the electronics firms the hypothesis three must be rejected, with a 15.41 % advantage of the creditor-controlled firms in x-efficiency over the owner-controlled ones. Here, too, the owner-controlled groups are equal for either variable. The food & beverages sector, while splitting the owner-controlled groups differently according to the agency variable used also rejects the third hypothesis with insignificant differences in x-inefficiency. The agency variables split the utilities firms, on the other hand, into 14 and 2 company strong groups. For these a difference in x-inefficiency of -51.71 % in favor of the owner-controlled firms is apparent. The result is significant, due to the staggering difference and the small group size involved.

The reason for the effectiveness of the ownership control for the utilities sector might lie in the fact that the sector is comparatively highly regulated, canceling out any monitoring effectiveness the sales market for utilities might have. Should the ownership be content to let the market forces exert their monitoring force where possible, here the owners find it necessary to become active themselves.

The next hypothesis that can be tested using the sectoral results is the fifth, that claims that firms in less competitive markets will be less x-efficient than those more exposed to competition. Table 5-37 gives an initial overview over the differences in *xineff* by sector. Pitting the results from different regressions against each other is not as clean a procedure as using the results from the single overall regression, since this operation approaches what in the extreme could turn into comparing phenomena from completely unrelated samples and regressions.

	mean			z value for difference to							
sector	(xineff)	std. dev	N	machinery	sig	electronics	sig	food	sig	utilities	sig
chemicals	25.76 %	9.60 %	20	-0.64381		0.32575		0.74610		-1.1707	
machinery	29.74 %	29.53 %	26			0.76713		1.01896		-0.3445	
electronics	24.18 %	17.40 %	16	-0.76713				0.17080		-1.2064	
food & bev	23.33 %	12.76 %	27	-1.01896		-0.17080				-1.5634	
utilities	32.44 %	20.47 %	15	0.34450		1.20636		1.56342			

N = number of companies; *** = significant at the 1 % level (** = 5 %; * = 10 %)

Table 5-37: T-Test for differences in sector means of *xineff*, separate regressions

A comparison of the differences in x-inefficiency for the sectors shows that the levels of *xineff* are very similar. Small numbers of companies and high standard deviations prohibit differences from being significant. Not even the difference of over 9 % from the most efficient sector, food & beverages, to the least efficient one, the utilities, is significant. The applicability of the fifth hypothesis concerning the monitoring effectiveness of the markets companies from each sector are operating can be read from Table 5-32 above.

As is also apparent from Table 5-37, no differences in *xineff* are significant between neighboring sectors. The two sectors machinery and food & beverages, the sectors with the smallest average company size, trade places when going from the ranking that hypothesis five postulated to the actual result here. The food & beverages companies are the least x-inefficient here, while the machinery firms come in second to last. The other sectors however follow hypothesis five exactly. In sum this means the hypothesis five must be rejected when rigidly judged, although the basic trend the hypothesis describes does shine through for three of the five sectors.

The rank by cost/asset ratio was added for comparison in the table. This ratio also favors the food & beverages industry while ranking the machinery companies very low, just like the rankings by *xineff*, and does not jibe with the fifth hypothesis. In fact, when checking closely it becomes apparent that the cost/asset ratio delivers rankings that are diametrically opposed to those that the fifth hypothesis.

The sixth hypothesis posits that the differences in x-inefficiency between owner and manager-controlled companies will be greater in uncompetitive markets. This hypothesis cannot be tested in a satisfactory way using the data available, as many sectors sometimes did not produce workable classifications; often only one or even zero companies were in one category. For the utilities the only useable categories were produced by the leverage and monitored debt ratio variables. Due to these circumstances, the evaluation of the sixth hypothesis should not be given too much weight in this section on efficiency.

	xineff	
paired sectors	difference	sig
machinery–electronics	.1644	***
electronics–chemicals	.0115	
chemicals–food & beverages	.0392	
food & beverages–utilities	-.2350	***

*** = significant at 1 %-level (** = 5 %; * = 10 %)

Table 5-38: T-tests for *xineff* mean differences, by sector pairs for the separate regressions

Table 5-38 shows the results of paired t-tests for the neighboring sector groups as defined by competitivity. The difference in x-inefficiency for the agency categories (ownership control and management control) for each of the agency variables and conglomerates respectively in the first (more competitive) sector is subtracted from the difference for the second sector. This produces up to 13 values, (for the six agency variables and seven conglomerates) which are then tested for significance. According to the sixth hypothesis, negative values are expected, with insignificant differences toward the top of the table, and significant differences at the bottom. Only for the last pair does the hypothesis hold, while it is rejected for the other sector pairs due to wrong signs. In the case of the machinery-electronics comparison, the significance of the difference is also contrary to expectations. Therefore the sixth hypothesis is rejected overall using the data from the separate regressions.

5.2.5.3.4.2 T-Tests for the Comprehensive Estimate by Sector

The overall regression of course also included the companies in the sectors treated above, making it possible to compare the results one would achieve if one tests the results from the comprehensive regression on a sectoral basis with the separate sectoral regression results. The separate regressions have the advantage of not supposing a common production function for all sectors in the dataset and producing one frontier per sector defined by companies from that sector. The disadvantage is the smaller number of cases included in each regression which can negatively affect the goodness of the results.[142]

From the results for the other sectors shown in Figure 5-25 and reported in the appendix it is clear that the trend of the comprehensive maximum likelihood regression to produce lower inefficiencies holds. This is only untrue for the food & beverages sector (23.33 % mean inefficiency in the separate regression vs. 27.38 % in the comprehensive one). The difference in the estimation of *xineff* differs most widely for the machinery firms, reaching about 12 %. For the other four sectors the difference is much smaller, in the range of one to four percent.

The reason for the tendency of the separate regressions to estimate higher levels of inefficiency than the comprehensive regression can be traced to the econometrical effect mentioned earlier. Introducing the sector dummy variables into the model, which is necessary in the comprehensive regression, adds more possibilities of reducing the error term which forms the basis of the inefficiency. Thus models using more variables can be expected to have lower inefficiency levels.

Table 5-39 shows the results of t-tests for differences in means of the sectors for the comprehensive regression. The machinery sector is significantly more efficient than all other sectors except the electronics firms, where the advantage is not significant. Despite its high average inefficiency, the utilities sector cannot

[142] For samples with less than 30 cases, a normal distribution may not be given (not tested for here). A corrective factor for finite samples may be omitted if the sample can be considered to be less than 5 % of the data. Cf. Bleymüller/Gehlert/Gülicher (1988), p. 78.

be said to be significantly less efficient than the other sectors (excluding the machinery sector). This is due to the high standard deviation of the results for the utilities. In the separate regression results reported in Table 5-37, there were no significant differences in x-inefficiency. The signs change in many cases, due to the new position of the machinery and food & beverages sectors in the ranking of sectors by *xineff*.

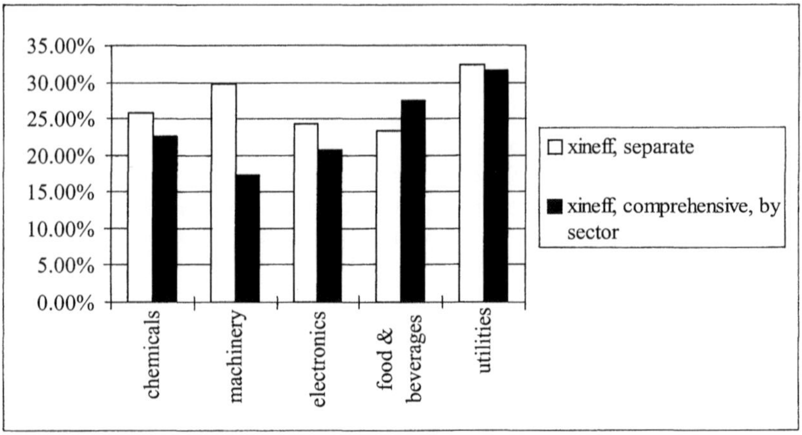

Figure 5-25: Comparison of *xineff*, by sector, for the separate and comprehensive regressions

	mean			z value for difference to							
sector	(xineff)	std. dev	N	machinery	sig.	electro.	sig.	food	sig.	utilities	sig.
chemicals	22.53 %	8.72 %	20	1.99133	**	0.58234		-1.1769		-1.2909	
machinery	17.29 %	9.00 %	26			-1.08523		-2.4992	**	-2.0538	**
electronics	20.66 %	10.21 %	16	1.08523				-1.5145		-1.5168	
food & bev.	27.38 %	18.87 %	27	2.49915	**	1.51454				-0.5477	
utilities	31.57 %	26.04 %	15	2.05379	**	1.51682		0.5477			

N = number of companies; *** = significant at the 1 % level (** = 5 %; * = 10 %)

Table 5-39: T-Test for differences in sector means of *xineff*, comprehensive regression

Nevertheless the utilities sector does remain the most inefficient sector of those studied more closely here, suggesting that the hypothesis might hold that regulations, or the restriction of market pricing mechanisms or competition as an instrument for controlling the management of a firm, lead to higher inefficiency in a firm.

The results of the t-tests for differences in inefficiency means by agency group for the **machinery** sector using the data from the comprehensive estimation over all sectors are given below in Table 5-40. As mentioned above, it is surprising to see that the overall level of inefficiency of 17.29 % is actually lower, and markedly so, than the one that the single-sector regression arrived at (29.74 %, Table 5-33). The opposite outcome would make sense if the machinery companies did not supply any of the frontier companies for the comprehensive regression. That could make them very inefficient in the overall regression. Then, once these companies would be regressed alone, they would naturally supply the frontier and emerge as more efficient in the mean.

As the case stands, the machinery firms actually are the most efficient sector in the overall regression. They are, in fact, so efficient that the other companies' relative positions forced the machinery firms closer to the border, and some of them even over it, which is possible due to the true error component included in the regression. Once the other companies are removed and the machinery companies are entered into their separate regression, the "pressure" that pushed the firms towards the border subsides and the efficiency estimates deteriorate. Figure 5-26 sketches this effect with fictitious datapoints. The companies marked by crosses stand for the machinery firms while the dots represent firms from all other sectors. When all firms are included in the regression, the efficient frontier runs closer to the center of the machinery firms (left graph) than when the machinery firms are taken alone (right graph).

More of the differences in the machinery sector results from the separate regression are significant than those from the overall regression, though. Most important is that the signs of the differences between the groups often change, even for significant results (block ownership, *agency5*). For the results presented in this section, the first hypothesis can be said to be confirmed, as opposed to the earlier statements for the separate regression.

The second hypothesis that draws upon the monitored debt ratio and the leverage is cannot be rejected by the results here. The differences between the manager- and creditor-controlled company classifications—under 5 % difference in x-inefficiency—are less drastic, and also insignificant. That hypothesis had been rejected in the separate regression for the machinery sector, meaning there is another reversal of results here. This implies that under more detailed scrutiny, the methodology applied, or even the parameters chosen in the context of the same methodology, can affect the results obtained. Above the opposite had been suggested for the aggregate results.

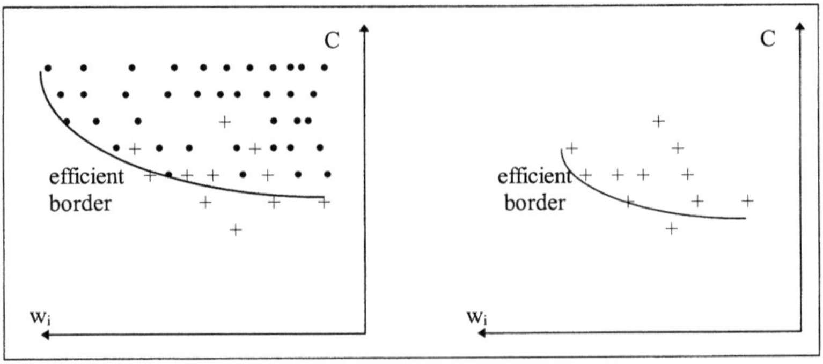

Figure 5-26: Sketch of efficient border in relation to machinery companies (+) with and without companies from other sectors (•) included in regression

mean(xineff) overall: **17.29 %**

variable	mean(xineff)	std. dev.	N	diff	z	sig
block own-	24.83 %		1	-9.50 %	-4.91539	***
ership	15.33 %	7.73 %	16			
size	16.29 %	5.69 %	4	1.19 %	0.33921	
	17.48 %	9.57 %	22			
market	16.52 %	6.45 %	10	1.26 %	0.37975	
segment	17.78 %	10.46 %	16			
dividend	10.04 %	1.76 %	3	8.20 %	3.79473	***
signal	18.24 %	9.14 %	23			
leverage	19.01 %	9.16 %	17	-4.97 %	-1.41238	
	14.05 %	8.18 %	9			
monitored	18.62 %	11.59 %	10	-2.15 %	-0.52563	
debt ratio	16.47 %	7.24 %	16			
agency1			0	15.89 %	N/A	N/A
	15.89 %	7.83 %	17			
agency2			0	15.89 %	N/A	N/A
	15.89 %	7.83 %	17			
agency3	16.23 %	7.03 %	11	-0.97 %	-0.21332	
	15.26 %	9.83 %	6			
agency4	18.04 %	8.53 %	2	-2.44 %	-0.38203	
	15.60 %	8.01 %	15			

mean(xineff) overall: **17.29 %**

variable	mean(xineff)	std. dev.	N	diff	z	sig
agency5	24.83 %		1	-9.50 %	-4.91539	***
	15.33 %	7.73 %	16			
agency6	19.51 %	6.08 %	4	-4.74 %	-1.24841	
	14.78 %	8.17 %	13			
agency7			0	-15.89 %	N/A	N/A
	15.89 %	7.83 %	17			

for each variable: first row = large agency problems, second row = low agency problems;
*** = significant at the 1 % level (** = 5 %; * = 10 %)

Table 5-40: T-tests for differences of means of *xineff* by agency variable over the machinery industry (comprehensive regression)

This reversal of the rejection of hypothesis two is again due to the omission of the other non-machinery firms from the regression. Not only did the position of the efficient frontier relative to the cloud of machinery companies change by moving to the border of that cloud (Figure 5-26), but also the slope of the curve shifted in such a way as to favor the manager-controlled firms in the separate regression. Figure 5-27 shows an attempt to sketch this, using new fictitious datapoints.

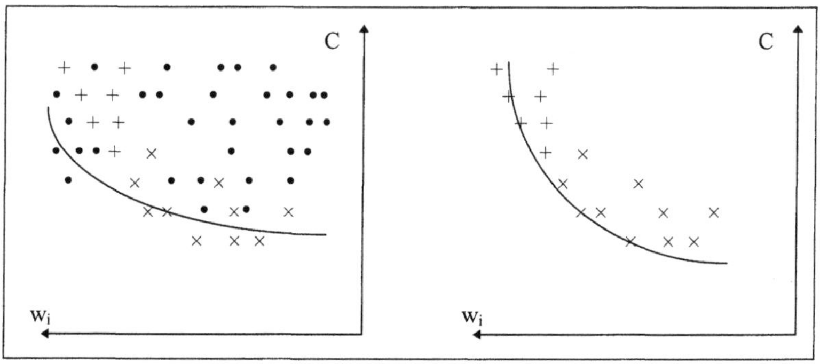

Figure 5-27: Sketch of efficient border in relation to management-controlled (+) and ownership-controlled (×) machinery companies with and without companies from other sectors (•) included in regression

If the management-controlled machinery firms are represented by the plusses (+) and the ownership-controlled machinery firms by the crosses (×), with all other companies represented by dots (•), then the position of the other firms in the comprehensive regression in the left graph puts the management-controlled firms at a disadvantage and makes the owner-controlled ones emerge as less inefficient. The bulk of the companies from other sectors pulls the frontier into the cloud of owner-controlled firms, making them very x-efficient. Removing the other companies from the procedure allows the frontier to more closely follow the management-controlled firms, while the efficient border no longer cuts through the owner-controlled firms.

This explanation should give the separate regression results more weight, as the influence of companies in other sectors should be nil. However, the dummy variables used to account for sectoral differences in this case were not sufficient. As mentioned before, the decreased reliability of the smaller sample used in the separate regression can be held against this and mitigates the criticism somewhat.

The machinery sector was found to produce many unlucky agency categorizations. With no or only one case in some subgroups, it is possible that single firms are responsible for the divergent results, not the choice of model as such. The other sector results could shed more light on this question, especially those from the chemicals, electronics and food & beverages sectors, where the companies are more evenly distributed among the agency categories.

The results of the t-tests for the differences in means of *xineff* for the **chemicals** sector are given above in Table 5-41. Checking the results for hypothesis one quickly confirms that the hypothesis must be rejected, with the vast majority of agency variables (except *agency3*) producing positive differences in *xineff*, where negative ones were postulated. Two of the differences are significant at the 1 %-level.

The second hypothesis is neither rejected by the leverage nor the monitored debt ratio variables, allowing the hypothesis that managers run their companies less efficiently when uncontrolled by creditors to stand. Neither difference is significant, as is mostly the case. The same result supporting the second hypothesis had been obtained for the comprehensive regression results for the machinery sector.

The other sector results are as usual in the appendix. The first hypothesis is not rejected for any of the major agency variables for the **electronics** sector. Also the second hypothesis concerning the management-controlled companies' x-efficiency and that of the creditor-controlled ones is not rejected due to the 8 % lower x-inefficiency of the creditor-controlled firms, significant at the 10 % level. The **food & beverages** sector is hard to judge as regards the first hypothesis. This is because the block ownership variable does not subdivide the dataset and the other two major variables *agency1* and *agency5* alternately reject and accept the hypothesis. The second hypothesis is rejected in the case of both agency variables. Finally, the **utilities** sector of course again classifies all cases into one group for all major variables used in hypothesis one. So no statement is possible with regard to that variable. As already stated for the food & beverages sector, the second hypothesis must be rejected for the utilities firms, too.

mean(xineff) overall: **22.53 %**

variable	mean(xineff)	std. dev.	N	diff	z	sig
block own-ership	18.65 %	10.81 %	5	3.53 %	0.6597	
	22.18 %	7.94 %	12			
size	20.12 %	5.78 %	4	3.01 %	0.80981	
	23.14 %	9.37 %	16			
market	14.99 %	5.49 %	4	9.42 %	2.71969	***
segment	24.42 %	8.45 %	16			
dividend	15.42 %	8.85 %	2	7.91 %	1.20183	
signal	23.32 %	8.59 %	18			
leverage	22.00 %	7.52 %	12	-1.68 %	-0.33862	
	20.32 %	10.92 %	6			
monitored	25.06 %	7.04 %	10	-5.05 %	-1.31988	
debt ratio	20.01 %	9.85 %	10			
agency1	20.53 %	2.71 %	3	0.75 %	0.24968	
	21.28 %	9.56 %	14			
agency2	17.28 %	6.86 %	4	5.05 %	1.18802	
	22.33 %	9.06 %	13			
agency3	21.59 %	7.75 %	11	-1.28 %	-0.25369	
	20.32 %	10.92 %	6			
agency4	17.48 %	2.87 %	3	4.45 %	1.48412	
	21.93 %	9.36 %	14			
agency5	18.65 %	10.81 %	5	3.53 %	0.6597	
	22.18 %	7.94 %	12			
agency6	19.251 %	8.86 %	6	2.52 %	0.56024	
	22.03 %	8.87 %	11			
agency7	8.35 %	1.14 %	2	14.50 %	6.75346	***
	22.85 %	7.71 %	15			

N =20; for each variable: first row = large agency problems, second row = low agency problems; *** = significant at the 1 % level (** = 5 %; * = 10 %)

Table 5-41: T-tests for differences of means of *xineff* by agency variable over the chemicals industry (comprehensive regression)

variable	mean(xineff)	std. dev.	N	diff	z	sig
block ownership	15.33 %	7.73 %	16	-1.14 %	-0.42954	
creditor	16.47 %	7.24 %	16			
agency5	15.33 %	7.73 %	16	-1.14 %	-0.42954	
creditor	16.47 %	7.24 %	16			

first row = ownership control according to the variable given, second row = creditor control; *** = significant at the 1 % level (** = 5 %; * = 10 %)

Table 5-42: T-tests for differences of means of *xineff* between owner-controlled and creditor-controlled companies, comprehensive regression for the machinery sector

The third hypothesis is tested for in the Table 5-42 above for the machinery sector and Table 5-43 below for the chemicals companies. For both sectors, the two ownership control classifying variables block ownership and *agency5* produce the same company groups. The owner-controlled machinery companies are 1.17 % more x-efficient than the creditor-controlled ones. This confirms hypothesis three, which postulated that tendency. The opposite result emerges for the chemicals industry, though, where creditor-controlled firms are 2.17 % more x-efficient than the owner-controlled ones. The differences are insignificant for both sectors.

variable	mean(xineff)	std. dev.	N	diff	z	sig
block ownership	22.18 %	7.94 %	12	2.17 %	0.5626	
creditor	20.01 %	9.85 %	10			
agency5	22.18 %	7.94 %	12	2.17 %	0.5626	
creditor	20.01 %	9.85 %	10			

first row = ownership control according to the variable given, second row = creditor control; *** = significant at the 1 % level (** = 5 %; * = 10 %)

Table 5-43: T-tests for differences of means of *xineff* between owner-controlled and creditor-controlled companies, comprehensive regression for the chemicals sector

For the electronics sector the third hypothesis is rejected, again with equal group classifications resulting from the two ownership control variables, while the third hypothesis cannot be rejected for either agency variable block ownership or *agency5* in the case of the food & beverages companies. The same can be said for the utilities companies, that the third hypothesis cannot be rejected. In total the third hypothesis is rejected for two of the sectors, the chemicals and the electronics industry, and is not rejected for the other three sectors.

sector	average *xineff*	rank	sig[+]	rank by degree of competition in sales market	rank by cost/asset ratio
machinery	17.29 %	1		1	5
electronics	20.66 %	2		2	4
chemicals	22.53 %	3		3	3
food & beverages	27.38 %	4		4	2
utilities	31.57 %	5		5	1

[+]of difference to next sector; *** = significant at the 1 % level (** = 5 %; * = 10 %)

Table 5-44: Average values for *xineff* for five sectors, comprehensive regression

paired sectors	*xineff* difference	sig
machinery–electronics	-.0118	
electronics–chemicals	-.0301	*
chemicals–food & beverages	-.0192	
food & beverages –utilities	-.2107	***

*** = significant at 1 %-level (** = 5 %; * = 10 %)

Table 5-45: T-tests for *xineff* mean differences, by sector pairs for the comprehensive regression

The fifth hypothesis is the next that can be tested with the data available here. The hypothesis states that companies offering their products in more competitive markets will be more x-efficient than companies in less competitive sales markets, be it due to regulation or imperfect market conditions such as oligopolies or intransparency. The ranking order of the sectors by *xineff* as estimated by the comprehensive panel regression exactly follows the ranking suggested by the hypothesis, as shown in Table 5-44. This supports the fifth hypothesis to the fullest possible degree, with the exception that the differences in *xineff* between neighboring sectors are never significant. In the table the exact reversal of the cost/asset rankings is also very clear to see. For the separate sectoral regressions, the fifth hypothesis is rejected since two sectors do not follow the prescribed ranking, see Tables A-56 to A-65 in the appendix.

Again, the sixth hypothesis is testable, with the same reservations toward the result as mentioned above, in that many categories are incomplete and could give a false impression of the situation. Negative differences with rising significance levels are demanded in hypothesis six. As the table shows, the negative signs are given in every case, and the differences do rise more or less, the farther one goes down in the table. The sixth hypothesis therefore is not rejected for the comprehensive regression results, contrary to the separate regression results (see Table 5-38 above).

5.2.5.3.5 Logistic Regressions

The logistic regressions for the machinery sector were often not possible, usually due to multiple solutions. The models for which this was the case are either marked with N/A (not applicable) in Table 5-46 or the coefficient is zero, if it could be computed. Table 5-46 shows the results of the regressions on the separately estimated sectoral x-inefficiencies, Table 5-47 features those from the overall comprehensive regression.

In Table 5-46, the first market segment dummy for the electronics sector and the dividend signal for the utilities sector were redundant and therefore omitted from the regression. In the first model with the six agency variables, support for the first hypothesis is only provided by the chemicals and utilities sectors, while the agency conglomerate models always support the hypothesis, except for the machinery sector as mentioned. Never are the coefficients consistently negative for all coefficients in the first model. Tests of the second hypothesis suffer from opposing signs for the coefficients of the two variables for every sector. Weighting the debt ratio coefficient more heavily gives slight overall support for the second hypothesis. The high classification scores clearly beat the benchmark of random classification, which reaches a maximum of 53.1 % (for the food & beverages industry).[143]

---

[143] The number of cases per sector is fairly small, though, whereas the logistic regression should really only be used on larger samples (N > 50). Cf. Urban (1993); Aldrich/Nelson (1984).

	chemicals	machinery	electronics	food & beverages	utilities
expected sign	–	–	–	–	–
		model 1			
block ownership	-.6547	1.1767	3.8843	N/A	-26.4799
size	-.4435	.4938	-.4258	N/A	-.2360
market segment 1	9.3323	3.0444	-1.3862	N/A	26.1309
market segment 2	17.7660	-7.8266	N/A⁺	N/A	32.4163
dividend signal	-2.7081	-11.3624	2.4886	N/A	N/A⁺
leverage	-.3580	2.2170 **	1.9762	N/A	-3.8011
-2 log likelihood‡	15.831	17.927 **	10.585	N/A	11.104
% correct classific.	66.67	83.33	80.00	N/A	78.57
		model 2			
leverage	-.0634	.6198	.1517	.2010	-2.1077
monitored debt ratio	.0922	-4.8031	-2.2507	-.6296	11.4041
-2 log likelihood‡	24.805	32.303 *	20.051	33.895	14.582 *
% correct classific.	61.11	51.85	46.67	42.31	71.43
		model 3			
agency1	-.1542	-1.0116 *	-.3185	.0000	-.2877
-2 log likelihood‡	20.72	17.40 *	32.80	13.86	19.12
% correct classific.	53.33	73.33	50.00	50.00	57.14
		model 4			
agency5	-.1823	-.9163	-.6285	.0000	-.2877
-2 log likelihood‡	20.70	18.14	31.10	13.86	19.12
% correct classific.	53.33	66.67	66.67	50.00	57.14

N = 20/27/16/26/15; *** = significant at the 1 % level (** = 5 %; * = 10 %); ⁺ redundant; ‡ = significance of model chi-square

Table 5-46: Coefficients and overall results of the logistic regressions on the *xineff* dummy variable, by sector (separate regressions) [144]

[144] The market segment dummy 1 is one for official continuous trade, the second dummy is one for official daily trade.

	chemicals	electronics	food & beverages	machinery	utilities
expected sign	–	–	–	–	–
			model 1		
block ownership	-1.9203	-1.0769	-1.9351	N/A	-9.1568
size	-.3013	.3840	.0157	N/A	-.5323
market segment 1	7.5046	-1.0176	-.4617	N/A	11.0394
market segment 2	-.3752	N/A+	8.2843	N/A	20.7764
dividend signal	-2.7948	-4.0903	.6444	N/A	N/A+
leverage	-.5970	.6097	.5889	N/A	4.3389
-2 log likelihood‡	14.535	12.327	26.859	N/A	9.614 *
% correct classifica.	80.00	60.00	70.83	N/A	85.71
			model 2		
leverage	-.1166	2.1218	.0363	-.6400	-4.0614 *
monitored debt ratio	-.2897	-12.8240 *	.3050	-.1976	10.3451
-2 log likelihood‡	23.853	13.093 **	37.337	27.183 **	11.244 **
% correct classifica.	66.67	80.00	40.74	65.38	78.57
			model 3		
agency1	-1.2040 *	-.5108	-.3185	-1.8718 **	-1.2993 **
-2 log likelihood‡	16.81 **	13.36	32.80	11.78 ***	14.54 **
% correct classifica.	73.33	70.00	54.17	86.67	78.57
			model 4		
agency5	-1.5040 *	-.5108	-.2624	-2.5648 **	-1.2993 **
-2 log likelihood‡	15.98 **	13.36	32.88	8.59 ***	14.55 **
% correct classifica.	73.33	70.00	54.17	93.33	78.57

N = 20/27/16/26/15; *** = significant at the 1 % level (** = 5 %; * = 10 %); + = redundant; ‡ = significance of model chi-square

Table 5-47: Coefficients and overall results of the logistic regressions on the *xineff* dummy variable, comprehensive regressions by sector[145]

The results for the comprehensive estimation (Table 5-47) are also beset by estimation problems for the machinery sector. A slight majority of coefficients are negative in the first model, with the most in the chemicals and the least in the

145 The market segment dummy 1 is one for official continuous trade, the second dummy is one for official daily trade.

food & beverages and utilities sectors. Six of the ten agency conglomerate regressions are significant, with the usual strong support for hypothesis one. The completed estimations follow the pattern that the first hypothesis is supported by the block ownership and agency conglomerates, but not confirmed by the other variables. The second hypothesis is supported by the chemicals, electronics, and machinery sectors, and rejected by the other two, if the coefficient of the monitored debt ratio is given preference. Overall, the high classification results confirm that agency control mechanisms are crucial to x-efficiency levels in a company.

Again, to finish the section an overview over the results of the hypothesis tests is presented below in Table 5-48. The table presents the results from tests of the applicable hypotheses one, two three and five for the separate sectoral cost function regressions in an overview format. Only the major agency variables are listed here; it should be remembered that the other variables provide a more varied picture that can belie seemingly clear-cut outcomes here. The table puts the sector results side by side for easy comparison, and adds overall rows and columns that aggregate the results for the major agency variables on a majority basis. For the second hypothesis concerning the relation of manager-controlled firms to creditor-controlled ones, the monitored debt ratio result was weighted more heavily than the leverage's, if the two did not agree in tendency. This hypothesis received some support, but not enough to consider it accepted. As can be seen, only the third hypothesis, comparing ownership control to creditor control, is confirmed, i. e., ownership control is the more effective of the two. This confirmation is only qualified (shown by the brackets), because of the rejection of the hypothesis for the chemicals and utilities sectors.

Table 5-49 gives the results for the same sectoral evaluation, this time of the comprehensive estimation. For the first hypothesis, the many non applicable results (N/A) are unfortunate, reducing the weight of the overall decisions for that hypothesis. In total, the hypothesis is not rejected for two of the major agency variables, block ownership (qualified acceptance) and *agency5*, plus the logistic regressions, and it is also not rejected for three of the sectors. This results in a majority of instances supporting the hypothesis and its acceptance.

The second hypothesis comparing management-controlled to creditor-controlled companies' x-inefficiency is almost cleanly rejected by the food & beverages and utilities sector results, but is not rejected by the other three. Overall, this means that the hypothesis cannot be rejected and is conditionally accepted.

hypothesis #	variable/ model	machinery	chemicals	electronics	food & beverages	utilities	overall
1	block ownership	☐	☐	☐	N/A	N/A	☐
	agency1	N/A	☐	☐	☐	N/A	☐
	agency5	☐	☐	☐	☑	N/A	☐
	logistic	N/A	☐	(☑)	(☑)	☑	(☑)
overall		☐	☐	☐	☐	N/A	☐
2	leverage	☐	☐	☐	☐	☐	☐
	monitored debt ratio	☐	☐	☑	☑	☐	(☐)
	logistic	(☑)	☐	(☑)	(☑)	☐	(☐)
overall		☐	☐	☑	☑	☐	(☐)
3	block ownership	☑	☑	☐	☐	☑	(☑)
	agency5	☑	☑	☐	☐	☑	(☑)
overall		☑	☑	☐	☐	☑	(☑)
5	overall						(☐)
6	overall						☐

Table 5-48: Overview over the validity of hypotheses one, two, three, five and six for five sectors; separate sectoral regressions[146]

The third hypothesis compares the ownership control to the creditor control and expects higher x-efficiency values to be found on the side of the ownership control. This is only rejected for the electronics industry, again leading to an overall non-rejection of the hypothesis. The fifth hypothesis, too, was not rejected due to the exact compliance of the *xineff* rankings of the sectors with those postulated in accordance with the degree of competition on the sales markets of each sector. Therefore, for the method of the comprehensive panel regression in combination with the separate analysis of the results by sector, all testable hy-

[146] T-tests for group differences by the variable given or logistic regressions. A check marks a hypothesis that could not be rejected for the sector given at the top of the column. N/A = not applicable, used where the agency variable does not subdivide the sample into two groups. For hypothesis three, the monitored debt ratio was used to identify creditor-controlled firms.

potheses are not rejected in the overall condensation of the results over all sectors. Finally, the sixth hypothesis is guardedly confirmed by the comprehensive regression, while the separate regression results reject that hypothesis. The support given by the comprehensive regressions was not perfect, though, so the checked box is put in parentheses in Table 5-49.

hypothesis #	variable/ model	machinery	chemicals	electronics	food & beverages	utilities	overall
1	block ownership	☑	☐	☑	N/A	N/A	(☑)
	agency1	N/A	☐	☑	☐	N/A	(☐)
	agency5	☑	☐	☑	☑	N/A	☑
	logistic	(☑)	☑	☑	☑	☑	☑
overall		☑	☐	☑	(☑)	N/A	☑
2	leverage	☑	☑	☐	☐	☐	(☐)
	monitored debt ratio	☑	☑	☑	☐	☐	(☑)
	logistic	☑	☑	☑	☐	(☑)	☑
overall		☑	☑	(☑)	☐	☐	(☑)
3	block ownership	☑	☑	☐	☑	(☑)	☑
	agency5	☑	☑	☐	☑	(☑)	☑
overall		☑	☑	☐	☑	(☑)	☑
5	overall						☑
6	overall						(☑)

Table 5-49: Overview over the validity of hypotheses one, two, three, five and six for five sectors; comprehensive panel regression[147]

[147] A check marks a hypothesis that could not be rejected for the sector given at the top of the column. N/A = not applicable, used where the agency variable does not subdivide the sample into two groups. For hypothesis three, the monitored debt ratio was used to identify creditor-controlled firms.

5.3 Summary of the Chapter

A final overview of the results of the hypothesis tests is given below in Table 5-50. Here, the three different models and versions thereof are compared, using the overall evaluations of the hypotheses that had been provided for each model (the rightmost column in the final overview tables for each model). The first model (5.2.5.1) is the cross-sectional model, requiring separate regressions for every year in the dataset. Sector dummies were necessary for the estimation of these seven cost functions. The comprehensive panel regression over all cases in the sample constitutes the second model (5.2.5.2), calling for the addition of both sectoral dummies and time index variables to the basic translog cost function. This model was processed in two versions. The first version was to take the full panel data as used for the regression and interpret the results for the x-inefficiency variable. The second version was a sector-specific analysis of the overall x-inefficiency estimates. The third model is the panel estimate of a cost function for each sector on its own, requiring time index variables in the model but of course no sector dummies (5.2.5.3).

The first hypothesis states that manager-controlled firms will operate less x-efficiently than owner-controlled companies. Taking the major agency variables, it is not rejected for the majority of the models, so overall the hypothesis is accepted, but the acceptance is marked as qualified. Only the separate sectoral model does not find support for the hypothesis except in the logistic evaluation. Seen from the point of view of the agency variables, the hypothesis is not rejected for the block ownership variable (qualified) and the *agency5* conglomerate.

The second hypothesis postulates that manager-controlled firms will also operate less x-efficiently than creditor-controlled companies. Allowing for lesser informational insight possibilities for the creditors of a firm in comparison to the owners calls for the difference in x-efficiency to be less pronounced than in the first hypothesis. The comprehensive panel model in its two versions, the overall interpretation of the results and the sectoral analysis, does not reject the hypothesis due to the results when using the ratio of monitored to unmonitored debt. The logistic models accept the hypothesis in three out of four models. In all other cases the hypothesis is rejected, leading to an overall rejection of the hypothesis. This result, too, is qualified by putting it in brackets, to show that there is some support for the hypothesis. In a sense this result confirms that the difference in x-inefficiency between management and creditor-controlled companies is only slight.

hypothesis #	variable/ model	cross-sectional model – yearly regressions	comprehensive panel model – overall results	comprehensive panel model – sectoral results	sectoral panel model – separate regressions	overall
1	block ownership	☑	☑	(☑)	☐	(☑)
	agency1	(☑)	☑	(☐)	☐	☐
	agency5	☑	☑	☑	☐	(☑)
	logistic	☑	☑	☑	(☑)	☑
overall		☑	☑	☑	☐	(☑)
2	leverage	☐	☐	(☐)	☐	☐
	monitored debt ratio	☐	☑	(☑)	(☐)	(☐)
	logistic	☑	☑	☑	(☐)	☑
overall		☐	☑	☐	(☐)	(☐)
3	block ownership	☑	☐	☑	(☑)	(☑)
	agency5	☑	☐	☑	(☑)	(☑)
overall		☑	☐	☑	(☑)	(☑)
4	overall	☐				☐
5	overall			☑	(☐)	(☑)
6	overall			(☑)	☐	(☐)

Table 5-50: Overview over the validity of the six hypotheses for all models[148]

The third hypothesis compares ownership and creditor control to each other and concludes that ownership control should be more effective than creditor control, with a subsequent advantage in x-efficiency on the ownership side. This hypothesis follows directly from the first and second hypotheses. Unlike the second hypothesis, though, the third one is not rejected for any method except the comprehensive panel regression. For the separate sectoral regressions, the support is not clear-cut, so altogether the hypothesis is marked as conditionally ac-

[148] A check marks a hypothesis that could not be rejected according to the model given at the top of the column.

cepted. The results for the second and third hypotheses suggest that creditor control alone is not effective. X-inefficiency measures are not statistically different for either management-controlled or creditor-controlled companies. With creditor control for the most part a domain of banks in Germany, since industrial bonds do not constitute a large fraction of corporate financing, this raises questions about the effectivity of this method of control.

The logistic regressions come out overall in support of hypotheses one and two, though the results are not clear-cut when looked at in detail. This is to be expected when many variables are used. The third hypothesis is only weakly supported.

The fourth hypothesis is time-related and thus could only be answered using the results of one method of cost function estimation, the cross-sectional one applied to the seven years of data separately. It postulates that manager-controlled firms will decrease their x-inefficiency at a slower rate than ownership-controlled companies, and increase it again at a faster rate, in effect maximizing the periods of high inefficiency. The tendency of the x-inefficiency is to decrease over the seven years, effectively making only the test of the decrease rate of x-inefficiency possible. That hypothesis is rejected for the sample.

The fifth hypothesis addresses the sector classifications of the firms. Assuming somewhat boldly that the competitive conditions on the sales markets of the companies can be judged using sector-wide data on the firms, an hypothesis was constructed that companies facing stiff competition would be forced to be more x-efficient than companies not so exposed to market forces. The reason for this lack of exposure is not central to the hypothesis, but could be due to such reasons as market regulation or oligopolistic developments on the sales markets.

Two of the models allowed this hypothesis to be tested. First, the separate panel regressions for each sector allow sector-specific cost frontiers to be estimated and average x-inefficiencies for each sector to be derived from the estimates. Second, the comprehensive panel regression including all sectors, but also sector dummies to account for sectoral differences, was used to compare the results from one sector to the next. In theory this is possible, too, for the cross-sectional regressions, but the small sample size prohibited this in practice. The results from the separate regressions lead to a rejection of the hypothesis, as two of the sectors do not rank as hypothesized. As the other three do follow the prediction, though, the rejection of the hypothesis is placed in parentheses. The comprehensive model evaluated by sector exactly replicates the ranking postulated, meaning that the fifth hypothesis cannot be rejected according to that estimation model. That means that overall, the hypothesis is not rejected, but the check is put in parentheses, signifying that sales market conditions (fifth hypothesis) have more monitoring power than creditor banks in holding the x-inefficiency at bay in industrial companies (second hypothesis).

The sixth and final hypothesis was also tested on the separate sectoral regression results and the comprehensive estimates, divided by sectors. The hypothesis states that the differences in x-inefficiency between owner and manager-controlled companies will be higher in sectors with little competition to act as an external control mechanism. This hypothesis is neatly rejected by the results from the separate sector regressions, while the comprehensive regression result gives it qualified support. On the whole the hypothesis is marked as rejected but placed in parentheses to reflect the mixed result that the two regressions produced.

6 Summary

The goal of this analysis was to test for the effects of agency problems between managers, owners, and creditors on the financial behavior, performance and efficiency of German stock corporations. In order to do this, it was necessary to identify and classify characteristics of a firm that point to the existence of agency problems. As is also the case in other research, it is not possible to prove that the agency variables unerringly mirror agency problems. This gave the empirical analyses the characteristic of joint hypotheses: If the agency variables are valid indicators of agency problems, the financial behavior, performance and efficiency differences of the companies in the various agency categories can be linked to agency problems.

Since information asymmetry between the principals and the agents are a precondition for agency problems, variables were sought that capture information levels of the principals. The **market segment** a company is traded in and the existence of **dividend signals** were identified as suitable variables, where the market segment determines the long-term level of information a principal can expect, and dividend signals constitute short-term deviations from that level. Control possibilities of the principals are measured by the **block ownership** variable for shareholders, while for creditors the **ratio of monitored to unmonitored debt** was applied. The latter variable in particular captured the influence of banks as creditors. In addition to that ratio, the **leverage** was used as another creditor control variable. This variable was important from another point of view, too, as it proxied for the internal control produced by the need to regularly service debit interest and amortization payment obligations. External monitoring and control finally was determined by both the corporate **size**, which is judged to be positively correlated with the public interest in and external monitoring of a company, and the **sector** classification which sheds light on the competitive situation a company faces in the product market. Five sectors provided large enough samples to be studied on their own. These sectors were the chemicals, machinery, electronics, food & beverages, and utilities firms. Of these, the utilities firms faced the least competition and therefore were expected to show the most agency problems overall. Payment incentives for the managers could not be captured with the data available.

The influence of each control variable was tested separately via **t-tests for differences in means**. These differences were posited for the comparison of the various agency control groups, where the companies were divided into manager-controlled companies, owner-controlled ones and creditor-controlled firms. The latter two groups are not mutually exclusive. In order to make the joint determination of the importance of the agency variables possible, both **multiple logistic regressions**, using the agency variables as independent variables, and **conglomerate agency variables** were used. The conglomeration of the variables was effected in two ways. The first was to give each agency variable an equal weight in the conglomerate variable, with the exception of the block ownership variable which was given more weight in accordance with its importance in other research as the central variable for identifying agency problems. The second was the employment of genetic algorithms to determine the weights most suitable to distinguish between the control groups' attributes.

The **data sample from 1986 to 1992** with over 1100 cases for 237 different firms was used in up to three fashions: first the total sample was analyzed with the t-tests and logistic regressions, using sector-based mean calculations to account for industry-wide characteristics. If time-related hypotheses were set up, then the data was also analyzed in yearly subsamples. Finally, the five sectors strongest in number were separately subjected to the statistical tests. Apart from testing the original not time-related hypotheses in these sectoral analyses, up to two other hypotheses were constructed that addressed the varying competitive conditions of the sectors, i. e., product markets of the firms.

***

In the first empirical chapter, the **financial behavior** of companies was the subject of attention. The financial instruments that were studied were divided into internal and external finance instruments. The internal cash flow method of financing was not studied, as the theory made this the equally preferred method of financing for all control groups. However, the **free cash flow** (that cash flow which remains after all investment outlays have been paid for) was included in the study. The external instruments comprise **equity issues** and **long-** and **short-term external debt**. For each of the three relations, those between owners and managers, between creditor and managers, and between owners and creditors, a hypothesis was set up to comparatively rank the financial preferences of either group and deduce expected directions of influence of each control group on each financial instrument.

Table 6-1 shows the results of the three agency group hypotheses plus the sectoral hypothesis for each of the four financial instruments.

The **first financial hypothesis** treated differences in financial preferences between owners and uncontrolled managers. Whereas managers were expected to prefer free cash flow over short-term debt, short-term debt over long-term debt, and long-term debt over equity issues in order to minimize the outside control over their activities, owners are expected to favor the two debt types over free cash flow for the opposite reason. Owners should dislike equity issues even more than the managers, as issues dilute either their control or cost them money. Only this greater dislike of the owners for equity issues allowing new shareholders into a firm could be consistently confirmed by the tests.

hypothesis #	sample	d_l/fa	d_s/fa	e/fa	fcf/fa	overall
1	compre-hensive	☐	(☐)	☑	☐	(☐)
	sectoral	(☐)	(☐)	☑	(☑)	(☐)
overall		☐	(☐)	☑	(☐)	(☐)
2	compre-hensive	(☐)	☐	(☐)	(☐)	(☐)
	sectoral	(☐)	(☐)	☐	(☑)	(☐)
overall		(☐)	☐	☐	(☐)	(☐)
3	compre-hensive	☑	☑	☑	☑	☑
	sectoral	☑	(☐)	(☑)	☑	(☑)
overall		☑	(☑)	(☑)	☑	(☑)
4	sectoral					☐

Table 6-1: Overview over the validity of the financial behavior hypotheses[1]

In the **second financial hypothesis**, the differences between creditors and managers were inspected. It was posited that creditors prefer long-term debt over short-term debt, this over equity issues, and least of all they accept free cash flows. For managers, the preference of instruments given for hypothesis one applied. There was marginal support for the notion that creditors prefer long-term debt and dislike free cash flow, but not enough to accept those sub-hypotheses or the second hypothesis in full.

The **third financial hypothesis** compared the ownership control with the creditor control, using the preference orders mentioned for hypotheses one and two. This is the only hypothesis that received at least conditional acceptance for every financial instrument. The owners do not favor long-term debt as much as creditors do. Due to the insights creditors, especially house banks, receive into corporate workings, it is entirely understandable that a creditor-controlled company has easier access to more debt. Owners, on the other hand, tolerate free cash flow more easily than creditors, which could be a sign that owners are more

[1] A check marks a hypothesis that could not be rejected according to the model given at the top of the column. Parentheses are used to show gradual differences. d_l/fa = growth of long-term debt to fixed assets; d_s/fa = growth of short-term debt to fixed assets; e/fa = growth of external equity to fixed assets; fcf/fa = free cash flow to fixed assets.

privy to future investment prospects requiring additional funds. In addition, owners are less partial to equity issues and equally or more interested in short-term debt than creditors, as hypothesized. These last two statements are only conditionally supported, though, leading to an only qualified acceptance of the third hypothesis in total.

In the **fourth financial hypothesis**, it was surmised that the varying levels of competition in the product markets could affect financial behavior. In sectors where the companies have to face stiff competition (machinery and electronics), this would force all control groups to follow the same financial policies, and cause the lack of distinctions found in the tests of the first three hypotheses. For the less competitive companies (food & beverages, utilities), the three hypotheses should be confirmed, though. This theory could not be corroborated by the statistical tests, leading to the rejection of the fourth hypothesis.

> Overall, the differences in preference postulated for the free cash flow instrument received the most support. Managers tend to prefer it more than owners, while creditors are most opposed to it. In their dislike of the equity finance, the shareholders are clearly offset from the other control groups. To a lesser degree this is also true for short-term debt finance, which shareholders prefer more than others. The creditors favor long-term debt finance more than the other control groups.

The investment side of corporate operations could not be analyzed here, but could contribute valuable additional insights into financial behavior in the light of the agency theory. For example, a question that remains to be studied in detail is if the investment volume depends on the control group of a company, i. e., if the under- or overinvestment problem can be observed in companies. Large differences in volume could affect the outcome of the hypotheses tested here. Additional information on incentive or control clauses in compensation or credit contracts, respectively, would also be important. House banks may have access to informal insights into companies, and further exercise influence over the companies through equity ownership. Also, the riskiness of investment policies was seen to be theoretically related to the risk propensity of the control group, and could affect the financial mix used in investment funding.

***

Agency problems are typically associated with decreases in **corporate performance** in the literature, although often the hypotheses were not validated in subsequent empirical analyses. In the second empirical chapter, four performance measures were selected to test six hypotheses. Two of the performance measures, the **return on equity** and the **return on capital**, are based on book valued data, while the other two, the **Sharpe ratio** and **Tobin's q** as a measure of the market value of assets to their book value, include market values in their calculation. The Sharpe ratio was expected to be unaffected by agency problems, meaning that non-significant results when using it as the performance measure act as a calibrating mechanism for the tests. This result was generally achieved. The return on capital is included as a measure that is more important to creditors than to the ownership of a firm. All performance measures have a high level of aggregation, as opposed to the concept of efficiency as used in the third empirical chapter.

The **first performance hypothesis** to be tested was that managers, when able to act uncontrolled by the ownership of a firm, will only achieve an inferior performance to the one that firms under ownership control produce. This effect should especially be visible in the return on equity and Tobin's q. In all three data sampling versions applied, using the comprehensive sample, the seven yearly subsamples, and the separate sector subsamples for the five most numerous sectors in the sample, this hypothesis was rejected. Tobin's q was the performance measure that most frequently uncovered differences in performance, which befits its status as a market-valued performance measure.

This negative result conforms to previous findings for the German market. A possible reason for this outcome lies in the aggregation of the performance measures. Especially the book measures are susceptible to manipulative measures in the accounting process which can be used to skew performance readings in the direction desired. If one assumes that the aggregate performance measures are more closely studied by investors than disaggregate numbers, then it makes immediate sense for unmonitored managers to apply their energy to maintaining certain performance levels instead of working to improve the disaggregate numbers.

A similar result also was found for the **second performance hypothesis**, which stated that creditor control is more effective than manager control, especially with regard to the return on capital. This hypothesis, too, was rejected, and the results even suggested that the exact opposite is true.

This being the case, then the **third performance hypothesis** that claims that ownership control, too, is better than creditor control should hold. This hypothesis indeed was consistently not rejected by the data. Creditors with their lesser involvement in a company's dealings and especially lower information levels concerning that company are apparently not able to secure the performance levels that owners or managers reach. They might not even be interested in doing so, as their lower interest demands for their loans can usually be met with non-maximal performance.

The **fourth performance hypothesis** was time-related and expected a tendency of performance measures to cling to lower levels in manager-controlled companies over the course of time. This hypothesis was not rejected, but the distinctions were too small to lay great store by this result.

hypothesis #	compre-hensive	yearly	sectoral	overall
1	☐	☐	(☐)	☐
2	☐	☐	(☐)	☐
3	☑	☑	☑	☑
4		(☑)		(☑)
5			(☑)	(☑)
6			☑	☑

Table 6-2: Overview over the validity of the performance hypotheses[2]

On the other hand, the sector-related hypotheses found more support and gave insights into the reasons for the rejection of the first hypothesis. The **fifth performance hypothesis** was formulated to say that both high and low levels of competition in the sales markets of companies are detrimental to performance. In the first case, intense competition does not allow any one company or type of company to greatly outperform any other company, while in the other case unchecked sloth prohibits monopolistic or near-monopolistic companies from maximizing profits and performance. Indeed, the highly competitive machinery firms and the uncompetitive utilities performed poorly. The medium-competition electronics and chemicals sectors exhibited the highest book performances, but were surpassed by the food & beverages sector with regard to the market performance measures. There, the electronics and chemicals firms came in second and third place. The food & beverages sector had been counted among the less competitive sectors, and indeed performed in last place by the book measures, so that result led to an only conditional acceptance of the fifth hypothesis.

The **sixth performance hypothesis** incorporated the high competition levels as external control mechanisms and stated that only in their absence would the other agency variables be of any importance. This was confirmed by the significant results for distinguishing performance levels by agency variables in the case of the utilities and food & beverages sectors (those facing the least competition), and the frequent rejection of the first hypotheses for the other three sectors. This means that the rejection of the first two hypotheses for the comprehensive and yearly samples could be due to the combination of companies facing varying

2 A check marks a hypothesis that could not be rejected according to the model given at the top of the column. Parentheses are used to show gradual differences.

levels of competition on the output markets, where the results of the more competitive sectors dominate those of the less competitive sectors.

> In sum, the creditor-controlled companies underperform in comparison with both the owner- and manager-controlled firms, whose performance scores do not differ statistically. The performance of manager-controlled firms reacts slightly faster to follow economic downswings than that of ownership-controlled firms. Both very high and low levels of competitive pressure reduce differences in performance, and only where the external control of competition is missing, the other control and monitoring mechanisms gain importance. This latter effect could explain the rejection of the first hypotheses.

In this sense, the analysis confirms the relevance of the agency theory for all sectors and companies. An interesting question for future research is if the lower performance levels of creditor-controlled firms are also associated with a corresponding lower variance in the performance of such firms. This should be desirable to creditors who do not participate in profits elevated higher than those needed to satisfy their fixed claims and wish to minimize the default risk of the company.

***

In the third empirical chapter, the **x-efficiency**, or the efficiency in the responsibility of the management, of the firms in each agency control group was compared. In contrast to the aggregate performance measures used in the second empirical chapter, x-efficiency was defined as a disaggregate measure based on the distance of a firm's cost level to its estimated cost level defined by a dual cost function. The underlying production function related output amounts and input prices to the costs of a firm. The process to extract the x-efficiency of a firm was more complicated than the procedures used in the other chapters. It involved the estimation of a stochastic translog frontier cost function with a split error term including a one-sided inefficiency component for the companies in the sample using maximum likelihood techniques.

For 848 cases in the sample 1986-1992 the employee figures necessary to estimate the cost function were available. An overview of the results of the hypothesis tests for is given below in Table 6-3. Here, the three different models and versions thereof are compared. The first model is the cross-sectional model, requiring seven separate regressions using sector dummies for every year in the dataset. The comprehensive panel regression over all cases in the sample constitutes the second model, calling for the addition of both sectoral dummies and time index variables to the basic translog cost function. This model was processed in two versions. The first version was to take the full panel data as used for the regression and interpret the results for the x-inefficiency variable. The second version was a sector-specific analysis of the overall x-inefficiency estimates.

The third model is the panel estimate of a cost function for each sector on its own, requiring time index variables in the model, but no sector dummies.

hypothesis #	variable/ model	cross-sectional model – yearly regressions	comprehensive panel model – overall results	comprehensive panel model – sectoral results	sectoral panel model – separate regressions	overall
1	block ownership	☑	☑	(☑)	☐	(☑)
	agency1	(☑)	☑	(☐)	☐	☐
	agency5	☑	☑	☑	☐	(☑)
	logistic	☑	☑	☑	(☑)	☑
overall		☑	☑	☑	☐	(☑)
2	leverage	☐	☐	(☐)	☐	☐
	monitored debt ratio	☐	☑	(☑)	(☐)	(☐)
	logistic	☑	☑	☑	(☐)	☑
overall		☐	☑	☐	(☐)	(☐)
3	block ownership	☑	☐	☑	(☑)	(☑)
	agency5	☑	☐	☑	(☑)	(☑)
overall		☑	☐	☑	(☑)	(☑)
4	overall	☐				☐
5	overall			☑	(☐)	(☑)
6	overall			(☑)	☐	(☐)

Table 6-3: Overview over the validity of the efficiency hypotheses[3]

The **first efficiency hypothesis** stated that manager-controlled firms will operate less x-efficiently than owner-controlled companies. Going by the major agency variables, it was not rejected for the majority of the models. The logistic regres-

3 A check marks a hypothesis that could not be rejected according to the model given at the top of the column. Parentheses are used to show gradual differences.

sion also supported the hypothesis, so overall the hypothesis was conditionally accepted. The separate sectoral model found no support for the hypothesis except in the logistic evaluation. Seen from the point of view of the agency variables, the first hypothesis was not rejected for the block ownership variable (qualified) and the *agency5* conglomerate.

The **second efficiency hypothesis** postulated that manager-controlled firms will also operate less x-efficiently than creditor-controlled companies. Allowing for lesser informational insight possibilities for the creditors of a firm in comparison to the owners called for the difference in x-efficiency to be less pronounced than in the first hypothesis. The comprehensive panel model in its two versions, the overall interpretation of the results and the sectoral analysis, did not reject the hypothesis due to the results when using the ratio of monitored to unmonitored debt. The logistic models accepted the hypothesis in three out of four models. In all other cases the hypothesis was rejected, though, leading to an overall rejection of the hypothesis. This result, too, was qualified by putting it in brackets, to show that there was some support for the hypothesis. This result confirmed that the difference in x-inefficiency between management and creditor-controlled companies is only slight.

The **third efficiency hypothesis** compared ownership and creditor control to each other and concluded that ownership control should be more effective than creditor control, with a subsequent advantage in x-efficiency on the ownership side. This hypothesis followed directly from the first and second hypotheses. Unlike the second hypothesis, though, the third one was not rejected for any method except the comprehensive panel regression. For the separate sectoral regressions, the support was not clear-cut, so altogether the hypothesis was marked as conditionally accepted. The results for the second and third hypotheses suggested that creditor control alone is not effective. The x-inefficiency measure was not statistically different for either management-controlled or creditor-controlled companies. With creditor control for the most part a domain of banks in Germany (industrial bonds do not constitute a large fraction of German corporate financing), this raises questions about the effectivity of this method of control.

The **fourth efficiency hypothesis** was again time-related and thus could only be answered using the results of one method of cost function estimation, the cross-sectional one applied to the seven years of data separately. It was postulated that manager-controlled firms would decrease their x-inefficiency at a slower rate than ownership-controlled companies, and increase it again at a faster rate, in effect maximizing the periods of inefficiency. The tendency of the x-inefficiency was to decrease over the seven years, effectively making only the test of the decrease rate of x-inefficiency possible. That hypothesis was rejected for the sample.

The **fifth efficiency hypothesis** addressed the sector classifications of the firms. The hypothesis stated that companies facing stiff competition would be forced to be more x-efficient than companies not as exposed to market forces. Two of the models allowed this hypothesis to be tested. First, the separate panel regressions for each sector allow sector-specific cost frontiers to be estimated and average x-inefficiencies for each sector to be derived from the estimates. Second, the comprehensive panel regression including all sectors, but also sector dummies to account for sectoral differences, was used to compare the results from one sector to the next. The results from the separate regressions led to a rejection of the hypothesis, as two of the sectors did not rank as hypothesized. As the other three did follow the prediction, though, the rejection of the hypothesis was placed in parentheses. The comprehensive model evaluated by sector exactly replicated the ranking postulated, meaning that overall, the hypothesis was not rejected, although the check was put in parentheses.

The **sixth efficiency hypothesis** was also tested on the separate sectoral regression results and the comprehensive estimates, divided by sectors. The hypothesis stated that the differences in x-inefficiency between owner and manager-controlled companies would be higher in sectors with little competition to act as an external control mechanism. This hypothesis was neatly rejected by the results from the separate sector regressions, while the comprehensive regression result gave it qualified support. On the whole the hypothesis is marked as rejected but placed in parentheses to reflect the mixed result that the two regressions produced.

> In overview, companies controlled by managers are less x-efficient than those controlled by the owners, but both groups are equally susceptible to prevailing economic conditions. Creditor control is only slightly more effective than manager control. Sales market conditions exercise more control than creditor banks in holding the x-inefficiency at bay in industrial companies. There is only slight evidence that competition reduces the differences in x-inefficiency between the control groups.

Thus this thesis shows that there are a number of possibilities for an external observer to identify agency problems in a firm. Their impact on the financial behavior, performance, and efficiency of German stock corporations could be statistically confirmed, although a number of hypotheses drawn from theoretical considerations were rejected. Many other avenues in this promising field remain that should prove fruitful in future research.

A Appendix

A.1 The Agency Theory and its Empirical Implementation

no.	security code number	name	sector
1.	500800	Adlerwerke	holding
2.	503800	AEG AG	electronics
3.	634800	AEG Kabel AG	electronics
4.	576300	Aeskulap AG	electronics
5.	502770	AG Kuehnle, Kopp & Kausch	machinery
6.	500990	AGAB, Gesellschaft für Anlagen	holding
7.	502820	AGIV, AG für Industrie und Verkehrswesen	holding
8.	542200	Aktiengesellschaft für chemische Industrie	chemicals
9.	503200	Alexanderwerk AG	machinery
10.	503490	Allweiler AG	machinery
11.	760080	Altana Industrie-Aktien und Anlagen-AG	holding
12.	504700	Andreae-Noris Zahn AG	trade
13.	505160	Antriebstechnik G. Bauknecht AG	machinery
14.	505710	ASKO Deutsche Kaufhaus AG	trade
15.	675700	AUDI AG	automotive
16.	725090	Axel Springer Verlag AG	other
17.	515600	Bad Salzschlirf AG	other
18.	515060	Badenwerk AG	utility
19.	556500	Balcke-Dürr AG	machinery
20.	515100	BASF AG	chemicals
21.	575200	Bayer AG	chemicals
22.	518300	Bayerische Brauerei-Schuck-Jaenisch AG	food
23.	519000	Bayerische Motoren Werke AG	automotive
24.	529100	BBC Brown Boverie AG	other
25.	520000	Beiersdorf AG	chemicals
26.	521450	Berliner Elektro- Beteiligungen	holding
27.	522100	Berliner Kindl Brauerei AG	food
28.	530300	Berliner Kraft-und Licht (Bewag)-AG	utility
29.	522950	Bijou Brigitte modische Accessoires AG	apparel
30.	590900	Bilfinger & Berger Bau AG	construction
31.	719500	Binding-Brauerei AG	food
32.	704200	Blaue Quellen Mineral- und Heilbrunnen AG	food
33.	555030	Brau und Brunnen AG	food
34.	529700	Brauerei Cluss AG	food
35.	524730	Brauerei Moninger AG	food
36.	525900	Breitenburger Portland-Cement-Fabrik AG	holding
37.	527100	Bremer Vulkan AG, Schiffbau und Maschinenfabrik	other
38.	527200	Bremer Woll-Kämmerei AG	apparel
39.	657600	Buckau-Walther AG	holding
40.	527800	Buderus AG	metallurgy

no.	security code number	name	sector
41.	717170	Carl Schenck AG	machinery
42.	527400	Carl Schlenk AG	chemicals
43.	540700	Cassella AG	chemicals
44.	620110	CEAG Industrie-Aktien und Anlagen AG	holding
45.	542400	Chemische Werke Brockhues AG	chemicals
46.	634100	Christian Adalbert Kupferberg & Co. CGaA	food
47.	558000	Christian Dierig AG	holding
48.	543770	Computer 2000 AG	electronics
49.	544400	Concordia-Chemie AG	chemicals
50.	550400	CONTIGAS Deutsche Energie AG	utility
51.	543900	Continental AG	plastics
52.	521300	Dahlbusch Verwaltungs-AG	holding
53.	550000	Daimler-Benz AG	automotive
54.	551200	Degussa AG	chemicals
55.	677200	DELME Grundbesitz und Beteiligungs-AG	holding
56.	550700	Deutsche Babcock AG	holding
57.	552700	Deutsche Spezialglas AG	ceramics
58.	552800	Deutsche Steinzeug- und Kunststoffwarenfabrik AG	holding
59.	521000	Deutsche Telefonwerke AG (DeTeWe)	holding
60.	550900	Deutsche Texaco AG	other
61.	553700	Didier-Werke AG	ceramics
62.	553830	Dinkelacker Brauerei AG	food
63.	551800	DLW AG	chemicals
64.	554800	Dortmunder Aktien-Brauerei AG	food
65.	554900	Dortmunder Ritterbrauerei AG	food
66.	775100	DUEWAG AG	automotive
67.	559100	Dyckerhoff AG, Wiesbaden	ceramics
68.	557550	DYWIDAG (Dyckerhoff & Widmann AG)	construction
69.	600000	Edelstahlwerk Witten AG	holding
70.	570600	Eichbaum Brauereien AG	food
71.	565800	Eisen- und Hüttenwerke AG, Köln	holding
72.	565600	Eisenbahn-Verkehrsmittel-AG für Transport und Lagerung (EVA)	other
73.	568300	Engelhardt-Brauerei AG	food
74.	762200	ENKA AG	chemicals
75.	569210	ESCADA AG	apparel
76.	569300	Eschweiler Bergwerks-Verein AG	other
77.	575470	FAG Kugelfischer Georg Schäfer	machinery
78.	558800	Flachglas AG	ceramics
79.	579700	FORD-Werke AG	automotive
80.	550430	Friedrich Deckel AG	machinery
81.	579040	Fuchs-Petrolub AG, Öl + Chemie	chemicals
82.	585340	Garny AG	holding
83.	585700	GEA AG	machinery
84.	585800	GEHE AG	chemicals
85.	776000	Gelsenwasser AG	utility
86.	587300	Gerresheimer Glas AG	ceramics

no.	security code number	name	sector
87.	587570	GESTRA	machinery
88.	587800	Gildemeister AG	machinery
89.	587900	Girmes-AG	apparel
90.	590670	Grünzweig + Hartmann AG	construction
91.	522500	H. Berthold AG	machinery
92.	600500	HAGEDA AG	chemicals
93.	601300	Hamborner Bergbau AG	holding
94.	601150	Hamburger Getreide-Lagerhaus AG	holding
95.	601200	Hamburgische Electricitäts-Werke AG (HEW)	utility
96.	601950	Hanfwerke Oberachern AG, Achern	apparel
97.	503400	Hannoversche Papierfabriken Alfeld-Gronau AG	wood
98.	603400	Harpener AG, Dortmund	other
99.	603600	Hartmann & Braun AG, Frankfurt	electronics
100.	604700	Heidelberger Zement AG	ceramics
101.	604300	Heilmann & Littmann	construction
102.	604400	Hein, Lehmann AG, Düsseldorf	machinery
103.	611800	Heinrich Industrie- und Handels-AG	holding
104.	610700	Henniger-Bräu AG, Frankfurt am Main	food
105.	605310	Herlitz AG, Berlin	other
106.	606400	Hindrichs-Auffermann AG, Wuppertal	metallurgy
107.	607000	Hochtief AG	construction
108.	575800	Hoechst AG	chemicals
109.	620000	Hoesch AG	holding
110.	607600	Hoffmanns Stärkefabriken AG	food
111.	608370	Horten AG, Düsseldorf	trade
112.	524550	Hugo Boss AG, Metzingen	apparel
113.	609900	Hussel Holding AG, Hagen	holding
114.	610200	Hutschenreuther AG, Selb	ceramics
115.	609400	Hüttenwerke Kayser AG	metallurgy
116.	620440	Industrie-Werke Karlsruhe Augsburg AG (IKWA)	machinery
117.	690310	Jean Pascale AG	holding
118.	765850	Joseph Vögele AG, Mannheim	machinery
119.	716200	Kali und Salz AG, Kassel	other
120.	635000	Kali-Chemie AG	chemicals
121.	627500	KARSTADT AG	trade
122.	781900	Kaufhof AG	trade
123.	608700	Kempinski AG	other
124.	628300	KERAMAG Keramische Werke AG	ceramics
125.	630500	Klöckner-Humboldt-Deutz AG	machinery
126.	678000	Klöckner-Werke AG	metallurgy
127.	600300	KM kabelmetal AG	electronics
128.	629900	Kochs Adler AG, Bielefeld	machinery
129.	719350	Koenig & Bauer AG	machinery
130.	630280	Koepp AG	chemicals
131.	632030	Kolbenschmidt AG	other
132.	631800	Kötitzer Ledertuch- und Wachstuch-Werke AG	holding
133.	701900	Kraftübertragungswerke Rheinfelden AG	utility
134.	632800	Kraftwerk Altwürttemberg AG	utility

no.	security code number	name	sector
135.	633200	Krauss-Maffei AG	machinery
136.	633400	Kromschröder AG	electronics
137.	629200	KSB Klein,Schanzlin & Becker AG	machinery
138.	633800	Küppersbusch AG	electronics
139.	645200	Lahmeyer AG für Energiewirtschaft	utility
140.	645500	Langbein-Pfanhauser Werke AG (LPW)	holding
141.	645800	Lech-Elektrizitätswerke AG, Augsburg (LEW)	utility
142.	646370	Leffers AG	trade
143.	646450	Leifheit AG, Nassau/Lahn	electronics
144.	648300	Linde AG	machinery
145.	648500	Lindener Gilde-Bräu AG, Hannover	food
146.	649600	Löwenbräu AG, München	food
147.	823210	Lufthansa AG	other
148.	655260	Maho AG, Pfronten	machinery
149.	655400	Main-Kraftwerke AG	utility
150.	655500	Mainzer Aktien-Bierbrauerei AG	holding
151.	593700	MAN AG	holding
152.	656000	Mannesmann AG	metallurgy
153.	656900	Markt- und Kühlhallen AG	other
154.	569700	Maschinenfabrik Esslingen AG	holding
155.	658030	Mauser Waldeck AG	other
156.	658280	MCS Modulare Computer und Software Systeme AG	electronics
157.	659860	Mercedes-Automobil-Holding AG	holding
158.	660200	Metallgesellschaft AG	holding
159.	767700	MG Vermögensverwaltungs-AG	metallurgy
160.	662100	Moenus AG, Frankfurt	holding
161.	662800	Mühle Rüningen AG	food
162.	675800	Neckarwerke Elektrizitätsversorgungs-AG	utility
163.	686500	O & K Orenstein & Koppel AG	machinery
164.	685160	Oberland Glas AG, Bad Wurzach	ceramics
165.	726900	Oelmühle Hamburg AG	food
166.	687300	Otavi Minen AG	ceramics
167.	688950	Papierfabrik Weissenstein AG	wood
168.	690200	Parkbrauerei AG Pirmasens-Zweibrücken	food
169.	690220	Patrizier-Bräu AG	food
170.	627800	Pfleiderer Kunststoff AG	other
171.	608200	Philipp Holzmann AG, Frankfurt	construction
172.	576700	Phillips Kommunikations Industrie AG (PKI)	electronics
173.	603100	Phoenix AG, Hamburg	plastics
174.	692420	Piper Generalvertretung Deutschland AG	other
175.	760200	Pirelli Deutschland AG	plastics
176.	692500	Pittler Maschinenfabrik AG	machinery
177.	695200	PREUSSAG AG	metallurgy
178.	696800	Progress-Werk Oberkirch AG	electronics
179.	688980	PWA Papierwerke Waldhof-Aschaffenburg AG	holding
180.	700700	Reichelbräu AG	food
181.	702600	Rheinelektra AG	utility

no.	security code number	name	sector
182.	703700	Rheinisch-Westfälisches Elektrizitätswerke AG	utility
183.	703000	Rheinmetall Berlin AG	holding
184.	704900	Riedel-de Haën AG	chemicals
185.	706200	Rosenthal AG, Selb	ceramics
186.	707200	Rütgerswerke AG, Frankfurt	chemicals
187.	730500	Salamander AG	apparel
188.	717100	Scheidemandel AG	holding
189.	717200	Schering AG	chemicals
190.	730200	SCHIESS AG	machinery
191.	524700	Schloßquellbrauerei AG	food
192.	719230	Schmalbach-Lubeca AG	metallurgy
193.	720800	Schubert & Salzer Maschinenfabrik AG	machinery
194.	721670	Schumag AG	machinery
195.	721870	Schwäbische Zellstoff AG	wood
196.	558700	Seebeckwerft AG	other
197.	568400	Seitz Enzinger Noll Maschinenbau AG (SEN)	machinery
198.	723600	Siemens AG	electronics
199.	724000	Sinalco AG	food
200.	500900	Sommer-Allibert Industrie AG	holding
201.	733100	Spinnstoffabrik Zehlendorf AG	chemicals
202.	725000	Stahlwerke Bochum AG	metallurgy
203.	620200	Stahlwerke Peine-Salzgitter AG	metallurgy
204.	661900	Standard Elektrik Lorenz AG	electronics
205.	727380	Stinnes AG	other
206.	727400	Stock AG	machinery
207.	727700	Stöhr & Co. AG	apparel
208.	727900	Stolberger Zink AG	holding
209.	728000	Stollwerck AG	food
210.	728300	STRABAG-AG	construction
211.	728200	Stumpf AG	chemicals
212.	731800	Stuttgarter Hofbräu AG	food
213.	729700	Süddeutsche Zucker-AG, Mannheim	food
214.	734660	Südwestdeutsche Salzwerke AG, Heilbronn	other
215.	589300	Th. Goldschmidt AG	chemicals
216.	748100	Thüga AG	other
217.	748500	Thyssen AG	holding
218.	703300	Thyssen Industrie AG	holding
219.	778300	TIW Beteiligungs- und Grundbesitz AG	ceramics
220.	748840	TRAUB AG	machinery
221.	749490	TRIUMPH INTERNATIONAL AG	apparel
222.	525100	Tucher Bräu AG	food
223.	756500	Überlandwerk Unterfranken AG	utility
224.	761440	VEBA AG	holding
225.	767800	Vereinigte Altenburger & Stralsunder Spielkarten-Fabrik AG	wood
226.	761200	Vereinigte Deutsche Nickel-Werke AG (VDN)	metallurgy
227.	762900	Vereinigte Kunstmühlen AG	food
228.	764400	VERSEIDAG AG	apparel

no.	security code number	name	sector
229.	761560	VGT AG	holding
230.	766400	Volkswagen AG	automotive
231.	775600	Wanderer-Werke AG	holding
232.	775700	WASAG-CHEMIE AG	holding
233.	777760	Westfälische Zellstoff AG	wood
234.	780300	WMF Württembergische Metallwarenfabrik AG	electronics
235.	779900	Württembergische Elektrizitäts-AG (WEAG)	utility
236.	785210	Zanders Feinpapiere AG	wood
237.	787200	Zeiss Ikon AG	electronics

Table A-1: Companies included in the analyses[1]

A.2 Financial Behavior in the Industrial Firm

	d_l/fa difference	sig	d_s/fa difference	sig	e/fa difference	sig	fcf/fa difference	sig
expected sign	+		+ (o)		–		–	
block ownership	.0465		-.1355		-.0015		.1924	
size	.0098		-.0569		-.1104		-.8265	*
market segment	.0490		-.5211		-.0919		.0062	
dividend signal	N/A		N/A		N/A		N/A	
leverage	.1237		.8721	***	-.0117		-.0283	
agency1	.0435		.2335		-.0859		.1104	
agency2	.0519		-.1015		-.1032	*	.0786	
agency3	.1211		.7814	**	-.0032		.0557	
agency4	.0256		-.0672		-.1768		-.8149	
agency5	.0456		-.0039		.0086		.0811	
agency6	.0563		.0099		-.0504		.0093	
agency7	.0380		-1.0811		.0719		.2587	
expected sign	+		o		+		–	
monitored debt ratio	.0932		.5482	**	-.0964	**	-.0319	

N = 118; *** = significant at 1 %-level (** = 5 %; * = 10 %)

Table A-2: T-tests for differences of means of finance measures for groups with and without agency problems, by agency variable, chemicals sector

1 The full names of the sectors are: **apparel** = leather, fabrics, apparel; **automotive** = automobiles and accessories; **ceramics** = mining, ceramics, glass; **construction**; **chemicals**; **electronics** = electronics and precision mechanics; **food** = food, beverages, tabacco; **holdings** = holdings, participation acquisition, and property administration; **machinery**; **metallurgy**; **other** = other sectors, including diversified firms; **plastics** = plastics and rubber; **trade**; **wood** = wood, paper, printing; **utility** = water and energy utilities.

	d_l/fa difference	sig	d_s/fa difference	sig	e/fa difference	sig	fcf/fa difference	sig
expected sign	+		+ (o)		–		–	
block ownership	.0182		.0144		.0637		.3307	
size	-.0447		-.0562		.0834		-.1843	
market segment	-.0175		-.0210		.0611		-.6281	*
dividend signal	.0203		.0542		-.2980		.3699	
leverage	.0201		.0855		-.1630	***	.0439	
agency1	.0198		.0332		-.0005		.2493	
agency2	.0198		.0332		-.0005		.2493	
agency3	.0161		.3941	***	-.1067		.0153	
agency4	-.0447		-.0562		.0834		-.1843	
agency5	.0184		.0053		-.0138		.7280	
agency6	.0212		.2575	**	.0147		-.5052	
agency7	.0113		-.1619		.1304		.1110	
expected sign	+		o		+		–	
monitored debt ratio	.0274		.0534		.0715		-.1607	

N = 79; *** = significant at 1 %-level (** = 5 %; * = 10 %)

Table A-3: T-tests for differences of means of finance measures for groups with and without agency problems, by agency variable, electronics sector

	d_l/fa difference	sig	d_s/fa difference	sig	e/fa difference	sig	fcf/fa difference	sig
expected sign	+		+ (o)		–		–	
block ownership	N/A		N/A		N/A		N/A	
size	.0006		.0675		-.0283		-.3255	**
market segment	.0123	*	-.0129		-.0460		-.0294	
dividend signal	.0203		.0255		-.0758		.2309	
leverage	-.0020		.1461	**	-.0820	***	-.0622	
agency1	.0135		.0690		-.0859		-.3554	
agency2	.0217	***	.0593		-.0634		-.2969	
agency3	.0033		.1378	***	-.1030	***	-.0886	
agency4	.0137	*	.0357		-.0692		-.2455	
agency5	.0203		.0255		-.0758		.2309	
agency6	.0053		.0809		-.0978	*	-.0052	
agency7	.0203		.0255		-.0758		.2309	
expected sign	+		o		+		–	
monitored debt ratio	.0118		.0876		.0083		-.1837	

N = 158; *** = significant at 1 %-level (** = 5 %; * = 10 %)

Table A-4: T-tests for differences of means of finance measures for groups with and without agency problems, by agency variable, food & beverages sector

	d_l/fa difference	sig	d_s/fa difference	sig	e/fa difference	sig	fcf/fa difference	sig
expected sign	–		+ (o)		–		+	
block ownership	-4.78 %		-43.72 %	*	6.72 %	*	9.58 %	
agency5	-5.00 %		-38.08 %		7.29 %	*	3.43 %	

*** = significant at 1 %-level (** = 5 %; * = 10 %)

Table A-5: T-tests for differences of means of the finance measures between owner-controlled and creditor-controlled companies, chemicals sector[2]

	d_l/fa difference	sig	d_s/fa difference	sig	e/fa difference	sig	fcf/fa difference	sig
expected sign	–		+ (o)		–		+	
block ownership	-1.33 %		-2.86 %		-3.27 %		13.34 %	
agency5	-1.44 %		-3.01 %		-4.16 %		13.76 %	

*** = significant at 1 %-level (** = 5 %; * = 10 %)

Table A-6: T-tests for differences of means of the finance measures between owner-controlled and creditor-controlled companies, electronics sector[3]

	d_l/fa difference	sig	d_s/fa difference	sig	e/fa difference	sig	fcf/fa difference	sig
expected sign	–		+ (o)		–		+	
block ownership	-0.79 %		-5.82 %		-0.55 %		12.21 %	
agency5	-0.71 %		-5.72 %		-0.84 %		13.09 %	

*** = significant at 1 %-level (** = 5 %; * = 10 %)

Table A-7: T-tests for differences of means of the finance measures between owner-controlled and creditor-controlled companies, food & beverages sector[4]

	dependent variable			
independent variables	d_l/fa	d_s/fa	e/fa	fcf/fa
expected sign	+	+ (o)	–	–
block ownership	.7236	.5419	1.2683	-.0730
size	.6061 ***	.9497 ***	.7915 **	-.5230 **
market segment 1	16.6136	.8472	4.5903	-5.6652
market segment 2	7.8927	-2.8235	.3909	-2.4321
dividend signal	-27.4410	-16.5225 ***	-18.6174	13.7180
leverage	1.0097 ***	.4002 *	-.5222	2.0431
-2 log likelihood‡	87.437 ***	76.354 ***	56.518 ***	84.157 ***
% correct	83.90	85.59	90.68	80.51

2 Differences are to the companies that count as monitored by creditors according to the ratio of monitored to unmonitored debt.

3 Differences are to the companies that count as monitored by creditors according to the ratio of monitored to unmonitored debt.

4 Differences are to the companies that count as monitored by creditors according to the ratio of monitored to unmonitored debt.

	dependent variable			
independent variables	d_l/fa	d_s/fa	e/fa	fcf/fa
expected sign	+	+ (o)	–	–
classification				
agency1	-1.7044 ***	-2.1690 ***	-2.9178 ***	2.1690 ***
-2 log likelihood‡	119.654 ***	104.265 ***	84.234 ***	104.265 ***
% correct classification	65.52	71.55	69.83	80.17
agency5	-1.6737 ***	-2.2882 ***	-2.8904 ***	2.1401 ***
-2 log likelihood‡	121.748 ***	102.174 ***	86.793 ***	106.599 ***
% correct classification	63.79	71.55	68.10	80.17
% random classification	69.66	70.74	83.09	68.62

N = 118; *** = significant on the 1 % level (** = 5 %; * = 10 %); ‡ = significance of model chi-square

Table A-8: Coefficients and overall results of the logistic seemingly unrelated regressions on the finance dummy variables for the first hypothesis, chemicals sector[5]

	dependent variable			
independent variables	d_l/fa	d_s/fa	e/fa	fcf/fa
expected sign	+	+ (o)	–	–
block ownership	-1.7301 *	-.0731	-2.8842 **	-.5669
size	-.1733	.0459	.0661	.4791 **
market segment	1.4693	1.1849	1.7203	-.5703
dividend signal	.2983	-3.1823 *	-2.6123 *	-6.3524 **
leverage	.9521 *	.7255	-1.7292	-.6571
-2 log likelihood‡	66.299 ***	75.184 ***	33.299 ***	76.487 ***
% correct classification	79.75	78.48	94.94	82.28
agency1	-1.4213 ***	-1.1741 ***	-2.5951 ***	1.8873 ***
-2 log likelihood‡	80.639 ***	88.408 ***	46.021 ***	96.628 ***
% correct classification	73.14	69.62	87.54	65.82
agency5	-1.4552 ***	-1.2098 ***	-2.6244 ***	-.9258 ***
-2 log likelihood‡	78.718 ***	86.696 ***	43.532 ***	95.212 ***
% correct classification	75.95	72.15	89.87	68.35

5 The market segment dummy 1 is one for official continuous trade, the second dummy is one for official daily trade.

	dependent variable			
independent variables	d_l/fa	d_s/fa	e/fa	fcf/fa
expected sign	+	+ (o)	–	–
% random classification	70.84	66.22	83.85	59.81

N = 79; *** = significant on the 1 % level (** = 5 %; * = 10 %); ‡ = significance of model chi-square

Table A-9: Coefficients and overall results of the logistic seemingly unrelated regressions on the finance dummy variables for the first hypothesis, electronics sector[6]

	dependent variable			
independent variables	d_l/fa	d_s/fa	e/fa	fcf/fa
expected sign	+	+ (o)	–	–
block ownership	-3.9809 ***	-2.1032 **	-1.5560	-4.7057 ***
size	.2093 *	.0473	.0226	.3454 ***
market segment 1	1.0632 *	.2439	-.2420	.1421
market segment 2	1.9315 **	.2796	.0554	-.0466
dividend signal	-2.0055 *	-.7956	.3599	-1.0501
leverage	.5713 **	.5703 **	-1.4062 ***	-.2040
-2 log likelihood[‡]	154.094 ***	164.452 ***	131.808 ***	178.987 ***
% correct classification	75.95	75.32	82.91	70.25
agency1	-1.0217 ***	-1.0598 ***	-1.6449 ***	-.5108 ***
-2 log likelihood[‡]	187.693 ***	185.612 ***	150.881 ***	210.444 ***
% correct classification	65.19	65.19	75.32	54.43
agency5	-1.0986 ***	-1.1340 ***	-1.5781 ***	-.6538 ***
-2 log likelihood[‡]	179.268 ***	177.035 ***	147.413 ***	203.614 ***
% correct classification	72.78	72.78	80.38	63.29
% random classification	62.82	64.13	71.66	55.84

N = 158; *** = significant on the 1 % level (** = 5 %; * = 10 %); ‡ = significance of model chi-square

Table A-10: Coefficients and overall results of the logistic seemingly unrelated regressions on the finance dummy variables for the first hypothesis, food & beverages sector[7]

6 The market segment dummy 1 is one for official (continuous trade), 0 for unofficial trade. The second dummy for official daily trade was omitted, as there are no companies traded this way in the sector.

7 The market segment dummy 1 is one for official continuous trade, the second dummy is one for official daily trade.

	dependent variable			
independent variables	d_l/fa	d_s/fa	e/fa	fcf/fa
expected sign	+	o	+	–
leverage	-.7129 ***	-.7367 ***	-4.6877 ***	3.3430 ***
monitored debt ratio	.3227	-.0693	-3.6094	-.6997
-2 log likelihood[‡]	144.424 ***	-.7129 ***	75.997 ***	98.832 ***
% correct classification	66.95	75.42	83.90	79.66
% random classification	69.66	70.74	83.09	68.62

N = 118; *** = significant on the 1 % level (** = 5 %; * = 10 %); ‡ = significance of model chi-square

Table A-11: Coefficients and overall results of the logistic seemingly unrelated regressions on the finance dummy variables for the second hypothesis, chemicals sector

	dependent variable			
independent variables	d_l/fa	d_s/fa	e/fa	fcf/fa
expected sign	+	o	+	–
leverage	-.3002	-.3231	-2.8451 ***	-.3595
monitored debt ratio	-4.3795 **	-4.2900 **	-8.8629 **	-10.1119 **
-2 log likelihood[‡]	96.814 ***	96.843 ***	57.743 ***	78.446 ***
% correct classification	79.75	75.95	91.14	72.15
% random classification	70.84	66.22	83.85	59.81

N = 79; *** = significant on the 1 % level (** = 5 %; * = 10 %); ‡ = significance of model chi-square

Table A-12: Coefficients and overall results of the logistic seemingly unrelated regressions on the finance dummy variables for the second hypothesis, electronics sector

	dependent variable			
independent variables	d_l/fa	d_s/fa	e/fa	fcf/fa
expected sign	+	o	+	–
leverage	-.3854 **	-.5086 ***	-2.1636 ***	-.3528 **
monitored debt ratio	-.8811	-.0623 ***	-.3750	-.5356
-2 log likelihood[‡]	206.387 ***	208.331 ***	140.128 ***	210.303 **
% correct classification	65.82	67.09	77.22	62.66
% random classification	62.82	64.13	71.66	55.84

N = 158; *** = significant on the 1 % level (** = 5 %; * = 10 %); ‡ = significance of model chi-square

Table A-13: Coefficients and overall results of the logistic seemingly unrelated regressions on the finance dummy variables for the second hypothesis, food & beverages sector

A.3 A Test of the Managerial Theory of Performance

	return on equity difference	sig	return on capital difference	sig	Sharpe ratio difference	sig	Tobin's q difference	sig
expected sign	+		+		o		+	
block ownership	.0687		.0085		-.4699		.1276	
size	-.0060		-.0035		.0898		-.0987	
market segment	-.0237		-.0088		-.1236		.0724	
dividend signal	.0217		.0192		.5758		.4901	
leverage	-.0671	*	-.0278	*	-.7375		-.8096	***
monitored debt ratio	-.0519	*	-.0083		.0305		-.5992	***
agency1	-.0868	*	-.0483		-1.0828		-.2023	
agency2	-.0368		-.0271		-.9550		-.0493	
agency3	-.0660	**	-.0264	***	-.3276		-.7028	***
agency4	-.0199		-.0132		-1.0672		-.0140	
agency5	.0127		.0011		-.4395		.0123	
agency6	-.0466		-.0233		-1.2895	**	-.2703	*
agency7	.0670		.0329		.0550		.5835	*

*** = significant at 1 %-level (** = 5 %; * = 10 %)

Table A-14: T-tests for differences of means of performance measures for groups with and without agency problems, by agency variable, 1986

	return on equity difference	sig	return on capital difference	sig	Sharpe ratio difference	sig	Tobin's q difference	sig
expected sign	+		+		o		+	
block ownership	.0776		.0128		.8528		.4455	***
size	.1040		.0298	**	-.2516		-.3394	***
market segment	-.0998		-.0074		.1977		.0270	
dividend signal	.0253		.0133		-2.0319	*	.1245	
leverage	-.1423	*	-.0503	***	-.5653		-.5049	***
monitored debt ratio	.0395		.0096		-.8144	*	-.4507	***
agency1	.0257		-.0058		-.7043		-.0674	
agency2	.0295		-.0031		-.6349		-.0264	
agency3	.0355		-.0207	*	.3654		-.1882	*
agency4	.0792		.0162		.3331		-.1465	
agency5	.0558		.0085		.0668		.3416	***
agency6	.0159		-.0109		.2595		.0518	
agency7	-.0040		-.0035		-1.1326		.2414	

*** = significant at 1 %-level (** = 5 %; * = 10 %)

Table A-15: T-tests for differences of means of performance measures for groups with and without agency problems, by agency variable, 1987

	return on equity difference	sig	return on capital difference	sig	Sharpe ratio difference	sig	Tobin's q difference	sig
expected sign	+		+		o		+	
block ownership	.0179		-.0054		-1.0771		.3816	***
size	.0224		.0087		.4447		-.1848	
market segment	-.0956		-.0213		.5168		.0703	
dividend signal	.0946		.0390		2.5121		.4373	
leverage	-.0579		-.0244	*	.9978		-.4090	***
monitored debt ratio	.0560		.0167	*	1.4105	***	-.4118	***
agency1	.0234		.0027		.4087		-.0831	
agency2	.0291		.0038		.2602		-.0397	
agency3	-.0728		-.0286	***	.7077		-.3761	***
agency4	.0117		.0008		.2857		-.1468	
agency5	.0214		-.0018		-.2756		.3568	**
agency6	-.1183		-.0308	*	.7033		-.0070	
agency7	-.0004		.0055		-.2432		.3864	

*** = significant at 1 %-level (** = 5 %; * = 10 %)

Table A-16: T-tests for differences of means of performance measures for groups with and without agency problems, by agency variable, 1989

	return on equity difference	sig	return on capital difference	sig	Sharpe ratio difference	sig	Tobin's q difference	sig
expected sign	+		+		o		+	
block ownership	.0323		.0048		.4601		.5628	***
size	-.0221		.0040		1.0438		-.4735	**
market segment	.0404		.0121		.5726		-.0299	
dividend signal	.0563		.0513		1.4982		-.2798	
leverage	-.0860	*	-.0166		.6285		-.2209	
monitored debt ratio	-.0401	*	-.0047		-1.1315	*	-.3199	**
agency1	.0090		.0044		.8359		.2922	
agency2	.0128		-.0017		1.2098		.2677	
agency3	-.0407		-.0091		.2368		-.1070	
agency4	-.0246		-.0002		-.0934		-.2277	
agency5	.0387		.0080		.7080		.5012	***
agency6	-.0037		.0005		.6760		.1198	
agency7	.1350	*	.0381		3.9087	*	.3721	

*** = significant at 1 %-level (** = 5 %; * = 10 %)

Table A-17: T-tests for differences of means of performance measures for groups with and without agency problems, by agency variable, 1991

	return on equity		return on capital		Sharpe ratio		Tobin's q	
	difference	sig	difference	sig	difference	sig	difference	sig
expected sign	+		–		o		+	
block ownership	3.35 %		0.51 %		-0.0692		30.81 %	
agency5	2.68 %		0.42 %		-0.0606		29.57 %	

*** = significant at 1 %-level (** = 5 %; * = 10 %)

Table A-18: T-tests for differences of means of the performance measures between owner-controlled and creditor-controlled companies, 1986[8]

	return on equity		return on capital		Sharpe ratio		Tobin's q	
	difference	sig	difference	sig	difference	sig	difference	sig
expected sign	+		–		o		+	
block ownership	-1.29 %		-0.39 %		0.5643		31.25 %	***
agency5	-1.60 %		-0.45 %		0.4673		29.77 %	***

*** = significant at 1 %-level (** = 5 %; * = 10 %)

Table A-19: T-tests for differences of means of the performance measures between owner-controlled and creditor-controlled companies, 1987[9]

	return on equity		return on capital		Sharpe ratio		Tobin's q	
	difference	sig	difference	sig	difference	sig	difference	sig
expected sign	+		–		o		+	
block ownership	-3.01 %		-1.03 %		-0.9232		28.05 %	***
agency5	-3.00 %		-0.98 %		-0.8257		27.36 %	***

*** = significant at 1 %-level (** = 5 %; * = 10 %)

Table A-20: T-tests for differences of means of the performance measures between owner-controlled and creditor-controlled companies, 1989[10]

	return on equity		return on capital		Sharpe ratio		Tobin's q	
	difference	sig	difference	sig	difference	sig	difference	sig
expected sign	+		–		o		+	
block ownership	2.71 %		0.32 %		0.7056		24.95 %	**
agency5	2.76 %		0.35 %		0.7291		23.95 %	**

*** = significant at 1 %-level (** = 5 %; * = 10 %)

Table A-21: T-tests for differences of means of the performance measures between owner-controlled and creditor-controlled companies, 1991[11]

8 Differences are to the companies that count as monitored by creditors according to the ratio of monitored to unmonitored debt.

9 Differences are to the companies that count as monitored by creditors according to the ratio of monitored to unmonitored debt.

10 Differences are to the companies that count as monitored by creditors according to the ratio of monitored to unmonitored debt.

independent variables	dependent variable: return on equity	return on capital	Sharpe ratio	Tobin's q
expected sign	+	+	o	+
block ownership	-.3706	-.1850	.1367	-.0714
size	-.0344	-.0222	.0074	.0747
market segment 1	-.1258	-.5987	-.0327	-.0410
market segment 2	-.2310	-.7114	.8097	-.0157
dividend signal	1.0471	1.2357	.0920	.6512
leverage	-.2829 **	-.5627 ***	-.2338 *	-1.1481 ***
-2 log likelihood‡	231.840	217.828 ***	234.317	195.963 ***
% correct classification	58.96	63.58	54.34	68.79
leverage	-.2949 ***	-.5880 ***	-.1753 *	-.3532 ***
monitored debt ratio	.6389 *	.9227 **	.4087	.2358
-2 log likelihood‡	229.593 ***	214.258 ***	235.024 *	227.121 ***
% correct classification	55.49	63.01	53.18	46.82
agency1	-.2059	-.4430 ***	-.0256	.1027
-2 log likelihood‡	238.185	232.359 ***	239.803	239.418
% correct classification	55.49	60.79	51.45	53.76
agency5	-.1681	-.3787 **	-.0129	.0904
-2 log likelihood‡	238.737	234.371 **	239.822	239.513
% correct classification	53.76	57.80	50.87	53.76

N = 173; *** = significant on the 1 % level (** = 5 %; * = 10 %); ‡ = significance of model chi-square

Table A-22: Coefficients and overall results of the logistic regressions on the performance dummy variables, 1986[12]

11 Differences are to the companies that count as monitored by creditors according to the ratio of monitored to unmonitored debt.

12 The market segment dummy 1 is one for official continuous trade, the second dummy is one for official daily trade.

independent variables	dependent variable: return on equity		return on capital		Sharpe ratio		Tobin's q	
expected sign	+		+		o		+	
block ownership	-1.0384	**	-.9088	*	1.5847	*	2.3252	***
size	.0309		-.0324		-.0593		-.2402	***
market segment 1	-.6204		-.7840	*	-.0856		.1729	
market segment 2	-.9691		-.8866		.9545		-.5293	
dividend signal	.8501		1.5404	*	-2.4825	***	.6064	
leverage	-.4106	**	-.7197	***	.2088		-.6185	**
-2 log likelihood‡	232.399	**	215.044	***	130.451	***	174.090	***
% correct classification	56.50		64.41		86.59		75.71	
leverage	-.4961	***	-.9609	***	-.8239	***	-.9027	***
monitored debt ratio	.8315	*	.8246	*	-2.2910	***	-2.1592	**
-2 log likelihood‡	235.317	***	219.442	***	200.034	***	195.747	***
% correct classification	51.98		57.63		80.45		74.01	
agency1	-.2348		-.6161	***	-1.8608	***	-1.1872	***
-2 log likelihood‡	243.265		231.422	***	155.146	***	199.371	***
% correct classification	54.80		62.71		77.75		70.62	
agency5	-.2059		-.5520	***	-1.8216	***	-1.0314	***
-2 log likelihood‡	243.730		233.926	***	156.644	***	208.820	***
% correct classification	53.67		60.45		77.65		66.10	

N = 177; *** = significant on the 1 % level (** = 5 %; * = 10 %); ‡ = significance of model chi-square

Table A-23: Coefficients and overall results of the logistic regressions on the performance dummy variables, 1987[13]

[13] The market segment dummy 1 is one for official continuous trade, the second dummy is one for official daily trade.

independent variables	dependent variable: return on equity		return on capital		Sharpe ratio		Tobin's q	
expected sign	+		+		o		+	
block ownership	-.9258	*	-1.6395	***	.4523		.6943	
size	-.0530		.0067		-.0173		-.0836	
market segment 1	-.5723		-.7832	*	.1192		.2300	
market segment 2	-.1454		-.3197		-1.0536		.0989	
dividend signal	1.9975	**	1.9282	*	1.6276		.9235	
leverage	-.5171	***	-.3741	*	1.7547	**	-.6251	***
-2 log likelihood‡	228.564	**	225.608	**	94.326	***	227.757	**
% correct classification	60.34		60.92		90.59		58.62	
leverage	-.4636	***	-.4346	**	3.2990	***	-.2201	
monitored debt ratio	.8372	*	1.9682	***	10.0203	***	-.7896	*
-2 log likelihood‡	232.060	**	224.904	***	106.167	***	232.382	**
% correct classification	56.90		60.34		90.59		52.30	
agency1	-.0263		.1054		2.5292	***	.0000	
-2 log likelihood‡	241.189		240.794		107.612	***	241.215	
% correct classification	48.85		52.30		90.59		50.57	
agency5	-.0256		.0513		2.3695	***	.1284	
-2 log likelihood‡	241.190		241.113		113.741	***	240.574	
% correct classification	48.85		52.30		90.59		50.57	

N = 174; *** = significant on the 1 % level (** = 5 %; * = 10 %); ‡ = significance of model chi-square

Table A-24: Coefficients and overall results of the logistic regressions on the performance dummy variables, 1989[14]

---

[14] The market segment dummy 1 is one for official continuous trade, the second dummy is one for official daily trade.

independent variables	dependent variable return on equity	 return on capital	 Sharpe ratio	 Tobin's q
expected sign	+	+	o	+
block ownership	.1313	-1.1848 *	.0594	1.4552 **
size	-.1849 *	-.0446	.1202	-.1405
market segment 1	-.4212	-.4750	-.5457	.4993
market segment 2	-.9470	-.3683	-.2001	-.2593
dividend signal	2.7331 *	2.1480	-1.8829	.0404
leverage	-.2640	-.1130	-.1477	-.3043
-2 log likelihood‡	202.858 *	204.984	181.755 ***	185.701 ***
% correct classification	61.94	61.94	68.46	67.10
leverage	-.2042	-.0394	-.4129 **	-.2184
monitored debt ratio	-.2131	.2941	-.4066	-2.5904 ***
-2 log likelihood‡	209.521 *	213.581	192.819 ***	184.015 ***
% correct classification	56.77	56.13	67.79	64.52
agency1	-.1452	.3216 *	-.8082 ***	-.6285
-2 log likelihood‡	214.150	211.353 *	186.492 ***	201.888 ***
% correct classification	50.97	57.42	65.10	60.00
agency5	-.1297	.2751	-.7386 ***	-.6079 ***
-2 log likelihood‡	214.292	212.270	189.585 ***	202.600 ***
% correct classification	50.32	57.42	62.42	59.35

N = 155; *** = significant on the 1 % level (** = 5 %; * = 10 %); ‡ = significance of model chi-square

Table A-25: Coefficients and overall results of the logistic regressions on the performance dummy variables, 1991[15]

[15] The market segment dummy 1 is one for official continuous trade, the second dummy is one for official daily trade.

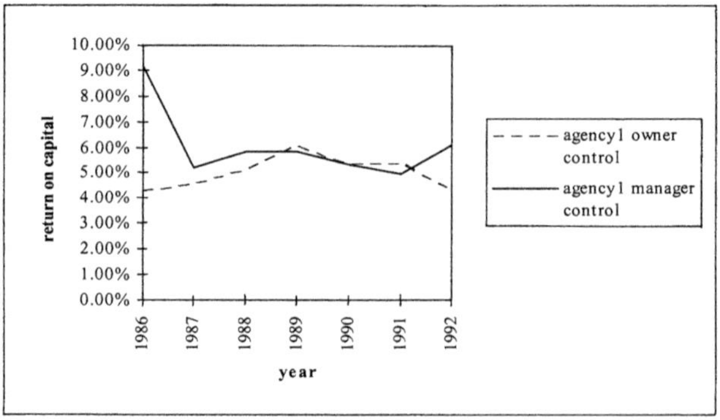

Figure A-1: Development of return on capital over time, by agency group (using *agency1* to distinguish)

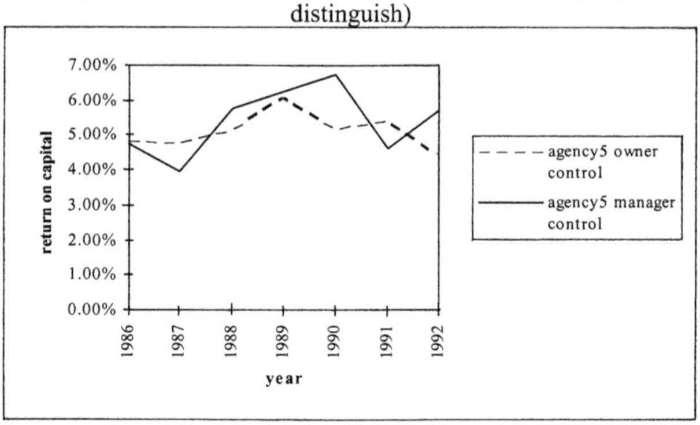

Figure A-2: Development of return on capital over time, by agency group (using *agency5* to distinguish)

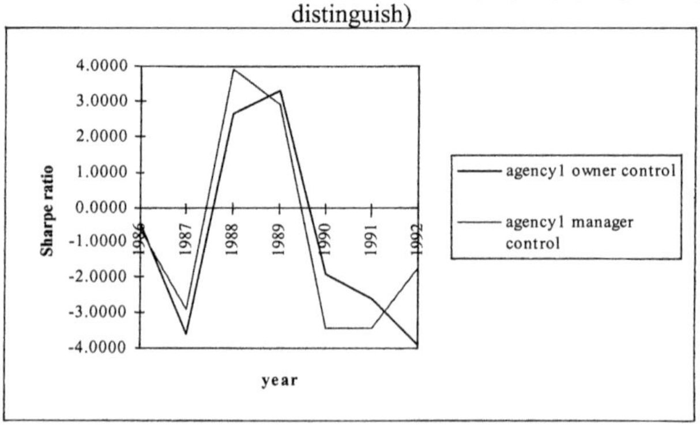

Figure A-3: Development of Sharpe ratio over time, by agency group (using *agency1* to distinguish)

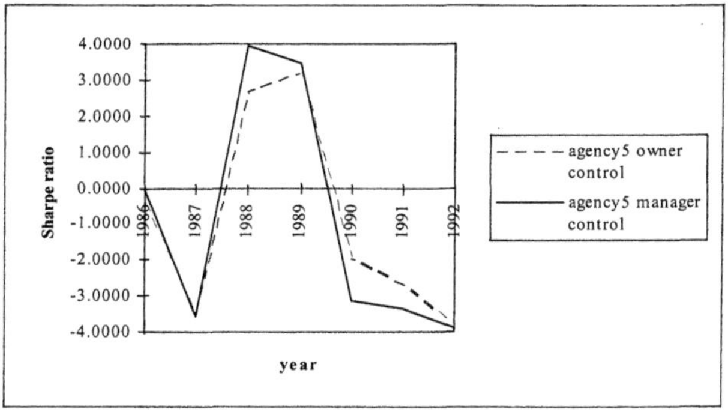

Figure A-4: Development of Sharpe ratio over time, by agency group (using *agency5* to distinguish)

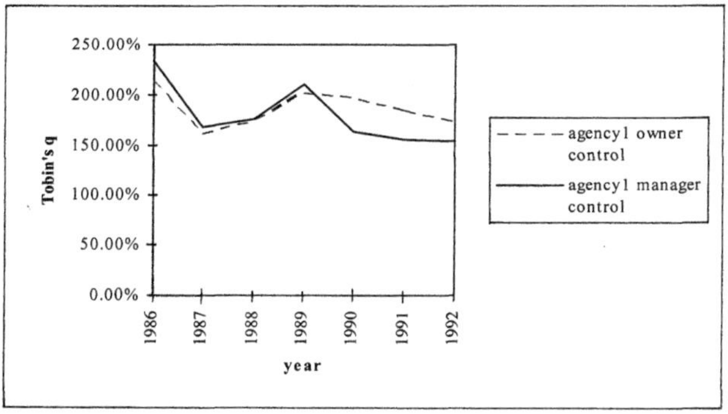

Figure A-5: Development of Tobin's q over time, by agency group (using *agency1* to distinguish)

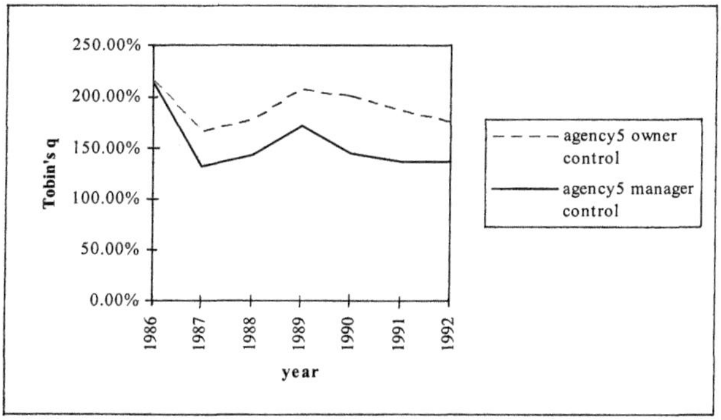

Figure A-6: Development of Tobin's q over time, by agency group (using *agency5* to distinguish)

	return on equity		return on capital		Sharpe ratio		Tobin's q	
	difference	sig	difference	sig	difference	sig	difference	sig
expected sign	+		+		o		+	
block ownership	.0450	**	-.0009		1.1155		.4818	***
size	.0367		.0231	*	-.3050		-.1382	
market segment	.0702	**	.0240	*	.2297		.0401	
dividend signal	N/A		N/A		N/A		N/A	
leverage	-.0669	***	-.0275	***	-.7210		-.6158	***
monitored debt ratio	-.0364	**	-.0163	**	.1216		-.4990	***
agency1	-.0116		-.0134	*	.2625		-.1930	
agency2	.0271		-.0023		.6211		.0655	
agency3	-.0281		-.0298		.5976		-.1339	
agency4	-.0564	**	-.0243	***	-.3482		-.6523	***
agency5	-.1690	**	-.0507	***	1.3530		-.1926	**
agency6	.1062		-.0143		.8607		-.2811	
agency7	.0428		.0254		1.3096		-.3670	*

*** = significant at 1 %-level (** = 5 %; * = 10 %)

Table A-26: T-tests for differences of means of performance measures for groups with and without agency problems, by agency variable, chemicals sector 1986-1992

	return on equity		return on capital		Sharpe ratio		Tobin's q	
	difference	sig	difference	sig	difference	sig	difference	sig
expected sign	+		+		o		+	
block ownership	.0723		.0081		-.2445		.4519	**
size	.0381		-.0035		-.3168		.4101	
market segment	-.1949		-.0157		-.5110		.0525	
dividend signal	.1336		.0409		1.3921		.1324	
leverage	-.1482		-.0283		1.8487		-.4075	
monitored debt ratio	.1501		.0221		-.2270		-.5823	***
agency1	.0964		.0238		.5073		.8302	***
agency2	.0964		.0238		.5073		.8302	***
agency3	.1062		-.0143		1.1224		-.2811	
agency4	.0381		-.0035		-.3168		.4101	
agency5	.0770		.0161		.5816		.6931	***
agency6	.0201		-.0148		.3971		-.0253	
agency7	.0875		.0269		-2.1787		.6823	***

*** = significant at 1 %-level (** = 5 %; * = 10 %)

Table A-27: T-tests for differences of means of performance measures for groups with and without agency problems, by agency variable, electronics sector 1986-1992

	return on equity		return on capital		Sharpe ratio		Tobin's q	
	difference	sig	difference	sig	difference	sig	difference	sig
expected sign	+		+		o		+	
block ownership	N/A		N/A		N/A		N/A	
size	.0551	***	.0288	***	.4078		.4633	***
market segment	.0041		.0058		-.1215		.4676	***
dividend signal	.0480	***	.0330	***	.3374		.1021	
leverage	-.0046		.0075		.7860		-.4317	**
monitored debt ratio	.0049		.0143	***	-.0667		-.9167	***
agency1	.0441	***	.0271	***	.4414		.0912	
agency2	.0529	***	.0309	***	.8122		.0870	
agency3	-.0031		.0018		.6005		-.0046	
agency4	.0314	***	.0209	***	-.3429		.3731	**
agency5	.0480	***	.0330	***	.3374		.1021	
agency6	.0109		.0106	*	.0659		.1898	
agency7	.0480	***	.0330	***	.3374		.1021	

*** = significant at 1 %-level (** = 5 %; * = 10 %)

Table A-28: T-tests for differences of means of performance measures for groups with and without agency problems, by agency variable, food & beverages sector 1986-1992

	return on equity		return on capital		Sharpe ratio		Tobin's q	
	difference	sig	difference	sig	difference	sig	difference	sig
expected sign	+		–		o		+	
block ownership	3.87 %	*	1.03 %		0.2944		48.46 %	***
agency5	3.20 %		0.86 %		0.3144		42.89 %	***

*** = significant at 1 %-level (** = 5 %; * = 10 %)

Table A-29: T-tests for differences of means of the performance measures between owner-controlled and creditor-controlled companies, chemicals sector 1986-1992[16]

	return on equity		return on capital		Sharpe ratio		Tobin's q	
	difference	sig	difference	sig	difference	sig	difference	sig
expected sign	+		–		o		+	
block ownership	-6.92 %		-1.06 %		0.0858		37.01 %	**
agency5	-7.39 %		-1.06 %		0.1602		35.54 %	**

*** = significant at 1 %-level (** = 5 %; * = 10 %)

Table A-30: T-tests for differences of means of the performance measures between owner-controlled and creditor-controlled companies, electronics sector 1986-1992[17]

---

16 Differences are to the companies that count as monitored by creditors according to the ratio of monitored to unmonitored debt.

17 Differences are to the companies that count as monitored by creditors according to the ratio of monitored to unmonitored debt.

	return on equity		return on capital		Sharpe ratio		Tobin's q	
	difference	sig	difference	sig	difference	sig	difference	sig
expected sign	+		–		o		+	
block ownership	-0.33 %		-0.96 %	**	0.0448		61.52 %	***
agency5	-0.14 %		-0.82 %	*	0.0584		61.93 %	***

*** = significant at 1 %-level (** = 5 %; * = 10 %)

Table A-31: T-tests for differences of means of the performance measures between owner-controlled and creditor-controlled companies, food & beverages sector 1986-1992[18]

independent variables	dependent variable: return on equity		return on capital		Sharpe ratio		Tobin's q	
expected sign	+		+		o		+	
block ownership	.9209		-.6710		-.2120		1.0120	
size	.1482		.0764		-.2267	*	-.2363	
market segment 1	-.2567		-.2925		1.0315		-1.9646	*
market segment 2	-8.2590		-7.7445		.5924		-9.4046	
dividend signal	-1.8253		-.1561		2.2550		4.6261	**
leverage	-.2023		-.2079		-.0251		-.8855	***
-2 log likelihood‡	141.321	***	144.614	**	152.475		117.272	***
% correct classification	69.57		65.22		59.29		71.30	
leverage	-1.1743	**	-.1695		-.1534		-.4777	*
monitored debt ratio	-2.3931		-.0005		.6794		-1.3168	
-2 log likelihood‡	83.298	***	156.452		154.144		133.774	***
% correct classification	81.94		53.91		52.21		66.96	
agency1	-.0953		-.3857	*	.1466		-.8587	**
-2 log likelihood‡	159.233		156.358	*	156.212		145.259	***
% correct classification	53.91		63.48		49.56		64.25	

18 Differences are to the companies that count as monitored by creditors according to the ratio of monitored to unmonitored debt.

independent variables	dependent variable: return on equity	return on capital	Sharpe ratio	Tobin's q
expected sign	+	+	o	+
agency5	.1466	-.2451	.2007	-.4463 **
-2 log likelihood‡	158.984	158.201	155.850	155.440 **
% correct classification	50.43	58.26	49.56	50.43

N = 115; *** = significant on the 1 % level (** = 5 %; * = 10 %); ‡ = significance of model chi-square

Table A-32: Coefficients and overall results of the logistic regressions on the performance dummy variables, chemicals sector 1986-1992[19]

independent variables	dependent variable: return on equity	return on capital	Sharpe ratio	Tobin's q
expected sign	+	+	o	+
block ownership	2.4179	-1.3793	.5605	1.8136 *
size	-.1511	-.2144	-.0266	.0200
market segment 1	-1.2170	-.1629	-.2821	.0326
dividend signal	-.7751	4.2406 *	.0828	-2.1991
leverage	-.1166	-1.0049 **	.1165	-.1391
-2 log likelihood‡	57.644 ***	91.618	98.325	88.135 **
% correct classification	81.94	68.06	54.17	65.28
leverage	-1.1743 **	-.9635 **	.0622	-.1021
monitored debt ratio	-2.3931	2.7114 *	-.0249	-4.4751 **
-2 log likelihood‡	83.298 ***	94.154 *	99.778	89.046 ***
% correct classification	81.94	58.33	47.22	65.28
agency1	-1.3863 ***	-.0924	.0308	-.4700 *
-2 log likelihood‡	74.756 ***	99.675	99.798	96.320 *
% correct classification	72.22	50.00	50.00	55.56

19 The market segment dummy 1 is one for official continuous trade, the second dummy is one for official daily trade.

independent variables	dependent variable return on equity		return on capital		Sharpe ratio		Tobin's q	
expected sign	+		+		o		+	
agency5	-1.4240	***	-.0896		.0299		-.5188	**
-2 log likelihood‡	72.861	***	99.679		99.798		95.452	**
% correct classification	75.00		50.00		50.00		58.44	

N = 72; *** = significant on the 1 % level (** = 5 %; * = 10 %); ‡ = significance of model chi-square

Table A-33: Coefficients and overall results of the logistic regressions on the performance dummy variables, electronics sector 1986-1992[20]

independent variables	dependent variable return on equity		return on capital		Sharpe ratio		Tobin's q	
expected sign	+		+		o		+	
block ownership	-4.2384	***	-5.6466	***	.7434		1.3685	
size	.2176	*	.3142	***	-.0730		-.0884	
market segment 1	-.5750		-.4025		.0206		.7167	*
market segment 2	.4686		.1377		1.1981	*	.0363	
dividend signal	1.1473		1.1142		.3182		-.6019	
leverage	-.5363	**	-.0390		-.1098		-.0280	
-2 log likelihood‡	179.675	***	171.213	***	201.236		199.172	
% correct classification	68.46		71.81		57.72		54.36	
leverage	-.4438	**	-.1840		.0618		.2188	
monitored debt ratio	1.0151	*	2.9967	**	-.5710		-3.3840	**
-2 log likelihood‡	198.474	*	193.185	***	204.963		191.718	***
% correct classification	59.06		67.69		47.65		58.39	
agency1	-.0953		.3202	*	.0635		-.1911	
-2 log likeli-	206.272		203.370	*	206.431		205.413	

20 The market segment dummy 1 is one for official continuous trade, the second dummy is one for official daily trade. The second market segment dummy was omitted, as its value was constant.

independent variables	dependent variable return on equity	return on capital	Sharpe ratio	Tobin's q
expected sign	+	+	o	+
hood‡				
% correct classification	45.64	50.34	51.68	53.69
agency5	-.2673	.0980	.0700	-.1542
-2 log likelihood‡	204.026	206.215	206.383	205.711
% correct classification	54.36	50.34	51.68	53.02

N = 149; *** = significant on the 1 % level (** = 5 %; * = 10 %); ‡ = significance of model chi-square

Table A-34: Coefficients and overall results of the logistic regressions on the performance dummy variables, food & beverages sector 1986-1992[21]

independent variables	dependent variable return on equity	return on capital	Sharpe ratio	Tobin's q
expected sign	+	+	o	+
block ownership	-2.1783	.1564	-1.3808	1.0522
size	-1.6031 ***	-.3112	.0092	-.5098 *
market segment 1	14.4012	-.9793	7.8074	6.8558
market segment 2	7.1565	-1.3507	8.5364	.2347
dividend signal	8.4029	6.9006	-7.4008	-.4969
leverage	2.0756 **	-3.8726 ***	.8429	-2.2882 **
-2 log likelihood‡	82.834 ***	84.570 ***	113.951	85.388 ***
% correct classification	75.28	82.02	62.50	78.65
leverage	-.5862	-2.6633 ***	.2524	-2.2967 ***
monitored debt ratio	.1626	2.8924 ***	.0714	.5968
-2 log likelihood‡	120.834	92.471 ***	121.318	95.928 ***
% correct classification	57.30	74.16	50.00	67.42

21 The market segment dummy 1 is one for official continuous trade, the second dummy is one for official daily trade.

independent variables	dependent variable: return on equity		return on capital		Sharpe ratio		Tobin's q	
expected sign	+		+		o		+	
agency1	-.2942		-.2029		.0000		-.8313	***
-2 log likelihood‡	121.475		122.469		121.994		109.237	***
% correct classification	57.30		55.06		50.00		69.66	
agency5	-.2336		-.1866		-.0235		-.7817	***
-2 log likelihood‡	122.215		122.635		121.982		111.182	***
% correct classification	53.93		53.93		51.14		66.29	

N = 89; *** = significant on the 1 % level (** = 5 %; * = 10 %); ‡ = significance of model chi-square

Table A-35: Coefficients and overall results of the logistic regressions on the performance dummy variables, utilities sector 1986-1992[22]

A.4 Agency Problems and Efficiency in the Firm

variable		minim.	median	mean	maxim.	std. dev.
	total assets*)	14.31	285.43	1694.07	27903.25	4415.16
C	costs*)	7.22	111.06	724.15	16150.30	2080.80
y_1	sales and self-constructed assets*)	9.80	396.45	2340.58	47628.65	6905.62
y_2	interest earnings and earnings from affiliated companies**)	35.72	5238.84	51903.63	992595.21	154805.00
x_1	labor***)	35	1317	7899.16	166523	21862.76
x_2	tangible and intangible fixed assets**)	2197.15	66800.63	544459.68	8386764.4	1299134.4
x_3	financial capital**)	.00	20501.40	251759.73	5134085.6	841920.05
w_1	salary or wages plus social costs**)	37.18	70.27	70.05	116.30	15.07
w_2	depreciation on tangible and intangible fixed assets****)	.046	.295	.309	1.139	.178
w_3	cost of financial assets (via stock return as opportunity earning*****)	-.719	.073	.087	1.513	.285

N =125 *) millions of 1992 DM **) thousands of 1992 DM ***) no. of employees ****) 1 = 100 % *****) ln(return + 1)

Table A-36: Netputs and 1986 summary statistics of the cross sectional cost functions

variable		minim.	median	mean	maxim.	std. dev.
	total assets*)	13.04	340.88	1407.96	31503.60	3849.86
C	costs*)	3.19	127.39	451.67	13330.97	1314.18
y_1	sales and self-constructed assets*)	12.67	460.51	1698.37	47640.60	4902.02
y_2	interest earnings and earnings from affiliated companies**)	11.50	7738.84	39637.13	883085.42	106988.84

22 The market segment dummy 1 is one for official continuous trade, the second dummy is one for official daily trade.

variable	minim.	median	mean	maxim.	std. dev.
x_1 labor***)	80	15400	5780.34	169234	16972.69
x_2 tangible and intangible fixed assets**)	2145.62	71782.85	448336.90	12258782.	1503593.3
x_3 financial capital**)	.00	31567.99	236551.32	4778777.2	630928.18
w_1 salary or wages plus social costs**)	40.53	74.14	73.46	124.05	17.60
w_2 depreciation on tangible and intangible fixed assets****)	.041	.288	.317	1.375	.190
w_3 cost of financial assets (via stock return as opportunity earning*****)	-.996	-.194	-.237	.379	.275

N =123 *) millions of 1992 DM **) thousands of 1992 DM ***) no. of employees ****) 1 = 100 % *****) ln(return + 1)

Table A-37: Netputs and 1987 summary statistics of the cross sectional cost functions

variable	minim.	median	mean	maxim.	std. dev.
total assets*)	8.33	335.09	1403.92	33086.14	3891.92
C costs*)	1.34	139.90	584.49	17728.81	1706.71
y_1 sales and self-constructed assets*)	2.16	413.50	1637.24	47478.18	4738.01
y_2 interest earnings and earnings from affiliated companies**)	2.27	6026.29	44892.47	1186188.9	133944.00
x_1 labor***)	19	1253	5602.51	170577	16598.47
x_2 tangible and intangible fixed assets**)	583.45	70994.23	369483.64	11993102.	1271316.8
x_3 financial capital**)	.00	30447.02	264473.68	5963860.0	791424.01
w_1 salary/wage rate plus social costs**)	38.43	74.33	74.82	131.60	18.36
w_2 depreciation rate on tangible and intangible fixed assets****)	.038	.273	.315	1.855	.210
w_3 cost of financial assets (via stock return as opportunity earning*****)	-.501	.237	.264	1.042	.239

N =135 *) millions of 1992 DM **) thousands of 1992 DM ***) no. of employees ****) 1 = 100 % *****) ln(return + 1)

Table A-38: Netputs and 1988 summary statistics of the cross sectional cost functions

variable	minim.	median	mean	maxim.	std. dev.
total assets*)	8.76	333.00	1633.16	53351.94	5268.54
C costs*)	1.91	160.23	731.68	24521.33	2337.37
y_1 sales and self-constructed assets*)	1.84	453.75	1528.28	46052.70	4522.91
y_2 interest earnings and earnings from affiliated companies**)	5.52	8353.04	58324.72	2083288.2	207533.49
x_1 labor***)	20	1287	5406.29	205300	18724.95
x_2 tangible and intangible fixed assets**)	43.08	75788.16	384027.15	11028502.	1244469.2
x_3 financial capital**)	.00	36347.08	364526.89	10848230.	1149061.1
w_1 salary/wage rate plus social costs**)	38.39	74.38	76.22	140.67	19.00
w_2 depreciation rate on tangible and intangible fixed assets****)	.045	.264	.453	20.298	1.711
w_3 cost of financial assets (via stock return as opportunity earning*****)	-.229	.369	.385	1.071	.242

N =139 *) millions of 1992 DM **) thousands of 1992 DM ***) no. of employees ****) 1 = 100 % *****) ln(return + 1)

Table A-39: Netputs and 1989 summary statistics of the cross sectional cost functions

variable	minim.	median	mean	maxim.	std. dev.
total assets*)	10.09	370.79	1510.19	53499.56	5043.55
C costs*)	.79	134.09	477.97	17640.61	1664.92
y_1 sales and self-constructed assets*)	1.88	467.65	1559.04	45137.59	4460.08
y_2 interest earnings and earnings from	3.23	9449.60	54506.90	2157211.0	201162.56

variable		minim.	median	mean	maxim.	std. dev.
	affiliated companies**)					
x_1	labor***)	20	1420.5	5510.06	206200	19619.82
x_2	tangible and intangible fixed assets**)	448.57	75623.39	327071.03	6741095.0	873662.58
x_3	financial capital**)	.00	54817.18	362393.13	15458360.	1432421.8
w_1	salary/wage rate plus social costs**)	39.56	77.13	79.18	135.00	19.65
w_2	depreciation rate on tangible and intangible fixed assets****)	.025	.269	.302	1.200	.184
w_3	cost of financial assets (via stock return as opportunity earning*****)	-.803	-.001	-.018	.660	.288

N =126 *) millions of 1992 DM **) thousands of 1992 DM ***) no. of employees ****) 1 = 100 % *****) ln(return + 1)

Table A-40: Netputs and 1990 summary statistics of the cross sectional cost functions

variable		minim.	median	mean	maxim.	std. dev.
	total assets*)	11.10	359.63	1674.10	52184.90	5077.16
C	costs*)	1.39	123.29	537.45	20443.24	1960.02
y_1	sales and self-constructed assets*)	2.31	466.65	1538.65	41351.99	4217.45
y_2	interest earnings and earnings from affiliated companies**)	51.99	9190.64	72570.83	2284844.5	235220.24
x_1	labor***)	22	1480	5469.16	184900	18286.71
x_2	tangible and intangible fixed assets**)	371.19	75636.40	406192.78	10029648.	1200629.0
x_3	financial capital**)	.00	70349.29	458681.06	16380175.	1593177.5
w_1	salary/wage rate plus social costs**)	34.18	78.09	79.96	141.69	21.41
w_2	depreciation rate on tangible and intangible fixed assets****)	.069	.268	.309	3.098	.298
w_3	cost of financial assets (via stock return as opportunity earning*****)	-.815	-.026	-.048	.554	.240

N =123 *) millions of 1992 DM **) thousands of 1992 DM ***) no. of employees ****) 1 = 100 % *****) ln(return + 1)

Table A-41: Netputs and 1991 summary statistics of the cross sectional cost functions

coefficient	1986	std. error		1987	std. error	
α	-4.419268	0.074583	***	9.804721	0.100083	***
β_1	0.026974	0.004987	***	-0.330671	0.007673	***
β_2	-0.081333	0.008385	***	0.817697	0.011498	***
γ_1	4.382630	0.015267	***	-1.733151	0.023332	***
γ_2	-0.322367	0.040709	***	2.053100	0.070419	***
γ_3	-3.060263	0.044160	***	0.680052	0.075960	***
β_{11}	0.073338	0.000435	***	-0.043098	0.000599	***
β_{12}	0.009704	0.000573	***	0.046390	0.000861	***
β_{22}	-0.003738	0.000832	***	-0.015738	0.001281	***
γ_{11}	-0.844267	0.003740	***	0.121997	0.005637	***
γ_{12}	-0.021702	0.011741	*	-0.115578	0.016434	***
γ_{13}	0.865969	0.012071	***	-0.006419	0.017604	
γ_{22}	-0.044428	0.010930	***	0.308086	0.043688	***
γ_{23}	-1.036022	0.250525	***	-2.587140	0.324978	***
γ_{33}	0.096822	0.237775		2.176992	0.327321	***
δ_{11}	-0.017774	0.001448	***	0.238747	0.001787	***
δ_{12}	0.079690	0.003566	***	-0.151027	0.005406	***
δ_{13}	-0.061916	0.003522	***	-0.087720	0.005833	***
δ_{21}	-0.014520	0.001725	***	-0.236241	0.002668	***

coefficient	1986	std. error		1987	std. error	
δ_{22}	-0.067658	0.005251	***	0.108109	0.008080	***
δ_{23}	0.082178	0.005487	***	0.128132	0.008728	***
ζ_1	-0.678205	0.068868	***	-0.427477	0.104278	***
ζ_2	0.266261	0.071957	***	0.830192	0.104295	***
ζ_3	-0.026732	0.097620		0.416275	0.104276	***
ζ_4	-0.398992	0.068546	***	0.182810	0.104289	*
ζ_5	0.028259	0.069509		0.539902	0.104174	***
ζ_6	-0.794669	0.073602	***	-0.047062	0.104294	
ζ_7	0.032607	0.069066		0.627573	0.104278	***
ζ_8	-0.280493	0.068740	***	0.303600	0.104294	***
ζ_9	0.154152	0.067616	**	0.311467	0.104291	***
ζ_{10}	-0.496538	0.068506	***	-0.188686	0.104212	*
ζ_{11}	0.067585	0.073462		0.417174	0.104290	***
ζ_{12}	-0.411742	0.092381	***	0.225170	0.104287	**
ζ_{13}	-0.382821	0.086186	***	-0.124137	0.104208	
ζ_{14}	0.103946	0.067411		0.345956	0.104240	***
λ	0.993145	0.225154	***	0.593539	0.103896	***
σ	0.416705	0.033537	***	0.522596	0.104324	***

N =125/123; *** = significant on the 1 % level (** = 5 %; * = 10 %)

Table A-42: Results of the cross-sectional maximum likelihood regressions for 1986 and 1987

coefficient	1989	std. error		1991	std. error	
α	4.874713	0.093881	***	5.547746	0.098280	***
β_1	0.147617	0.007302	***	-1.447301	0.007470	***
β_2	1.323519	0.010585	***	0.730266	0.010694	***
γ_1	-2.190373	0.021944	***	2.512041	0.022255	***
γ_2	0.535823	0.064048	***	-0.891492	0.067726	***
γ_3	2.654549	0.069499	***	-0.620549	0.071451	***
β_{11}	0.019303	0.000573	***	0.136520	0.000592	***
β_{12}	-0.080730	0.000806	***	-0.104929	0.000831	***
β_{22}	0.118383	0.001152	***	0.092782	0.001162	***
γ_{11}	0.239838	0.005194	***	-1.385911	0.005291	***
γ_{12}	-0.214506	0.015079	***	0.350877	0.015533	***
γ_{13}	-0.025332	0.016119		1.035034	0.016455	***
γ_{22}	-0.042936	0.038637		0.066278	0.040068	*
γ_{23}	-0.720647	0.179204	***	-1.741379	1.608785	
γ_{33}	0.003608	0.174780		1.988647	1.621780	
δ_{11}	0.220470	0.001708	***	0.323140	0.001708	***
δ_{12}	0.026636	0.004982	***	-0.005497	0.005206	
δ_{13}	-0.247106	0.005410	***	-0.317643	0.005535	***
δ_{21}	-0.227071	0.002463	***	-0.033408	0.002457	***
δ_{22}	0.027932	0.007117	***	-0.024331	0.007348	***
δ_{23}	0.199139	0.007749	***	0.057739	0.007744	***
ζ_1	-0.672843	0.097011	***	0.486112	0.101793	***
ζ_2	-0.385210	0.097032	***	1.199265	0.101843	***
ζ_3	-0.078768	0.097024		1.104111	0.101744	***
ζ_4	-0.115931	0.097025		1.120452	0.101827	***
ζ_5	0.127292	0.096940		1.223917	0.101352	***
ζ_6	-0.626026	0.097032	***	-0.139554	0.101847	
ζ_7	-0.084848	0.097010		1.111461	0.101827	***

coefficient	1989	std. error		1991	std. error	
ζ_8	-0.203281	0.097030	**	0.625617	0.101932	***
ζ_9	-0.411086	0.097028	***	0.528048	0.101886	***
ζ_{10}	-0.349986	0.096986	***	0.191314	0.100819	*
ζ_{11}	-0.562389	0.097029	***	1.047421	0.101879	***
ζ_{12}	0.198006	0.097026	***	0.989693	0.101844	***
ζ_{13}	-0.067322	0.096997		0.993476	0.101995	***
ζ_{14}	-0.198342	0.096973	**	0.763506	0.101490	***
λ	0.593819	0.096744		0.573690	0.105319	***
σ	0.525405	0.097009		0.524160	0.038078	***

N =139/123; *** = significant on the 1 % level (** = 5 %; * = 10 %)

Table A-43: Results of the cross-sectional maximum likelihood regressions for 1989 and 1991

mean(xineff) overall: **33.02 %**

	mean(xineff)	std. dev.	n	diff	z	sig
block	29.03 %	8.80 %	11	4.32 %	1.28034	
	33.35 %	21.98 %	111			
size	31.10 %	21.24 %	36	2.69 %	0.64471	
	33.79 %	20.97 %	89			
market segment	31.18 %	21.18 %	39	2.67 %	0.65598	
	33.85 %	20.99 %	86			
dividend signal	30.28 %	18.80 %	54	3.71 %	1.04440	
	33.99 %	20.56 %	70			
leverage	33.32 %	18.79 %	71	-0.49 %	-0.12419	
	32.83 %	23.94 %	53			
monitored debt ratio	34.34 %	21.33 %	58	-2.48 %	-0.65512	
	31.87 %	20.80 %	67			
agency1	33.05 %	21.68 %	18	-0.87 %	-0.15837	
	32.18 %	19.74 %	103			
agency2	33.65 %	22.70 %	19	-1.59 %	-0.28577	
	32.06 %	19.51 %	102			
agency3	33.03 %	18.77 %	70	-1.71 %	-0.45375	
	31.32 %	21.61 %	51			
agency4	32.05 %	22.39 %	29	0.34 %	0.07394	
	32.39 %	19.24 %	92			
agency5	34.33 %	22.44 %	17	-2.35 %	-0.40735	
	31.98 %	19.61 %	104			
agency6	35.55 %	20.88 %	28	-4.21 %	-0.94821	
	31.33 %	19.67 %	93			
agency7	31.06 %	23.63 %	16	1.43 %	0.23093	
	32.50 %	19.45 %	105			

for each variable: first row = high agency problems, second row = low agency problems;
*** = significant on the 1 % level (** = 5 %; * = 10 %)

Table A-44: T-tests for differences of means of xineff by agency variable, 1986

	mean(xineff)	std. dev.	n	diff	z	sig
block	33.35%	21.98%	111	1.49%	0.45259	
creditor	31.87%	20.80%	67			
agency5	31.98%	19.61%	104	0.11%	0.03505	
creditor	31.87%	20.80%	67			

first row = ownership control according to the variable given, second row = creditor control;
*** = significant on the 1 % level (** = 5 %; * = 10 %)

Table A-45: T-tests for differences of means of xineff between owner-controlled and creditor-controlled companies, 1986

mean(xineff) overall: **29.08 %**

	mean(xineff)	std. dev.	n	diff	z	sig
block	33.23 %	9.89 %	10	-4.92 %	-1.46545	
	28.31 %	12.12 %	98			
size	26.97 %	10.28 %	32	2.86 %	1.38772	
	29.83 %	9.32 %	91			
market segment	28.45 %	9.33 %	35	0.89 %	0.4813	
	29.34 %	8.91 %	88			
dividend signal	30.35 %	8.76 %	45	-1.99 %	-1.08283	
	28.36 %	11.39 %	78			
leverage	29.09 %	10.02 %	72	0.34 %	0.17608	
	29.43 %	10.72 %	48			
monitored debt ratio	28.06 %	8.90 %	58	1.95 %	1.19583	
	30.00 %	9.13 %	65			
agency1	31.12 %	10.50 %	15	-2.73 %	-0.91417	
	28.39 %	12.04 %	93			
agency2	29.43 %	9.24 %	14	-0.76 %	-0.29023	
	28.67 %	8.24 %	94			
agency3	28.67 %	9.89 %	62	0.24 %	0.11848	
	28.91 %	10.52 %	46			
agency4	26.65 %	8.47 %	18	2.54 %	1.16096	
	29.19 %	8.51 %	90			
agency5	30.66 %	9.86 %	15	-2.19 %	-0.78087	
	28.47 %	11.33 %	93			
agency6	30.10 %	9.40 %	26	-1.75 %	-0.79192	
	28.35 %	11.11 %	82			
agency7	30.28 %	9.19 %	12	-1.70 %	-0.57715	
	28.58 %	12.68 %	96			

for each variable: first row = high agency problems, second row = low agency problems;
*** = significant on the 1 % level (** = 5 %; * = 10 %)

Table A-46: T-tests for differences of means of xineff by agency variable, 1987

	mean(xineff)	std. dev.	n	diff	z	sig
block	28.31%	12.12%	98	-1.69%	-1.01184	
creditor	30.00%	9.13%	65			
agency5	28.47%	11.33%	93	-1.54%	-0.94117	
creditor	30.00%	9.13%	65			

first row = ownership control according to the variable given, second row = creditor control;
*** = significant on the 1 % level (** = 5 %; * = 10 %)

Table A-47: T-tests for differences of means of xineff between owner-controlled and creditor-controlled companies, 1987

mean(xineff) overall: **24.82 %**

	mean(xineff)	std. dev.	n	diff	z	sig
block	28.03 %	7.01 %	11	-3.52 %	-1.576	
	24.51 %	7.24 %	101			
size	23.85 %	6.90 %	37	1.32 %	0.9654	
	25.17 %	7.78 %	102			
market segment	23.43 %	6.72 %	43	2.01 %	1.59538	
	25.44 %	7.14 %	96			
dividend signal	26.03 %	8.28 %	20	-1.42 %	-0.71215	
	24.61 %	7.86 %	119			
leverage	23.69 %	6.72 %	73	2.72 %	2.4939	**
	26.41 %	5.69 %	57			
monitored debt ratio	24.49 %	6.88 %	60	0.59 %	0.5127	
	25.08 %	6.43 %	78			
agency1	25.49 %	7.47 %	14	-0.57 %	-0.26546	
	24.92 %	7.53 %	96			
agency2	25.68 %	6.74 %	13	-0.77 %	-0.38505	
	24.91 %	7.08 %	97			
agency3	23.94 %	6.80 %	59	2.27 %	1.92139	*
	26.21 %	5.60 %	51			
agency4	25.55 %	7.86 %	16	-0.65 %	-0.30139	
	24.90 %	8.34 %	94			
agency5	27.70 %	6.56 %	12	-3.04 %	-1.48084	
	24.67 %	7.77 %	98			
agency6	26.04 %	6.65 %	26	-1.36 %	-0.92482	
	24.67 %	6.25 %	84			
agency7	27.97 %	6.97 %	12	-3.34 %	-1.50726	
	24.63 %	9.10 %	98			

for each variable: first row = high agency problems, second row = low agency problems;
*** = significant on the 1 % level (** = 5 %; * = 10 %)

Table A-48: T-tests for differences of means of xineff by agency variable, 1989

	mean(xineff)	std. dev.	n	diff	z	sig
block	24.51%	7.24%	101	-0.56%	-0.55025	
creditor	25.08%	6.43%	78			
agency5	24.67%	7.77%	98	-0.41%	-0.38431	
creditor	25.08%	6.43%	78			

first row = ownership control according to the variable given, second row = creditor control;
*** = significant on the 1 % level (** = 5 %; * = 10 %)

Table A-49: T-tests for differences of means of xineff between owner-controlled and creditor-controlled companies, 1989

mean(xineff) overall: **25.78 %**

	mean(xineff)	std. dev.	n	diff	z	sig
block	26.42 %	7.45 %	6	-1.00 %	-0.30398	
	25.42 %	11.96 %	92			
size	21.81 %	10.27 %	26	5.04 %	2.17361	**
	26.85 %	11.33 %	97			
market segment	25.03 %	11.63 %	37	1.07 %	0.47446	
	26.11 %	11.16 %	86			
dividend signal	31.16 %	16.68 %	9	-5.80 %	-1.02685	
	25.36 %	10.72 %	114			
leverage	24.76 %	8.83 %	73	2.51 %	1.0155	
	27.27 %	14.86 %	44			
monitored debt ratio	24.30 %	7.63 %	56	2.73 %	1.40599	
	27.03 %	13.52 %	67			
agency1	21.84 %	7.99 %	9	4.01 %	1.36085	
	25.85 %	11.99 %	89			
agency2	22.00 %	8.51 %	8	3.79 %	1.16199	
	25.80 %	11.94 %	90			
agency3	24.10 %	8.76 %	58	3.40 %	1.29922	
	27.50 %	14.89 %	40			
agency4	20.96 %	11.29 %	15	5.34 %	1.67643	*
	26.30 %	11.66 %	83			
agency5	28.78 %	7.52 %	7	-3.54 %	-1.14048	
	25.23 %	11.96 %	91			
agency6	23.19 %	9.44 %	23	2.99 %	1.23379	
	26.19 %	12.29 %	75			

mean(xineff) overall: **25.78 %**

	mean(xineff)	std. dev.	n	diff	z	sig
agency7	31.39 %	13.69 %	5	-6.22 %	-0.99702	
	25.17 %	11.59 %	93			

for each variable: first row = high agency problems, second row = low agency problems;
*** = significant on the 1 % level (** = 5 %; * = 10 %)

Table A-50: T-tests for differences of means of xineff by agency variable, 1991

	mean(xineff)	std. dev.	n	diff	z	sig
block	25.42%	11.96%	92	-1.60%	-0.77347	
creditor	27.03%	13.52%	67			
agency5	25.23%	11.96%	91	-1.79%	-0.86437	
creditor	27.03%	13.52%	67			

first row = ownership control according to the variable given, second row = creditor control;
*** = significant on the 1 % level (** = 5 %; * = 10 %)

Table A-51: T-tests for differences of means of xineff between owner-controlled and creditor-controlled companies, 1991

	variable	**minim.**	**median**	**mean**	**maxim.**	**std. dev.**
	total assets*)	19.22	512.40	1375.54	20236.83	3274.04
C	costs*)	10.54	169.89	486.21	7756.16	1191.94
y_1	sales and self-constructed assets*)	38.87	709.94	2120.24	21765.19	4008.85
y_2	interest earnings and earnings from affiliated companies**)	35.72	14814.32	55414.94	748621.23	116465.50
x_1	labor***)	20	1784	4323.22	64518	10102.18
x_2	tangible and intangible fixed assets**)	371.19	70416.45	247775.39	3744811.3	615195.67
x_3	financial capital**)	.00	90432.96	395443.56	5134085.6	851722.86
w_1	salary/wage rate plus social costs**)	40.73	82.80	77.75	132.58	20.26
w_2	depreciation rate on tangible and intangible fixed assets****)	.072	.296	.319	1.855	.227
w_3	cost of financial assets (via stock return as opportunity earning*****)	-.531	.121	.101	.783	.288

N =73 *) millions of 1992 DM **) thousands of 1992 DM ***) no. of employees ****) 1 = 100 %
*****) ln(return + 1)

Table A-52: Netputs and summary statistics of the panel cost function data for the chemicals sector

	variable	**minim.**	**median**	**mean**	**maxim.**	**std. dev.**
	total assets*)	30.79	445.02	4076.36	55437.00	12423.20
C	costs*)	9.57	296.50	1723.75	24521.33	4752.61
y_1	sales and self-constructed assets*)	33.29	744.30	3850.87	46052.70	10186.11
y_2	interest earnings and earnings from affiliated companies**)	9.68	7935.22	173291.26	2714000.3	540684.72
x_1	labor***)	91	3930	17839.17	206200	45179.76
x_2	tangible and intangible fixed assets**)	258.48	75797.05	520976.41	6990612.9	1507006.0
x_3	financial capital**)	.00	19069.33	1086104.2	18151000.	3607167.0
w_1	salary/wage rate plus social costs**)	38.39	67.45	70.60	105.85	17.60
w_2	depreciation rate on tangible and intan-	.069	.329	.648	20.298	2.395

variable	minim.	median	mean	maxim.	std. dev.
gible fixed assets****)					
w_3 cost of financial assets (via stock return as opportunity earning*****)	-.924	.022	.034	1.513	.387

N =70 *) millions of 1992 DM **) thousands of 1992 DM ***) no. of employees ****) 1 = 100 % *****) ln(return + 1)

Table A-53: Netputs and summary statistics of the panel cost function data for the electronics sector

variable	minim.	median	mean	maxim.	std. dev.
total assets*)	15.52	89.85	245.94	3619.44	557.33
C costs*)	5.33	44.79	72.43	804.15	107.99
y_1 sales and self-constructed assets*)	20.955	149.59	285.04	2153.07	405.97
y_2 interest earnings and earnings from affiliated companies**)	17.67	1988.70	7857.12	148212.40	20684.14
x_1 labor***)	46	418.5	539.94	3193	633.07
x_2 tangible and intangible fixed assets**)	2904.58	39814.94	60129.65	510246.00	88289.51
x_3 financial capital**)	.00	30160.50	80764.26	1746891.0	236224.38
w_1 salary/wage rate plus social costs**)	58.53	80.35	79.70	102.38	9.18
w_2 depreciation rate on tangible and intangible fixed assets****)	.145	.349	.395	1.375	.202
w_3 cost of financial assets (via stock return as opportunity earning*****)	-.420	.066	.087	1.071	.220

N =138 *) millions of 1992 DM **) thousands of 1992 DM ***) no. of employees ****) 1 = 100 % *****) ln(return + 1)

Table A-54: Netputs and summary statistics of the panel cost function data for the food sector

variable	minim.	median	mean	maxim.	std. dev.
total assets*)	319.14	1036.60	3432.99	26665.53	5164.22
C costs*)	8.28	239.71	717.67	9240.23	1271.73
y_1 sales and self-constructed assets*)	184.15	849.66	2275.56	19525.47	3744.36
y_2 interest earnings and earnings from affiliated companies**)	1805.35	22110.07	73166.12	824257.80	139173.79
x_1 labor***)	402	1845	3558.65	24590	4780.42
x_2 tangible and intangible fixed assets**)	63091.13	635822.88	1861866.1	12258782.	2750653.6
x_3 financial capital**)	1364.40	179848.34	671033.43	5344204.2	1076473.1
w_1 salary/wage rate plus social costs**)	62.04	93.98	95.68	146.17	16.32
w_2 depreciation rate on tangible and intangible fixed assets****)	.046	.161	.151	.250	.051
w_3 cost of financial assets (via stock return as opportunity earning*****)	-.548	.047	.079	.674	.216

N =80 *) millions of 1992 DM **) thousands of 1992 DM ***) no. of employees ****) 1 = 100 % *****) ln(return + 1)

Table A-55: Netputs and summary statistics of the panel cost function data for the utilities sector

mean(xineff) overall: **24.18 %**

	mean(xineff)	std. dev.	n	diff	z	sig
block	20.34 %	12.06 %	2	10.31 %	0.93076	
	30.65 %	23.47 %	11			
size	20.97 %	18.03 %	3	3.96 %	0.32109	
	24.93 %	23.85 %	13			
market segment	20.57 %	24.01 %	6	5.79 %	0.4788	
	26.35 %	22.38 %	10			
dividend signal	1.88 %	1.72 %	2	25.49 %	4.21952	***
	27.37 %	22.15 %	14			
leverage	22.75 %	21.78 %	9	7.42 %	0.60387	
	30.18 %	24.31 %	6			
monitored debt ratio	33.13 %	23.59 %	8	-17.88 %	-1.69478	*
	15.24 %	18.29 %	8			
agency1	20.34 %	12.06 %	2	10.31 %	0.93076	
	30.65 %	23.47 %	11			
agency2	20.34 %	12.06 %	2	10.31 %	0.93076	
	30.65 %	23.47 %	11			
agency3	25.56 %	21.48 %	8	9.12 %	0.68893	
	34.67 %	24.23 %	5			
agency4	31.28 %	3.43 %	2	-2.63 %	-0.34274	
	28.66 %	24.10 %	11			
agency5	20.34 %	12.06 %	2	10.31 %	0.93076	
	30.65 %	23.47 %	11			
agency6	26.76 %	22.25 %	5	3.75 %	0.29003	
	30.50 %	23.33 %	8			
agency7	14.76 %	19.94 %	2	16.90 %	1.0823	
	31.66 %	22.25 %	11			

N =16; for each variable: first row = high agency problems, second row = low agency problems;
*** = significant on the 1 % level (** = 5 %; * = 10 %)

Table A-56: T-tests for differences of means of xineff by agency variable over the electronics industry (separate regression)

	mean(xineff)	std. dev.	n	diff	z	sig
block	30.65%	23.47%	11	15.41%	1.60737	
creditor	15.24%	18.29%	8			
agency5	30.65%	23.47%	11	15.41%	1.60737	
creditor	15.24%	18.29%	8			

N =16; first row = ownership control according to the variable given, second row = creditor control;
*** = significant on the 1 % level (** = 5 %; * = 10 %)

Table A-57: T-tests for differences of means of *xineff* between owner-controlled and creditor-controlled companies, separate regression for the electronics sector

mean(xineff) overall: **20.66 %**

	mean(xineff)	std. dev.	n	diff	z	sig
block	25.04 %	3.31 %	2	-3.87 %	-1.0889	
	21.17 %	8.89 %	11			
size	18.10 %	10.23 %	3	3.15 %	0.47815	
	21.25 %	10.53 %	13			
market segment	20.38 %	12.06 %	6	0.45 %	0.07791	
	20.83 %	9.64 %	10			
dividend signal	11.23 %	7.61 %	2	10.78 %	1.79369	*
	22.01 %	10.01 %	14			
leverage	17.98 %	7.55 %	9	4.05 %	0.71422	
	22.03 %	12.46 %	6			
monitored debt ratio	24.71 %	7.61 %	8	-8.09 %	-1.67828	*
	16.62 %	11.32 %	8			
agency1	25.04 %	3.31 %	2	-3.87 %	-1.0889	
	21.17 %	8.89 %	11			
agency2	25.04 %	3.31 %	2	-3.87 %	-1.0889	
	21.17 %	8.89 %	11			
agency3	19.33 %	6.80 %	8	6.33 %	1.26992	
	25.66 %	9.76 %	5			
agency4	23.59 %	5.36 %	2	-2.16 %	-0.4643	
	21.43 %	8.89 %	11			
agency5	25.04 %	3.31 %	2	-3.87 %	-1.0889	
	21.17 %	8.89 %	11			
agency6	20.24 %	8.54 %	5	2.47 %	0.50694	
	22.72 %	8.59 %	8			
agency7	16.62 %	15.22 %	2	6.08 %	0.55364	
	22.70 %	7.30 %	11			

N =16; for each variable: first row = high agency problems, second row = low agency problems; *** = significant on the 1 % level (** = 5 %; * = 10 %)

Table A-58: T-tests for differences of means of xineff by agency variable over the electronics industry (comprehensive regression)

	mean(xineff)	std. dev.	n	diff	z	sig
block	21.17%	8.89%	11	4.55%	0.94506	
creditor	16.62%	11.32%	8			
agency5	21.17%	8.89%	11	4.55%	0.94506	
creditor	16.62%	11.32%	8			

N =16; first row = ownership control according to the variable given, second row = creditor control; *** = significant on the 1 % level (** = 5 %; * = 10 %)

Table A-59: T-tests for differences of means of *xineff* between owner-controlled and creditor-controlled companies, comprehensive regression for the electronics sector

mean(xineff) overall: **23.33 %**

	mean(xineff)	std. dev.	n	diff	z	sig
block			0	24.80 %	N/A	N/A
	24.80 %	16.40 %	25			
size	24.81 %	20.22 %	14	-3.07 %	-0.48107	
	21.74 %	12.25 %	13			
market segment	22.37 %	18.54 %	11	1.61 %	0.23601	
	23.99 %	15.76 %	16			
dividend signal	29.34 %	23.42 %	7	-8.12 %	-0.86649	
	21.23 %	13.67 %	20			
leverage	20.96 %	17.77 %	20	9.15 %	1.57555	
	30.10 %	11.20 %	7			
monitored debt ratio	26.13 %	18.73 %	17	-7.56 %	-1.2953	
	18.57 %	11.60 %	10			
agency1	21.06 %	24.20 %	6	4.92 %	0.47445	
	25.98 %	13.77 %	19			
agency2	23.26 %	26.37 %	5	1.92 %	0.15727	
	25.18 %	13.87 %	20			
agency3	22.73 %	17.86 %	18	7.37 %	1.23445	
	30.10 %	11.20 %	7			
agency4	20.88 %	20.84 %	9	6.12 %	0.79218	
	27.00 %	13.57 %	16			
agency5	31.14 %	33.68 %	3	-7.20 %	-0.36612	
	23.93 %	13.88 %	22			
agency6	21.87 %	20.49 %	9	4.58 %	0.59562	
	26.45 %	14.08 %	16			
agency7	31.14 %	33.68 %	3	-7.20 %	-0.36612	
	23.93 %	13.88 %	22			

N =27; for each variable: first row = high agency problems, second row = low agency problems; *** = significant on the 1 % level (** = 5 %; * = 10 %)

Table A-60: T-tests for differences of means of xineff by agency variable over the food & beverage industry (separate regression)

	mean(xineff)	std. dev.	n	diff	z	sig
block	24.80%	16.40%	25	6.23%	1.26606	
creditor	18.57%	11.60%	10			
agency5	23.93%	13.88%	22	5.37%	1.13835	

	mean(xineff)	std. dev.	n	diff	z	sig
creditor	18.57%	11.60%	10			

N =27; first row = ownership control according to the variable given, second row = creditor control; *** = significant on the 1 % level (** = 5 %; * = 10 %)

Table A-61: T-tests for differences of means of *xineff* between owner-controlled and creditor-controlled companies, separate regression for the food & beverages sector

mean(xineff) overall: **27.38 %**

	mean(xineff)	std. dev.	n	diff	z	sig
block			0	26.72 %	N/A	N/A
	26.72 %	18.50 %	25			
size	27.50 %	23.78 %	14	-0.23 %	-0.03204	
	27.26 %	12.59 %	13			
market segment	23.91 %	17.41 %	11	5.87 %	0.80948	
	29.78 %	20.00 %	16			
dividend signal	25.20 %	18.40 %	7	2.94 %	0.35905	
	28.15 %	19.44 %	20			
leverage	25.02 %	17.12 %	20	9.13 %	0.95079	
	34.14 %	23.29 %	7			
monitored debt ratio	23.67 %	13.21 %	17	10.02 %	1.15676	
	33.69 %	25.46 %	10			
agency1	23.36 %	20.76 %	6	4.42 %	0.46813	
	27.79 %	18.22 %	19			
agency2	26.78 %	21.23 %	5	-0.07 %	-0.00721	
	26.71 %	18.38 %	20			
agency3	23.84 %	16.14 %	18	10.30 %	1.07469	
	34.14 %	23.29 %	7			
agency4	21.90 %	18.28 %	9	7.54 %	0.98274	
	29.44 %	18.65 %	16			
agency5	32.15 %	26.07 %	3	-6.16 %	-0.39689	
	25.99 %	17.94 %	22			
agency6	22.04 %	18.76 %	9	7.31 %	0.94164	
	29.36 %	18.43 %	16			
agency7	32.15 %	26.07 %	3	-6.16 %	-0.39689	
	25.99 %	17.94 %	22			

N =27; for each variable: first row = high agency problems, second row = low agency problems; *** = significant on the 1 % level (** = 5 %; * = 10 %)

Table A-62: T-tests for differences of means of xineff by agency variable over the food & beverage industry (comprehensive regression)

	mean(xineff)	std. dev.	n	diff	z	sig
block	26.72%	18.50%	25	-6.97%	-0.78666	

	mean(xineff)	std. dev.	n	diff	z	sig
creditor	33.69%	25.46%	10			
agency5	25.99%	17.94%	22	-7.71%	-0.86504	
creditor	33.69%	25.46%	10			

N =27; first row = ownership control according to the variable given, second row = creditor control; *** = significant on the 1 % level (** = 5 %; * = 10 %)

Table A-63: T-tests for differences of means of *xineff* between owner-controlled and creditor-controlled companies, comprehensive regression for the food & beverages sector

mean(xineff) overall: **32.44 %**

	mean(xineff)	std. dev.	n	diff	z	sig
block			0	33.52 %	N/A	N/A
	33.52 %	29.55 %	14			
size			0	32.44 %	N/A	N/A
	32.44 %	28.78 %	15			
market segment	68.82 %		1	-38.98 %	-5.21105	***
	29.84 %	27.99 %	14			
dividend signal	4.55 %		1	29.88 %	3.88543	***
	34.43 %	28.78 %	14			
leverage	28.53 %	19.53 %	4	6.99 %	0.48525	
	35.52 %	33.45 %	10			
monitored debt ratio	24.32 %	20.47 %	13	60.91 %	5.99866	***
	85.23 %	11.91 %	2			
agency1			0	33.52 %	N/A	N/A
	33.52 %	29.55 %	14			
agency2			0	33.52 %	N/A	N/A
	33.52 %	29.55 %	14			
agency3	28.53 %	19.53 %	4	6.99 %	0.48525	
	35.52 %	33.45 %	10			
agency4			0	33.52 %	N/A	N/A
	33.52 %	29.55 %	14			
agency5			0	33.52 %	N/A	N/A
	33.52 %	29.55 %	14			
agency6			0	33.52 %	N/A	N/A
	33.52 %	29.55 %	14			
agency7			0	33.52 %	N/A	N/A
	33.52 %	29.55 %	14			

N =15; for each variable: first row = high agency problems, second row = low agency problems; *** = significant on the 1 % level (** = 5 %; * = 10 %)

Table A-64: T-tests for differences of means of xineff by agency variable over the utilities industry (separate regression)

	mean(xineff)	std. dev.	n	diff	z	sig
block	33.52%	29.55%	14	-51.71%	-4.47931	***
creditor	85.23%	11.91%	2			
agency5	33.52%	29.55%	14	-51.71%	-4.47931	***
creditor	85.23%	11.91%	2			

N =15; first row = ownership control according to the variable given, second row = creditor control; *** = significant on the 1 % level (** = 5 %; * = 10 %)

Table A-65: T-tests for differences of means of *xineff* between owner-controlled and creditor-controlled companies, separate regression for the utilities sector

mean(xineff) overall: **31.57 %**

	mean(xineff)	std. dev.	n	diff	z	sig
block			0	31.74 %	N/A	N/A
	31.74 %	27.01 %	14			
size			0	31.57 %	N/A	N/A
	31.57 %	26.04 %	15			
market segment	60.78 %		1	-31.30 %	-4.55989	***
	29.48 %	25.68 %	14			
dividend signal	5.09 %		1	28.37 %	4.09416	***
	33.46 %	25.93 %	14			
leverage	20.21 %	9.63 %	4	16.13 %	1.48997	
	36.34 %	30.67 %	10			
monitored debt ratio	23.24 %	13.96 %	13	62.44 %	4.2884	***
	85.68 %	19.85 %	2			
agency1			0	31.74 %	N/A	N/A
	31.74 %	27.01 %	14			
agency2			0	31.74 %	N/A	N/A
	31.74 %	27.01 %	14			
agency3	20.21 %	9.63 %	4	16.13 %	1.48997	
	36.34 %	30.67 %	10			
agency4			0	31.74 %	N/A	N/A
	31.74 %	27.01 %	14			
agency5			0	31.74 %	N/A	N/A
	31.74 %	27.01 %	14			
agency6			0	31.74 %	N/A	N/A
	31.74 %	27.01 %	14			
agency7			0	31.74 %	N/A	N/A
	31.74 %	27.01 %	14			

N =15; for each variable: first row = high agency problems, second row = low agency problems; *** = significant on the 1 % level (** = 5 %; * = 10 %)

Table A-66: T-tests for differences of means of xineff by agency variable over the utilities industry (comprehensive regression)

	mean(xineff)	std. dev.	n	diff	z	sig
block	31.74%	27.01%	14	-53.94%	-3.41796	***
creditor	85.68%	19.85%	2			
agency5	31.74%	27.01%	14	-53.94%	-3.41796	***
creditor	85.68%	19.85%	2			

N =15; first row = ownership control according to the variable given, second row = creditor control; *** = significant on the 1 % level (** = 5 %; * = 10 %)

Table A-67: T-tests for differences of means of *xineff* between owner-controlled and creditor-controlled companies, comprehensive regression for the utilities sector

B References

Adam, Dietrich (1993)
Produktions-Management, Wiesbaden.

Aghion, Philippe; Bolton, Patrick (1989)
The Financial Structure of the Firm and the Problem of Control, in: European Economic Review, Vol. 33, 286-293.

Agrawal, Anup; Mandelker, Gershon N. (1987)
Managerial Incentives and Corporate Investment and Financing Decisions, in: Journal of Finance, Vol. 42, 823-837.

Aigner, Dennis J.; Chu, S. F. (1968)
On Estimation the Industry Production Function, in: The American Economic Review, 826-839.

Aigner, Dennis; Lovell, C.A. Knox; Schmidt, Peter (1977)
Formulation and Estimation of Stochastic Frontier Production Function Models, in: Journal of Econometrics, 21-37.

Akerlof, George A. (1970)
The Market for "Lemons": Quality Uncertainty and the Market Mechanism, in: Quartely Journal of Economics, Vol. 84, 488-500.

Akhigbe, Aigbe; Madura, Jeff; Tucker, Alan L. (1996)
Market-Controlled Stock Options: A New Approach to Executive Compensation, in: Journal of Applied Corporate Finance, Vol. 9, 93-97.

Albach, Horst (1975)
Zur Entwicklung der Kapitalstruktur deutscher Unternehmen, in: Zeitschrift für Betriebswirtschaft, Vol. 45, 1-12.

Alchian, Armen A. (1965)
Some Economics of Property Rights, in: Il Politico, Vol. 30, 816-829.

Alchian, Armen A.; Demsetz, Harold (1973)
The Property Rights Paradigm, in: Journal of Economic History, Vol. 33, 16-27.

Aldrich, John H.; Nelson, Forrest D. (1992)
Linear Probability, Logit, and Probit Models, Newbury Park et al.

Alessi, Louis de (1980)
The Economics of Property Rights: A Review of the Evidence, in: Research in Law and Economics, Vol. 2, 1-47.

Amihud, Yakov; Kamin, Jacob Y.; Ronen, Joshua (1983)
'Managerialism', 'Ownerism' and Risk, in: Journal of Banking and Finance, Vol. 7, 189-196.

Amihud, Yakov; Lev, B.; Travlos, Nikolaos G. (1990)
Corporate Control and the Choice of Investment Financing: The Case of Corporate Acquisitions, in: Journal of Finance, Vol. 45, 603-616.

Amihud, Yakov; Murgia, Maurizio (1997)
Dividends, Taxes, and Signaling: Evidence from Germany, in: Journal of Finance, Vol. 52, 397-408.

Aptech Systems (ed.) (1994)
Gauss. 2 volumes, Maple Valley, WA.

Arrow, Kenneth J. (1976)
Essays in the Theory of Risk-Bearing, Amsterdam.

Arrow, Kenneth J. (1985)
The Economics of Agency, in: J. Pratt, R. Zeckhauser (eds.): Principals and Agents: The Structure of Business, Boston, 37-59.

Arrow, Kenneth J. (1986)
Agency and the Market, in: Arrow, Kenneth J.; Intriligator, Michael D. (eds.), Handbook of Mathematical Economics, Vol. III, Amsterdam et al.

Badrinath, S. G.; Kini, Oneshi (1994)
The Relationship between Securities Yields, Firm Size, Earnings/Price Ratios and Tobin's q, in: Journal of Business Finance and Accounting, Vol. 21, S. 109-131.

Baker, George P.; Jensen, Michael C.; Murphy, Kevin J. (1988)
Compensation and Incentives: Practice versus Theory, in: Journal of Finance, Vol. 43, 593-616.

Balakrishnan, Srinivasan; Fox, Isaac (1993)
Asset Specificity, Firm Heterogeneity and Capital Structure, in: Strategic Management Journal, Vol. 14, 3-16.

Ball, V. Eldon; Chambers, Robert G. (1982)
An Economic Analysis of Technology in the Meat Products Industry, in: American Journal of Agricultural Economics, Vol. 64, 699-709.

Banker, Rajiv; Conrad, Robert F.; Strauss Robert P. (1986)
A Comparative Application of Data Envelopment Analysis and Translog Methods: An Illustrative Study of Hospital Production, in: Management Science, Vol. 32, 30-44.

Barber, Brad M.; Lyon, John D. (1996)
Detecting Abnormal Operating Performance: The Empirical Power and Specification of Test Statistics, in: Journal of Financial Economics, Vol. 41, 359-399.

Barber, Brad M.; Lyon, John D. (1997)
Detecting Long-Run Abnormal Stock Returns: The Empirical Power and

Specification of Test Statistics, in: Journal of Financial Economics, Vol. 43, 341-372.

Barnea, Amir; Haugen, Robert A.; Senbet, Lemma W. (1980)
A Rationale for Debt Maturity Structure and Call Provisions in the Agency Theoretic Framework, in: Journal of Finance, Vol. 35, 1223-1234.

Barnea, Amir; Haugen, Robert A.; Senbet, Lemma W. (1985)
Agency Problems and Financial Contracting, Englewood Cliffs, New Jersey.

Bartoldy, Jan; Boyle, Glenn W.; Stover, Roger D. (1996)
Corporate Capital Structure and Regulation of Bank Equity Holdings: Some International Evidence, working paper, University of Otago.

Battese, George E.; Coelli, Tim J. (1988)
Prediction of Firm-Level Technical Efficiencies with a Generalized Frontier Production Function and Panel Data, in: Journal of Econometrics, Vol. 38, 387-399.

Battese, George E.; Coelli, Tim J. (1992)
Frontier Production, Technical Efficiency and Panel Data: With Application to Paddy Farmers in India, in: The Journal of Productivity Analysis, Vol. 3, 149-165.

Bauer, Paul W.; Berger, Allen N.; Ferrier, Gary D.; Humphrey, David B. (1998)
Consistency Conditions for Regulatory Analysis of Financial Institutions: A Comparison of Frontier Efficiency Methods, in: Journal of Economics and Business, Vol. 50, 85-114.

Bauer, Paul W.; Hancock, Diana (1993)
The Efficiency of the Federal Reserve in Providing Check Processing Services, in: Journal of Banking and Finance, Vol.17, 287-311.

Baumol, William (1967)
Business Behavior, Value and Growth, 2nd edition, New York.

Baxter, Nevins D. (1967)
Leverage, Risk of Ruin and the Cost of Capital, in: Journal of Finance, Vol. 22, 395-403.

Becht, Marco ; Boehmer, Ekkehart (1997)
Transparency of Ownership and Control in Germany, working paper, Humboldt University, Berlin.

Beiker, Hartmut (1993)
Überrenditen und Risiken kleiner Aktiengesellschaften, Cologne.

Bellgardt, Egon (1997)
Statistik mit SPSS, München.

Berens, James L.; Cuny, Charles J. (1995)
The Capital Structure Puzzle Revisited, in: The Review of Financial Studies, Vol. 8, 1185-1208.

Berger, Allen N. (1993)
"Distribution-Free" Estimates of Efficiency in the U.S. Banking Industry and Tests of the Standard Distributional Assumptions, in: The Journal of Productivity Analysis, Vol. 4, 261-292.

Berger, Allen N.; Humphrey David B. (1991)
The Dominance of Inefficiencies over Scale and Product Mix Economies in Banking, in: Journal of Monetary Economics, Vol. 28, 117-148.

Berger, Allen N.; Mester, Loretta J. (1997)
Inside the Black Box. What Explains Differences in the Efficiency of Financial Institutions?, in: Journal of Banking and Finance, Vol. 21, 895-947.

Berger, Matthias (1993)
Management-Buyout und Mitarbeiterbeteiligung, Cologne.

Bergman, Yaacov Z.; Callen, Jeffrey L. (1991)
Opportunistic Underinvestment in Debt Renegotiation and Capital Structure, in: Journal of Financial Economics, Vol. 29, 137-171.

Berkovitch, Elazar; Israel, Ronen; Spiegel, Yossef (1996)
Managerial Compensation and Capital Structure, working paper, Tel Aviv University.

Berkovitch, Elazar; Kim, E. Han (1990)
Financial Contracting and Leverage Induced Over- and Under-Investment Incentives, in: Journal of Finance, Vol. 45, 765-794.

Bernhart, Wolfgang; Witt, Peter (1997)
Stock Options und Shareholder Value, in: Zeitschrift für Betriebswirtschaft, Vol. 67, 85-101.

Berle, Adolf A. (1954)
The 20th Century Capitalist Revolution, New York.

Berle, Adolf A.; Means, Gardiner C. (1932)
The Modern Corporation and Private Property, New York.

Bertero, Elisabetta; Rondi, Laura (1997)
Does Debt Discipline State-Owned Firms? Evidence from a Panel of Italian Firms, working paper, London School of Economics/Ceris-CNR Turin.

Bester, Helmut (1987a)
Die Anreizfunktion von Kreditsicherheiten, in: Schneider, Dieter (ed.), Kapitalmarkt und Finanzierung, Berlin, 225-236.

Bester, Helmut (1987b)
The Role of Collateral in Credit Markets with Imperfect Information, in: European Economic Review, Vol. 31, 887-899.

Bester, Helmut; Scheepens, Joris P. J. F. (1996)
Internal Finance versus Bank Debt: The Gains from Establishing a Debt History, in: Kredit und Kapital, Vol. 38, 565-591.

Bhattacharya, Sudipto (1988)
Corporate Finance and the Legacy of Miller and Modigliani, in: Journal of Economic Perspectives, Vol. 2, 135-147.

Bieg, Helmut (1997)
Der Einfluß der Besteuerung auf Außenfinanzierungsentscheidungen, in: Wirtschaftswissenschaftliches Studium, Vol. 26, 175-182.

Binmore, K. G. (1977)
Mathematical Analysis, Cambridge.

Black, Fischer (1976)
The Dividend Puzzle, in: Journal of Portfolio Management, Vol. 2, 5-8.

Black, Fischer; Scholes, Myron (1973)
The Pricing of Options and Corporate Liabilities, in: Journal of Political Economy, Vol. 81, 637-654.

Bleymüller, Josef; Gehlert, Günther (1988)
Statistische Formeln, Tabellen und Programme, 4th edition, Munich.

Bleymüller, Josef; Gehlert, Günther; Gülicher, Herbert (1988)
Statistik für Wirtschaftswissenschaftler, 5th edition, Munich.

Bleymüller, Josef; Gehlert, Günther; Küting, Karlheinz (1987)
Konzentrationsmessung, in: Dichtl, Erwin; Issing, Otmar (eds.), Vahlens großes Wirtschaftslexikon, four volumes, Munich, 1070-1071.

Blickle-Liebersbach, Marina (1991)
Agency-Theorie: Rahmenbedingungen und Entlohnung, Ulm.

Blohm, Hans; Lüder, Klaus (1995)
Investition, 8th edition, Munich.

Böbel Ingo; Dirrheimer, Manfred (1984)
Eigentumsrechte, Managementmotivation und Managerverhalten: Ein Beitrag zur Erweiterung der Theorie der Unternehmung, in: Neumann, Manfred (ed.): Ansprüche, Eigentums- und Verfügungsrechte, Schriften des Vereins für Socialpolitik, Neue Folge Vol. 140, Berlin, 157-187.

Böhm, Jürgen (1992)
Der Einfluß der Banken auf Großunternehmen, Hamburg.

Börner, Christoph J. (1996)
Entstehung und strukturelle Problemfelder des deutschen Bankensystems,

in: Institut für Bankwirtschaft und Bankrecht an der Universität zu Köln (ed.), Mitteilungen und Berichte, Vol 27, 32-60.

Bolton, Patrick; Scharfstein, David S. (1996)
Optimal Debt Structure and the Number of Creditors, in: Journal of Political Economy, Vol. 104, 1-25.

Botta, Volkmar (1997)
Kennzahlensysteme als Führungsinstrumente, 5th edition, Berlin.

Bouderaux, Kenneth J. (1973)
"Managerialism" and Risk-Return Performance, in: Southern Economic Journal, Vol. 39, 366-372.

Bowen, Robert M.; Daley, Lane A.; Huber, Charles C. (1982)
Evidence on the Existence and Determinants of Inter-Industry Differences in Leverage, in: Financial Management, Vol. 11, 10-20.

Bradford, William D. (1987)
The Issue Decision of Manager-Owners under Information Asymmetry, in: Journal of Finance, Vol. 42, 1245-1260.

Bradley, Michael; Jarrell, Gregg A.; Kim, E. Han (1984)
On the Existence of an Optimal Capital Structure: Theory and Evidence, in: Journal of Finance, Vol. 39, 857-878.

Brakmann, Heinrich (1993)
Aktienemissionen und Kurseffekte, Wiesbaden.

Brander, James A.; Poitevin, Michel (1992)
Managerial Compensation and the Agency Costs of Debt Finance, in: Managerial and Decision Economics, Vol. 13, 55-64.

Brandi, Ernst (1977)
Informationswirkungen der Jahresabschlußveröffentlichung auf Entscheidungen am Aktienmarkt, dissertation, Augsburg.

Brealey, Richard A.; Myers, Stewart C. (1996)
Principles of Corporate Finance, 5th edition, New York et al.

Breslaw, Jon (1995)
GaussX, Montreal.

Breuer, Ralf (1994)
Probleme der Risikosteuerung im Rahmen der Marktzinsmethode, Berlin.

Bruckmann, Gerhart (1988)
Konzentrationsmessung, in: Bleymüller, Josef; Gehlert, Günther; Gülicher, Herbert, Statistik für Wirtschaftswissenschaftler, 5th edition, Munich, 189-194.

Bühler, Wilhelm; Göppl, Hermann; Möller, Hans Peter (1993)
Die deutsche Finanzdatenbank, in: Bühler, Wilhelm (ed.), Zeitschrift für betriebwirtschaftliche Forschung, Sonderheft 31 'Empirische Kapitalmarktforschung', Düsseldorf/Frankfurt, 287-333.

Bühner, Rolf (1984)
Rendite-Risiko-Effekte der Trennung von Eigentum und Leistung im diversifizierten Großunternehmen, in: Zeitschrift für betriebswirtschaftliche Forschung, Vol. 36, 812-824.

Bühner, Rolf (1989)
Möglichkeiten der unternehmerischen Gehaltsvereinbarung für das Top-Management, in: Die Betriebswirtschaft, Vol. 42, 2181-2186.

Bühner, Rolf (1996)
Kapitalmarktorientierte Unternehmenssteuerung, in: Wirtschaftswissenschaftliches Studium, Vol. 25, 334-338, 392-396.

Bühner, Rolf; Tuschke, Anja (1997)
Zur Kritik am Shareholder Value—eine ökonomische Analyse, in: Betriebswirtschaftliche Forschung und Praxis, 499-516.

Bühner, Rolf; Weinberger, Hans-Joachim (1991)
Cash Flow und Shareholder Value, in: Betriebswirtschaftliche Forschung und Praxis, 187-208.

Buhbe, Matthes (1980)
Ökonomische Analyse von Eigentumsrechten. Der Beitrag der economics of property rights zur Theorie der Institutionen, Frankfurt.

Bundesministerium der Finanzen (ed.) (1979)
Grundsatzfragen der Kreditwirtschaft: Bericht der Studienkommission, Bonn.

BVI Bundesverband Deutscher Investment-Gesellschaften e. V. (ed.) (1994)

Investment 94—Daten, Fakten, Entwicklungen, Frankfurt/Main.

Campbell, Tim S; Kracaw, William A. (1990)
Corporate Risk Management and the Incentive Effects of Debt, in: Journal of Finance, Vol. 45, 1673-1686.

Campell, John Y. (1996)
Understanding Risk and Return, in: Journal of Political Economy, Vol. 104, No. 2, 298-345.

Campell, John Y.; Lo, Andrew W.; MacKinlay, A. Craig (1997)
The Econometrics of Financial Markets, Princeton.

Cantner, Uwe; Hanusch, Horst; Westermann, Georg (1995)
Effizienz, öffentlicher Auftrag und Deregulierung, in: Jahrbuch für Nationalökonomie und Statistik, Stuttgart, Vol. 214/3, 257-274.

Capasso, Arturo (1996)
Stakeholders or Virtual Shareholders? Exploring the Border between Business and Ethics, working paper, University of Naples.

Carleton, Willard T.; Silberman, Irwin H. (1977)
Joint Determination of Rate of Return and Capital Structure: An Econometric Analysis, in: Journal of Finance, Vol. 32, 811-821.

Carney, William J. (1997)
Large Bank Stockholders in Germany: Saviors or Substitutes?, in: Journal of Applied Corporate Finance, Vol. 9, 74-81.

Carpenter, Robert E. (1994)
Finance Constraints or Free Cash Flow? The Impact of Asymmetric Information on Investment, working paper, Emory University.

Castanias, Richard (1983)
Bankruptcy Risk and Optimal Capital Structure, in: Journal of Finance, Vol. 38, 1617-1635.

Cauglan, Anne T.; Schmidt, Ronald M. (1985)
Executive Compensation, Management Turnover, and Firm Performance, in: Journal of Accounting and Economics, Vol. 7, 43-66.

Chambers, Robert G. (1988)
Applied Production Analysis. A Dual Approach, Cambridge.

Charnes, A.; Cooper, W. W.; Rhodes, E. (1978)
Measuring the Efficiency of Decision Making Units, in: European Journal of Operational Research, Vol. 2, 429-444.

Chen, Haiyang; Hexter, Lawrence J.; Hu, Michael Y. (1993)
Management Ownership and Corporate Value, in: Managerial and Decision Economics, Vol. 14, S. 335-346.

Chirinko, Robert S.; Elston, Julie Ann (1996)
Banking Relationships in Germany: Empirical Results and Policy Implications, working paper, Federal Reserve Bank of Kansas City.

Cho, Myeong-Hyeon (1998)
Ownership Structure, Investment, and the Corporate Value: An Empirical Analysis, in: Journal of Financial Economics, Vol. 47, 103-121.

Chung, Kee H. (1993)
Asset Characteristics and Corporate Debt Policy: An Empirical Test, in: Journal of Business & Accounting, Vol. 20, 83-98.

Chung, Kee H.; Pruitt, Stephen W. (1996)
Executive Ownership, Corporate Value, and Executive Compensation: A Unifying Framework, in: Journal of Banking & Finance, Vol. 20, 1135-1159.

Clemenz, Gerhard (1988)
Informationsökonomische Theorie der Kreditrationierung, in: Wirtschaftswissenschaftliches Studium, Vol. 17, 598-604.

Coase, Ronald (1937)
The Nature of the Firm, in: Economica, Vol. 4, 386-405.

Coase, Ronald (1960)
The Problem of Social Cost, in: Journal of Law and Economics, Vol. 3, 1-44.

Coenenberg, Adolf G.; Schmidt, F.; Werhand, M. (1983)
Bilanzpolitische Entscheidungen und Entscheidungswirkungen in manager- und eigentümerkontrollierten Unternehmen, in: Betriebswirtschaftliche Forschung und Praxis, Vol. 35, 321-343.

Constantinides, George M.; Grundy, Bruce D. (1989)
Optimal Investment with Stock Repurchase and Financing as Signals, in: Review of Financial Studies, Vol. 2, 445-465.

Cooney, John W. Jr.; Kalay, Avner (1993)
Positive Information from Equity Issue Announcements, in: Journal of Financial Economics, Vol. 33, 149-172.

Cornell, Bradford; Shapiro, Alan C. (1987)
Corporate Stakeholders and Corporate Finance, in: Financial Management, Vol. 16, 5-14.

Cornwell, Christopher; Schmidt, Peter; Sickles, Robin C. (1990)
Production Frontiers with Cross-Sectional and Time-Series Variation in Efficiency Levels, in: Journal of Econometrics, Vol. 46, 185-200.

Crutchley, Claire E.; Hansen, Robert P. (1989)
A Test of the Agency Theory of Managerial Ownership, Corporate Leverage, and Corporate Dividends, in: Financial Management, Vol. 18, 36-46.

Darrough, Masako N.; Stoughton, Neal M. (1986)
Moral Hazard and Adverse Selection: the Question of Financial Structure, in: Journal of Finance, Vol. 41, 501-513.

Decker, Rolf O. A. (1994)
Eine Prinzipal-Agenten-theoretische Betrachtung von Eigner-Manager-Konflikten in der Kommanditgesellschaft auf Aktien und in der Aktiengesellschaft, Bergisch-Gladbach/Cologne.

DeFond, Mark L.; Park, Chul W. (1996)
Do Managers Smooth Incomes in Anticipation of Future Earnings? working paper, University of Southern California/Hong Kong University of Science and Technology.

Demsetz, Harold (1967)
Toward a Theory of Property Rights, in: American Economic Review, Vol. 57, 347-359.

Demsetz, Harold; Lehn, Kenneth (1985)
The Structure of Corporate Ownership: Causes and Consequences, in: Journal of Political Economy, Vol. 93, 1155-1177.

Denis, David J.; Denis, Diane K.; Sarin, Atulya (1994)
The Information Content of Dividend Changes: Cash Flow Signaling, Overinvestment, and Dividend Clienteles, in: Journal of Financial and Quantitive Analysis, Vol. 29, 567-587.

DeYoung, Robert (1998)
Management Quality and X-Inefficiency in National Banks, forthcoming in: Journal of Financial Services Research, Vol. 13, No. 1.

Deutsche Bundesbank (various years)
Monatsberichte, Statistischer Teil V., Geldmarktsätze.

Deutsche Bundesbank (1997)
Monatsbericht, Vol. 49, Heft 1.

Devereux, Michael; Schiantarelli, Fabio (1990)
Investment, Financial Factors, and Cash Flow: Evidence from U.K. Panel Data, in: Hubbard, R. Glenn (ed.), Asymmetric Information, Corporate Finance, and Investment, Chicago/London, 279-306.

Diamond, Douglas W. (1984)
Financial Intermediation and Delegated Monitoring, in: Review of Economic Studies, Vol. 51, 393-414.

Diamond, Douglas W. (1989)
Reputation Acquisition in Debt Markets, in: Journal of Political Economy, Vol. 97, 828-862.

Dichtl, Erwin; Issing, Otmar (eds.) (1987)
Vahlens großes Wirtschaftslexikon, four volumes, Munich.

Diewert, W. E.; Wales, T. J. (1987)
Flexible Functional Forms and Global Curvature Conditions, in: Econometrica, Vol 55, 43-68.

Doerks, Wolfgang (1992)
Der Kursunterschied zwischen Stamm- und Vorzugsaktien in der Bundesrepublik Deutschland, Cologne.

Donaldson, Gordon (1961)
Corporate Debt Capacity, Boston.

Drukarczyk, Jochen (1981)
Verschuldung, Konkursrisiko, Kreditverträge und Marktwert von Aktiengesellschaften, in: Kredit und Kapital, Vol. 14, 287-319.

Drukarczyk, Jochen; Schmidt, Hartmut (1997)
Lenders as a Force of Corporate Governance, working paper, University of Regensburg.

Dufrene, Uric; Wong, Alan (1996)
Stakeholders Versus Stockholders and Financial Ethics: Ethics to Whom?, in: Managerial Finance Vol. 22, No. 4, S. 1-10.

DVFA/SG (1990)
Ergebnis nach DVFA/SG. Gemeinsame Empfehlung, Darmstadt.

Eakins, Stan; Mishra, Chandrasekhar (1996)
Ethics, Institutions, and Business Relations: A Study of Collusive Incentives for Institutional Shareholders to Monitor Firm Managers, in: Managerial Finance, Vol. 22, No. 4, S. 11-19.

Easterbrook, F. (1984)
Two Agency-Cost Explanations of Dividends, in: American Economic Review, 650-659.

Eberhardt, Stefan (1998)
Wertorientierte Unternehmensführung, Wiesbaden.

Edwards, Jeremy; Fischer, Klaus (1994)
Banks, Finance and Investment in Germany, Cambridge.

Eisenhardt, Kathleen M. (1989)
Agency Theory: An Assessment and Review, in: Academy of Management Review, Vol. 14, 57-74.

Elschen, Rainer (1991)
Gegenstand und Anwendungsmöglichkeiten der Agency-Theorie, in: Zeizschrift für betreibwirtschaftliche Forschung, Vol. 43, 1002-1012.

Evans, David S.; Heckman, James J. (1984)
A Test for Subadditivity of the Cost Function with an Application to the Bell System, in: The American Economic Review, Vol. 74, 615-623.

Fama, Eugene F. (1970)
Efficient Capital Markets: A Review of Theory and Empirical Work, in: Journal of Finance, Vol. 25, 383-417.

Fama, Eugene F. (1980)
Agency Problems and the Theory of the Firm, in: Journal of Political Economics, Vol. 88, 288-307.

Fama, Eugene F. (1991)
Efficient Capital Markets: II, in: Journal of Finance, Vol. 46, 1575-1617.

Fama, Eugene F.; French, Kenneth R. (1992)
The Cross Section of Expected Stock Returns, in: The Journal of Finance, Vol. 47, 427-465.

Fama, Eugene F.; French, Kenneth R. (1995)
Size and Book-to-Market Factors in Earnings and Returns, in: The Journal of Finance, Vol. 50, 131-155.

Fama, Eugene F.; Jensen, Michael C. (1983)
Separation of Ownership and Control, in: Journal of Law and Economics, Vol. 26, 301-325.

Fandel, Günter (1985)
Die Erfassung produktiver Gesetzmäßigkeiten durch Technologien, in: Wirtschaftswissenschaftliches Studium, Vol. 14, 57-62.

Färe, Rolf; Primont, Daniel (1995)
Multi-Output Production and Duality: Theory and Applications, Boston/London/Dordrecht.

Farrell, M. J. (1957)
The Measurement of Productive Efficiency, in: Journal of the Royal Statistical Society A 120, part 3, 253-281.

Faught, Jacqueline G.; Kale, Jayant R.; Rebello, Michael J. (1996)
On the Relative Efficacy of Tobin's q and other Firm Quality Measures, working paper, Georgia State University.

Fischer, Edwin O.; Zechner, J. (1990)
Die Lösung des Risikoanreizproblems durch Ausgabe von Optionsanleihen, in: Zeitschrift für betriebswirtschaftliche Forschung, Vol. 42, 334-342.

Fischer, Klaus (1990)
Hausbankbeziehungen als Instrument der Bindung zwischen Banken und Unternehmen: Eine theoretische und empirische Analyse, dissertation, Bonn.

Fischer, Marc (1994)
Der Property-Rights-Ansatz, in: Wirtschaftswissenschaftliches Studium, Vol. 23, 316-318.

Fluck, Zsusanna (1998)
Optimal Financial Contracting: Debt versus Outside Equity, in: Review of Financial Studies, Vol. 11, 383-418.

Förschle, Gerhart; Glaum, Martin; Mandler, Udo (1998)
Gesetz zur Kontrolle und Transparenz im Unternehmensbereich: Umfrage

unter Führungskräften börsennotierter Unternehmungen, in: Der Betrieb, Vol. 51, 889-895.

Førsund, Finn R.; Lovell, C.A. Knox; Schmidt, Peter (1980)
A Survey of Frontier Production Functions and of their Relationship to Efficiency Measurement, in: Journal of Econometrics, Vol. 13, 5-25.

Forsyth, Joetta (1996)
Corporate Control, Leverage, and Managerial Incentives, working paper 96-4, University of Michigan.

Francfort, Alfred J.; Rudolph, Bernd (1992)
Zur Entwicklung der Kapitalstrukturen in Deutschland und den Vereinigten Staaten von Amerika, in: Zeitschrift für betriebswirtschaftliche Forschung, Vol. 44, 1059-1079.

Franke, Günter (1995)
Kapitalstruktur, Theorie der, in: Gerke, Wolfgang; Steiner, Manfred (eds.), Handbuch des Bank- und Finanzwesens, 2nd edition, Stuttgart, 1178-1193.

Franks, Julian; Mayer, Colin (1997)
Ownership, Control and the Performance of German Corporations, working paper, London Business School/University of Oxford.

Frantzmann, Hans-Jörg (1987)
Der Montags-Effekt am deutschen Aktienmarkt, in: Zeitschrift für Betriebwirtschaft, Vol. 57, 611-635.

Freeman, R. E. (1984)
Stategic Management. A Stakeholder Approach, Boston.

Friend, Irwin; Hasbrouck, Joel (1988)
Determinants of Capital Structure, in: Research in Finance, Vol. 7, 1-19.

Friend, Irwin; Lang, Larry H. P. (1988)
An Empirical Test of the Impact of Managerial Self-Interest on Corporate Capital Structure, in: Journal of Finance, Vol. 43, 271-281.

Frisse, Kenneth; Funke, Michael; Lankes, Fidelis (1991)
An Empirical Analysis of West German Corporate Investment Decisions Using Company-Level Panel Data, working paper, London Business School.

Gäfgen, Gérard (1984)
Entwicklung und Stand der Theorie der Property Rights: Eine kritische Bestandsaufnahme, in: Neumann, Manfred (ed.): Ansprüche, Eigentums- und Verfügungsrechte, Schriften des Vereins für Socialpolitik, N. F. Vol. 140, Berlin, 43-62.

Galai, D.; Masulis, Ronald W. (1976)
The Option Pricing Model and the Risk Factor of Stock, in: Journal of Financial Economics, Vol 3, 53-81.

Garvey, Gerald T.; Hanka, Gordon (1997)
The Management of Corporate Capital Structure: Theory and Evidence, working paper, University of British Columbia.

Gehrke, Norman (1994)
Tobins q. Die Beziehung zwischen Buch- und Marktwerten deutscher Aktiengesellschaften, Wiesbaden.

Gerke, Wolfgang; Oerke, Marc; Sentner, Arnd (1997)
Der Informationsgehalt von Dividendenänderungen auf dem deutschen Aktienmarkt, in: Die Betriebswirtschaft, 810-822.

Girgensohn, Thomas; Calmbach, Jürgen (1980)
Der Einfluß der Aktionärsstrukturen auf Kapitalerhöhungen deutscher Industriegesellschaften, in: Zeitschrift für Betriebswirtschaft, Vol. 50, 426-440.

Gorton, Gary; Schmid, Frank A. (1996)
Universal Banking and the Performance of German Firms, Working Paper 96-11, Wharton School.

Green, Richard C. (1984)
Investment Incentives, Debt, and Warrants, in: Journal of Financial Economics, Vol. 13, S. 115-136.

Green, Richard C.; Talmor, Eli (1986)
Asset Substitution and the Agency Costs of Debt Financing, in: Journal of banking and Finance, Vol. 10, 391-399.

Greene, William H. (1980)
Maximum Likelihood Estimation of Econometric Frontier Functions, in: Journal of Econometrics, Vol. 13, 27-56.

Greene, William H. (1981)
Maximum Likelihood Estimation of Stochastic Frontier Production Models, in: Journal of Econometrics, Vol. 18, 285-289.

Greene, William H. (1990a)
A Gamma-Distributed Stochastic Frontier Model, in: Journal of Econometrics, Vol. 46, 141-163.

Greene, William H. (1990b)
Multiple Roots of the Tobit Log-Likelihood, in: Journal of Econometrics, Vol. 46, 365-380.

Greene, William H. (1993)
The Econometric Approach to Efficiency Analysis, in: Fried, Harold O.;

Lovell, C. A. Knox; Schmidt, Shelton S. (eds): The Measurement of Productive Efficiency, New York, Oxford, 68-119.

Greene, William H. (1997)
Econometric Analysis, 3rd edition, Upper Saddle River, NJ.

Grinblatt, Mark; Titman, Sheridan (1989)
Adverse Risk Incentives and the Design of Performance-Based Contracts, in: Management Science, Vol. 35, 807-822.

Griner, Emmeth H.; Gordon, Lawrence A. (1995)
Internal Cash Flow, Insider Ownership, and Capital Expenditures: A Test of the Pecking Order and Managerial Hypotheses, in: Journal of Business Finance & Accounting, Vol. 22, 179-199.

Grossman, Sanford J.; Hart, Oliver D. (1982)
Corporate Financial Structure and Mangerial Incentives, in: McCall, John J. (ed.), The Economics of Information and Uncertainty, Conference Report Universities-National Bureau for Economic Research Number 32, Chicago/London, 107-140.

Gorman, W. M., (1968)
Measuring the Quantities of Fixed Factors, in: Wolfe, J. N. (ed.), Value, Capital and Growth, Edinburgh, 141-172.

Guilkey, David; Lovell, C. A. Knox (1980)
On the Flexibility of the Translog Approximation, in: International Ecomic Review, Vol. 21, 137-147.

Hackel, Kenneth S.; Livnat, Joshua; Rai, Atul (1994)
The Free Cash Flow/Small-Cap Anomaly, in: Financial Analysts Journal, 33-41.

Hackett, John T. (1985)
Concepts and Practice of Agency Theory within the Corporation, in: Altman, Edward I.; Subrahmanyam, Marti G. (eds.), Recent Advances in Corporate Finance, Homewood, 163-171.

Halbinger, Josef (1980)
Erfolgsausweispolitik, Berlin.

Hannan, Timothy H.; Mavinga, Ferdinand (1980)
Expense Preference and Managerial Control: The Case of the Banking Firm, in: Bell Journal of Economics, Vol. 10, 671-682.

Hansen, Herbert (1997)
Die Kopflastigkeit des deutschen Kurszettels, in: Die Aktiengesellschaft, Vol. 42, 78-82.

Harris, Milton; Raviv, Artur (1988)
Corporate Control Contests and Capital Structure, in: Journal of Financial Economics, Vol. 20, 55-86.

Harris, Milton; Raviv, Artur (1991)
The Theory of Capital Structure, in: Journal of Finance, Vol. 46, 297-355.

Harris, Milton; Raviv, Artur (1992)
Financial Contracting Theory, in: Laffont, Jean-Jacques (ed.), Advances in Economic Theory Sixth World Congress, Vol. 2, 64-150.

Hartmann-Wendels, Thomas (1986)
Dividendenpolitik bei asymmetrischer Informationsverteilung, Wiesbaden.

Hartung, Joachim (1986)
Statistik, 5th edition, Munich at al.

Haugen, Robert A.; Senbet, Lemma W. (1981)
Resolving the Agency Problems of External Capital through Options, in: Journal of Finance, Vol. 36, 629-647.

Hawawini, Gabriel (1984)
European Equity Markets: Price Behavior and Efficiency, New York.

Hax, Herbert (1981)
Die arbeitsgeleitete Unternehmung—Probleme der Unternehmensführung und Überwachung, in: Gerhard Seicht (ed.): Management und Kontrolle, Festgabe für Erich Loitlsberger, Berlin, 337-364.

Hax, Herbert; Hartmann-Wendels, Thomas; von Hinten, Peter (1988)
Moderne Entwicklung der Finanzierungstheorie, in: Christians, F. Wilhelm (ed.), Finanzierungshandbuch, 2nd edition, Wiesbaden, 689-713.

Heinke, Volker (1998)
Bonitätsrisiko und Credit Rating festverzinslicher Wertpapiere. Eine empirische Untersuchung am Euromarkt, Bad Soden.

Heinkel, Robert; Zechner, Josef (1990)
The Role of Debt and Preferred Stock as a Solution to Adverse Investment Incentives, in: Journal of Financial and Quantitative Analysis, Vol. 25, 1-24.

Henderson, James M.; Quandt, Richard E. (1983)
Mikroökonomische Theorie, 5th edition, Munich.

Hildebrand, George H.; Liu, Ta-Chung (1965)
Manufacturing Production Functions in the United States, 1957, Ithaca.

Hill, Charles W. L.; Jones, Thomas M. (1992)
Stakeholder-Agency Theory, in: Journal of Management Science, Vol. 29, 132-154.

Hindley, Brian (1970)
Separation of Ownership and Control in the Modern Corporation, in: Journal of Law and Economics, Vol. 13, 185-221.

Hodges, Charles W.; Taylor, Walton R. L.; Yoder, James A. (1997)
Stocks, Bonds, the Sharpe Ratio, and the Investment Horizon, in: Financial Analysts Journal, 74-80.

Holl, Peter (1975)
Effect of Control Type on the Performance of the Firm in the UK, in: Journal of Industrial Economics, Vol. 23, 257-271.

Holl, Peter (1977)
Control Type and the Market for Corporate Control in Large U.S. Corporations, in: Journal of Industrial Economics, Vol. 25, 259-273.

Homaifar, Ghassem; Zietz, Joachim; Benkato, Omar (1994)
An Empirical Model of Capital Structure: Some New Evidence, in: Journal of Business Finance & Accounting, Vol. 21, 1-14.

Hoppenstedt GmbH (ed.) (1986-1991)
Saling Aktienführer, Darmstadt et al.

Hoppenstedt GmbH (ed.) (1996)
CD-ROM Bilanzdatenbank, Darmstadt.

Horn, Ernst-Jürgen (1994)
Neuere Entwicklungen auf dem deutschen Kapitalmarkt, Tübingen.

Hughes, Joseph P.; Mester, Loretta J. (1993)
A Quality and Risk-Adjusted Cost Function for Banks. Evidence on the "Too-Big-To-Fail" Doctrine, in: Journal of Productivity Analysis, 293-315.

Iber, Bernhard (1985)
Zur Entwicklung der Aktionärsstruktur in der Bundesrepublik Deutschland (1963-1983), in: Zeitschrift für Betriebswirtschaft, Vol. 55, 1101-1119.

Iber, Bernhard (1987)
Zur Entwicklung der Aktionärsstruktur börsennotierter deutscher Aktiengesellschaften, Kiel.

Institut der deutschen Wirtschaft (ed.) (1996)
Zahlen zur wirtschaftlichen Entwicklung der Bundesrepublik Deutschland, Cologne.

Israel, Ronen (1991)
Capital Structure and the Market for Corporate Control: The Defensive Role of Debt Financing, in: Journal of Finance, Vol. 46, 1391-1409.

Jaffee, Dwight M.; Russell, Thomas (1976)
Imperfect Information, Uncertainty, and Credit Rationing, in: Quarterly Journal of Economics, 651-666.

Jarrell, G.; Poulsen, A. (1987)
Shark Repellents and Stock Prices: The Effects of Antitakeover Amendments since 1980, in: Journal of Financial Economics, Vol. 19, 127-168.

Jeger, Matthias (1994)
Dynamik von Unternehemensrenditen in der Schweiz, Chur.

Jehle, Egon (1982)
Reformvorschläge zur Verstärkung der eigentümerbezogenen Managementkontrolle in Publikumsgesellschaften, in: Zeitschrift für betriebswirtschaftliche Forschung, Vol. 34, 1065-1084.

Jenkinson, Tim; Ljungqvist, Alexander (1997)
Hostile Satkes an the Role of Banks in German Corporate Governance, working paper, Oxford University.

Jensen, Gerald R.; Johnson, James M. (1995)
The Dynamics of Corporate Dividend Reductions, in: Financial Management, Vol. 24, 31-51.

Jensen, Michael C. (1983)
Organization Theory and Methodology, in: The Accounting Review, Vol. 58, 319-339.

Jensen, Michael C. (1986)
Agency Costs of Free Cash Flow, Corporate Finance, and Takeovers, in: American Economic Review, Papers and Proceedings, Vol. 76, 323-329.

Jensen, Michael C. (1988)
Takeovers: Their Causes and Consequences, in: Journal of Economic Perspectives, Vol. 2, 21-48.

Jensen, Michael C. (1993)
The Modern Industrial Revolution, Exit, and the Failure of Internal Control Systems, in: Journal of Finance, Vol. 48, 831-880.

Jensen, Michael C.; Meckling, William H. (1976)
Theory of the Firm: Managerial Behavior, Agency Costs and Ownership Structure, in: Journal of Financial Economics, Vol. 3, 305-360.

Jensen, Michael C.; Meckling, William H. (1979)
Rights and Production Functions: An Application to Labor-Managed Firms and Codetermination, in: Journal of Business, Vol. 52, 469-506.

Jensen, Michael C.; Murphy, Kevin (1990)
Performance Pay and Top Management Incentives, in: Journal of Political Economy, Vol. 98, 225-264.

Jensen, Michael C.; Ruback, Richard S. (1983)
The Market for Corporate Control. The Scientific Evidence, in: Journal of Financial Economics, Vol. 11, 5-50.

Jensen, Michael C.; Smith, Clifford W. (1985)
Stockholder, Manager, and Creditor Interests: Applications of Agency Theory, in: Altman, Edward I.; Subrahmanyam, Marti G. (eds.), Recent Advances in Corporate Finance, Homewood, 95-131.

John, Kose (1987)
Risk-Shifting Incentives and Signalling Through Corporate Capital Structure, in: Journmal of Finance, Vol. 42, 623-641.

John, Teresa A.; John, Kose (1993)
Top-Management Compensation and Capital Structure, in: Journal of Finance, Vol. 48, 949-974.

Johnson, Shane A. (1997)
An Empirical Analysis of the Determinants of Corporate Debt Ownership Structure, in: Journal of Financial and Quantitative Analysis, Vol. 32, 47-69.

Jondrow, James; Knox Lovell, C. A.; Materov, Ivan S.; Schmidt, Peter (1982)
On the Estimation of Technical Inefficiency in the Stochastic Frontier Production Function Model, in: Journal of Econometrics, Vol. 19, 233-238.

Jorgenson, D. W.; Fraumeni, B. M. (1981)
Relative Prices and Technical Change, in: Berndt, E.; Field, B. (eds.) Modeling and Measuring Natural Resource Substitution, Cambridge, MA, 17-47.

Jung, Kooyul; Kim, Yong-Cheol; Stulz, René M. (1996)
Timing, Investment Opportunities, Mangerial Discretion, and the Security Issue Decision, in: Journal of Financial Economics, Vol. 42, 159-185.

Kalay, Avner (1982)
Stockholder-Bondholder Conflict and Dividend Constraints, in: Journal of Financial Economics, Vol. 10, 211-233.

Kallfass, Hermann H. (1992)
Managementkontrolle in Publikumsgesellschaften, in: Kantzenbach, E.; Molitor, B.; Mayer, O. (eds.), Hamburger Jahrbuch für Wirtschafts- und Gesellschaftspolitik, Tübingen, 277-290.

Kamerschen, David R. (1968)
The Influence of Ownership and Control on Profit Rates, in: American Economic Review, Vol. 58, 432-447.

Kamin, Jacob Y.; Ronen, Joshua (1978)
The Effects of Corporate Control on Apparent Profit Performance, in: Southern Economic Journal, Vol. 45, 181-191.

Kang, Jun-Koo; Stulz, René M. (1997)
Is Bank-Centered Corporate Governance Worth it? A Cross-Sectional

Analysis of the Performance of Japanese Firms during the Asset Price Deflation, working paper Korea University/Ohio State University.

Kania, John J.; McKean, John R.; (1976)
Ownership, Control and the Contemporary Corporation: A General Behavior Analysis, in: Kyklos, Vol. 29, 272-291.

Kaplan, Steven (1997)
Corporate Governance and Corporate Performance: A Comparison of Germany, Japan, and the U.S., in: Journal of Applied Corporate Finance, Vol. 9, No. 4, 86-93.

Karmann, Alexander (1992)
Principal-Agent-Modelle und Risikoallokation, in: Wirtschaftswissenschaftliches Studium, Vol. 21, 557-562.

Kaulmann, Thomas (1987)
Property Rights und Unternehmungstheorie: Stand und Weiterentwicklung der empirischen Forschung, Munich.

Kessel, Anette (1995)
Der Leveraged Buyout in den USA und der Bundesrepublik Deutschland, Frankfurt et al.

Kim, Chang Soo (1996)
Changes in Corporate Capital Structures: Evidence from the 1986 Tax Reform Act, in: Managerial Finance, Vol. 22, 53-68.

Kim, Wi S.; Sorensen, Eric H. (1986)
Evidence on the Impact of the Agency Costs of Debt on Corporate Debt Policy, in: Journal of Financial and Quantitative Analysis, Vol. 21, 131-144.

Kmenta, Jan (1967)
On Estimation of the CES Production Function, in: International Economic Review, Vol. 8, No. 2, 180-189.

Kmenta, Jan (1986)
Elements of Econometrics, 2nd edition, New York, London.

Köhne, Dietmar; Tebroke, Hermann-Josef (1995)
Managementkontrolle in Kreditinstituten—eine vergleichende Analyse aus Sicht der Sparkassen, in: Zeitschrift für öffentliche und gemeinwirtschaftliche Unternehmen, Vol. 18, 312-333.

Kole, Stacey R. (1993)
Mangerial Ownership and Firm Performance: Incentives or Rewards? working paper FR 93-10, University of Rochester.

Kopp, Raymond J.; Diewert, W. Erwin (1982)
The Decompositions of Frontier Cost Function Deviations into Measures of

Technical and Allocative Efficiency, in: Journal of Econometrics, Vol. 19, 319-331.

Koutsoyiannis, Anne (1981)
Theory of Econometrics, 2nd edition, London/Basingstoke.

Kovenack, Dan; Phillips, Gordon (1995)
Capital Structure and Product-Market Rivalry: How Do We Reconcile Theory and Evidence?, in American Economic Association Papers and Proceedings, Vol. 85, 403-408.

Krahnen, Jan Pieter (1985)
Kapitalmarkt und Kreditbank, Berlin.

Krahnen, Jan Pieter (1988)
Zur Wahl der Vertragsdauer bei Kreditarrangemants unter asymmetrischer Information, in: Wirtschaftswissenschaftliches Studium, Vol. 17, 343-349.

Kürsten, Wolfgang (1993)
Finanzkontrakte und Risikoanreizproblem. Mißverständnisse im informationsökonomischen Ansatz der Finanztheorie. Wiesbaden.

Küting, Karl-Heinz (1997)
Der Wahrheitsgehalt deutscher Bilanzen, in: Deutsches Steuerrecht, 84-91.

Lang, Günter; Welzel, Peter (1994)
Skalenerträge und Verbundvorteile im Bankensektor. Empirische Bestimmung für die bayerischen Genossenschaftsbanken, working paper no. 109, Institut für Volkswirtschaftslehre, University of Augsburg.

Lang, Günter; Welzel, Peter (1996)
Efficiency and Technical Progress in Banking. Empirical Results for a Panel of German Cooperative Banks, in: Journal of Banking and Finance, Vol. 20, 1003-1023.

Lang, Günter; Welzel, Peter (1997)
Größe und Kosteneffizienz im deutschen Bankensektor, in: Zeitschrift für Betriebswirtschaft, 67. Jg., H. 3, 269-283.

Langendijk, Henk P. A. J.; Praag, Bart van (1996)
An Empirical Analysis of Income Smoothing Behaviour in France, Germany, the Netherlands and the United Kingdom, working paper, University of Amsterdam.

Larner, Robert J. (1966)
Ownership and Control in the 200 Largest Nonfinancial Corporations, 1929-1963, in: American Economic Review, Vol. 56, 777-787.

Lasfer, Ameziane M. (1995)
Agency Costs, Taxes and Debt: The UK Evidence, in: European Financial Management, Vol. 1, 265-285.

Lau, L. J.; Yotopoulos, P. A. (1971)
A Test for Relative Efficiency and Application to Indian Agriculture, in: American Economic Review, Vol. 61, 95-109.

Leffson, Ulrich (1984)
Bilanzanalyse, 3rd edition, Stuttgart.

Leibenstein, H. W. (1966)
Allocative versus 'X-efficiency', in: American Economic Review, Vol. 56, 392-415.

Leimkühler, Claudia (1996)
Ist die öffentliche Kritik am deutschen Aufsichtsratssystem gerechtfertigt? in: Die Wirtschaftsprüfung, Vol. 49, 305-313.

Leland, Hayne E.; Toft, Klaus Bjerre (1996)
Optimal Capital Structure, Endogenous Bankruptcy, and the Term Structure of Credit Spreads, in: Journal of Finance, Vol. 51, 987-1019.

Lerbinger, Paul (1984)
Die Leistungsfähigkeit deutscher Aktieninvestmentfonds–eine empirische Untersuchung zur Informationseffizienz des deutschen Aktienmarktes, in: Zeitschrift für betriebwirtschaftliche Forschung, Vol. 36, 60-73.

Lewellen, Wilbur G.; Badrinath, S. G. (1997)
On the Measurement of Tobin's q, in: Journal of Financial Economics, Vol 44, 77-122.

Lin, Laura (1996)
The Effectiveness of Outside Directors as a Corporate Governance Mechanism: Theories and Evidence, in: Northwestern University Law Review, Vol. 90, 898-976..

Linde, R. (1981)
Produktionsfunktionen, in: Handwörterbuch der Wirtschaftswissenschaften, Vol. 6, Stuttgart 1981, 276-295.

Lintner, John (1956)
Distribution of Incomes of Corporations among Dividends, Retained Earnings, and Taxes, in: American Economic Review, Vol. 61, 97-113.

Lintner, John (1965)
The Valuation of Risk Assets and the Selection of Risky Investments in Stock Portfolios and Capital Budgets, in: Review of Economics and Statistics, Vol. 47, 13-37.

Lipka, Sabine (1995)
Managementeffizienz und Kapitalmarktkontrolle, Frankfurt.

Lipsey, R; Lancaster, K. (1956)
The General Theory of Second Best, in: Review of Economic Studies, Vol. 24, 11-32.

Loderer, Claudio; Martin, Kenneth (1997)
Executive Stock Ownership and Performance. Tracking Faint Traces, in: Journal of Financial Economics, Vol. 45, 223-255.

Lovell, C. A. Knox (1993)
Production Frontiers and Productive Efficiency, in: Fried, Harold O.; Lovell, C. A. Knox; Schmidt, Shelton S. (eds.): The Measurement of Productive Efficiency, New York, Oxford, 3-67.

Macey, Jonathan R.; Miller, Geoffrey P. (1997)
Universal Banks are not the Answer to America's Corporate Governance "Problem": A Look at Germany, Japan, and the U.S., in: Journal of Applied Corporate Finance, Vol. 9, 57-73.

MacKie-Mason, Jeffrey K. (1990)
Do Firms Care Who Provides Their Financing?, in: Hubbard, R. Glenn (ed.), Asymmetric Information, Corporate Finance, and Investment, Chicago/ London, 63-103.

Marris, Robin (1968)
The Economic Theory of "Managerial" Capitalism, New York.

Marris, Robin (1971)
An Introduction to Theories of Corporate Growth, in: Marris, Robin; Wood, Adrian (eds.): The Corporate Economy: Growth, Competition and Innovative Potential, London, 1-31.

Marsh, Paul (1979)
Equity Rights Issues and the Efficiency of the UK Stock Market, in: Journal of Finance, Vol. 34, 839-862.

McAllister, Patrick H.; McManus, Douglas (1993)
Resolving the Scale Efficiency Puzzle in Banking, in: Journal of Banking and Finance, Vol. 17, 389-405.

McEachern, William A. (1975)
Managerial Control and Performance, Lexington.

McFadden, D. M. (1978)
Cost, Revenue, and Profit Functions, in: Fuss, M.; McFadden, D. M. (eds.), Production Economics. A Dual Approach to Theory and Applications, Vol. 1, Amsterdam, 3-110.

McKean, John R.; Kania, John J. (1978)
An Industry Approach to Owner-Manager Control and Profit Performance, in: Journal of Business, Vol. 51, 327-342.

Meffert, Heribert (1998)
Marketing: Grundlagen marktorientierter Unternehmensführung, 8th edition, Wiesbaden.

Mehran, Hamid (1992)
Executive Incentive Plans, Corporate Control, and Capital Structure, in: Journal of Financial and Quantitative Analysis, Vol. 27, 539-560.

Merton, Robert C. (1974)
The Pricing of Corporate Debt: The Risk Structure of Interest Rates, in: Journal of Finance, Vol. 29, 449-470.

Meeusen, Wim; van den Broeck, Julien (1977)
Efficiency Estimation from Cobb-Douglas Production Functions with Composed Error, in: International Economic Review, Vol. 18, 435-444.

Mester, Loretta J. (1987)
A Multiproduct Cost Study of Savings and Loans, in: Journal of Finance, Vol. 42, 423-445.

Mester, Loretta J. (1994)
Efficieny of Banks in the Third Federal Reserve District, working paper 94-13, The Wharton School, University of Pennsylvania.

Milde, Hellmuth (1990)
Dividendenhöhe als Signal, in: Wirtschaftwissenschaftliches Studium, Vol. 19, 334-339.

Milde, Hellmuth (1995)
Napoleon und Goethe über Agency-Probleme, in: Österreichisches Bank-Archiv, 519-523.

Milgrom, Paul R.; Roberts, John (1992)
Economics, Organizations, and Management, Englewood Cliffs.

Miller, Merton H. (1988)
The Modigliani-Miller Propositions after Thirty Years, in: Journal of Economic Perspectives, Vol. 2, 99-120.

Modigliani, Franco (1988)
MM—Past, Present, Future, in: Journal of Economic Perspectives, Vol. 2, 149-158.

Modigliani, Franco; Miller, Merton H. (1958)
The Cost of Capital, Corporate Finance, and the Theory of Investment, in: American Economic Review, Vol. 48, 261-297.

Modigliani, Franco; Miller, Merton H. (1963)
Corporation Income taxes and the Cost of Capital: A Correction, in: American Economic Review, Vol. 53, 433-443.

Monsen, R. Joseph; Chiu, John S.; Cooley, David E. (1968)
The Effect of Separation of Ownership and Control on the Performance of the Large Firm, in: Quarterly Journal of Economics, Vol. 82, 435-451.

Morck, Randall; Shleifer, Andrei; Vishny, Robert W. (1988)
Management Ownership and Market Valuation. An Empirical Analysis, in: Journal of Financial Economics, Vol. 20, 293-315.

Morck, Randall; Shleifer, Andrei; Vishny, Robert W. (1989)
Alternative Mechanisms for Corporate Control, in: American Economic Review, Vol. 79, 842-852.

Morrison, D. G. (1969)
On the Interpretation of Discriminant Analsysis, in: Journal of Marketing Research, Vol. 6, 156-163.

Moses, O. Douglas (1991)
Cash Flow Signals and Analysts' Earnings Forecast Revisions, in: Journal of Business & Financial Accounting, Vol. 18, 807 - 832.

Mossin, J. (1966)
Equilibrium in a Capital Asset Market, in: Econometrica, Vol. 34, 768-783.

Mühlbradt, Frank W. (1978)
Chancen und Risiken der Aktienanlage—Untersuchungen zur "Efficient-Market"-Theorie in Deutschland, Cologne.

Mühlhaupt, Ludwig (1956)
Umsatz-, Kosten- und Gewinnplanung einer Kreditbank, in: Zeitschrift für betriebwirtschaftliche Forschung, Vol. 8, 7-74.

Mülbert, Peter O. (1997)
Bank Equity Holdings in Non-Financial Firms and Corporate Governance: The Case of German Universal Banks, working paper, University of Trier.

Münchow, Malte-Maria (1995)
Bankenmacht oder Kontrolle durch Banken, Sinzheim.

Murali, Ramaswami; Welch, Johnathan B. (1989)
Agents, Owners, Control and Performance, in: Journal of Business Finance & Accounting, Vol. 16, 385-398.

Murphy, Kevin (1985)
Corporate Performance and Managerial Remuneration: An Empirical Analysis, in: Journal of Accounting and Economics, Vol. 7, 11-42.

Myers, Stewart C. (1977)
The Determinants of Corporate Borrowing, in: Journal of Financial Economics, Vol. 5, 147-175.

Myers, Stewart C. (1984)
The Capital Structure Puzzle, in: Journal of Finance, Vol. 39, 575-592.

Myers, Stewart C.; Majluf, Nicholas S. (1984)
Corporate Financing and Investment Decisions when Firms have Information that Investors do not have, in: Journal of Financial Economics, Vol. 13, 187-221.

Myerson, Roger B (1991)
Game Theory. Analysis of Conflict, Cambridge, MA/London.

Narayanan, M. P. (1988)
Debt versus Equity under Asymmetric Information, in: Journal of Financial and Quantitative Analysis, Vol. 23, 39-51.

Neuberger, Doris (1989)
Finanzstruktur, Wettbewerb und Kapitalakkumulation, Frankfurt/New York.

Neuberger, Doris (1994)
Kreditvergabe durch Banken, Tübingen.

Neumann, John von; Morgerstern, Oskar (1947)
The Theory of Games and Economic Behavior, 2nd edition, Princeton.

Neus, Werner (1989)
Ökonomische Agency-Theorie und Kapitalmarktgleichgewicht, Wiesbaden.

Noe, Thomas H. (1988)
Capital Structure and Signaling Game Equilibria, in: The Review of Financial Studies, Vol. 1, 331-355.

Noth, Corinna (1996)
Die Eigenkapitalausstattung deutscher Gesellschaften mit beschränkter Haftung, Cologne.

Oberender, Peter (1987)
Marktformen, in: Dichtl, Erwin; Issing, Otmar (eds.), Vahlens großes Wirtschaftslexikon, four volumes, Munich, 1240-1241.

Oberender, Peter (1994)
Industrieökonomik, in: Wirtschaftwissenschaftliches Studium, Vol. 23, 65-73.

Olson, Jerome A.; Schmidt, Peter; Waldmann, Donald M. (1980)
A Monte Carlo Study of Estimators of Stochastic Frontier Production Functions, in: Journal of Econometrics, Vol. 13, 68-82.

Opitz, Otto (1995)
Mathematik, 5th edition, Munich.

Opler, Tim C.; Titman, Sheridan (1996)
Financial Distress and Corporate Performance, in: Journal of Finance, Vol. 49, 1015-1040.

Osterloh, Margit; Löhr, Albert (1994)
Ökonomik oder Ethik als Grundlage der sozialen Ordnung? in: Wirtschaftswissenschaftliches Studium, Vol. 23, 401-406.

Padberg, Max (1995)
Der Einfluß von Kapitalerhöhungen auf den Marktwert deutscher Aktiengesellschaften, Cologne.

Pagano, Marco; Jappelli, Tullio (1993)
Information Sharing in Credit Markets, in: Journal of Finance, Vol. 48, 1693-1718.

Palmer, John (1973)
The Profit-Performance Effects of the Separation of Ownership from Control in Large U.S. Industrial Corporations, in: The Bell Journal of Economics and Management Science, Vol.4, 293-303.

Parrino, Robert; Weisbach, Michael S. (1997)
On the Magnitude of Stockholder-Bondholder Conflicts, working paper, University of Chicago and University of Arizona.

Partch, M. Megan (1987)
The Creation of a Class of Limited Voting Common Stock and Shareholder Wealth, in: Journal of Financial Economics, Vol. 18, 313-339.

Payne, Thomas H.; Millar, James A.; Glezen, G. William (1994)
Fiduciary Responsibility and Bank-Firm Relationships: An Analysis of Shareholder Voting by Banks, working paper, University of Arkansas, Fayetteville.

Perotti, Enrico C.; Spier, Kathryn E. (1993)
Capital Structure as a Bargaining Tool: The Role of Leverage in Contract Renegotiation, in: American Economic Review, Vol. 83, 1131-1141.

Petersen, Thomas (1989)
Optimale Anreizsysteme, Wiesbaden.

Pfaffmann, Eric (1996)
Die vertragstheoretische Perspektive in der Neuen Institutionenökonomik, in: Wirtschaftswissenschaftliches Studium, Vol. 25, 646-648.

Pi, Lynn; Timme, Stephen G. (1993)
Corporate Control and Bank Efficiency, in: Journal of Banking and Finance, Vol. 17, 515-530.

Picot, Arnold (1982)
Transaktionskostenansatz in der Organisationstheorie: Stand der Diskussion und Aussagewert, in: Der Betrieb, Vol. 42, 267-284.

Picot, Arnold (1991)
Ökonomische Theorien der Organisation—Ein Überblick über neuere

Ansätze und deren betriebwirtschaftliches Anwendungspotential, in: Ordelheide, Dieter; Rudolph, Bernd; Büsselmann; Elke (eds.), Betriebwirtschaftslehre und ökonomische Theorie, Stuttgart, 144-170.

Pitelis, Christos N.; Sugden, Roger (1985)
The Separation of Ownership and Control in the Theory of the Firm, in: International Journal of Industrial Organization, Vol. 4, 69-86.

Pitt, Mark M.; Lee, Lung-Fei (1981)
The Measurement and Sources of Technical Inefficiency in the Indonesian Weaving Industry, in: Journal of Development Economics, Vol. 9, 43-64.

Popper, Karl (1966)
Logik der Forschung, Tübingen.

Pottschmidt, Günter (1995)
Kreditsicherheiten, in: Gerke, Wolfgang; Steiner, Manfred (eds.), Handwörterbuch des Bank- und Finanzwesens, 2nd edition, Stuttgart, 1290-1304.

Pratt, John W.; Zeckhauser, Richard J. (1985)
Principals and Agents: An Overview, in: Pratt, John W.; Zeckhauser, Richard J. (eds.), Principals and Agents: The Structure of Business, Boston, 1-35.

Pulley, Lawrence B.; Braunstein, Yale M. (1992)
A Composite Cost Function for Multiproduct Firms with an Application to Economies of Scope in Banking, in: The Review of Economic and Statistics, Vol. 74, 221-230.

Qualls, David P. (1976)
Market Structure and Managerial Behavior, in: Masson, Robert T.; Qualls, David P. (eds.), Essays on the Industrial Organization in Honor of Joe S. Bain, Cambridge, (Mass.), 89-104.

Radcliffe, Nicholas J. (1993)
Genetic Set Recombination, in: Whitley, Darrell L. (ed.): Foundations of Genetic Algorithms 2, San Mateo, CA, 203-220.

Radice, Hugo K. (1971)
Control Type, Profitability and Growth in Large Firms: An Empirical Study, in: Economic Journal, Vol. 81, 547-562.

Rathenau, Walter (1916)
Von kommenden Dingen, Berlin.

Ravid, S. Abraham (1988)
On Interactions of Production and Financial Decisions, in: Financial Management, Vol. 17, 87-99.

Rayton, Bruce (1996)
Firm Performance and Compensation Structure: Performance Elasticities of

Average Employee Compensation, working paper, Nottingham Trent University.

Reagan, Patricia B.; Stulz, René M. (1983)
Risk Sharing, Labor Contracts and Capital Markets, working paper, University of Rochester.

Rees, Ray (1985)
The Theory of Principal and Agent I, in: Bulletin of Economic Research, Vol. 37, 3-26.

Reifschneider, David; Stevenson, Rodney (1991)
Systematic Departures from the Frontier: A Framework for Analysis of Firm Inefficiency, in: International Economic Review, Vol. 32, 715-723.

Riahi-Belkaoui, Ahmed (1992)
Executive Compensation, Organizational Effectiveness, Social Performance and Firm Performance: An Empirical Investigation, in: Journal of Business Finance & Accounting, Vol. 19, 25-38.

Richmond, J. (1974)
Estimating the Efficiency of Production, in: International Economic Review, Vol.15, 515-521.

Richter, Rudolf (1990)
Sichtweise und Fragestellung der Neuen Institutionenökonomik, in: Zeitschrift für Wirtschafts- und Sozialwissenschaften, Vol. 110, 571-591.

Ridder-Aab, Christa-Maria (1980)
Die moderne Aktiengesellschaft im Lichte der Theorie der Eigentumsrechte, Frankfurt.

Ritter, C.; Simar, L. (1994)
Pitfalls of Normal-Gamma Stochastic Frontier Models, working paper, Louvain.

Rosen, Sherwin (1990)
Contracts and the Market for Executives, NBER working paper no. 3542, Cambridge, MA.

Ross, Stephen A. (1977)
The Determination of Financial Structure: The Incentive-Signalling Approach, in: Bell Journal of Economics, Vol. 8, 23-40.

Ross, Stephen A. (1978)
Some Notes on Financial Incentive-Signalling Models, Activity Choice, and Risk Preferences, in: Journal of Finance, Vol. 33, 777-794.

Rozeff, M. S. (1982)
Growth, Beta and Agency Costs as Determinants of Dividend Payout Ratios, in: Journal of Financial Research, 249-259.

Sahling, Claus (1981)
Die Reaktion des Aktienmarktes auf wesentliche Ausschüttungsänderungen – Empirische Untersuchung zur Überprüfung der mittelstarken Form der "efficient market"-Theorie für die deutschen Börsen im Zeitraum 1971-1977, Schwarzenbek.

Schalk, Hans Joachim; Untiedt, Gerhard; Lüschow, Jörg (1994)
Technische Effizienz, Wachstum und Konvergenz in den Arbeitsmarktregionen der Bundesrepublik Deutschland (West): Eine ökonometrische Analyse für die Verarbeitende Industrie mit einem „Frontier Production Function" - Modell, in: Volkswirtschaftliche Diskussionsbeiträge Westfälische Wilhelms-Universität Münster, Beitrag Nr. 192, 1994.

Schefczyk, Michael (1996)
Data Envelopment Analysis, in: Die Betriebswirtschaft, Vol. 56, 167-183.

Schenk, Karl-Ernst (1984)
Property Rights and Industrial Organization: Towards a Double Interface Concept, in: Boettcher, E.; Herder-Dorneich, P.; Schenk, K. E. (eds.): Jahrbuch für Neue Politische Ökonomie, Vol. 3, 17-30.

Scheper, W. (1981)
Produktionstheorie, in: Handwörterbuch der Wirtschaftswissenschaften, Vol. 6, Stuttgart, 256-276.

Schierenbeck, Henner (1987)
Grundzüge der Betriebswirtschaftslehre, 9th edition, Munich.

Schierenbeck, Henner (1997)
Ertragsorientiertes Bankmanagement, 5th edition, Wiesbaden.

Schmid, Frank A. (1996)
Banken, Aktionärsstruktur und Unternehmenssteuerung, parts I and II, in: Kredit und Kapital, Vol. 29, 402-427, 545-564.

Schmid, Helmut (1994)
Leveraged Management Buy-Out—Begriff, Gestaltungen, optimale Kapitalstruktur und ökonomische Bewertung, Frankfurt am Main et al.

Schmidt, Peter; Sickles, Robin C. (1984)
Production Frontiers and Panel Data, in: Journal of Business & Economic Statistics, Vol. 2, No. 4, 367-374.

Schmidt, Reinhard H. (1981a)
Ein "neo-institutionalistischer Ansatz" der Finanzierungstheorie, in: Rühli, Edwin; Thommen, Jean-Paul (eds.), Unternehmensführung aus finanz- und bankbetreibwirtschaftlicher Sicht, Stuttgart, 135-154.

Schmidt, Reinhard H. (1981b)
Grundformen der Finanzierung—eine Anwendung des neo-institutionali-

stischen Ansatzes der Finanzierungstheorie, in: Kredit und Kapital, 186-221.

Schmidt, Reinhard H. (1988)
Neuere Property Rights-Analysen in der Finanzierungstheorie, in: Dietrich Budäus; Elmar Gerum; Gebhard Zimmermann (eds.): Betriebswirtschaftslehre und Theorie der Verfügungsrechte, Wiesbaden, 239-267.

Schmidt, Reinhard H.; Terberger, Eva (1996)
Grundzüge der Finanzierungs- und Investitionstheorie, 3rd edition, Wiesbaden.

Schmidt, Reinhart (1976)
Capital Structure and Bankruptcy, in: European Finance Association 1975 Proceedings, 309-328.

Schmidt, Reinhart; May, Axel (1993)
Erklärung von Aktienindizes durch Pressemitteilungen, in: Zeitschrift für Betriebwirtschaft, Vol. 63, 61-88.

Schneider, Dieter (1987)
Agency Costs and Transaction Costs: Flops in the Principal-Agent-Theory of Financial Markets, in: Bamberg, Günter; Spremann, Klaus (eds.), Agency Theory, Information, and Incentives, Heidelberg, 481-494.

Schneider, Kristian (1991)
Erfolgswirkungen der Kapitalstruktur, Frankfurt et al.

Schnittge, Jürgen (1989)
Überrenditeeffekte am deutschen Aktienmarkt. Eine theoretische und empirische Analyse, Cologne.

Schrader, Alexander (1991)
Hostile Takeover Bids and Bank Control. An Anglo-German Comparison of Corporate Restructuring and Control toward the Single Market, working paper, Freie Universität Berlin.

Schreyögg, Georg; Steinmann, Horst (1981)
Zur Trennung von Eigentum und Verfügungsgewalt. Eine empirische Analyse der Beteiligungsverhältnisse in deutschen Großunternehmen, in: Zeitschrift für Betriebswirtschaft, Vol. 51, 533-557.

Schüller, Alfred (ed.) (1983)
Property Rights und ökonomische Theorie, Munich.

Schumann, Jochen (1987)
Grundzüge der mikroökonomischen Theorie, 5th edition, Berlin et al.

Seiford, Lawrence M.; Thrall, Robert, M. (1990)
Recent Developments in DEA. The Mathematical Programming Approach to Frontier Analysis, in: Journal of Econometrics, Vol. 46, 7-38.

Servaes, Henri; Zenner, Marc (1994)
Ownership Structure, in: Finanzmarkt und Portfolio Management, Vol. 8, 184-196.

Sharpe, William F. (1964)
Capital Asset Prices: A Theory of Market Equilibrium under Conditions at Risk, in: Journal of Finance, Vol. 19, 425-442.

Shavell, Steven (1979)
Risk Sharing and Incentives in the Principal and Agent Relationship, in: Bell Journal of Economics, Vol. 10, 55-73.

Sheldon, George (1993)
Skalenerträge, Verbundvorteile und Ineffizienz im Schweizer Bankengewerbe, in: ifo-Studien, Vol. 38, 351-379.

Sheldon, George (1994)
Nichtparametrische Messung des technischen Fortschrittes im Schweizer Bankensektor, in: Schweizer Zeitschrift für Volkswirtschaft und Statistik, 691-707.

Shephard, Ronald W. (1981)
Cost and Production Functions. Lecture Notes in Economics and Mathematical Systems, Vol. 194, reprint of the first edition, Berlin.

Shyam-Sunder, Lakshmi; Myers, Stewart (1994)
Testing Static Trade-Off Against Pecking Order Models of Capital Structure, Working Paper Series (No. 4722), National Bureau of Economic Research.

Sloan, Richard G. (1996)
Using Earnings and Free Cash Flow to Evaluate Corporate Performance, in: Journal of Applied Corporate Finance, Vol. 9, 70-78.

Slovin, Myron B.; Sushka, Marie E. (1993)
Ownership Concentration, Corporate Control Activity, and Firm Value: Evidence from the Death of Inside Blockholders, in: Journal of Finance, Vol. 48, 1293-1321.

Smith, Adam (1986)
An Inquiry into the Nature and Causes of the Wealth of Nations, facsimile of the original published in London in 1776, Düsseldorf.

Smith, Clifford W.; Warner, Jerold B. (1979)
On Financial Contracting. An Analysis of Bond Covenants, in: Journal of Financial Economics, Vol. 7, 117-161.

Smith, Clifford W.; Watts, Ross (1982)
Incentive and Tax Effects of Executive Compensation Plans, in: Australian Journal of Management, Vol. 7, 139-157.

Sorensen, Robert L. (1974)
The Separation of Ownership and Control and Firm Performance: An Empirical Analysis, in: Southern Economic Journal, Vol. 41, 145-148.

Spiegel, Yossef; Spulber, Daniel F. (1994)
The Capital Structure of a Regulated Firm, in: Rand Journal of Economics, Vol. 25, 424-440.

Spiegel, Yossef; Spulber, Daniel F. (1997)
Capital Structure with Countervailing Incentives, in: Rand Journal of Economics, Vol. 28, 1-24.

Spremann, Klaus (1990)
Asymmetrische Information, in: Zeitschrift für Betriebswirtschaft, Vol. 60, 561-586.

SPSS Inc. (ed.) (1991)
Statistical Algorithms, 2nd edition, Chicago.

Stano, Miron (1976)
Monopoly Power, Ownership and Corporate Performance, in: Bell Journal of Economics, Vol. 7, 672-679.

Statistisches Bundesamt (ed.) (1992)
Unternehmen und Arbeitsstätten, Fachserie 2, Reihe 2.2, Zahl und Nominalkapital der Kapitalgesellschaften–1991, Wiesbaden.

Statistisches Bundesamt (ed.) (1994)
Statistisches Jahrbuch 1994 für die Bundesrepublik Deutschland, Wiesbaden.

Statistisches Bundesamt (ed.) (1995)
Statistisches Jahrbuch 1995 für die Bundesrepublik Deutschland, Wiesbaden.

Stehle, Richard (1994)
Eigenkapitalquoten und Fremkapitalstruktur börsennotierter deutscher Aktiengesellschaften, in: Zeitschrift für Betriebswirtschaft, Vol. 64, 811-837.

Stein, Heinz-Gerd (1994)
Die deutsche Bilanzierung vor neuen Herausforderungen, in: Zeitschrift für betriebswirtschaftliche Forschung, Vol. 46, 658-670.

Stein, Jeremy C. (1995)
Rational Capital Budgeting in an Irrational World, working paper, Massachusets Institute of Technology, Cambridge, MA.

Steinbeck, Claudia (1992)
Überwachungspflicht und Einwirkungsmöglichkeiten des Aufsichtsrats in der Aktiengesellschaft, Berlin.

Steiner, Manfred (1994)
Unternehmensfinanzierung in Krisensituationen, in: Berndt, Ralph (ed.), Management-Qualität contra Rezession und Krise, Berlin et al., 223-240.

Steiner, Manfred; Bruns, Christoph (1998)
Wertpapiermanagement, 6th edition, Stuttgart.

Steiner, Manfred; Kleeberg, Jochen (1991)
Zum Problem der Indexauswahl im Rahmen der wissenschaftlich-empirischen Anwendung des Capital Asset Pricing Model, in: Die Betriebswirtschaft, Vol. 51, 171-182.

Steiner, Manfred; Heinke, Volker G. (1996)
Rating aus Sicht der modernen Finanzierungstheorie, in: Büschgen, Hans E.; Everling, Oliver, Handbuch des Ratings, Wiesbaden, 579-628.

Steiner, Manfred; Schneider, Sebastian; Wolf, J. Benedict (1998)
An Analysis of the Financing Behavior of German Stock Corporations Using Artificial Neural Networks, in: Bol, G.; Nakhaeizadeh, G.; Vollmer, K.-H. (eds.), Risk Measurement, Econometrics and Neural Networks, Heidelberg/New York, 105-146.

Steiner, Manfred; Wittrock, Carsten (1995)
Performance Messung ohne Rückgriff auf kapitalmarkttheoretische Renditeerwartungsmodelle, Eine Analyse des Anlageerfolgs deutscher Aktieninvestmentfonds, in: Kredit und Kapital, 1995, 1-45.

Steinmann, Horst; Gerum, Elmar (1980)
Unternehmenspolitik in der mitbestimmten Unternehmung. Empirische Befunde zum Einfluß des Aufsichtsrates von Aktiengesellschaften, in: Die Aktiengesellschaft, Vol. 25, 1-10.

Steinmann, Horst; Schreyögg, Georg; Dütthorn, Carola (1983)
Managerkontrolle in deutschen Großunternehmen – 1972 und 1979 im Vergleich, in: Zeitschrift für Betriebswirtschaft, Vol. 53, 4-25.

Stevenson, Rodney E. (1980)
Likelihood Functions for Generalized Stochastic Frontier Estimation, in: Journal of Econometrics, Vol. 13, 57-66.

Stiglitz, Joseph E. (1985)
Credit Markets and the Control of Capital, in: Journal of Money, Credit and Banking, Vol. 17, 133-152.

Stiglitz, Joseph E.; Weiss, Andrew (1981)
Credit Rationing in Markets with Imperfect Information, in: American Economic Review, Vol. 71, 393-410.

Strickland, Deon; Wiles, Kenneth W.; Zenner, Marc (1996)
A Requiem for USA. Is Small Shareholder Monitoring Effective?, in: Journal of Financial Economics, Vol. 40, 319-338.

Strock Bagnani, Elizabeth; Milonas, Nikolaos, T.; Saunders, Anthony; Travlos, Nickolaos G. (1994)
Managers, Owners, and the Pricing of Risky Debt: An Empirical Analysis, in: The Journal of Finance, Vol. 49, 453-477.

Strong, Norman; Walker, Martin (1987)
Information and Capital Markets, Oxford/New York.

Stulz, René M. (1988)
Managerial Control of Voting Rights: Financing Policies and the Market for Corporate Control, in: Journal of Financial Economics, Vol. 20, 25-54.

Stulz, René M. (1990)
Managerial Discretion and Optimal Financing Policies, in: Journal of Financial Economics, Vol. 26, 3-27.

Stulz, René M. (1997)
Rethinking Risk Management, in: Journal of Applied Corporate Finance, Vol. 9, 8-24.

Stulz, René M.; Johnson, Herb (1985)
An Analysis of Secured Debt, in: Journal of Financial Economics, Vol. 19, 3-27.

Swank, Job (1996)
How Stable ist the Multiproduct Translog Cost Function? Evidence from the Dutch Banking Industry, in: Kredit und Kapital, 153-172.

Swoboda, Peter (1985)
Der Risikograd als Abgrenzungskriterium von Eigen- versus Fremdkapital, in: Stöppler, S. (ed.), Information und Produktion, Festschrift zum 60. Geburtstag von Prof. Dr. Waldemar Wittmann, Stuttgart, 343-361.

Swoboda, Peter (1987)
Kapitalmarkt und Unternehmensfinanzierung – Zur Kapitalstruktur der Unternehmung, in: Dieter Schneider (ed.): Kapitalmarkt und Finanzierung, Berlin, 49-68.

Syswerda, Gilbert (1993)
Simulated Crossover in Genetic Algorithms, in: Whitley, Darrell L. (ed.): Foundations of Genetic Algorithms 2, San Mateo, CA, 239-256.

Taggart, R. A. (1985)
Effects of Regulation on Utility Financing: Theory and Evidence, in: Journal of Industrial Economics, Vol. 33, 257-276.

Terberger, Eva (1987)
Der Kreditvertrag als Instrument zur Lösung von Anreizproblemen, Heidelberg.

Theuvsen, Ludwig (1997)
Interne Organisation und Transaktionskostenansatz, in: Zeitschrift für Betriebwirtschaft, Vol. 67, 971-996.

Thompson, R. S.; Wright, M (1989)
Bonding, Agency Costs and Management Buyouts: A Note, in: Bulletin of Economic Research, Vol. 41, 69-75.

Thonet, Peter J. (1977)
Managerialismus und Unternehmenserfolg, dissertation, Saarbrücken.

Thonet, Peter. J.; Poensgen, Otto H. (1979)
Managerial Control and Economic Performance in Western Germany, in: Journal of Industrial Economics, Vol. 28, 23-37.

Titman, Sheridan (1984)
The Effect of Capital Structure on a Firm's Liquidation Decision, in: Journal of Financial Economics, Vol. 13, 137-151.

Titman, Sheridan; Wessels, Roberto (1988)
The Determinants of Capital Structure Choice, in: Journal of Finance, Vol. 43, 1-19.

Todd, Douglas (1985)
Productive Performance in West German Manufacturing Industry 1970-80: A Farrel Frontier Characterisation, in: The Journal of Industrial Economics, Vol. 33, No. 3 (March), 295-316.

Trosper, R. L. (1978)
American Indian Relative Ranching Efficiency, in: American Economic Review Vol 68, 503-516.

Urban, D. (1993)
Logit-Analyse: Statistische Verfahren zur Analyse von Modellen mit qualitativen Response-Variablen, Stuttgart/Jena/New York.

Valentiner-Branth, Klaus; Weiler, Frank (1991)
Dialog zum Arbeitgeber-Arbeitnehmer-Verhältnis als Principal-Agent-Beziehung, in: Wirtschaftswissenschaftliches Studium, Vol. 20, 257-260.

Varian, Hal R. (1984)
The Nonparametric Approach to Production Analysis, in: Econometrica, Vol. 52, 579-597.

Varian, Hal R., (1992)
Microeconomic Analysis, 3rd edition, New York, London.

Vermaelen, Theo (1981)
Common Stock Repurchases and Market Signalling, in: Journal of Financial Economics, Vol. 9, 139-183.

Vogel, C. Wolfgang (1980)
Aktienrecht und Aktienwirklichkeit. Organisation und Aufgabenteilung von Vorstand und Aufsichtsrat, Baden-Baden.

Vollmer, Lothar; Lorch, Bernhard (1991)
Der Ausschluß des Bezugsrechts von Minderheitsaktionären auf Genußscheine und andere stimmrechtlose Titel, in: Der Betrieb, Vol. 44, 1313-1318.

Wallmeier, Martin (1997)
Prognose von Aktienrenditen und -risiken mit Mehrfaktorenmodellen, Bad Soden.

Ward Systems Group, Inc. (ed.) (1995)
GeneHunter, Frederick, MD.

Ware, Robert F. (1975)
The Performance of Manager vs. Owner Controlled Firms in the Food and Beverage Industry, in: Quarterly Review of Economics and Business, Vol. 15, 81-92.

Wenger, Ekkehard (1987)
Managementanreize und Kapitalallokation, in: Boettcher, Erich; Herder-Dorneich, Philipp; Schenk, Karl-Ernst (eds.): Jahrbuch für Neue Politische Ökonomie, Vol. 6, Tübingen, 217-240.

Wenger, Ekkehard (1990)
Die Rolle der Banken in der Industriefinanzierung und in der Unternehmenskontrolle am Beispiel der Bundesrepublik Deutschland, in: Wirtschaftspolitische Blätter, Vol. 37, 155-168.

Wenger, Ekkehard (1994)
Markt für Unternehmenskontrolle, in: Gerke, Wolfgang; Steiner, Manfred (eds.), Handwörterbuch des Bank- und Finanzwesens, 2nd edition, Stuttgart, 1410-1420.

Wenger, Ekkehard; Terberger, Eva (1988)
Die Beziehung zwischen Agent und Principal als Baustein einer ökonomischen Theorie der Organisation, in: Wirtschaftswissenschaftliches Studium, Vol. 17, 506-514.

Werner, Joachim (1989)
Grundlagen der Inferenzstatistik, in: Frenzel, G.; Hermann, D. (eds.), Statistik mit SPSS-X: eine Einführung nach M. J. Norusis, Stuttgart et al.

Westermann, Georg; Pröll, Raimund; Canter, Uwe (1996)
DEA—effektives Instrument zur Effizienzmessung, in: Betriebswirtschaftliche Blätter, Vol. 46, 77-81.

Wiegers, Anton (1987)
Kapitalmarktpolitik und Unternehmensfinanzierung in der Bundesrepublik Deutschland, Frankfurt am Main.

Wiendieck, Markus (1992)
Unternehmensfinanzierung und Kontrolle durch Banken – Der Einfluß der Kontrolle durch Banken auf die Unternehmensfinanzierung in Deutschland, Japan und den USA, dissertation, Cologne.

Williams, Joseph (1987)
Perquisites, Risk, and Capital Structure, in: Journal of Finance (1987), Vol. 42, 29-48.

Williamson, Oliver E. (1963)
Managerial Discretion and Business Behavior, in: American Economic Review, Vol. 53, 1032-1057.

Williamson, Oliver E. (1969)
Corporate Control and the Theory of the Firm, in: Manne, H. (ed.), Economic Policy and the Regulation of Corporate Securities, Washington, D.C., 281-336.

Williamson, Oliver E. (1974)
The Economics of Discretionary Behavior—Managerial Objectives in a Theory of the Firm, London.

Williamson, Oliver E. (1985)
The Economic Institutions of Capitalism, New York/London.

Williamson, Oliver E. (1988)
Corporate Finance and Corporate Governance, in: Journal of Finance, Vol. 43, 567-591.

Wittkemper, Hans-Georg (1993)
Neuronale Netze als Hilfsmittel zur Rendite- und Risikoschätzung von Aktien, Cologne.

Wittrock, Carsten (1995)
Messung und Analyse der Performance von Wertpapierportfolios. Eine theoretische und empirische Untersuchung, Bad Soden.

Wohlschieß, Volker (1996)
Unternehmensfinanzierung bei asymmetrischer Informationsverteilung, Wiesbaden.

Wohlschieß, Volker (1997)
Die Determinanten der Kapitalstruktur, in: Finanzmarkt und Portfolio Management, Vol. 11, 282-308.

Wolf, Joachim (1995a)
Die Messung des Diversifikationsgrads von Unternehmen (I), in: Das Wirtschaftsstudium, 439-445.

Wolf, Joachim (1995b)
Die Messung des Diversifikationsgrads von Unternehmen (II), in: Das Wirtschaftsstudium, 519-523.

Wosnitza, Michael (1991)
Das Agency-theoretische Unterinvestitionsproblem in der Publikumsgesellschaft, Heidelberg.

Yotopoulos, P. A.; Lau, L. J. (1973)
A Test for Relative Economic Efficiency, in: American Economic Review, Vol. 63, 214-223.

Zantout, Zaher (1994)
External Capital Market Control, Corporate Restructuring, and Firm Performance During the 1980s, in: Journal of Business Finance & Accounting, Vol. 21, 37-64.

Zeckhauser, Richard J.; Pound, John (1990)
Are Large Shareholders Effective Monitors? An Investigation of Share Ownership and Corporate Performance, in: Hubbard, R. Glenn (ed.), Asymmetric Information, Corporate Finance, and Investment, Chicago/ London, 149-180.

Zhang, Guochang (1995)
Ownership Concentration, Risk Aversion and the Effect of Financial Structure on Investment Decisions, working paper, Hong Kong University of Science & Technology.